MBA ACCOUNTING

MBA ACCOUNTING

Roger Hussey
*Emeritus Professor, University of the West of England
and the University of Windsor, Canada*

First published 2014 by
PALGRAVE MACMILLAN

Palgrave Macmillan in the UK is an imprint of Macmillan Publishers Limited, registered in England, company number 785998, of Houndmills, Basingstoke, Hampshire RG21 6XS.

Palgrave Macmillan in the US is a division of St Martin's Press LLC, 175 Fifth Avenue, New York, NY 10010.

Palgrave Macmillan is the global academic imprint of the above companies and has companies and representatives throughout the world.

Palgrave® and Macmillan® are registered trademarks in the United States, the United Kingdom, Europe and other countries.

ISBN 978–0–230–30337–9

This book is printed on paper suitable for recycling and made from fully managed and sustained forest sources. Logging, pulping and manufacturing processes are expected to conform to the environmental regulations of the country of origin.

A catalogue record for this book is available from the British Library.

A catalog record for this book is available from the Library of Congress.

Printed in China

To

Louise
Mathew
Benjamin
Liliane

CONTENTS

GUIDE TO THE CHAPTERS

Each chapter has the same structure. It commences with the learning objectives, executive summary and the conceptual and practical issues. At the end of each chapter are the conclusions, recommended readings and a case study.

The following outlines the main topics in each chapter.

CHAPTER 1 INTRODUCTION TO ACCOUNTING AND ITS ETHICAL DIMENSIONS

Learning Objectives
Executive Summary
Conceptual and Practical Issues
The Discipline of Accounting
The Professional Accountant
The Role of Auditors
The Individual Accountant and Ethics
Accounting Firms and Ethics
Regulatory Bodies and Ethics
Boundaries of Accounting
Conclusions
Recommended Reading
Case Study – The Dilemma of Friendships

PART I   FINANCIAL ACCOUNTING

CHAPTER 2 THE NATURE AND SCOPE OF FINANCIAL ACCOUNTING AND REPORTING

Learning Objectives
Executive Summary
Conceptual and Practical Issues
The Six Stages of Accounting
Users and Uses of Financial Statements
The UK Regulatory System
The Growth of Internationalization
Anatomy of an International Standard
The Future of Internationalization
Conclusions

PART II   MANAGEMENT ACCOUNTING

TABLES AND FIGURES

FIGURES

PREFACE

MBA Accounting explains how both financial and management accounting are used to assess business performance and to plan, control and make decisions on business activities. The ability to be able to interpret, analyse and use accounting information is critical to the personal success of individuals and the organizations for which they work.

The emphasis in each chapter is on the concepts and practices of accounting in the business context. This focus enables the inputs and outputs of the accounting process to be critically explored without a prior knowledge of accounting or spending efforts in mastering every aspect of bookkeeping.

The introductory chapter introduces accounting generally, its ethical dimensions and its widening boundaries. The two main parts of this book examine financial accounting and management accounting in detail.

Financial accounting is normally concerned with the activities of the entire organization, and for several companies the information will be in the public domain. The intended user of financial statements is external to the organization.

Because of the public availability of a company's financial statements, most countries have regulations on the generation and dissemination of these statements. This may be by law, stock exchange regulations and accounting standards. These three forces combined together are known as Generally Accepted Accounting Principles (GAAP), and the most influential and pervasive is accounting standards. In this book, we explain the impact of International Financial Reporting Standards (IFRSs) which are being increasingly used globally.

Management accounting is directed towards internal activities and managements' needs for information, which helps them to plan and control activities and to make decisions. The information is rarely publicly available, and the methods and techniques are developed to meet the requirements of the organization. However, management accounting reflects several of the financial accounting concepts and, in many organizations, management accounting information is drawn from the same database as that used for financial accounting.

Each chapter has a similar structure starting with an Executive Summary. This is followed by a section which explains the conceptual and practical issues of the particular topic. The main part of the chapter examines the various aspects of the topic in detail with worked examples. The chapter concludes with a list of recommended readings and a case study.

Chapters contain two main features: Discussion Points and Links to Practice. Discussion Points have few 'right' answers but are intended to encourage the students to reflect on what they have read and to determine their own opinions. It is to encourage the development of a critical decision-making faculty. The Links to Practice provide company examples and results of surveys which demonstrate how companies are responding to the challenges and opportunities of developments in both financial and management accounting.

Each chapter ends with a case study. Additionally, the companion website contains progress tests and detailed PowerPoint slides for each chapter that cover the main learning outcomes, as well as other teaching and learning materials.

ACKNOWLEDGEMENTS

I am indebted to colleagues and students at the University of Windsor, Canada, and the University of the West of England for enriching my understanding of financial and management accounting. In particular, heartfelt thanks to Tom Krizanovic and Dr Audra Ong of Windsor University for their comments on the draft manuscript. In addition, I am also grateful to Business Expert Press for allowing me to use, as a basis for Chapter 15, extracts from *Strategic Cost Analysis* (2012) by R. Hussey and A. Ong. Figure 1.3: Copyright © December 2013 by the International Integrated Reporting Council (IIRC). All rights reserved. Used with permission of the IIRC. Figure 2.1: © The Financial Reporting Council Limited (FRC). Adapted and reproduced with the kind permission of the FRC, 5th Floor, Aldwych House, 71–91 Aldwych, London WC2B 4HN. All rights reserved. For further information please visit www.frc.org.uk.

The team at Palgrave Macmillan provided excellent guidance and support throughout the production process and I wish to express my gratitude.

ACKNOWLEDGEMENTS

CHAPTER 1
INTRODUCTION TO ACCOUNTING AND ITS ETHICAL DIMENSIONS

LEARNING OBJECTIVES

At the end of this chapter you should be able to:

- Describe and contrast financial and management accounting
- Explain the ethics education and training which prospective professional accountants receive
- Summarize the rights and duties of auditors
- Identify the national and international bodies which have a major role in ethical conduct by accountants
- Explain the developments which are introducing an increase in the range of matters on which a company should report

EXECUTIVE SUMMARY

This chapter first examines the relationship between financial and management accounting. These are two separate and distinct branches of accounting but there are some similarities.

Financial accounting is primarily aimed at an external audience. It is concerned with the entire organizational activities and has little specific data about the daily operations. Financial accounting is governed by regulations, and financial statements are produced regularly, at least annually.

There are no legal requirements placed on businesses to have a management accounting system; it is a purely voluntary activity. The information is for internal purposes to assist managers in their responsibilities of planning, control and decision making. The information is also used for performance evaluation.

To ensure that the information has value, the information must be generated in time to be used and it may be necessary to relax the need for the reliability of the information to ensure that it is relevant to managers' needs. Cost estimation techniques and forecasts are widely used in management accounting.

The individual accountant, both those who have studied a degree in accounting at college or university and those who have studied further to qualify as a member of one of the professional accounting bodies, have received instruction on ethical issues.

Professional accounting bodies expect their members to have a knowledge base for ethical decision making, the cognitive skills to support them and a strong sense of moral responsibility.

Many professionally qualified accountants will work as auditors and, as such they have specific rights and duties. Standards and guidance are issued by the Financial Reporting Council (FRC) and it also covers ethical standards and guidance for auditors' and reporting accountants' integrity, objectivity and independence.

The most important regulatory body in the United Kingdom for accounting matters is the FRC. It is the primary independent regulator responsible for promoting high-quality corporate governance and reporting.

At the international level there are several bodies which are influential, although they have no direct regulatory powers in the United Kingdom. The International Federation of Accountants seeks to reinforce professional accountants' adherence to ethical values through the International Ethics Standards Board for Accountants' *Code of Ethics for Professional Accountants*.

The expanding areas of interest in accounting reflect a wider ethical view of organizations' responsibilities than just the financial statements. Environmental Accounting and Reporting, Sustainability Accounting and Reporting, Green Accounting, Corporate Social Responsibility (CSR) all are on the accounting agenda.

The International Integrated Reporting Council is a global coalition of regulators, investors, companies, standard setters, the accounting profession and non-governmental organizations (NGOs). It promotes the adoption by organizations of an integrated report. This contains details of how an organization's strategy, governance, performance and prospects lead to the creation of value over the short, medium and long term. Integrated reports are aimed at the providers of financial capital but contain information of interest to a wide range of stakeholders.

CONCEPTUAL AND PRACTICAL ISSUES

As you read through this chapter, regardless of your preconceptions, you will appreciate that accounting is dominated by the concepts and conventions used in the discipline. Subsequent chapters will examine these in greater detail. This is not to deny that the actual recording of economic transactions by the use of 'bookkeeping' is not important. However, it is a mundane activity which only addresses a small part of the entire accounting discipline.

In this chapter we examine the structure of the accounting profession in the United Kingdom and explain the ethical aspects of the work. This chapter does not attempt to define ethics in the broad sense. To do so adequately would require a discussion of various philosophies through the ages. Instead the chapter concentrates on how accountants view ethics and the importance they attach to it. This is demonstrated in their education and training, the methods they adopt to carry out their work, the regulations and guidance they follow and the pronouncements by various accounting bodies and institutions.

Towards the end of this chapter we discuss the shifting boundaries of accounting and how this reflects the concerns and issues of society. For example, large-scale business activities, particularly connected with energy production and mineral extraction, can be extremely profitable but sometimes at a social and environmental cost. Should this be taken into the equation and companies compelled to disclose the full benefits and burdens of their activities? Our final section describes the most recent initiatives in this area.

THE DISCIPLINE OF ACCOUNTING

> ## Definition – Accounting
> The process of identifying, measuring, recording and communicating economic events and transactions to those who require the information.

Most definitions of accounting are similar to the one given above but newcomers to the study of the discipline tend to concentrate on the recording of financial numbers. Unfortunately, this is a narrow view of the accounting process. Numbers are certainly important but, as we will see in this book, accounting draws heavily on concepts and conventions, some of which are debatable. The numbers attempt to capture complex business activities but it is how we determine what to capture and how to measure it which is the most substantial aspect.

The discipline is also separated into several sub-disciplines which have different purposes. The main division is into financial accounting and management accounting. The relationship between the two accounting systems and the process is shown in Figure 1.1).

The purpose of financial accounting is to provide information on the performance, position and cash activities of an organization over a period of time. This will be at least annually, but could be half-yearly or quarterly.

The information is communicated in the form of financial statements. The users of the financial statements are the owners of the business and individuals and groups external to the organization. These users are discussed in Chapter 2.

The main financial statements generated by financial accounting are:

- The statement of cash flows which shows the actual cash which has flowed into the organization during the financial period. It also shows the cash which has been expended. We examine this statement in Chapter 5.

- The income statement or profit and loss account which shows the financial performance over a period of time. The key information is the revenue for that period, the costs which were incurred and, by subtracting the costs from the revenue, showing the profit or loss for the period. We explain this statement in Chapter 6.

- The balance sheet or statement of financial position can, with reservations, be considered a snapshot of the business at one specific point of time: the last day of the financial period. It will show the resources the organization has to conduct its activities and its sources of finance and liabilities. We explain this statement in Chapter 7.

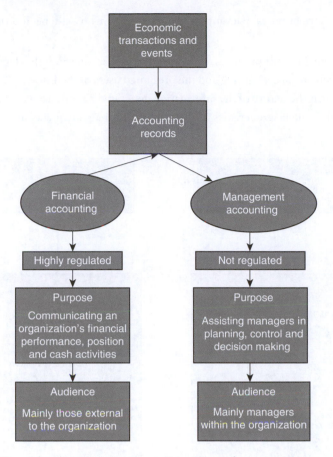

Figure 1.1 Financial and management accounting compared

Financial accounting is highly regulated and the information disclosed is expected to be very reliable. It is also the aim of financial accounting to make the information relevant to the external user.

Management accounting is aimed at providing highly relevant information for managers inside the company. This information should assist them with their responsibilities of planning and controlling the activities of the organization and making decisions. Clearly, there must be a need to ensure a certain level of information reliability, but timeliness in providing the information enhances relevance.

As timing is important, estimates and forecasts can be more useful than the preciseness of the information. For the busy manager, the time frame for receiving information they can use may be only days or even hours.

In Part II of this book, the various methods and techniques of management accounting are explained. The range of techniques means that the information generated and communicated will have many forms. It is essential that the information is relevant to the recipients who will be internal to the organization.

Given the different purposes of the two forms of accounting, the degree of regulation for financial accounting and the presumed users of the information, it is not surprising that the nature of the information generated has different characteristics. In Figure 1.2, the characteristics of financial and management accounting data are compared.

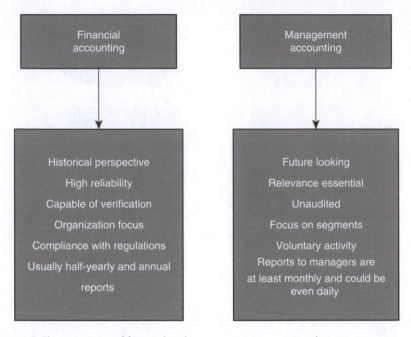

Figure 1.2 Characteristics of financial and management accounting data

THE PROFESSIONAL ACCOUNTANT

In the United Kingdom, the title accountant does not have the same protection as, for example, lawyers. Anybody can describe themselves as an accountant, but a person claiming to be a 'qualified' or 'professional' accountant is normally a member of one of the main professional bodies of accountants in the United Kingdom. The maturity and size of the accounting bodies is reflected in Table 1.1.

All but the Association of International Accountants (AIA) has received a Royal Charter at some stage in their history, but not all the members of the above bodies are able to conduct audits of companies' accounts. It is possible that they did not

Name	Date founded	Number of members	Number of students
Association of Chartered Certified Accountants	1905	154,000	432,000
Association of International Accountants	1928	7,000	8,500
Chartered Accountants Ireland	1888	22,000	6,000
Chartered Institute of Management Accountants	1919	203,000	
Chartered Institute of Public Finance and Accountancy	1885	14,000	2,800
Institute of Chartered Accountants in England and Wales	1880	140,000	20,000
Institute of Chartered Accountants of Scotland	1854	19,000	3,000

Table 1.1 UK professional accounting bodies 2012

do the necessary training or their career has followed a different direction. It is the recognition of the professional body by the FRC which is essential to the status of the accountant as an auditor.

Table 1.1 separates the groups into members and students. Members are those who have passed all the examinations required of the professional body and undertaken the appropriate training. Students are exactly that. They will have their undergraduate degree and are at some stage in the long trek of becoming a qualified accountant. This will require passing various examinations, and the pass rates are much lower than those for a degree from a university.

If that professional accounting body is registered and the individual has studied specific subjects during their training, they can conduct audits.

Definition – Audit

An independent examination of, and the subsequent expression of opinion on, the financial statements of an organization.

The FRC has statutory powers delegated to it by the government for the recognition, supervision and de-recognition of those accountancy bodies responsible for supervising the work of auditors or offering an audit qualification. The FRC provides independent oversight of the regulation of the auditing profession by the recognized supervisory and qualifying bodies (RQBs and RSBs) in the United Kingdom.

There are currently five Recognized Supervisory Bodies (RSB) and six Recognized Qualifying Bodies (RQB) recognized by the FRC, and these are:

Recognized Supervisory Bodies (RSBs)

1. Association of Authorised Public Accountants (AAPA)
2. Association of Chartered Certified Accountants (ACCA)
3. Chartered Accountants Ireland (CAI)
4. Institute of Chartered Accountants in England and Wales (ICAEW)
5. Institute of Chartered Accountants of Scotland (ICAS)

Recognized Qualifying Bodies (RQBs)

1. Association of Chartered Certified Accountants (ACCA)
2. Association of International Accountants (AIA)
3. Institute of Chartered Accountants in England and Wales (ICAEW)
4. Chartered Accountants Ireland (CAI)
5. Institute of Chartered Accountants of Scotland (ICAS)
6. Chartered Institute of Public Finance and Accountancy (CIPFA). CIPFA's status as an RQB is currently in abeyance.

A major UK accountancy body not recognized by the FRC is the Chartered Institute of Management Accountants (CIMA). CIMA is the world's largest professional body of management accountants and its members do not undertake studies and training on auditing. This does not detract from the status of the members of that professional body but reflects the direction of their training and work.

Discussion point

Do you consider that there should be only one body of professionally qualified accountants to conduct audits rather than the present system?

The various bodies of professional accountants have substantial influence on the business activities of organizations. This is not only because of their work within an organization but because of their representations at national and international levels.

Due to their knowledge and skills, accountants serve on numerous committees and boards concerned with national economic policy. The bodies of professional accountants are also extremely active in conducting research into issues of public interest.

THE ROLE OF AUDITORS

It is possibly in the role of auditor of a public limited company that many perceive accountants. In that role, the comments in the above section on individual accountants still apply. Auditors, however, have certain statutory rights and duties which are summarized below.

An auditor's rights

- Access at all times to the company's books, accounts and vouchers.
- The provision of necessary information or explanations from key personnel.
- The receipt of all communications given to a member of the company in relation to a written resolution under the relevant statutory provisions.
- The receipt of all notices of and other communications relating to any general meeting that a member of the company is entitled to receive.
- Attendance at any general meeting of the company.
- To be heard at any general meeting on any part of the business of the meeting that concerns the auditor.

An auditor's duties

- To ensure all the necessary information and explanations for the audit have been obtained.
- To ensure that proper books of accounts have been kept and maintained by the organization.
- To confirm that the accounts dealt with in the report are in agreement with the books of accounts and are in conformity with UK Generally Accepted Accounting Principles (GAAP) or International Financial Reporting Standards.
- To confirm that the financial statements derived from the books of accounts give a 'true and fair view' of the organization.
- To issue an auditor's report which should contain a clear written expression of opinion on the financial statements taken as a whole.

The most publicly visible part of the auditors' work is the audit report which can be found in every annual report and accounts issued by a company that is not exempt from an audit for some reason. All the companies listed on the London Stock Exchange publish in their annual report and accounts an audit report. We have extracted below specific paragraphs from the audit report for J Sainsbury plc.

LINK TO PRACTICE

Independent Auditors' report to the members of J Sainsbury plc.

We have audited the financial statements of J Sainsbury plc. for the 52 weeks ended 17 March 2012 which comprise the Group income statement, the Group and Company Statements of comprehensive income, the Group and Company Balance sheets, the Group and Company Cash flow statements, the Group and Company statements of changes in equity and the related notes. The financial reporting framework that has been applied in their preparation is applicable law and International Financial Reporting Standards ('IFRSs') as adopted by the European Union and, as regards the Company financial statements, as applied in accordance with the provisions of the Companies Act 2006.

Respective responsibilities of Directors and Auditors

As explained more fully in the Statement of Directors' responsibilities, the Directors are responsible for the preparation of the financial statements and for being satisfied that they give a true and fair view. Our responsibility is to audit and express an opinion on the financial statements in accordance with applicable law and International Standards on Auditing (UK and Ireland). Those standards require us to comply with the Auditing Practices Board's Ethical Standards for Auditors . . .

Opinion on financial statements

In our opinion:

- the financial statements give a true and fair view of the state of the Group's and of the Company's affairs as at 17 March 2012 and of the Group's profit and Group's and Company's cash flows for the 52 weeks then ended;

- the Group financial statements have been properly prepared in accordance with IFRSs as adopted by the European Union;

- the Company financial statements have been properly prepared in accordance with IFRSs as adopted by the European Union and as applied in accordance with the provisions of the Companies Act 2006; and

- the financial statements have been prepared in accordance with the requirements of the Companies Act 2006 and, as regards the Group financial statements, Article 4 of the IAS Regulation . . .

Richard Hughes (Senior Statutory Auditor)
for and on behalf of PricewaterhouseCoopers LLP
Chartered Accountants and Statutory Auditors
London
8 May 2012

The key messages to be gained from this statement are:

- The report is addressed to the members, that is shareholders of J Sainsbury plc.
- The Directors are responsible for the preparation of the financial statements and for being satisfied that they give a true and fair view.
- The auditors have agreed that the financial statements give a 'true and fair view' and comply with accounting standards.
- The auditors are required to comply with the Auditing Practices Board's *Ethical Standards for Auditors*.

There are four types of audit opinion.

1. Unqualified opinion

The report for J Sainsbury plc. is known as an Unqualified Opinion. The auditors have concluded that the Financial Statements give a true and fair view in accordance with the financial reporting framework used for the preparation and presentation of the Financial Statements. This is the type of audit opinion companies wish to receive.

2. A Qualified Opinion

This is when the auditor encountered one of two types of circumstances. One is where the auditor could not audit one or more areas of the financial statements, but the rest of the financial statements were audited and they conform to regulations. The other is where one or more areas of the financial statements do not conform to regulations (e.g. are misstated), but do not affect the rest of the financial statements from being fairly presented when taken as a whole.

3. An Adverse Opinion

This report is issued when the auditor determines that the financial statements of an auditee are materially misstated and, when considered as a whole, do not conform to GAAP.

4. A Disclaimer of Opinion

Commonly referred to simply as a Disclaimer, such a report is issued when the auditor could not form an opinion and consequently refuses to present an opinion on the financial statements.

Despite the apparent preciseness of the audit report, it may not convey to the reader exactly what is intended because of the 'expectations gap'. This is a term coined by Liggio (1974) and refers to the difference between what the public and financial statement users believe the responsibilities of auditors to be and what auditors believe their responsibilities to be.

It is argued (Humphrey and Turley, 1992) that an expectation gap has been with us since the nineteenth century. Several researchers have investigated the reasons for the presence of the gap, and Lee, Ali and Bien (2009) have summarized the findings of three studies conducted in three different countries. These are Porter (1993) in New Zealand, Porter and Gowthorpe (2004) in the United Kingdom and Lee et al. (2007) in Malaysia.

There is considerable similarity in the perceived deficiencies in the performance by auditors with the failure to detect theft and distortion of the figures in the company's financial statements. The three studies also identified what were considered to be unreasonable expectations of auditors. Prominent was a guarantee by the auditors that the financial statements were accurate.

Examining the studies, the conclusion is that there are various reasons for the expectations gap, 'such as misconceptions and misunderstandings of the auditing functions and excessive expectations and insufficient performance of auditors' (Lee et al., 2009, p.29).

The disconnect between auditors and the users of financial statements has also been identified in a study by Asare and Wright (2012). They investigate the understanding of auditors, bankers and non-professional investors of the messages conveyed by the standard audit report. There were several differences in understanding between the auditors and the users of the messages conveyed by the standard audit report. These were not due to interpreting the technical terms but related to the perceived roles and responsibilities of the auditors.

Discussion point

What do you consider to be reasonable expectations of an auditor's duties?

One issue which did not arise in the extract from the J Sainsbury report is that of 'going concern'. Generally a company is considered a going concern if it has, or is able to raise, the resources to continue in operation into the near future. Auditors are required to consider the going concern of a company before issuing a report.

If the auditor judges that the company is not a going concern, the auditor must include an explanatory paragraph in the audit report explaining the situation.

Auditors' doubts on whether a company is a going concern is likely to disturb investors and others linked to the company's future. There are several ways in which the auditor may report their doubts. The FRC (2006) described the following examples.

As can be seen, the auditor may give a qualified opinion, disclaimer of opinion or adverse opinion depending on the circumstances. Two of the examples arise because the company failed to comply with financial accounting and reporting standards. Remember it is the responsibility of the directors to draw up the financial statements in accordance with accounting standards.

The standards which auditors must follow are issued by the Audit and Assurance team within the Codes and Standards Division of the FRC. The standards are as follows:

- Standards and guidance for auditors;
- Standards and guidance for reviews of interim financial information performed by the auditor of the entity;
- Standards and guidance for the work of reporting accountants in connection with investment circulars;
- Ethical standards and guidance for auditors' and reporting accountants' integrity, objectivity and independence;

- Guidance for the provision of assurance on client assets; and
- Statements that set out its views on particular matters of relevance to audit and other assurance engagements.

Some audit firms are small practitioners, whereas others are very substantial organizations. There are four major firms, known as the Big4, which are international in their scope. Some notion of their size and influence can be gained from the following worldwide figures (Table 1.2).

Discussion point

Do you consider that the Big4 could have excessive influence on accounting and auditing matters?

Name of firm	Deloitte LLP	PwC	Ernst & Young LLP	KPMG
Number of employees	182,000	168,000	152,000	145,000
Revenue 2011 (US$)	28.8 billion	29.223 billion	22.880 billion	22.710 billion

Table 1.2 The Big4

Source: The 2012 Big4 firm performance analysis, January 2013, www.Big4.com.

THE INDIVIDUAL ACCOUNTANT AND ETHICS

In this section, we examine the ethical component of the education and training of those who have studied accounting. This includes both those who have studied a degree in accounting at college or university and those who have studied further to qualify as a member of one of the professional accounting bodies.

In all business degrees, at some stage students will be instructed on business ethics. If it is an accounting degree, it is very likely that ethics will have a more important status than in other business degrees. Research (Keller et al., 2007) has indicated that a university education has a positive effect on accounting students' ethical standards. A more recent study by Thomas (2012) confirms this by demonstrating that accounting students improve their ethical decisions during their degree.

The study compared senior accounting students (with approximately four accounting courses to complete) with first-year students. The results showed that senior students exhibited higher deliberative reasoning, made more frequent use of post-conventional modes of deliberative reasoning and made more ethical decisions than first-year accounting students.

The finding on deliberative reasoning is important as it describes the level of ethical consideration applied to resolving issues, as opposed to cognitive moral capability and prescriptive reasoning that describe the ethical consideration of which an individual is capable.

These results indicate that accounting students benefit from studying ethics. Another study (Siegel et al., 2011) using a mail survey suggests that the accounting professors may be an important ingredient. The survey was directed towards marketing educators and accounting educators in the United States.

The results showed that in their roles as teachers, accounting and marketing educators were significantly different in their responses to the unacceptability of seven behaviours included in the survey. The authors claim that the behaviours which accountants viewed as more unacceptable reflected the accounting profession's attachment to the concepts of independence, confidentiality and objectivity.

Investigating the demographics of the accounting educators versus the marketing educators, the findings suggested that accounting educators may be bringing more professional experience into the classroom. Accounting educators in the survey were significantly older than marketing educators and could have had professional practice experience before entering the classroom.

We are not claiming that the research demonstrates that accounting students, once qualified, behave more ethically than students from other disciplines. The various studies, however, point to the influence of the professional accounting bodies in establishing criteria that would lead to ethical decision making.

All of the professional accounting bodies give ethical behaviour a priority, both in their examinations and working practices. The competencies that a professional accountant requires to be ethical have been identified by Powell (2012).

1. Knowledge

An information base for ethical decision making, including knowledge of:

- ethical standards and guidelines;
- legal and other obligations/guidance; and
- monitoring and regulatory aspects of the profession.

2. Cognitive skills

The necessary cognitive skills to support ethical decision making. These skills are acquired by:

- general cognitive development;
- learning to deal with uncertainty and change; and

- understanding and building skills in applying decision-making frameworks.

3. Moral responsibility

A strong sense of moral responsibility comprising:

- an innate sense of right and wrong, a moral compass;
- self-awareness – particularly a consciousness of what motivates or drives a decision at the personal level;
- free will – the ability of individuals to have the appropriate information and to choose to make the most ethically valid decision.

ACCOUNTING FIRMS AND ETHICS

It is possible that many view accountants in the role of auditor of a public limited company. In that role, the comments in the above section on the training and ethics of individual accountants still apply. There is also substantial encouragement from other quarters and Jorgen Holmquist, the Chairman of the International Ethics Standards Board for Accountants, claims 'Accountants and Auditors have a strong role in the public interest, and that makes ethics very important' (Fisher, 2013).

Looking at the United Kingdom, the Big4 audit approximately 99 per cent of FTSE 100 companies, and they have a significant influence on the development and practice of accounting. An examination of their websites shows the importance attached to ethics and CSR. As an illustration, a brief example is given from each of their websites.

LINK TO PRACTICE

Deloitte

The Ethics Programme has three parts:

1. **The Deloitte Code** – a practical guide setting out our ethical framework and principles.
   Continuous Learning – an online learning programme undertaken by everyone in our Firm, using real-life examples to translate independence and ethical questions into practical actions. In addition, ethics is woven into all stages of our existing milestone training programmes, for example when our people are promoted to a higher grade or receiving induction into the Firm as an experienced hire.

Ethics helpline – all our people can request information, ask questions or report issues regarding ethical dilemmas confidentially to senior members of the ethics team.

http://www.deloitte.com/view/en_GB/uk/index.htm

LINK TO PRACTICE

PwC (formerly known as PriceWaterhouse Cooper)

As a professional services firm, our success depends on our ability to build and sustain trust.

To help maintain this trust, we've created an ethical framework that incorporates applicable standards, laws and regulations – such as the legal and regulatory standards set to maintain our independence from our audit clients.

But we've chosen to go beyond these legal requirements and establish a culture that upholds integrity, objectivity and professional ethics, and professional competence. We've captured how we do this in our Code of Conduct which covers all our work, as well as a supplementary tax code of conduct for our tax practice.

http://www.pwc.co.uk/

LINK TO PRACTICE

Ernst & Young

Our Global Code of Conduct provides a clear set of standards for our business conduct. It presents each of us with an ethical and behavioural framework to guide our response to the challenging and sometimes difficult choices we face. It also reflects the commitments outlined in our values.

Whenever we encounter an ethical issue, each of us has the responsibility to respond in a manner that reflects our values in action. While most issues can be resolved locally, you will find information within this Code about additional support and resources available to all of us.

Full compliance with the Global Code of Conduct is essential and I ask each of you to make a personal commitment to abide by it.

http://www.ey.com/UK/en/home

The declared intentions of the Big4 are very similar and, one can claim, laudable. Unfortunately, as in all walks of life, there are transgressors, or at least behaviours which can be challenged. As with other professional bodies, accounting has its share of misdemeanours and these are well publicized in the financial press:

> If a firm of accountants does not conduct itself according to the responsibilities placed on them, the penalties can be heavy. Deloitte's US financial advisory unit is to pay a $10m (£6.4m) fine and refrain for one year from new business with certain New York banks as part of an agreement to settle accusations over its review of money laundering controls at Standard Chartered Bank.
>
> The state department said Deloitte, which was working as a consultant to Standard Chartered, omitted critical information in a report to regulators on its independent review of the bank's anti-money laundering policies.
>
> (Accountancy Live, 2013)

A far more drastic penalty was suffered by Arthur Andersen, one of the most stable and successful firms in the world. In 2002, Andersen was indited by the US Department of Justice on one account of obstruction of justice in connection with its destruction of documents of Enron, for whom it was the auditor. The blow to Andersen's reputation was cataclysmic; companies no longer wanted their services as auditors and the firm disappeared completely.

REGULATORY BODIES AND ETHICS

As we mentioned earlier, individual accountants and the professional accounting bodies are very active in informing and supporting various committees. Frequently, this work will enter the public domain through the actions of a regulatory body. The most important regulatory body in the United Kingdom for accounting matters is the FRC. It is the primary independent regulator responsible for promoting high-quality corporate governance and reporting to foster investment. In Chapter 2 we discuss more thoroughly the structure and role of the FRC.

The FRC has issued a Corporate Governance Code (FRC, 2010). The Code concentrates on how companies are managed and the accountability of the board of directors to the owners of the company. This is a narrower perspective than CSR which we discuss in a subsequent section.

The Code identifies 18 different matters which the company should disclose in its annual report. Companies listed on the stock exchange take these seriously as can be appreciated by the following extract from the website of AstraZeneca PLC.

LINK TO PRACTICE

We apply all the main and supporting principles of good corporate governance in the UK Corporate Governance Code (formerly the Combined Code) and related guidance.

As a foreign issuer with American Depositary Shares listed on the New York Stock Exchange (NYSE), we must also disclose any significant ways in which our corporate governance practices differ from those followed by US companies under the NYSE's corporate governance listing standards.

Source: astrazeneca.com/Investors/Corporate-governance

Corporate Governance Reports are lengthy and AstraZeneca's 2012 annual report devotes 12 pages of fairly dense text in making its disclosures.

Discussion Point

Do you consider company's Corporate Governance Reports a valuable disclosure or an exercise in information overload?

At the international level there are several bodies which are influential, although they have no direct regulatory powers in the United Kingdom. The International

Federation of Accountants (IFAC) currently has 134 members and 24 associate member organizations. Members of the IFAC are national accounting organizations rather than individual professional accountants or accounting firms.

IFAC's governing bodies, staff and volunteers are committed to the values of integrity, transparency and expertise. IFAC also seeks to reinforce professional accountants' adherence to these values through the International Ethics Standards Board for Accountants' Code of Ethics for Professional Accountants (IESBA Code).

The International Ethics Standards Board for Accountants (IESBA) is an independent standard-setting body that serves the public interest by setting high-quality ethical standards for professional accountants and by facilitating the convergence of international and national ethical standards, including auditor independence requirements, through the development of a robust, internationally appropriate code of ethics.

The International Auditing and Assurance Standards Board (IAASB) is an independent standard-setting body that serves the public interest by setting high-quality international standards for auditing, assurance and other related standards and by facilitating the convergence of international and national auditing and assurance standards.

Although auditors, for practical reasons, are remunerated directly by the company for which they are conducting the audit, they are reporting not to the company but to the owners, usually the shareholders, of the company. It is argued that their responsibility is even wider than this and there is a public responsibility. Accountants are not the only professional group to be in this position. Engineers may be paid and appointed by the government but have a responsibility to act in the interests of the public who are affected by their work. This can be compared to lawyers who only have a responsibility to their client.

In 2012 the IESBA issued the Handbook of the Code of Ethics for Professional Accountants. It states that a professional accountant's responsibility is not exclusively to satisfy the needs of an individual client or employer but to act in the public interest. To do this a professional accountant should comply with the Code of Ethics.

The Code sets out five fundamental principles with which a professional accountant should comply.

Fundamental principles

Integrity – to be straightforward and honest in all professional and business relationships.

Objectivity – to not allow bias, conflict of interest or undue influence of others to override professional or business judgements.

Professional competence and due care – to maintain professional knowledge and skill at the level required to ensure that a client or employer receives competent professional services based on current developments in practice, legislation and techniques and act diligently and in accordance with applicable technical and professional standards.

Confidentiality – to respect the confidentiality of information acquired as a result of professional and business relationships and, therefore, not disclose any such information to third parties without proper and specific authority, unless there is a legal or professional right or duty to disclose, nor use the information for the personal advantage of the professional accountant or third parties.

Professional behaviour – to comply with relevant laws and regulations and avoid any action that discredits the profession.

There are potential threats which may prevent or deter full compliance with the Code of Ethics. These threats can be created by a broad range of relationships and circumstances. The threats to compliance are listed and described as follows in the IESBA Code:

Threats to the fundamental principles

Self-interest threat – the threat that a financial or other interest will inappropriately influence the professional accountant's judgement or behaviour.

Self-review threat – the threat that a professional accountant will not appropriately evaluate the results of a previous judgement made or service performed by the professional accountant, or by another individual within the professional accountant's firm or employing organization, on which the accountant will rely when forming a judgement as part of providing a current service.

Advocacy threat – the threat that a professional accountant will promote a client's or employer's position to the point that the professional accountant's objectivity is compromised.

Familiarity threat – the threat that due to a long or close relationship with a client or employer, a professional accountant will be too sympathetic to their interests or too accepting of their work.

> **Intimidation threat** – the threat that a professional accountant will be deterred from acting objectively because of actual or perceived pressures, including attempts to exercise undue influence over the professional accountant.

A professional accountant shall take qualitative as well as quantitative factors into account when evaluating the significance of a threat. This is a matter of judgement and the matters that form part of the evaluation depends on the type of threat that exists. Some examples are given below for several types of threat to illustrate the evaluation.

THE USE OF SAFEGUARDS

Safeguards are necessary when the auditor concludes that the identified threats are at a level at which compliance with the fundamental principles is compromised. In other words, safeguards should be applied, when necessary, to eliminate the threats or reduce them to an acceptable level. Safeguards fall into two broad categories:

1. **Safeguards created by the profession, legislation or regulation** – this may include for example, the requirements of professional standards, corporate governance regulations and education and training of auditors.
2. **Safeguards in the work environment** – the IESBA Code gives examples of two types of safeguards in the work environment – those that are firm-wide, and those that are engagement specific.

A situation may occur where threats cannot be eliminated or reduced to an acceptable level, either because the threat is too significant or because appropriate safeguards are not available or cannot be applied. In such situations, the IESBA Code requires the auditor to decline or discontinue the specific professional service involved or, when necessary, resign from the audit engagement.

BOUNDARIES OF ACCOUNTING

> ### Discussion point
>
> Can you identify another business discipline which has similar fundamental principles?

In recent years, accounting interests have developed from a very narrow perspective of an organization and its key business activity. Influenced by societies' concerns and also by contributing to national and international debate on various issues, the boundaries of accounting have expanded. This is not only in the attention paid to those ethical issues which directly affect the work of accountants but by issues which are debated at national and international levels.

One issue which initially revolved around the debate on the environment has expanded into the subject of corporate social reporting and the information which large companies should disclose. Although much of the additional information cannot be regarded as strictly 'financial' in the traditional sense, it is strongly attached to the term and is, therefore, of interest to the accountants.

The proposed content of annual corporate reports is being extended far wider than the financial statements. Advances such as environmental accounting and sustainability reporting have encouraged thinking on what matters businesses should report and to whom. This has led to proposals which not only substantially extend the content of corporate reports and their users but also challenge opinions on the societal responsibilities of companies.

In this final section we will discuss those techniques and methods which are mainly focussed on environmental matters. We will complete that section by looking at the recent developments in integrated reporting.

ENVIRONMENTAL ACCOUNTING AND REPORTING

The above title is an umbrella term and the US Environmental Protection Agency (1995) gives three different contexts (Table 1.3).

Type of environmental accounting	Focus	Audience
National income accounting	Nation	External
Financial accounting	Firm	External
Management accounting	Firm, division, facility, product line or system	Internal

Table 1.3 The contexts of environmental accounting

The national level is important as environmental accounting can use physical or monetary units to refer to the consumption of the nation's natural resources, both renewable and non-renewable. For our purposes, of greatest relevance to us are the firm and various subsets of it.

At the firm or entity level, an estimation of the financially material environmental liabilities and costs can be made. Environmental reporting has been an increasing trend for several years.

In 2010, the European Commission renewed its efforts to further develop CSR to encourage long-term employee and consumer trust. Environmental issues were seen as a priority subject for greater disclosures.

A research study (Gîrbina, Albu and Albu, 2011) examined the public documents issued by the IFAC and of the Federation of European Expert Accountants (FEE). Their conclusions were that both accounting bodies had intensive activity and initiated political actions in the corporate social and environmental reporting field. The specific areas where the two bodies were identified as being active are:

- publication of assurance, education and ethics standards,

- development of educational and web materials,

- cooperation with other organizations in the development of reporting and assurance standards,

- research projects to support decision making and

- encouraging member bodies to develop similar policies, public statements inviting responsible parties to act.

SUSTAINABILITY ACCOUNTING AND REPORTING

This has been defined as 'the generation, analysis and use of monetarised environmental and socially related information in order to improve corporate environmental, social and economic performance' (Bent and Richardson, 2003).

This is a more inclusive concept than environmental accounting and involves economic viability, social responsibility and environmental responsibility. This has been described as the Triple Bottom Line (Elkington, 1998) and is frequently used in relation to CSR.

Although environmental accounting is sometimes the main concentration, sustainability accounting also includes the economic and social context of doing business using protocols to ensure long-term value creation.

The organization, The Global Reporting Initiative (GRI), has proposed a sustainability report framework (2011), which it suggests companies should publish. The adoption of this report would allow companies to report sustainability information in a way that is similar to financial reporting.

The framework can be used by organizations of any size, sector or location. The GRI Reporting Framework contains general and sector-specific content that has been agreed by a wide range of stakeholders around the world to be generally applicable for reporting an organization's sustainability performance. Standard disclosures are suggested with performance indicators and other disclosure items.

One example of such a report which has won awards is issued by Potash Corp. Since 2002, the company has followed the guidelines for sustainability reporting set out by the GRI. The main sustainability topics that Potash Corporation report on are:

CORPORATE SOCIAL RESPONSIBILITY

This refers to an organization's acceptance of responsibility for the impact of its activities on the environment, consumers, employees, communities and stakeholders. The final group is far wider than the term 'shareholder' and includes all those who are affected by the company's activities. Various organizations have issued documents giving advice on the adoption of CSR by a company. One of the most comprehensive is ISO 26000 issued by the International Organization for Standardization in November 2010.

This is not a compulsory standard but a guidance document providing advice and recommendations to those organizations wishing to embrace CSR. It is recognized as an authorative international standard for CSR and it discusses seven core subjects.

- Organizational governance
- Human rights
- Labour practices
- The environment
- Fair operating practices

- Consumer issues
- Community involvement and development

The above methods and techniques in some aspects require the skill and knowledge of the accountant in determining the financial aspects of a company's activities.

It would be easy to disregard the above proposals by arguing that only a few organizations, such as Potash Corp, will put these into action. A recent international survey of large company by KPMG contradicts this argument as demonstrated by the following extract.

LINK TO PRACTICE

- Ninety-five per cent of the 250 largest companies in the world (G250 companies) now report on their corporate responsibility (CR) activities, two-thirds of non-reporters are based in the US.

- Traditional CR reporting nations in Europe continue to see the highest reporting rates, but the Americas and the Middle East and Africa region are quickly gaining ground. Only around half of Asia Pacific companies report on their CR activities.

- For the 100 largest companies in each of the 34 countries we studied (N100 companies), CR reporting by the consumer markets, pharmaceuticals and construction industries more than doubled since KPMG's last survey in 2008, but overall numbers in some sectors – such as trade and retail and transportation – continue to lag stubbornly behind.

- Of the N100 companies, 69 per cent of publicly traded companies conduct CR reporting, compared to just 36 per cent of family-owned enterprises and close to 45 per cent for both cooperatives and companies owned by professional investors such as private equity firms.

Source: KPMG Survey of Corporate Responsibility Reporting 2011

Of course, what develops as a voluntary practice can become law if there are enough supporters. The European Union (EU) already has a directive requesting companies to provide non-financial information in their annual reports, where appropriate and the extent necessary, to explain the company's development, performance or position. Such a vaguely worded requirement does not attract compliance. This could change.

In April 2013 an amendment was put forward to the EU's fourth directive (78/660/EEC) and seventh directive (83/3449/EEC). If this goes ahead, companies with over 500 employees will be required to inform on policies, risks and results on environmental, social, employee aspects. Also companies will have to make similar disclosures on human rights, anti-corruption and bribery issues and diversity on the board of directors.

Discussion point

What do you consider to be the appropriate boundaries of business accountability?

INTEGRATED REPORTING

A new body, the International Integrated Reporting Council (IIRC), has been formed to promote company adoption of integrated reporting. The IIRC is a global coalition of regulators, investors, companies, standard setters, the accounting profession and NGOs.

In February 2013 it was announced that the International Accounting Standards Board (IASB) and IIRC agreed that the two organizations deepen their cooperation on the IIRC's work to develop an integrated corporate reporting framework.

An integrated report is far broader that the present financial statements. It contains details of how an organization's strategy, governance, performance and prospects lead to the creation of value over the short, medium and long term. Integrated reports are aimed at the providers of financial capital but contain information of interest to a wide range of stakeholders.

Over the years there has been an increasing requirement for companies to report financial information, but the boundaries are now being extended beyond the financial statements and investors. Two reasons for this development have been suggested (Adams, 2013) as:

1. The medium- to long-term likelihood of the financial consequences of severe climate change and
2. The recent tendency for stock markets (and employers) to prioritize a short-term view of corporate reporting.

One could also argue that the spread of international accounting has introduced other cultures and values into business relationships.

The IIRC has developed a Prototype of the International Framework (IIRC, 2012) which has been issued. It is anticipated that there will be a period of consultation and a final version will be issued late in 2013. The framework establishes the fundamental concepts that underpin Integrated Reporting, guiding principles on content and presentation, content elements to be included in a report and other issues on preparation and presentation.

The fundamental concepts are concerned with the various capitals that the organization uses and affects, the organization's business model and the creation of value over time. The capitals the organization uses are regarded as financial, manufactured, human, intellectual, natural and social and relationship capitals. How the organization interacts with these capitals and external factors to create value over the short, medium and long term are shown in Figure 1.3.

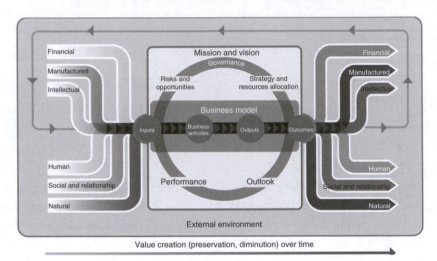

Figure 1.3 The integrated view of organizations
Source: Copyright © December 2013 by the International Integrated Reporting Council (IIRC). All rights reserved. Used with permission of the IIRC.

Where possible, the material components of value creation and the relationships between them should be described and measured. This will capture all the relevant capitals on which value creation depends, how the organization uses those capitals and its effects on them.

There are six guiding principles for an integrated report which are:

1. Insight should be given into the organization's strategy, and how that relates to its ability to create value in the short, medium and long term and to its use of and effects on the capitals.

2. It should demonstrate, as a comprehensive value creation story, the combination, inter-relatedness and dependencies between the components that are material to the organization's ability to create value over time.

3. Insight should be given into the quality of the organization's relationships with its key stakeholders and how and to what extent the organization understands, takes into account and responds to their legitimate needs, interests and expectations.

4. Concise information should be disclosed that is material to assessing the organization's ability to create value in the short, medium and long term.

5. The information in an integrated report should be reliable.

6. The information in an integrated report should be presented in a way that enables comparison with other organizations.

The first four principles are directed at the types of information to be given. For a large organization, this would be a considerable volume of information to aggregate and present in a single report. The last two are concerned with the characteristics of the information: reliability and comparability.

Although the framework proposes the description and measurement of the material components of value creation and the relationships between them, it takes a principles-based approach. In other words, there are no rules for measurement or disclosure of individual matters or identification of specific key performance indicators (KPIs) or key risk indicators (KRIs).

The framework's intent is to achieve an appropriate balance between flexibility and prescription that recognizes the wide variation in individual circumstances of different organizations but enables a sufficient degree of comparability across organizations to meet relevant information needs.

As far as the actual content is concerned, the framework lists the following Content Elements:

1. Organizational overview and operating context

2. Governance

3. Opportunities and risks

4. Strategy and resource allocation

5. Business model

6. Performance and outcomes

7. Future outlook.

This is not necessarily the order they should be presented and the framework proposes that the information should be arranged in a way that makes the interconnections between the Content Elements apparent. In the framework, each one of the seven Content Elements is stated in the form of a question rather than a list of specific items. It is for management to determine what should be reported.

Initiatives similar to the IIRC's current proposal have been made previously and have not won overwhelming support. However, Dzinkowski (2013) argues that there is evidence that this time may be different. She gives the following reasons for her views:

1. The IIRC's framework is the work of the world's leading accounting associations.

2. The International Organization of Securities Commissions, a powerful body representing security regulators, supports it.

3. There are an increasing number of examples around to demonstrate how it can be done.

It is too early to know whether the proposals will be successful, but the actions by the EU and the proposals by the IIRC show where corporate reporting is moving, and accountants are fully involved in these developments.

One example which draws together many of the issues discussed in this chapter is Rio Tinto. On their website they commit themselves to seven main areas.

LINK TO PRACTICE

Rio Tinto's commitment

Safety and health

Environment

Community

Our people

Human rights

Local sustainable development

REACH compliance

Source: riotinto.com/our-commitment-107.aspx

In 2007 the EU enacted EU Regulation for Registration, Evaluation, Authorisation and Restriction of Chemicals (REACH). The purpose is to manage the risks that chemicals can pose to human health and the environment throughout the EU. REACH places a duty on companies which produce or import chemicals (as defined in the legislation) into the EU and take appropriate measures to manage any identified risks.

Rio Tinto also provides considerable detail on the US$11.6 billion of taxes it paid worldwide in 2012. In summary it states:

> The distribution of taxes paid by the Group reflects the geographical spread of the Group's businesses. Accordingly the majority of the tax was paid in Australia and North America. However the tax amounts paid in South

America, Europe, Southern Africa, Mongolia and the rest of Asia are significant in the context of the tax receipts of some of the countries in these regions.

CONCLUSIONS

Professional accountants have been conducting their discipline for well over 100 years. The number of members of professional accounting bodies has increased, and the main accounting firms are influential on national and international debates. Accountants, in various ways, have a substantial impact on how businesses conduct and report their activities.

This chapter has demonstrated that a considerable amount of education, training and effort is directed to assist accountants to make ethical decisions. There are also bodies at the national and international levels which issue guidance and advice on the ethical practice of accounting. This is not to claim that accountants behave more ethically than those from other business disciplines, but there is a substantial framework which attempts to achieve a high standard.

Developments in accounting, such as sustainability accounting and reporting, and the Integrated Report have extended the boundaries of traditional accounting. Although there is reluctance by some companies to provide information of such a broad nature, the indications are that voluntary practice is increasing and some form of legislation, at least in the EU, is a possibility.

RECOMMENDED READING

IRRC (2012) Integrated Reporting (IR) *Prototype Framework*, http://www.theiirc.org/wp-content/uploads/2012/11/23.11.12-Prototype-Final.pdf

Global Reporting Initiative (2011) *Sustainability Reporting Guidelines*, www.globalreporting.org/Pages/default.aspx

International Ethics Standard Board for Accounting (2012) *Handbook of the Code of Ethics for Professional Accountants*

Ball, Ray (2009) "Market and Political/Regulatory Perspectives on the Recent Accounting Scandals 2009". *Journal of Accounting Research*, Vol. 47, No. 2, May pp.277–323.

Fisher, L (2013). "Importance of Ethics". *Accounting and Business International*, March pp.23–25.

Wearing, Robert (2005) *Cases in Corporate Governance*. Sage Publications.

Jenkins, Gregory, J. (2003) *The Enron Collapse*. Prentice Hall.

CASE STUDY THE DILEMMA OF FRIENDSHIPS

Annie Dorret works as an auditor for a medium-sized firm based in London. As part of an audit of Nocost plc., she travels to one of the company's stores in Lancashire. This is her first visit to the store and on her arrival she is delighted to discover that the store manager is an old friend from her childhood, Geoff Bowen.

Geoff and Annie have grown up in adjacent houses and were inseparable. However, they lost all contact when Annie left for university. She had heard that Geoff had drifted around in dead end jobs but had not received any news of him for many years. She was pleased to meet him again and the first few hours they spent together catching up on what they were doing.

Annie explained that she is now an audit junior and had her sights set on becoming an audit manager and, possibly, one day a partner at the firm of accountants. She lived on the outskirts of London with a colleague. They were planning to get married but could not find the time to arrange the wedding.

Geoff was reticent about his experiences but said he had started as a warehouse worker for Nocost about five years ago. He had married four years ago and he joked that meant he had to settle down. It obviously had paid off as Geoff had been the store manager for two years and enjoyed the work.

As part of her audit duties at Nocost, Annie gives meticulous attention to cash transactions. She was disturbed to find that there was a £2000 deficit. She queried Geoff on this and was horrified with his explanation and the transcript of their discussion is as follows.

Annie: I need to know what happened to that £2000.

Geoff: I will be straight with you – it's me. Last year was a terrible year for me personally. My old car had broken down, and I had to replace it, otherwise I could not get to work. My wife became very ill and was in and out of doctor's surgeries, and we had to pay a child minder for the two kids. We were really going under so I had no choice.

Annie: Look Geoff, I am very sympathetic, but I have no choice but to report it.

Geoff: Wait a minute. If you do that I will lose my job and with my past record it might be prison this time. It would kill my family. I promise I will pay it back.

Annie: This is really hard, Geoff, but if I do not report it, I will be an accessory and I will lose my job.

Geoff: Wait a minute. I am paying it back. It was £10,000 I took last year, but I have managed to put back £8000 of it. I promise I can put back the balance in the next few months. My wife is better now and has a part-time job. The kids are going to school and our finances are better. Please say yes.

Annie: If you took £10,000 why was that not picked up last year?

Geoff: The guy who came last year was pretty casual. He spent most of his time going to the local races and texting on his Blackberry. He didn't go through the books with a fine tooth comb like you do. For old times' sake and the family, please give me a break.

Annie: This is a shock. Give me time to look at the figures again and we will meet again tomorrow.

That evening, Annie ruminates on what to do. She is sorry for Geoff and knows that his salary as a store manager is just over half of what she gets. She realizes it must be hard to raise two children and with the problems he had, there were no easy answers. But theft was theft, and it was her responsibility to identify problems in the accounts. Finally she listed the possible implications of reporting or not reporting the fraud.

Reporting

1. Geoff will lose his job which will be devastating on the family.

2. The auditor who missed it last year will be, at best, reprimanded and possibly dismissed.

3. She will be praised for her thorough work.

Not reporting

1. Geoff keeps his job.

2. Last year's auditor was negligent but gets away scot-free.

3. If it is later discovered she is in a very difficult position. Either she admits to covering it up or she will be regarded as being negligent.

The next afternoon Annie sees Geoff. She hands him an envelope and says:

There is £2000 cash in the envelope. Put it back in the system. I will check the cash again next week and it had better balance. I don't want to talk about it but you must pay me back as soon as you can. Whatever, you do keep quiet about this or I lose my job.

CASE STUDY QUESTIONS:

1. What is your opinion of Annie's action?

2. In view of her responsibilities as an auditor, what should she have done?

3. What would you do in these circumstances?

PART I
FINANCIAL ACCOUNTING

CHAPTER 2
THE NATURE AND SCOPE OF FINANCIAL ACCOUNTING AND REPORTING

LEARNING OBJECTIVES

At the end of this chapter you should be able to:

- Explain the six stages of accounting
- Discuss the users and uses of financial statements
- Describe the UK regulatory system for financial accounting and reporting
- Explain the impact of international regulations on financial accounting and reporting

EXECUTIVE SUMMARY

Financial accounting is not only about numbers, it also deals with concepts: what the numbers are supposed to represent. Accounting is attempting to capture and record the activities of complex, fast-moving organizations possibly operating on an international scale in different time zones and in different currencies.

There are six main stages in the financial accounting process: recognition, initial measurement, subsequent measurement, recording, derecognition and disclosure. When all of these stages have been completed, an organization can construct financial statements.

The objective of businesses issuing financial statements and who the potential users are has been debated over the years. For a small business, the owner will want to assess the financial position and performance of the business. It is certain that the tax authorities and probably the bank will also show interest. The position is less definite for a public limited company which is listed on the Stock Exchange. Although investors and lenders are recognized as the prime users, some argue that customers, suppliers, employees and others could also be users.

All UK companies come under the Companies Act 2006 which sets out the broad regulations and, in particular, the requirement that financial statements must give a 'true and fair view'. Detailed requirements are given in accounting standards and, for listed companies, the requirements of the Stock Exchange.

Accounting standards in the United Kingdom are a mixture of standards set by the UK authority, the Accounting Standards Board and the International Accounting Standards Board. In 2012 the Financial Reporting Council announced that in 2015 there would be adoption of international accounting standards as endorsed by the EU and that UK-generated standards would be withdrawn.

International Financial Reporting Standards can be very lengthy and complex. Fortunately, a similar structure is adopted which makes it easier to find your way around. In this chapter the structure of IAS 2 Inventories is given.

CONCEPTUAL AND PRACTICAL ISSUES

Accounting for generations had been essentially a practical discipline. The person responsible for keeping financial records usually reported directly to the owner who made all decisions. Most of the business transactions conducted were reasonably straightforward in nature and attention was paid to keeping meticulous records.

The increasing size and complexity of business and the types of transactions entered into required a more sophisticated approach. This need was originally addressed by the professional accounting bodies which would send reports, recommendations and guidance to their individual members on how to account for certain types of transactions and events.

Although this met the immediate problems, the resources available and the lack of any method for resolving disagreements and addressing emerging economic practices meant that there were many weaknesses. To establish credibility of financial accounting and reporting and to meet the needs of users of financial statements, many countries began, in the 1970s, to issue pronouncements that come under the general term of accounting standards. The national bodies setting the standards were sometimes established by the government and in other countries formed by the professional accounting bodies in that country.

Definition – Accounting standards

Regulations governing financial accounting and reporting. These pronouncements are issued by a national or international standard-setting body and there is normally some form of national legal procedures that will ensure compliance with the requirements of the standards by organizations.

In attempting to establish their own national standards, countries confronted the difficulty that there was no overarching theory of accounting. The problems which were arising were not those of calculations, the mere adding and subtracting numbers, but conceptual ones. To resolve the conceptual dilemmas the following questions needed to be answered:

1. What is the purpose or objective of accounting?
2. Who are the users of accounting information?
3. What is the information which users require?
4. How should we prepare accounts that meet the users' needs?

A significant contribution to the debate is Agency Theory (Jensen and Mekling, 1976). This states that an agency relationship is present when one or more principals, such as shareholders or other investors, employ other persons, such as directors or managers, to manage an organization on their behalf. Unfortunately, agents may well pursue such goals as increasing their own financial benefits, reducing the amount of effort expended on their responsibilities and other perks such as corporate jets, chauffeur-driven cars and extended travelling to exotic 'business' destinations.

Mechanisms need to be in place that aligns the interests of agents with principals. Remuneration packages and incentives for agents can be effective but they may create potential new agency problems related to performance measurement. One monitoring mechanism is financial reporting that requires the agent to give, at least annually, a report to the owners on the conduct of the business.

In the United Kingdom, a structure of Company Law, EU Directives, Accounting Standards and Stock Exchange Regulations has developed to form Generally Accepted Accounting Principles (GAAP). These are the regulations that govern accounting. This can be a complex area and we list below the acronyms used in this chapter to assist you in following the subsequent discussions.

Acronyms used in this chapter

ASB	Accounting Standard Board
ASC	Accounting Standards Committee
ASSC	Accounting Standards Steering Committee
DP	Discussion Paper
ED	Exposure Draft
FASB	Financial Accounting Standards Board
FRC	Financial Reporting Council
FRS	Financial Reporting Standard
IASB	International Accounting Standards Board
IASC	International Accounting Standards Committee
NYSE	New York Stock Exchange
SEC	Securities and Exchange Commission
SSAP	Statement of Standard Accounting Practice

THE SIX STAGES OF ACCOUNTING

There are six well defined stages of accounting. Both large and small organizations go through the same process. Depending on the size of the company and the nature of its business transactions, some stages may be more troublesome than others. But the entire process attempts to capture and record business transactions. The six stages are:

1) Recognition

2) Initial Measurement

3) Subsequent Measurement

4) Recording

5) Derecognition

6) Disclosure

RECOGNITION

> ### Definition – Recognition
>
> The process of incorporating economic transactions and events into the financial statements of an organization. Both the nature of the transaction or event and the timing need to be recognized, that is in which financial period it should be recognized.

Accounting is concerned with the economic transactions and events that are undertaken by business or that affect them in some way. Economic transactions usually cause few problems because they are mainly the day-to-day operations of the business. Raw materials are purchased, the workforce is paid and sales are made. There may be payments for insurance, rent and advertising.

Economic events can be varied and outside of the control of the company. One of the office buildings burns down and it is uninsured. The national currency weakens against the currencies of the business's trading partners, inflation is on the increase, and the chairman of the company unexpectedly resigns without explanations. Many of these events may affect the share price of the company but the question arises as to how, and whether, we account for them.

Recognition is not only about whether there is an economic transaction or event but identifying in which financial period it took place. That is essential for calculating the profit or loss for the period and understanding the financial position of the company at the end of the period.

> ### Definition – Financial period
>
> The period of time between one balance sheet date for which financial statements are prepared and the next balance sheet date. The period is normally 12 months and annual financial statements are prepared. In some countries, companies may be encouraged, or required, to publish summary financial statements more frequently, either quarterly or half-yearly.

Definition – Initial measurement

The determination of the monetary amounts of economic transactions and events that are to be recognized and entered into the records of the organization at the date of the transaction or event.

We may have been able to recognize our economic event or transaction, but the next question is whether we can measure it in financial terms with reliability. Traditionally, accountants have used a method known as historical cost accounting to record the value of items in the accounts and this is still the dominant method. The value of the economic transaction or event at the time that it took place is the value that is used and, with some exceptions, stays at that amount in the accounting records. This method has the great advantage of being very reliable (you know what was paid and should have documentary evidence). Unfortunately this method has some weaknesses if the information is used for decision making.

Imagine that you had purchased a computer and a house on the same date five years ago. It is almost certain that the value of your computer will be a lot less that you paid for it as developments in technology will have made it obsolete. On the other hand, it is likely that the value of the house has increased if you have a property market which is extremely active with many buyers. In both cases, the historic cost is different from the present value of the items and, therefore, of little value for any decisions you wish to make now.

With some transactions and events we may have great difficulty in measuring the current value. For example, if you have purchased the right to drill for oil and you have struck lucky, how much is that oil worth? It's obviously worth less while it is still in the ground, but how much less? Another example of difficulties in measurement is with brand names. Many of us will purchase clothes or equipment because it has a 'brand' name. If that name attracts us to buying the item then that brand must have value for the company that owns it. But how do we measure that value?

SUBSEQUENT MEASUREMENT

The problem of the lack of relevance with historic cost accounting for decision making has resulted in some relaxation for certain assets where companies can remeasure (value) them. Subsequent measurement is the later determination of the monetary amount of economic transactions and events which will change the amount of initial measurement. This will be discussed in following chapters but a major issue is the method to be used for assessing the current values of the items.

RECORDING

> ### Definition – Recording
>
> Entering into the records of the organization the economic transactions and events. These records are still sometimes referred to as the 'books of account', although it is now normal practice to maintain these records on a computerized system, even for a small business.

Economic transactions and events must be recorded if we are to have confidence in our books of account and be able to produce information that is reliable. The usual method for recording transactions is known as double-entry bookkeeping. This method was developed in the fourteenth century and a book written by Luca Pacioli, explaining its application, was published in Venice in 1494. The same principles are still used today irrespective of a manual or computerized system being employed.

You do not need a thorough knowledge of bookkeeping to understand the book you are now reading. In this chapter we explain and demonstrate the basic principles. For further study you will find explanations and examples on the companion website to this book.

DERECOGNITION

> ### Definition – Derecognition
>
> The removal from the Statement of Financial Position of an organization of assets and liabilities that had previously been recognized.

Determining if and when an asset or liability should be removed from the organization's accounting records normally causes no problems. However, situations arise where it is not evident that an organization has completely or partially disposed of an asset or liability. In these complex situations, guidance is required and this can be found in the relevant accounting standard.

> ### Definition – Disclosure
>
> The publication of financial and non-financial information to those interested in the financial, operational and economic activities of an organization.

Disclosure is the communication of financial information to those who have a right to receive it or have an interest in the activities of the entity. In most countries, certain people do have a right to specific financial information. These are usually the shareholders or those who have loaned money, such as banks, to the company.

All business, even the smallest ones, will have to prepare some form of accounts to satisfy the tax authorities in the country where the business is situated. The larger the business entity, more people are likely to be interested in seeing financial information. With companies that have shares or other securities quoted on a stock exchange, there will be a requirement by the exchange to produce financial statements, at least annually, and possibly summary financial statements half-yearly or every three months.

USERS AND USES OF FINANCIAL STATEMENTS

If financial statements are intended to convey information, the questions are to whom and for what purposes. The answers to these questions have bothered the standard setters for many decades and the controversy is very much alive. One cause of the debate is that individual countries each developed their own approach. This is based on their history, culture, business practices, types of organizations and the existing legislative framework. Not surprisingly, they came up with different answers. This is best exemplified by comparing the developments in the United States and the United Kingdom and how this is proving a barrier to accord.

In November 1978 the Financial Accounting Standards Board (FASB) in the United States published Financial Accounting Concepts No 1 entitled *Objectives of Financial Reporting by Business Enterprises* (FASB, 1978). This states that 'financial reporting should provide information that is useful to present and potential investors and creditors and other users in making rational investment and similar decisions'. This tenet has been adhered to by the United States.

An earlier paper published in 1975 by the UK's Accounting Standards Steering Committee (ASSC, 1975) considered to whom companies should report and identified the following seven groups which the authors of the report believed had a 'reasonable right to information and whose information needs should be recognised by corporate reports' (ASSC, 1975, p.17).

1. The equity investor group
2. The loan creditor group
3. The employee group
4. The analyst-adviser group
5. The business contact group
6. The government
7. The public

Interestingly, the last group was included because of the perceived societal need for information on the economic activities of entities. This issue is very much alive today as we see in the rest of this chapter.

The United Kingdom's thinking is also reflected in the International Accounting Standards Committee's (IASC) Framework for the Presentation and Preparation of Financial Statements issued in 1989. Much of that document is repeated and retained in IAS 1 Presentation of Financial Statements, first issued in 1997, which states:

> The objective of financial statements is to provide information about the financial position, financial performance and cash flows of an entity that is useful to a wide range of users in making economic decisions. Financial statements also show the results of the management's stewardship of the resources entrusted to it.
>
> (IASC, 1997)

The two objectives identified in the previous paragraph are often referred to as the decision model and the stewardship model. It is argued that the decision model must provide information that is relevant and the most interested users would be the providers of capital, that is, shareholders and lenders. Relevant information would show, for example, current values for the assets held by the company. It is of no use to know the cost of a piece of land purchased 20 years ago. It is much more relevant to have an estimate of its current value, even if that is not 100 per cent reliable.

Advocates of the stewardship model contend that what is most important is the reliability of the information and that there is a moral, if not a legal, obligation for entities to provide information to a wide range of users who may be interested in its activities. Current employees and suppliers and customers are good examples.

Reliability is achieved by providing the original cost of assets, no matter what their current value is assumed to be.

Traditionally, accountants would always use the original cost of an asset in the financial statements of an organization, known as the historic cost. Over recent years there have been attempts to introduce accounting standards that capture the current values of such assets. It is not claimed that, theoretically, one method is better than another. The method the accountant will use will depend on assumptions about the users of financial statements and their information needs. And there's the rub!

In the United Kingdom a degree of ambivalence has appeared in documents. The Statement of Principles (ASB, 1999) stated the objective of financial statements is to provide information that is useful to a wide range of users for assessing the stewardship of the entity's management and for making economic decisions. It continued to contend that present and potential investors were the defining class of users and information provided to them would usually meet the needs of other users.

However, the document continued by stating that although financial statements were not specifically prepared for a wide range of users 'there is no doubt that they are prepared for a range of persons that extends far beyond existing investors' (para 1.2). It proceeded to identify the users as:

> Present and potential investors
> Lenders
> Suppliers and other trade creditors
> Employees
> Customers
> Governments and their agencies

The ASB concluded that those wanting information would be taking decisions based on economic data and that 'Even present investors assessing the stewardship of the entity's management do so in order to decide whether, amongst other things, to hold or sell their investment in the entity and to reappoint or replace the management' (para 1.4).

As we will explain later in this chapter and in greater detail in Chapter 3, the FASB and the IASB are attempting to achieve an agreed Conceptual Framework. This is proving to be a lengthy process but the position currently taken in discussion between the two bodies is that the objective of general purpose financial reporting is to provide financial information about the reporting entity that is useful to existing and potential investors, lenders and other creditors in making decision about providing resources to the entity.

THE UK REGULATORY SYSTEM

Financial accounting and reporting is heavily regulated and accountants and businesses must comply with GAAP, sometimes referred to as Generally Accepted Accounting Principles.

Definition – Generally Accepted Accounting Principles

Generally Accepted Accounting Principles (GAAP), are a set of regulations with substantial authoritative support. GAAP is the framework which accountants and businesses use to record their economic transactions and events and to produce financial statements.

The main components of GAAP are company legislation, stock exchange rules and accounting standards. Both company legislation and stock exchange rules require companies to comply with accounting standards. In the first part of this book, accounting standards will be extensively examined.

In the United Kingdom, most small unincorporated businesses are not subject to all the rigours of GAAP. For such business the most interested recipient of financial statements will be the owner and the tax authorities. However, all incorporated business, that is those that have been formed into private or public companies must comply with the provisions of the Companies Act 2006 in preparing their financial statements and additionally with the requirements of accounting standards.

Company legislation provides a very basic structure detailing how companies limited by shares should conduct themselves. It requires directors to prepare annual financial statements consisting of a profit and loss account (comprehensive income statement) and balance sheet (statement of financial position). These must be filed at Companies House together with a Directors' Report and Auditors Report. An important aspect of the legislation is that small- or medium-sized companies are allowed to file abbreviated accounts but must still provide full accounts to their shareholders.

Those incorporated businesses that are public and are listed on a Stock Exchange must follow the requirements of the Stock Exchange. The rules require extensive disclosures by public limited companies (PLC). In addition to the annual report and accounts, PLCs must issue interim reports covering the first six months of the year. This information is easily available and in this book we draw on the published annual reports and accounts and websites of PLCs to provide the examples.

The annual financial report must be published no later than four months after the end of each financial year and must include at least:

- audited financial statements prepared in accordance with the applicable accounting standards;
- a management report;
- an appropriate statement of assurance from persons responsible in the issuer; and
- provide an indication from which website the annual financial report is available.

Accounting standards are accorded legal definition in the Companies Act and are regarded as intended to apply to all financial accounts which are intended to give a true and fair view of the financial position and profit and loss of the entity.

The first standard-setting body, the Accounting Standards Committee (ASC), was established by the accounting profession. In total it issued 41 accounting standards, known as Statements of Standard Accounting Practice (SSAPs), and some of these are still in operation.

The ASC was replaced by the Accounting Standards Board (ASB). The ASB adopted all the SSAPs issued by the ASC and continued to issue standards entitled Financial Reporting Standards (FRSs). Unlike its predecessor body, the ASB could issue accounting standards on its own authority, without the approval of any other body.

Financial Reporting Standards (FRSs) are applicable to public and private companies. Since 1997, smaller companies have been relieved of the burden of complying with FRSs and can adopt the Financial Reporting Standard for FRSSE. Since 2005, all public companies listed on an EU Stock Exchange should comply with International Financial Reporting Standards (IFRSs) as endorsed by the EU. The impact of internationalization on financial accounting and reporting is examined in the next section.

The Accounting Standards Board was subsumed into The Financial Reporting Council which assumed responsibility for accounting standards on 2 July 2012. The Financial Reporting Council is the United Kingdom's independent regulator responsible for promoting high-quality corporate governance and reporting. Among other responsibilities it issues standards for corporate reporting and monitors and enforces accounting and auditing standards. It oversees the regulatory activities of the professional accountancy bodies and operates independent disciplinary arrangements for public interest cases involving accountant. Figure 2.1 shows the structure of the FRC.

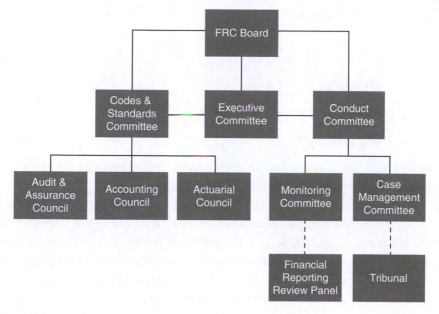

Figure 2.1 Structure of the financial reporting council

The Accounting Council which replaces the Accounting Standards Board reports into the Codes and Standards Committee and has the following responsibilities.

- Providing strategic input and thought leadership, both in the field of accounting and financial reporting and in the work-plan of the FRC as a whole.

- Considering and advising the FRC Board upon draft codes and standards (or amendments thereto) to ensure that a high-quality, effective and proportionate approach is taken.

- Considering and commending upon proposed developments in relation to international codes and standards and regulations.

- Considering and advising on research proposals and other initiatives undertaken to inform the FRC on matters material to its remit and any resultant publications.

The Codes & Standards Committee is responsible for advising the FRC Board on maintaining an effective framework of UK codes and standards for Corporate Governance, Stewardship, Accounting, Auditing and Assurance and Actuarial technical standards. Codes & Standards Committee also advises on influencing the wider regulatory framework and on the FRC's research programme.

These structural changes have been accompanied by substantial shifts in policy. Essentially, the FRC has confirmed its commitment to international accounting standards and 2015 will be a year of change in the United Kingdom. The importance of these changes is discussed in the following section.

THE GROWTH OF INTERNATIONALIZATION

Towards the end of the twentieth century some very profitable companies in Europe wished to list shares on the New York Stock Exchange (NYSE). To meet the requirements of the NYSE, the European company had to redraft its financial statements drawn up according to its own national standards to comply with US regulations. In some instances, the previously declared profit for a financial year turned into a loss. Thus, a conceptual inconsistency exists as the activities of a particular company in a specific financial period can show either a profit or loss depending on which national accounting regime applies.

Possibly the most famous case is that of Daimler Benz AG, a German company that wished to list its shares on the US Stock Exchange in the early 1990s. To do so it had to reconcile the profit it had shown for 1993 using German GAAP with what the profit would have been if it had used US GAAP. The net income, or profit, the company had reported in its German financial statements was DM615 million. After the company had made all the adjustments to comply with US GAAP the reported net income turned to a net loss of DM1839 million.

Such a huge difference demonstrated that accounting at the international level did not make sense. To declare that Daimler Benz either made a respectable profit or massive loss depending on which country's regulations were adopted generates little confidence in accounting. If you are investing or trading internationally, it is essential that financial statements are comparable irrespective of the accounting regulations applied.

Although Daimler Benz highlighted the problem, the issue of significant differences in national accounting standards had been recognised at an early stage. In 1973, national accountancy bodies from Australia, Canada, France, Germany, Mexico, the Netherlands, the United Kingdom and Ireland, and the United States established the International Accounting Standards Committee (IASC).

Although the IASC made considerable progress, the major national economies were still using national accounting standards. What was required was either a complete overhaul of all aspects of the IASC or the formation of a new body. The latter was the course of action chosen.

The IASB was established formally in April 2001 with the objectives of:

- developing in the public interest, a single set of high-quality, understandable and enforceable global accounting standards;
- helping participants in the world's capital markets and other users make economic decisions by having access to high-quality, transparent and comparable information;
- promoting the use and vigorous application of those standards;
- bringing about convergence of national accounting standards and International Accounting Standards to high-quality solutions.

Its present structure is shown in Figure 2.2.

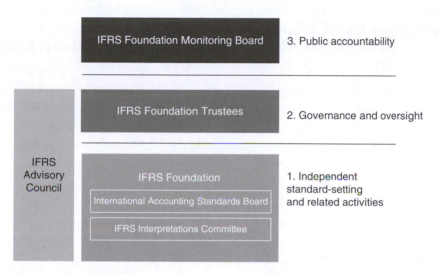

Figure 2.2 The IFRS foundation

Our interest is focussed on the International Accounting Standards Board, the body responsible for issuing International Financial Reporting Standards. The process in issuing a standard has the following six stages:

1. Establishing an agenda

The IASB evaluates the merits of adding a potential item to its agenda mainly by reference to the needs of investors.

2. Planning the project

In developing a plan to conduct the work the Board will decide whether to conduct the work by itself or jointly with another standards-setting body.

3. Issuing a Discussion Paper (DP)

It is usual for the Board to issue a discussion paper and ask for comments. The discussion paper provides a comprehensive review of the issue, possible ways to address it and the preliminary views of the Board.

4. Publishing the Exposure Draft (ED)

The ED is the IASB's main vehicle for consulting the public. The ED sets out a specific proposal in the form of a proposed standard (or amendment to an existing standard).

5. Publishing the standard

The Board has to decide whether to publish revised proposals for comments as a second ED or whether to proceed to issuing a standard. When the IASB is satisfied that it has reached a conclusion on the issues arising from the ED, it instructs the staff to draft the IFRS.

6. Implementation of the standard

After an IFRS is issued, the staff and the IASB members hold regular meetings with interested parties, including other standard-setting bodies, to help understand unanticipated issues related to the practical implementation and potential impact of its proposals.

The IASB has made substantial progress with the acceptance of international standards. Member states of the EU agreed that all companies issuing consolidated financial statements must comply with IFRSs as endorsed by the EU since 2005. The international standards have to be endorsed by the EU and there are standards that have not been fully endorsed.

There are some difficulties confronting companies and the users of financial statements. In the following example from GlaxoSmithKline, the company has followed UK company law but added another dimension.

LINK TO PRACTICE

GlaxoSmithKline

Directors are required to prepare the Group financial statements in accordance with International Financial Reporting Standards (IFRS) as adopted by the European Union. In preparing the Group financial statements, the Directors have also elected to comply with IFRS, as issued by the International Accounting Standards Board (IASB).

www.gsk.com/content/dam/gsk/globals/documents/pdf/
GSK-Annual-Report-2012.pdf

The company is meeting the United Kingdom requirements, but as an international company has decided to meet the interests of the international audience by issuing two sets of accounts, one complying with IFRSs.

The United Kingdom is not the only country where the adoption of IFRSs is not as complete as one may think. Where a company has interests in other countries, including being listed on their stock exchange, it can result in the disclosure as in the following example.

LINK TO PRACTICE

Rio Tinto

The Group's financial statements have been prepared in accordance with IFRS as adopted by the European Union (EU IFRS), which differs in certain respects from the version of IFRS that is applicable in Australia, referred to as Australian Accounting Standards (AAS).

http://www.riotinto.com/documents/rio_tinto_2012_annual_report.pdf

One implication that could be made from this note is that the EU has not fully adopted IFRSs whereas Australia has. There is considerable debate on how some countries have fully adopted IFRSs and Zeff and Nobes (2010, p.182) argue that, 'Australia changes the designation of the standard, makes various textual changes, adds a few disclosure requirements, and (initially) removed early adoption and deleted options. Even now, there is a short delay between the issue of a standard by the IASB and its emergence from the Australian process. In our view, for these reasons, it is misleading to call this Australian implementation 'adoption of IFRS'."

There is a danger in becoming entangled in semantics, but there is a possibility of differences between a country which takes on an international standard exactly as it stands and a country which implements a standard using its own regulatory processes.

Definition – Consolidated financial statements

Consolidated financial statements, also known as group statements, are the aggregated financial results of a parent company and its subsidiaries. They provide an overall view of an entire group of companies as opposed to one company's stand-alone position.

It is claimed that there are over 100 countries that have adopted international standards but caution should be expressed about the rigour and extent of that adoption.

In some instances it is only partial adoption, with only certain types of organizations in a particular country compelled to comply with the international standards. A few countries maintain that their standards are similar to and are based on international standards but this does not mean that there is full compliance.

A useful list of countries that claim to have adopted international standards and the scope is given on the website http://www.iasplus.com/en/jurisdictions. Two research papers that have investigated the characteristics of adopting and non-adopting companies have arrived at interesting conclusions.

Ramanna and Sletten (2009) examined 102 non-EU countries. They found more powerful countries are less likely to adopt IFRS and suggested that more powerful countries are less willing to surrender standard-setting authority to an international body. They also found that a country is more likely to adopt IFRS if its trade partners or countries within in its geographical region are IFRS adopters.

In a later publication, Johnson and Hicks (2012) took a different perspective and examined how standards were accepted and implanted. Their sample was 183 nations of the world. They gave significant focus to the 25 largest nations according to gross national product. They concluded that the probability of assuring strict implementation of accounting and reporting standards may be affected by weak national cultural ethics, unstable authoritarian forms of government and economic power measured by high debt levels and rapid growth rates.

Of course, adoption is only one part of the process and for standards to be effective, some form of monitoring and enforcement is required. The IASB does not have direct powers or procedures to ensure this but some mechanisms are already available or are being created. The IASB, however, has to rely on the mechanisms in place in individual countries to ensure enforcement.

Definition – Internal audit

An examination of the procedures and records of an organization carried out on its own behalf to ensure that its own internal controls are operating satisfactorily. The internal audit may also be used to conduct investigations to detect any possible theft or fraud.

The first stage of monitoring for compliance is at the internal level in an organization where control systems, including internal audit, can ensure that standards are applied. This may be reinforced by external auditors who are independent and have necessary expertise. The commitment of management is also required to ensure that financial statements fairly represent the financial performance and position of the organization.

A second stage in ensuring compliance with international accounting standards is an audit conducted by an auditor who is deemed to be independent of the company. An audit will involve an examination of the procedures, processes and records of the company and the financial statements that are drawn from those records. The auditor will express an opinion on those financial statements in a standard audit report. Unfortunately, research indicates that there are important differences in the understanding between auditors and users of the broad messages conveyed by the audit report (Asare and Wright, 2012).

There are different national rules on the status of organizations that require an external audit. At a minimum, an external audit is usually required by those companies whose shares are listed on a stock exchange and the auditors are reporting their opinion to the shareholders.

The final and critical stage is a monitoring and enforcement mechanism held by a regulator. There are models currently employed at the national level. There are security commissions, such as the SEC in the United States, stock exchanges that can de-list companies for regulatory transgressions and other bodies that have some legal support.

Copies of all standards, both IASs and IFRSs can be found (for a fee) on the IFRS Foundation and the IASB website International Financial Reporting Standards website http://www.ifrs.org/Pages/default.aspx.

The position in the United Kingdom had become complex with a mixed set of UK accounting standards, with some based on IFRSs endorsed by the EU and others developed independently by the ASB. In 2012 the FRC issued proposals and these will become mandatory in 2015. The revised proposals recommend:

(a) replacing all extant FRSs, Statements of Standard Accounting Practice and Urgent Issues Task Force Abstracts (current FRSs) in the United Kingdom and Republic of Ireland with a single FRS;

(b) introducing a reduced disclosure framework for the financial reporting of certain qualifying entities; and

(c) retaining the current Financial Reporting Standard for Smaller Entities (FRSSE) and, when planned changes to financial reporting for small companies is made at the EU level, revising the FRSSE to conform to EU policy.

The consequences of the FRC decision is over 30 UK SSAPs and FRSs will be withdrawn in 2015. Companies currently required to comply with international standards endorsed by the EU will continue to do so.

In this book it would be impossible to cover all of the standards issued by the ASB in the United Kingdom and the IASB. We use, therefore, the international standard as this reflects thinking presented by the Financial Reporting Council in 2012. We have chosen to explain in some detail the principles of the key international standards that impact on the three main financial statements. We have selected those standards that are most likely to be encountered by an MBA student or a manager.

As far as the present standards themselves are concerned, there is some confusion for new students because of the change of names and the apparent duplication of some individual standards. The present position is that the IASC issued 41 standards between 1975 and 2000. The standards were numbered consecutively starting with one and each standard also had a descriptive title, for example IAS 7 Statement of Cash Flows. Many of the IASC standards are still in force.

When the IASB took over from the IASC it 'adopted' the IASs still in force and started to issue its own standards which were titled International Financial Reporting Standards (IFRSs). Once again these standards are numbered consecutively, starting with one and have a descriptive title, for example, IFRS 7 Financial Instruments.

The term International Accounting Standards or International Financial Reporting Standards may be used when referring to all the standards that have been issued. It is essential, however, to use correctly the term IAS or IFRS when referring to a specific standard, for example, IAS 2 Inventories or IFRS 2 Share-Based Payment.

The standards we discuss in subsequent chapters are shown in Table 2.1.

Chapter	IASB standard
C5 The statement of cash flows	IAS 7
C6 The income statement	IAS 1 Presentation of Financial Statements IAS 2 Inventories IAS 18 Revenue
C5 The statement of financial position	IAS 16 Property plant and equipment IAS 23 Borrowing costs IAS 38 Intangible assets IAS 36 Impairment of assets
Chapter 8	IFRS 3 Business Combinations IFRS 10 'Consolidated Financial Statements' IFRS 11 'Joint Arrangements' IFRS 12 'Disclosure of Interests in Other Entities' IAS 27 'Separate Financial Statements' IAS 28 'Investments in Associates and Joint Ventures'

Table 2.1 IASB Standards by chapter

ANATOMY OF AN INTERNATIONAL STANDARD

Copies of all standards, both IASs and IFRSs can be found in the IASB website. There is an access fee. Many universities, colleges and professional organizations subscribe to this website, so access is available for most students and professional accountants. In addition to the website the IASB publishes all standards, interpretations and a glossary of terms in a large book of over 2500 pages. This is sometimes referred to as the 'bound volume' and is published annually. A fairly recent innovation has been the issue of a CD containing all the standards.

In the Preface to the bound volume, the IASB states that IFRS (and also IASs) apply to general purpose financial statements of profit-orientated entities. These include those organizations in commercial, industrial, financial and similar activities. All standards refer to 'entities' and this includes organizations in corporate or other forms. In other words, it is a very inclusive term.

Although IFRSs are not intended specifically for not-for-profit organizations, they may find them appropriate. If we look at the list of companies adopting international standards, several forms of profit and not-for-profit organizations are included.

Standards have paragraphs in bold type and in plain type. They have equal authority. The paragraphs in bold type indicate the main principles but they do not have greater authority than other paragraphs.

Individual standards have a similar structure and we will describe how a standard is organized. We will use as our example IAS 2 *Inventories* which was first issued in 1975 with a revised version being issued in 2003. The objective of the standard is to establish the methods to be used for valuing most types of inventory. The standard requires inventories to be measured at the lower of cost and net realisable value (NRV) and outlines acceptable methods of determining cost, including first-in first-out (FIFO) and weighted average cost.

The main sections of IAS 2 are:

OBJECTIVES

A standard cannot be understood properly without an appreciation of what it is trying to do. In the case of IAS 2 it is to set out the accounting treatment for inventories. It identifies what the problem is and explains how the standard addresses it.

SCOPE

This explains what transactions and events are covered by the standard and which are excluded. IAS 2, for example, applies to all inventories except work in progress in construction contracts, financial instruments and biological assets. Exclusions usually arise because they are dealt with in another standard.

DEFINITIONS

The key terms used in the standard are defined. This is extremely important as some standards are very technical and the definitions assist in the correct application of the standards.

MEASUREMENT OF INVENTORIES

In many standards the topic of measurement is the longest section. IAS 2 states that the cost of inventories comprises all costs of purchase, costs of conversion and other costs incurred in bringing the inventories to their present and condition. These terms are subsequently explained and guidance given on the application of the terms in measuring the value of inventories.

RECOGNITION AS AN EXPENSE

This is a timing issue. It is essential that you know when to deal with inventories as an expense as this will determine the profit for the financial period.

DISCLOSURES

The standard very carefully lists all the information that must be disclosed by an entity in its financial statements. With inventories the list is fairly short, starting with the disclosure of 'accounting policies used in measuring inventories' and ending with 'the carrying amount of inventories pledged as securities'.

Some standards are primarily concerned with the appropriate disclosure of information and will contain a lengthy list of requirements.

EFFECTIVE DATE

It is essential for entities to know when they must start complying with the standard. Usually the IASB permits at least 12 months to allow companies to adapt their accounting records and procedures so that the information can be captured. It is also usual for the standard to encourage entities to adopt the standard early if they so wish.

APPENDICES

In the appendices there is a basis for conclusions explaining the reasons for the IASB's requirements. With some standards there may be several examples of how the standard should be applied in different circumstances.

In this book our interest is on IFRSs and IASs and these are intended for large companies. In 2009, the International Accounting Standards Board recognized the need for guidance for smaller entities by issuing the IFRS for Small and Medium-sized Entities (IFRS for SMEs).

This guidance is based on IFRSs but simplified by

- removing some accounting treatments permitted under full IFRSs,
- eliminating topics and disclosure requirements that are not generally relevant to SMEs,
- simplifying requirements for recognition and measurement.

It is a complete standard, that is, not a series of separate standards, and cuts down the volume of accounting requirements by more than 90 per cent when compared with the full set of IFRSs.

In our discussions we do not incorporate considerations of IFRS for SMEs. However, the complete IFRS for SMEs (together with basis for conclusions, illustrative financial statements and presentation and disclosure checklist) can be downloaded free from the IASB website.

THE FUTURE OF INTERNATIONALIZATION

The IASB has made substantial progress in promoting international standards, but Zeff (2012) has identified four major challenges facing the IASB.

1. How to respond to the Security Exchange Commission's long-awaited decision on convergence. Not only will that decision affect the work of the IASB but also will influence the direction and strength of the commitment that has been made by other countries. In 2012 the United States still refused to commit to convergence.

2. The analysis and management of feedback to accounting changes made by recently formed regional standard setter groups. These groups are becoming more active and aware of the significant, and sometimes unwanted, consequences of international standards to corporate reporting in their own countries.

3. Although not an IASB responsibility, there is the issue of ensuring compliance with IFRSs. Each country should have its own mechanisms to monitor and correct deficient financial reporting, but the authority and commitment of national regulators differs.

4. Currently, there is some ambiguity in the way that companies and their auditors state that their financial reports comply with IFRSs. It is not always

clear whether it is the IFRSs issued by the IASB or those 'modified' by the country. As you can imagine on a global basis there is considerable variation, even with those countries that have adopted international accounting standards completely.

Zeff makes a final point that the method in which business is conducted and the corporate structures in some countries are very different. In the development of standards some way should be found to reflect these differences without compromising global comparability. This is a pertinent comment but it is difficult to envisage how it can be achieved.

There have been criticisms from practitioners and academics on the convergence project of the FASB and the IASB. Three leading academics argue that the two boards have a structure designed for debating technical issues and this is inadequate. They believe that the 'ultimately political nature of the social welfare issues may be better suited for broader social institutions reflecting social norms of the kind that the idea of *generally accepted accounting principles* was originally meant to encapsulate' (Bromwich et al., 2010, p.366).

Bruce (2013), discussing the complexity of international standards, argues that the 'result has been a standard-setting process which produces outcomes which outsiders cannot understand and which then produce financial reporting which is less than obviously understandable'.

This view is shared by many and there is a feeling that the IASB's desire for the United States to adopt international standards should now come to an end. In July 2012 the SEC issued their final report on the work plan started in 2010 which was intended to give direction on how and when to incorporate IFRSs into US GAAP. However, the final report did not commit to the United States adopting international accounting standards.

The ICAEW, responding to the failure of the SEC to decide on convergence, proposed that the project should be ended formally, in months not years. The argument was made that the IASB should concern itself with the 100 plus countries that have adopted international standards and assist those countries, such as China, which are making moves to convergence (ICAEW, 2012).

The final word on the convergence project must be left to Chairman of the IASB, Hans Hoogervorst. He is quoted as saying that

Five years ago, it (lack of US adoption) might have led to a disintegration of the whole project. I am not worried about that now. But I am worried that the US finds it so hard to make a decision and that it might lead to a growing divergence between IFRS and US GAAP.

(Perrin, 2013, p.30)

CONCLUSIONS

A continuing issue, and fundamental to the preparation of financial statements, is the perceived users and uses of financial statements. The debate on this will reappear in the following chapters.

The development of national accounting standards has contributed significantly to the quality of financial statements at the national level, but revealed the problems of comparing companies at the international level. The growth of internationalization of standard setting has established considerable comparability of financial statements, but even where countries have adopted or implemented IFRSs there may still be differences in accounting treatments.

Although progress has been made at the international level, not everyone is in agreement on how we tackle some of the more intractable issues. It is generally agreed that a conceptual framework would resolve these issues but work on this project, after many years, is still far from completion.

In the next chapter we examine in greater depth the concepts and assumptions used by accountants.

RECOMMENDED READING

Financial Reporting Council. (November 2012) *Foreword to Accounting Standards*. London.

Accounting Standards Board (1999) *Statement of Principles*. December London.

Zeff, Stephen A. (2012) 'The Evolution of the IASC into the IASB, and the Challenges it Faces', *The Accounting Review*, Vol. 73, No 3. pp.807–837.

CASE STUDY A VOTE FOR INTERNATIONAL ACCOUNTING

Louise Harrow attended a conference on Internationalization of Accounting. A speaker from the United States spoke very well and convincingly on the reasons why internationalization would not work. He argued that the most that could be achieved would be some removal of the greater differences.

When Louise returned to the office, she was asked to give her opinions on the conference to a group of trainee accountants. As the

United Kingdom is committed to adopting IFRS, Louise considered she needed to offer a rebuttal to the US speaker. She consulted her notes and wrote down the main points which had been made.

1. United States is a legalistic society and is most comfortable following a rules-based approach. A principles-based approach would never be accepted.

2. The SEC and the FASB would not wish to cede the financial controls they had over the US economy. That is the reason they were formed. Even the United Kingdom had refused to adopt the Euro!

3. Business practices varied in different countries. There may be several similarities between the United States and the United Kingdom but there were vast differences with many other countries.

4. International standards were best suited to those smaller countries which could not resource their own standard-setting process.

5. Although claims were made about the many countries adopting IFRSs, the evidence on the extent of that adoption suggested it was not full adoption in many cases.

6. There was little evidence on how rigorously the IFRs were applied. The country may have adopted IFRSs but we do not know if there is a good enforcement mechanism in that country compelling companies to follow them.

7. Countries differed considerably in their business activities. There was little point in making the financial statements of a large US manufacturing company comparable to a plantation in the far east.

8. Countries had different financial institutions with different levels of sophistication – we are not all on the same playing field.

Finally, the speaker argued that international accounting should not be decided by an organization which nobody had been able to vote for and the rules were decided by self-appointed accountants. It was a political and social decision. If an international body were to be set up, then we should all be allowed to vote who sits on it.

Louise found some of the arguments forceful but needed to give the other point of view. Knowing your strong support of international accounting she has asked you to write her presentation.

CHAPTER 3
CONCEPTS, ASSUMPTIONS AND PRINCIPLES

LEARNING OBJECTIVES

At the end of this chapter you should be able to:

- Explain the difference between the principles-based approach and the rules-based approach to accounting.

- Discuss the reasons for creating a Conceptual Framework and the problems involved.

- Describe the two underlying assumptions of financial statements which have been identified: the accruals concept and the going concern concept.

- Summarize the qualitative characteristics of information.

- Explain the business entity concept.

- Contrast the four measurement concepts.

EXECUTIVE SUMMARY

Accounting is based on assumptions and concepts. Some of the assumptions have been formalized by various national accounting standards setters in their Conceptual Frameworks. One of the purposes of a Conceptual Framework is to assist standard setters in establishing appropriate standards. As we move to international standards a major hurdle is that countries can have different views on the conceptual basis of standards.

The IASB has a principles-based approach which applies fundamental concepts to ensure financial statements are not misleading. The burden is placed on the preparer and auditors of the financial statements to use their judgement and experience to ensure the financial statements give a true and fair view. The United States has a rules-based approach which is based on the premise that if you follow the rules strictly when preparing financial statements they will not be misleading.

In 2002 the FASB and the IASB commenced a convergence project, part of which is to develop an agreed Conceptual Framework. The first phase of this dealt with the objectives of financial statements. The second phase is concerned with the qualitative characteristics of information. Two underlying assumptions of financial statements have been identified: the accruals concept and the going concern concept.

The accruals assumption states that transactions and other events are recognized as they occur and not when cash or any other consideration such as cheques are given or received. Financial statements are usually prepared using the assumption that the business is a going concern and will remain so in the foreseeable future.

The Conceptual Framework also identifies the qualitative concepts of information. There are two fundamental characteristics. For information to be useful to the decision maker it must be relevant and faithfully represent what it purports to represent. There are also enhancing qualitative characteristics such as comparability and timeliness.

The third phase of the project attempts to define what is meant by the Business Entity. There have been major problems in arriving at a definition that is comprehensible and acceptable. Although the problems may be overcome, there are strong indications that the convergence project will come to an end.

Although the FASB has been working with the IASB since 2002 to converge standards, there has been no commitment for the United States to adopt IFRSs. It was anticipated that the SEC would make a final decision on the time of adoption in 2012. It did not do so and the response from some other major groups is that the IASB should cease the convergence project and direct its attentions to the rest of the world.

CONCEPTUAL AND PRACTICAL ISSUES

When one examines a company's financial statements, there is an aspect of completeness about them. The additions and subtractions of columns of numbers are invariably correct and the Statement of Financial Position balances.

Caution must be exercised. Many of the figures you see are based on estimates and assumptions which may affect the financial statements as shown in the following example.

LINK TO PRACTICE

Tesco plc

The preparation of the consolidated financial statements requires management to make judgements, estimates and assumptions that affect the application of policies and reported amounts of assets and liabilities, income and expenses. The estimates and associated assumptions are based on historical experience and various other factors that are believed to be reasonable under the circumstances. Actual results may differ from these estimates.

Tesco Annual Report 2011

Every set of published accounts contains a note similar to the above. Despite the apparent precision of the numbers, the preparation of financial statements requires management to make judgements, estimates and assumptions which affect the reported amounts of assets, liabilities, income and expenses.

To carry out their work, accountants have made certain assumptions or developed concepts to define and categorize which economic transactions and events are to be recorded. Over the years it has been found necessary to formalize these concepts so that accountants apply the same basis in preparing financial statements and the users of those statements can better understand the information that is being communicated.

There are many concepts which are also referred to as assumptions, conventions, principles and axioms. Some of these concepts are known as 'qualitative characteristics'. This means the attributes the information should have in order to make it a valuable communication. For example, you would not expect the information to be biased or so incomplete that you might misinterpret it.

At this stage we are going to consider some basic assumptions used by accountants. Most of these are contained in the accounting literature. Some of the assumptions explained now will be understood better in later chapters which explain how these are applied in practice to the financial statements themselves.

BUSINESS ENTITY CONCEPT

This assumption means that the accountant is preparing financial statements only for the activities of the business and not for the personal financial activities of the owners. The financial statements will inform us about the financial performance and position of the business but very little about that of the owners. We will be able to obtain information about transactions between the owners and the business, for example the owners investing money into the business, but we will not have information about the activities of the owners that are not related to the business. For this reason when you are preparing financial statements it is useful to think of the business as an 'entity' separated completely from the owners.

Unfortunately, the complexity of modern business relationships has made it more difficult to define the business entity for reporting purposes. It is no longer possible to think of a physical entity such as a factory or shop. Companies enter into agreements and relationships which they consider to be mutually beneficial. This raises the problem as to which corporate body has financial responsibility for specific activities and should therefore report them.

THE CONSISTENCY CONCEPT

This concept has two aspects to it. The first is that there must be a uniformity of treatment for transactions and events of a similar nature. An accountant cannot treat a transaction in one way and then change to another method for a similar transaction.

Secondly, an accountant must use the same accounting treatment from one accounting period to another unless there is a very good reason to change. If a company has a policy of deciding that funds spent on certain items are considered long-term assets, it cannot then choose to treat the funds as day-to-day expenses. The consistency concept reassures the users of the financial statements that accountants do not change their accounting methods to show a more favourable picture of the organization.

Of course, there may be a very good reason for a company deciding to change its accounting policy. There is an accounting standard (IAS 8 *Accounting Policies, Changes in Accounting Estimates and Errors*) which sets out the circumstances where companies can change their accounting policies and the information that must be disclosed in such situations.

THE MATCHING CONCEPT

If we want to know the financial performance of an entity for a financial period (how much profit or loss it has made), we need to account for the expenses it has incurred in that period and match them with the revenue it has generated. By doing this we calculate the profit or loss for the financial period.

THE MONEY MEASUREMENT CONCEPT

This assumes that only the items that are capable of being measured reliably in financial terms are included in the financial records. This usually causes no problems. If a company buys 20 tonnes of steel at £500 per tonne £10,000 is entered into the financial records. If a company has 100 employees and pays them each £300 per week, the weekly wage bill is £30,000. What the company is unable to do is to enter into its records how much those employees are 'worth'. They may be highly skilled and the company may not be able to operate without them, but a money measurement cannot be calculated reliably to account for this asset.

Another example is where a successful business has built up a good 'reputation'. It is known for making excellent products, keeping to delivery times and offering an excellent after-sales service. You will not find a money measurement for these attributes. Reliability in measurement is normally a requirement to recognize an economic transaction or event and to be able to enter the economic activity into the accounting records of the appropriate organization.

HISTORICAL COST CONCEPT

The principle of this concept is that the values of assets are based on their original cost, which is when the original transaction or event took place. No adjustments are made for subsequent changes in price or value. The concept has the great merit of being extremely reliable. If you wanted to know how much a company had paid for an item of equipment, you would only need to look at the actual payment.

This method also has some great disadvantages. A company may purchase some land in 1970 for £750,000. It may decide in 2012 to buy an additional piece of land which is identical in all ways to the original purchase but the price is now £1,000,000. How is the user expected to interpret this information in 2012? In the financial statements the value of the land will be added together and the company will disclose it has land worth £1,750,000. The most obvious question the user will ask is 'What is the current value of the two pieces of land?'

There have been some attempts to replace historical cost accounting with a different method which better reflects current values. There are several methods each with their own advantages and disadvantages. These methods make the information more relevant to the decisions being made by the user but the reliability of the information may be uncertain.

PRINCIPLES VERSUS RULES

A substantial part of this chapter will be discussing the convergence project undertaken by the FASB and the IASB, particularly the part on the Conceptual Framework. If international accounting is to be achieved, there must be agreement on the assumptions and concepts that are to serve as the basis for setting standards. Unfortunately, the IASB (and the United Kingdom) has a very different starting position than the United States. The IASB uses a principles-based approach to standard setting and the United States uses a rules-based approach.

The difference between a principles-based approach and a rules-based approach to setting standards is that the former approach applies fundamental concepts to ensure financial statements are not misleading. The burden is placed on the preparer and auditors of the financial statements to use their judgement and experience to ensure the financial statements give a true and fair view. A rules-based approach states that if you follow the rules strictly when preparing financial statements they will not be misleading.

The problem with adhering strictly to the rules is that it excludes professional judgement resulting in decisions that are consistent with the rules but inconsistent with the principle of providing the most useful financial information to users.

There is also the danger that the preparers of financial statements may comply with the rules, and are beyond criticism, but may stretch the limits of what is permissible under the law, even though it may not be ethically or morally acceptable or even good accounting.

Conversely it can be argued that the principles-based approach gives too much scope to preparers and auditors for creative accounting. Also, without strict rules to be followed, individual companies will choose different accounting treatments and the characteristic of comparability will be lost. It is difficult to compare the financial results of companies if they use different methods to account for transactions and events.

The thinking of the IASB may have been influenced by the long-held tenet in the United Kingdom that financial statements should give a 'true and fair view'. The concept of true and fair view first appeared in the United Kingdom in the Joint Stock Companies Registration and Regulation Act of 1844 (McGregor, 1992). Over the years there has been debate over its meaning and in 1983 the Accounting Standards Committee in the United Kingdom took counsel's opinion.

The advice was that in the end the decision would be made by a judge but courts would consider compliance with accounting principles as prima facie evidence that the accounts are true and fair (Hoffman and Arden, 1983). The implication of this advice is that the obligation to give a true and fair view takes precedence over all other accounting requirements of company legislation and accounting standards.

In 2005 the Financial Reporting Council confirmed that following the adoption of IAS 1 and 'fair presentation' in the EU, the concept of 'true and fair view' remained a cornerstone of financial reporting and auditing in the United Kingdom (FRC, 2005).

This position has been reconfirmed by the Financial Reporting Council (2012) and the consequences of its application explained.

Para 18 The requirement to give a true and fair view may in special circumstances require a departure from accounting standards. However, because accounting standards are formulated with the objective of ensuring that the information resulting from their application faithfully represents the underlying commercial activity, the FRC envisages that only in exceptional circumstances will departure from the requirements of an accounting standard be necessary in order for financial statements to give a true and fair view.

Para 19 If in extremely rare circumstances compliance with the requirements of an accounting standard is inconsistent with the requirement to give a true and fair view, the requirements of the accounting standard should be departed from to the extent necessary to give a true and fair view.

Although IAS 1 used the term 'financial presentation', the ability to 'override' the requirements of accounting standards was maintained, although some argued that its interpretation was very different from true and fair. Evans (2003) critically examined the evidence and concluded that the override in IAS 1 should be viewed in its narrowest possible interpretation and not as an independent all-pervasive fundamental concept.

A different and more philosophical stance was taken by Alexander and Jermakowicz (2006). They contended that the 'underlying economics of any company, as a "reality", cannot exist independently of a conceptual scheme agreed between human actors' (p.137). Subsequent articles by other authors have also made suggestions and counterclaims. On a more practical basis it is argued that 'the "true and fair view" is not easy as ever-evolving regulation and changes in accounting standards mean that the "true and fair" goalposts keep moving' (O'Keeffe and Hackett (2012, p.31).

Given the above background, it is not surprising that the debate on the principles/rules approach is so heated and explains the problems that some countries have in adopting International Financial Reporting Standards completely. It is not just a case of exchanging one set of regulations for another. National regulators differ in their authority, size of budget, thoroughness of process and competence of staff and, the 'regulatory culture' differs from country to country. Additionally, some countries have a principles-based approach to regulations; others are more comfortable with a rules-based approach.

Discussion point

Do you consider the concept of 'true and fair' worth retaining or should it be abandoned?

CREATING A CONCEPTUAL FRAMEWORK

The debate on the purpose and users of financial statement has increased in intensity over recent years as the search for global standards has developed. We have already discussed the issues of users and uses of financial statements in Chapter 1. The debate has continued and is a joint project of the FASB and the IASB known as the Conceptual Framework.

This project attempts to converge the two different Conceptual Frameworks but there are difficulties. The project has been divided into eight phases and in 2006 a Discussion Paper was issued which addressed the objective of financial reporting.

> The objective of general purpose external financial reporting is to provide financial information that is useful to present and potential investors, and creditors and others in making investment, credit, and similar resource allocation decisions (IASB, 2006, p.18).

It is evident from this extract that the objective of financial reporting is perceived as a decision-making one. The users as well as the types of decision that they take are identified. However, several respondents to the Discussion Paper claimed the financial reporting has two objectives: decision making and stewardship.

There are various opinions on the meaning of stewardship, but 'the contemporary concept of stewardship is synonymous with the notion of accountability to both internal and external parties for the purposes of revealing and evaluating the past actions of both the enterprise and its management and, to some extent, influencing future actions' (O'Connell, 2007, p.218).

The UK Accounting Standards Board is a strong proponent of the stewardship objective. It issued a discussion paper (2007) after a detailed review of all the comment letters to the IASB 2006 Discussion Paper and argued that:

- there is a broad consensus among the majority of the respondents that the stewardship/accountability objective should be a separate objective of financial reporting;

- stewardship/accountability is linked to agency theory and is a broader notion than resource allocation as it focuses on both past performance and how the entity is positioned for the future. It should therefore be retained as a separate objective of financial reporting to ensure that there is appropriate emphasis on company performance as a whole and not just on potential future cash flows; and

- stewardship/accountability has implications for financial reporting which can be demonstrated by way of examples.

A Project Summary and Feedback report (FASB, 2010) explained the responses from external parties to the converged IASB/FASB opinion on objectives. Undoubtedly, the concept of stewardship was troublesome and the FASB stated that, in view of the comments received, the wording of the chapter would be changed to describe what stewardship encapsulates, even if that word would not be used.

Discussion points

Should financial statements serve a stewardship model, a decision-making model or attempt to serve both?

Although the objectives of financial reports may continue to be debated, the project on the Conceptual Framework has addressed other issues. Two underlying assumptions of financial statements have been identified: the accruals concept and the going concern concept. These concepts are not new and were first formally identified in the 'Framework for the Preparation and Presentation of Financial Statements'.

THE ACCRUALS ASSUMPTION

The concept

The IASB states that financial statements must be prepared on the accruals basis. It explains that transactions and other events are recognized as they occur and not when cash or any other consideration such as cheques are given or received. These transactions and events must be recorded in the accounting records when they occur and not when payment is made or received. In simple terms: profit and cash are not necessarily the same.

The application

In some instances the transaction and payment may take place at the same time. You go and have your haircut and you pay for it immediately. However, frequently the transaction and the payment of cash occur at different times. For example, you may decide to buy a new bed in the last month of 2011, although you will not pay until January 2012. Assuming the year end of the dealer is 31 December, using the accruals basis, the dealer must record the transaction in the accounts for 2011 although the cash will not be received until 2012.

The consequences

In March a store buys £1000 worth of goods and sells them in the same month for £1250. The profit is £250 but this tells us nothing about the cash position of the transactions. If cash is paid and received at the same time as the transaction the amount of cash surplus will be the same as the amount of profit £250. Let us take two scenarios where there is a difference in the timing of the cash movements.

A. The customers have not yet paid for the goods but the store has paid for the goods.

B. The customers have paid for the goods but the store has not yet paid its supplier.

The Cash Position

	Scenario A	Scenario B
Cash from customers	£0	£1,250
Cash paid to suppliers	£1,000	£0
Cash surplus/(deficit)	(£1,000)	£1,250

This is not merely a conceptual consequence but a major issue for the business. In scenario B the business appears to be cash rich with £1250 but, of course, the supplier still has to be paid. In scenario A the business has a serious problem with a cash deficit of £1000. If it has cash in the bank or can get a temporary loan, the matter is solved. If that is not the case it brings us to the next underlying assumption

THE GOING CONCERN ASSUMPTION

The concept

Financial statements are usually prepared using the assumption that the business is a going concern and will remain so in the foreseeable future. It is assumed that the business does not intend to or need to close down: it is going to continue trading. If there is evidence that this is not the case, for example, the company may have so much debt it has to close, the accounts will be drawn up on a different basis. This will often entail looking at the 'break-up' value of the business which is likely to be much less than its value if it were a going concern. If the company does not prepare its financial statements on a going concern basis, it must be disclosed, as should the reasons for making that decision.

The practice

It is the responsibility of the management to determine the organization's status as a going concern. If the management is aware that there are material uncertainties that may cast significant doubt upon the organization's ability to continue, those uncertainties should be disclosed. In making their decision, management must consider all available future information which is not necessarily restricted to the following 12 months.

The consequences

The responsibility for determining the going concern basis is firmly placed on the management. The signs that a business is probably experiencing difficulties are:

Financial problems

Default on loan or similar agreements, arrears in dividends, denial of usual trade credit from suppliers, restructuring of debt, noncompliance with statutory capital requirements and a need to seek new sources or methods of financing or to dispose of substantial assets.

Internal management problems

Work stoppages or other labour difficulties, substantial dependence on the success of a particular project, uneconomic long-term commitments and a need to significantly revise operations.

External problems

Legal proceedings, disadvantageous changes in legislation or similar matters that might jeopardize an entity's ability to operate; loss of a key franchise, license or patent; loss of a principal customer or supplier; and an uninsured or underinsured catastrophe such as a drought, earthquake or flood.

It is understandable if the management, in considering these factors, may take a more optimistic view than a less involved individual. It may then be left to the external auditors to state that in their opinion the business is not a 'going concern'. The above list is not exhaustive and the auditors will make a full investigation where they have doubts.

When it is known that the business may not be a going concern then that business is normally finished. No other organization will wish to trade or lend money to a business that is on the verge of failure. There are some examples, however, where such a business has been able to turn itself around. It would seem that the sound of the final nail in the coffin has compelled management to take the drastic actions that they have been avoiding.

QUALITATIVE CHARACTERISTICS OF INFORMATION

In addition to these fundamental assumptions the Framework for the Preparation and Presentation of Financial Statements (IASB, 2010) refers to the qualitative characteristics of information. These are the attributes that make the information in financial statements useful. In the 1997 Framework there were ten characteristics with no particular ranking. The 2010 revisions divide the characteristics into two groups: those that are fundamental and those that are enhancing qualitative characteristics.

It is not clear whether there is a ranking with these two groups, although the terminology suggests that fundamental characteristics are the most important. For information to be useful to the decision maker it must be relevant and faithfully represent what it purports to represent. Faithful representation appears to be very similar to reliable but, as we will see later, the text explains its choice of wording.

As well as the two fundamental characteristics, the usefulness of financial information is enhanced if it is comparable, verifiable, timely and understandable. These qualities do not of themselves make the financial information useful: there must be relevance and faithful representation. Innumerable academic papers have been written debating whether 'faithful representation' has the same meaning as the UK 'true and fair'. We discuss these in the following section.

The explanation of relevance follows on from other definitions. If the financial information is capable of affecting the decisions made by users it is relevant. To do this the financial information should have predictive value, confirmatory value or both. The information itself need not be predictive but it has predictive value if others can use it in making their own predictions. Confirmatory value is where the information provides feedback about previous evaluations.

Normally, the same financial information will have both confirmatory and predictive value. The actual financial results for the current year can be compared with previous predictions either to confirm or change them as well as serving as an input to future predictions.

To complete the explanation of 'relevance' the IASB incorporates the concept of 'materiality'. If information is omitted or misstated and this could influence the decision of the user, that information is considered material. It is impossible to specify what the term 'material' signifies as it will depend on the company and the event.

The claim for the importance of relevance is based on opinions on the information required by the user and standard setters have introduced more fair value accounting measures. However, a a study by Pike and Chui (2012) demonstrated, reliability is a more important factor influencing individuals' intentions to use/rely on financial statements for decision making. Some caution must be used with these results as the sample consisted of students.

FAITHFUL REPRESENTATION

Although one may be tempted to consider that faithful representation is the same as reliable, this would be a mistake. The IASB affirms that to give a perfectly faithful representation the information should be complete, neutral and free from error. This sounds like the concept of 'reliability', but wording elsewhere in the document suggests otherwise.

In discussing the information required for a group of assets the possibility of other than historical cost measurement is opened up. It states that, at a minimum, companies should disclose a description of the nature of the assets in the group, a numerical depiction of all of the assets in the group and a description of what the numerical depiction represents.

The Conceptual Framework also introduces the potential for using estimates to provide useful information that gives faithful representation. It contends that an estimate of an unobservable price or value cannot be determined to be accurate or inaccurate. However, a representation of that estimate can be faithful if the amount is described clearly and accurately as being an estimate, the nature and limitations of the estimating process are explained and no errors have been made in selecting and applying an appropriate process for developing the estimate.

> ### Discussion point
>
> Do you consider that financial information should promote relevance rather than reliability?

ENHANCING QUALITATIVE CHARACTERISTICS
Comparability

A major argument in favour of international accounting was comparability. Every country in the world would use the same accounting and therefore investors, creditors and trading partners could compare the financial statements of companies in different countries. That notion of comparability is the first of the four enhancing characteristics.

Comparability is regarded as the characteristic that enables users to identify and understand similarities in, and differences among, items. To make a comparison there must be at least two items. If alternative accounting methods are used for the same economic phenomenon, comparability will be diminished. Accounting aims to achieve comparability and consistency helps to achieve that aim.

Verifiability

Although the Conceptual Framework posits that verifiability helps assure users that information faithfully represents the economic phenomenon, it is not too clear what action the user should pursue, if any. One could assume that it is the management's responsibility to ensure this characteristic, but the paper refers to knowledgeable and independent observers being able to reach consensus. Only auditors could carry out the checks given in the examples in the document and therefore there is little change from existing practices.

A reference is made to the verification of future information and it is recommended that the underlying assumptions, the methods for compiling the information and other factors and circumstances are disclosed so that users can assess whether they wish to use the information. Once again, existing practices, at least by the major companies, usually adopt this approach.

Timeliness

This characteristic only merits a few sentences in the document and timeliness means having information available to decision makers in time to be capable of influencing their decisions. This raises some issues that are not addressed. The timeliness of the information can mean two different things. One can be the time taken to communicate the information to the user. The second can mean the recency of the data's values.

As far as the timing of the release of information to the users, the requirement of the London Stock Exchange is that companies should release their Annual Financial Report within four months of the financial year end. It is questionable whether this is timely, and when we discuss management accounting in the second half of this book, the timeliness of information will be a key factor in managerial decision making.

The recency of the data's values raises a greater problem which is discussed in more detail later. Essentially, accounting has traditionally followed the historical cost model. We record transactions on the date they occur. If I buy some land in the year 2000 and I communicate this information to you now, using the historical model I would tell you the price I paid in 2000, not what the land is now worth.

The historical cost model still dominates accounting practices, but as the conceptual model develops, there is every indication that the thinking of accounting standard setters will move further away from historical cost model and start to require current prices.

Discussion point

Does the time allowed by the Stock Exchange for the release of annual financial reports detract from their relevance?

Understandability

Nobody would claim that the lay person would be able to understand fully financial statements without training. The information is about complex economic phenomenon and uses concepts and assumptions that are not always well understood or articulated. Certainly, classifying, characterizing and presenting information clearly and concisely can make it understandable, but there can remain information that is intelligible to only the most financially sophisticated user.

The Conceptual Framework argues that such information should not be omitted as the reports would be incomplete and misleading. The paper recommends that even the reasonably knowledgeable user may need to seek an adviser to understand information about complex economic phenomenon. Interestingly, the standard setters only ever refer to the disclosure of financial information and not to the communication of such information. It could be argued that the term 'communication' implies that an effort is made to ensure that the recipient understands the message.

Discussion point

Should the IASB make a greater effort to ensure that information is communicated in a way that is understandable?

THE COST CONSTRAINT ON USEFUL FINANCIAL REPORTING

Producing annual financial reports is a costly business. The requirements and recommendations of the IASB for various disclosures of information are circumscribed by the need for the costs of reporting information to be outweighed by the benefits the users receive. This equation is difficult to calculate for the following reasons.

- The company may prepare the information but the user suffers the cost in the form of reduced financial returns from the company (e.g. a lower dividend).

- If the needed information is not provided, the user will incur additional costs in obtaining that information by other means.
- Disclosure of financial information that has relevance and faithful representation makes for a more efficient capital market with lower costs for everyone.

In concentrating on the financial disclosures, it is easy to forget that for most companies the Annual Report and Accounts is a promotional document. For most major companies, possibly less than one-third of the document contains the financial reports.

Much of the document is concerned with products, corporate strategy, successful projects and charitable involvements and so on. Most of these disclosures are accompanied by excellent photographs and are printed on high-quality paper. To a large extent, the total cost of the Annual Report and Accounts is in the control of the companies and is little influenced by the disclosure requirements of accounting standards.

THE BUSINESS ENTITY CONCEPT

This is the current phase of the new Conceptual Framework and is causing some difficulties. The main problem is how to define the term 'entity', particularly when we consider a group of companies. It could be argued that in developing the Conceptual Framework it might have been preferable to determine who has to give the information and then identify the users.

Entities listed on Stock Exchanges are usually Groups, that is a number of separate companies either wholly owned or partly owned by a holding company. As users of the financial statements we are interested in seeing the financial statements for the group and that is our reporting entity.

There are, however, two main theories or perspective as to what a group is: the proprietary theory and the entity theory.

The proprietary theory views the group from the perspective of the proprietors – the major owners of the group. The financial statements of the group should show the total interest owned by the proprietor. In some of the subsidiaries, the holding company will own the major part of the subsidiary, but not 100 per cent, the minor part being held by other investors. In this instance, the financial statements of the group will show the total interest owned by the holding company either directly or indirectly via the proportional ownership of the subsidiary.

The entity theory perceives the group as a single economic entity. In these circumstances the financial statements of the group show the total resources managed by the group for the purpose of providing useful information to all the group's stakeholders, including those with only the minor ownership.

The deliberations by the FASB and the IASB have tended to avoid this issue or at least delay its resolution to a later date. The current position is the following definition.

> ## Definition – Entity
>
> A circumscribed area of economic activities whose financial information has the potential to be useful to existing and potential equity investors, lenders and other creditors who cannot directly obtain the information they need in making decisions about providing resources to the entity and in assessing whether the management and the governing board of that entity have made efficient and effective use of the resources provided (FASB, 2011).

This tells us more about the reporting process than the reporting entity but the FASB document identifies the following three features of a reporting entity:

a. Economic activities of an entity are being conducted, have been conducted, or will be conducted.

b. Those economic activities can be objectively distinguished from those of other entities and from the economic environment in which the entity exists.

c. Financial information about the economic activities of that entity has the potential to be useful in making decisions about providing resources to the entity and in assessing whether the management and the governing board have made efficient and effective use of the resources provided.

This explanation lacks the preciseness that is required to define an entity and the position is not helped by the final line in the document which states 'These features are necessary but not always sufficient to identify a reporting entity.'

The preliminary views of the project were exposed for public comment. Many respondents believed that the IASB had not adequately discussed or debated the issue of presenting financial statements from a given perspective (i.e. entity, proprietary and parent company approach).

MAIN MEASUREMENT CONCEPTS

The Conceptual Framework identifies four different methods for determining how to measure the transactions and events to be recognized and shown in the financial statements. There have been other proposals and some changes in the terms used since the Framework was issued. Each method has its advocates and its detractors and we currently use a mixed measurement approach with historic cost accounting being the most dominant method. The four methods given in the Framework are summarized and explained below.

HISTORIC COST

Traditionally, this has been the approach favoured by accountants. Using this method assets are recorded at the amount paid for them at the time of their acquisition. Liabilities are recorded at the amount of proceeds received in exchange for the obligations or the amount of cash to be paid to satisfy the liability in the normal course of business.

The great advantage of historical cost is its reliability. You know exactly how much was paid for the asset and there will in all probability be a paper trail that can be used to verify the cost. You know how much you have to pay to settle any liability you have incurred. Bookkeeping records the cost at the date of the transaction and that amount appears in our financial statements.

The disadvantage of the historic cost approach is the poor input that the information gives to users for decision making, particularly after the passage of time. Companies may have acquired premises, land and machinery over the years. If they were recorded at historic cost they will remain in the records at that amount. After several years because of changes in prices, the values the assets are shown at will be out of date.

Some companies still have properties in their accounts at the price they were purchased at over 20 years ago. It is highly probable that the value of these has increased considerably. They may also have machines and equipment and it is highly likely that now these are not worth the original price. We explain in Chapter under the section 'depreciation' the accounting treatment of these items, but the objective of depreciation is not to reveal the current value.

CURRENT COST

This is sometimes referred to as replacement value or current entry value. For assets, it is the amount that would have to be paid if the same or similar asset was acquired currently, in other words how much it would cost to replace that asset. Liabilities are valued at the amount of cash that would be needed to settle the liability.

Some technical issues relate to this method. The asset you now own may be a few years old. It would be unfair to use the price of a brand new asset as the current replacement value; so adjustments need to be made. Additionally, prices may have increased or decreased due to inflation/deflation or other reasons. How is that to be factored into the calculation? It may be that the particular asset you own, for example, a specialized piece of machinery, is no longer available.

There are proposals to deal with some of these issues, but the amount of work that may need to be undertaken by companies to arrive at the current cost of their assets may not be worth the effort in terms of the relevance or reliability of the answers.

REALIZABLE VALUE

This is sometimes known as current exit value. Assets are shown at the amount that could be obtained if the asset were sold in an orderly disposal, that is, not in a bankruptcy. Liabilities are valued at the amount of cash that would be needed to settle the liability.

If there is an active market for the asset, it should be possible to assess the realizable value. But if there is no active market, what is the procedure? It could even be possible that the realizable value is zero although the company regards the asset capable of generating future economic benefits.

PRESENT VALUE

This is sometimes known as value in use. Money has a time value. If you invest £100 now you would expect to receive more than £100 back in one year's time. You can reverse this approach and say that if you expect to receive £100 in one year's time and the interest rate is 10 per cent that future £100 is only worth approximately £90 now.

In applying the present value method, assets are not shown in the balance sheet at what they cost. Instead the discounted value of the future cash flows that the asset is expected to generate in the normal course of business is used. Liabilities are carried at the present discounted net value of the future cash flows expected to be required to settle the liabilities in the normal course of business.

Obviously, these calculations require estimates of future cash flows and a decision made on the rate used to discount those future cash flows. Reliability is, to a large extent, being abandoned in preference to relevance.

We will use an introductory example to demonstrate how these concepts might be applied.

EXAMPLE

Company A needs a loan but the only asset it has is a machine that is used in production. Company A knows that the bank manager will want to use the machinery for security and will ask its value. The company has managed to obtain the following information.

HISTORICAL COST

The machine cost £250,000 five years ago and is expected to continue to produce for a further five years. The machine will have no scrap value at the end of that time.

CURRENT COST

As prices have increased over the last five years it would cost £300,000 to replace the machine. This would be basically the same model of machine.

REALIZABLE VALUE

As industry is booming and the machine has been well maintained; the company is confident that it could sell the machine for £175,000.

PRESENT VALUE

The company believes that after deducting all costs of running the machine, it will receive £100,000 in cash each year for the next five years from the output it will sell.

The problem is to decide what the value of the machine is. If we use historic cost we have the reliable purchase cost of £250,000, but the machine is half way through its useful life. As we explain in Chapter 7, the company will depreciate the machine so the amount shown in the company's accounts is likely to be £125,000. They will have written off half of the cost of the machine over the first five years and will write off the remaining half over the next five years. But the amount of £125,000 is not intended to show the 'value' of the machine. Under present practices, it is an indication of the proportion of the original cost that has not been written off in the financial statements.

The current cost is the value of a new machine, but the machine the company owns is five years old. We could arrive at a calculated, but arbitrary, value by taking just half of the value of the new machine to represent the age of the old machine. This gives a value of £150,000.

The realizable value of £175,000 looks a useful guide to the value. Of course, there are often many circumstances where the company is unable to sell the machine. Also, how confident are we that there are likely purchasers willing to complete the transactions. This also poses the question as to why the company does not sell the machine as it would receive £25,000 more than the amount it has in its books. The answer to that is in the final method of measurement.

By keeping the machine and continuing to sell the output the company will receive an annual cash surplus of £100,000 for the next five years. It is obviously better for the company to keep the machine rather than to sell it. There is one refinement that we need to make to this amount and that is the calculation of the present value of the future cash flows known as 'discounting'.

In making its predictions, the company is deciding that it will receive £100,000 in year five. The problem is that £100,000 in five years' time is not worth as much as £100,000 now. If you had £100,000 now you could invest it and by year five you would have significantly more than £100,000.

We need, therefore, to take all of the future cash flows of £100,000 and turn them into present values. For example, at 10 per cent interest you would only need to invest £90,909 now to receive £100,000 in one year's time. That future £100,000 is therefore discounted to its present value of £90,909. This procedure is applied to all future years and the further away in time the £100,000 is received, the less its value now.

FAIR VALUE

This method of measurement has recently been formalized in an accounting standard. IFRS 13 *Fair Value Measurement* applies to IFRSs that require or permit fair value measurements or disclosures. It also provides a single IFRS framework for measuring fair value and requires disclosures about fair value measurement. The standard represents the completion of the IASB project to align the IFRS and US GAAP fair value requirements (with some minor exceptions).

IFRS 13 does not prescribe which assets or liabilities should be measured at fair value. It only gives guidance for measuring fair value when another IFRS requires or permits fair value measurements or disclosures about fair value measurements. It does not apply to:

- share-based payment transactions within the scope of IFRS 2 *Share-based Payment*;
- leasing transactions within the scope of IAS 17 *Leases*;
- measurements that have some similarities to fair value but that are not fair value, such as net realizable value in IAS 2 *Inventories* or value in use in IAS 36 *Impairment of Assets*.

It is too early to determine the impact of the standard but the companies most likely to be affected are:

- Acquisitive companies
- Those with significant goodwill and indefinite-lived intangible assets on the balance sheet.
- Financial services and other companies with financial instruments at fair value.
- Those companies which elect to revalue theirtangible assets.
- Real estate developers, retail companies and others with investment properties at fair value.
- Investment companies measuring subsidiaries or other investments at fair value.

In future chapters we will be looking again at the various methods of measurement, but you can appreciate the difficulty in determining the 'value' of an asset. The fact that different standards can require different methods of measurement adds another layer of complexity for the user of the information. You can produce values that are more up to date and more relevant to users' needs but you are going to sacrifice the reliability and understandability of historic cost.

Discussion point

Which measurement method do you consider should be used and why?

CONCLUSIONS

Accounting uses concepts and assumptions and mostly these terms can be regarded as synonyms. To a great extent, the accepted concepts and assumptions have proved useful, but the attempts by the IASB and the FASB to develop a common Conceptual Framework have exposed where there are problems.

The principle- and rule-based approaches are a divide which is proving hard to breach. The discussions involve agreement on the users and uses of financial statements and it is not evident that there is an unambiguous agreement. The protracted search for a Conceptual Framework now appears to be faltering. The documents issued to date have only confronted the basic assumptions and the business entity concept and the measurement concepts are far from completion.

The unwillingness, in 2012, of the United States to commit fully to international accounting standards did not cause the anguish that may have been expected. The United Kingdom has clearly spelt out its commitment and the IASB is putting its efforts into other parts of the world. It is difficult to predict the impact on the Convergence Project, but one suspects that the IASB will continue to develop the Conceptual Framework with or without the US partner.

RECOMMENDED READING

The Bruce Column on the IAS Website.

http://www.iasplus.com/en/news/2013/01/bruce-column.

Institute of Chartered Accountants in England and Wales. (2012) *The Future of IFRS*.

The Financial Reporting Council. (2012) *The Future of UK GAAP*.

http://www.frc.org.uk/Our-Work/Codes-Standards/Accounting-and-Reporting-Policy/
The-future-of-UK-GAAP.aspx

CASE STUDY ELEON PLC.

Eleon plc is a smaller public company that has been in existence for approximately 25 years. It has five factories in the United Kingdom with the newest and most expensive being in the North of England.

There has been a strong rumour that a major, international company intends to launch a hostile takeover. Eleon's managing director has decided to lessen the potential takeover threat by visiting each factory and, in his words, 'Wave the flag'. He intends to address employees, unions, financial institutions and analysts.

Part of his speech will concentrate on the 'true' value of the company. He regards the factory in the North as the big attraction and has asked the PR Director, Bill Crosby, to prepare the speech. The MD has instructed Bill to ensure that his figures are correct, with explanations, because he does not want any awkward questions. Bill has no accounting background.

To gather information, Bill visits the Northern factory and meets Pam Argent, the Management Accountant, and Dave Seward, the Plant Manager. The following is part of their discussions.

Bill: 'How much is the machinery we have in this factory really worth?'

Pam: 'Well, it's only about 4 years old and we have it in our books at about £25 million.'

Bill: 'Is that what we paid for it or what we could sell it for?'

Pam: 'Neither, it's the amount we paid for it 4 years ago less the depreciation charge – you can think of that as the wear and tear of using the machinery for as long as they last. It doesn't tell you what the machinery is now worth. We reckon the machinery will be scrapped after 10 years and then it will be worth nothing.'

Bill: 'OK – so it's like a fictitious figure. Would we get more if we sold them?'

Dave: 'I doubt it. Most of the machinery is built in so I suspect that after getting it ready for transporting to the buyer we could only get £20 million after all costs, if that.'

Bill: 'It seems a bad investment if we can only get less for them than what is shown in our books. I doubt if there will be a takeover if that's the sort of decisions we are making.'

Dave: 'We bought the machines to work and make money. They should bring in lots of cash over the next six years. It should be at least

£10 million cash each year. But be careful. We still have costs of materials, wages and administration so that is not profit.'

Pam: 'And also remember that we have to discount that £10 million each year to its present value.'

Bill decides not to pursue Pam's comment as he fears further explanation will only confuse him at this stage. He thanks Pam and Dave and returns to Head Office. Once there he asks you to prepare a speech, with clear explanations and diagrams, explaining the different ways of valuing the machinery. You should also select the valuation method you consider best for the speech by the MD and prepare the presentation for him to give to the various audiences.

CHAPTER 4
CONSTRUCTING FINANCIAL STATEMENTS

LEARNING OBJECTIVES

At the end of this chapter you should be able to:

- Record business transactions using double entry bookkeeping.
- Construct a Trial Balance.
- Draw up a simple Income Statement and Balance Sheet from the Trial Balance.
- Describe the main financial statements.
- Discuss the requirements and issues regarding provisions.
- Explain the action a company should take in respect of events after the reporting period.

EXECUTIVE SUMMARY

One of the main stages in accounting is recording economic transactions and events. This is a mechanistic procedure relying on good original documentation. Essentially, each transaction is recorded in two accounts in the ledger on opposite sides of the accounts. The accounts will be two sided, the left-hand side being for debit entries and the right-hand side for credit entries.

As each transaction will generate a debit entry on one account and a credit entry on another account, at the end of the financial period the total of the debit entries should be the same as the total of the credit entries. The next stage is to balance all the accounts and then draw a Trial Balance. This is a financial statement which lists of all the closing balances on the accounts of an organization with debit balances in one column and credit balances in the other. If all the entries have been correctly made to the individual accounts, the total of the debit balances on the Trial Balance should agree with the total of the credit balances.

From the Trial Balance, an Income Statement can be drawn up which will show the profit or loss of the organization for the financial period. We will discuss this statement in Chapter 6. Finally, a Balance Sheet can be constructed which will show the capital, assets and liabilities of the organization on the last day of the period. The Balance Sheet is based on the accounting equation. We will discuss this statement in Chapter 7.

The logical procedure of recording transactions must not obscure the fact that the financial statements of a company will contain assumptions and estimates. Two areas of potential problems are provisions and events after the reporting period and standards have been issued on these topics.

IAS 37 *Provisions, Contingent Liabilities and Contingent Assets* was first issued in 1998 and last revised in 2005. Under the standard certain criteria must be met to create a provision. There must be a present obligation (legal or constructive), it must have arisen as a result of a past event, payment is probable in order to settle the obligation, and the amount can be estimated reliably.

IAS 10 *Events After The Reporting Period* was reissued in December 2003 and applies to annual periods beginning on or after 1 January 2005. There was a small revision in 2007. The purpose of the standard is to set out the requirements for those events, both favourable and unfavourable, that occur between the reporting date and the date on which the financial statements are authorized by the board for issue. The standard divides these events into adjusting events and non-adjusting events.

Adjusting events give new evidence on conditions as at the date of the Balance Sheet. The financial statements must be changed to show this new information before they can be authorized. Non-adjusting events occur after the year-end of the company but before the financial statements are authorized. They do not provide new evidence on the conditions as at the Balance Sheet date but they should be disclosed by means of a note to the accounts.

CONCEPTUAL AND PRACTICAL ISSUES

The concept underpinning the method of recording economic transactions and events is that of duality of transactions. This means that every financial transaction has two aspects to record in the book of accounts. At its simplest you can consider those two aspects as giving and receiving by the organization. If a company purchases goods to be sold then it will give cash and receive the goods. If it sells some of those goods on credit to a customer, then the organization will give the customer the goods and receive a promise of payment at a later date. The process of recording these activities is known as double-entry bookkeeping.

The stage of recording economic transactions and events uses double-entry bookkeeping. An account is opened for every type of transaction undertaken. Every transaction has a debit entry and a corresponding credit entry. At the end of the financial period, if the records have been kept correctly, the sum of all the debit entries equals the credit entries.

From the bookkeeping records maintained, periodically a Trial Balance can be constructed. This is a list of all the debit and credit balances on the accounts. If individual transactions have been entered correctly in the books of account, the debit column in the Trial Balance should agree with the credit column. From the Trial Balance an Income Statement to show the profit of the organization and a Statement of Financial Position also known as a Balance Sheet can be constructed.

Transactions can be much more complicated than the above examples, but the same principles hold true and we will set out some basic rules and provide examples. It is assumed that all the economic events and transactions will generate some form of source document such as an invoice or a receipt. These source documents are used by the accounting staff to record the transaction. The authenticity of the transaction is therefore the key to a good bookkeeping system.

Definition – Ledger

Traditionally a book containing accounts of a similar type. For example, the Debtors Ledger would contain a separate account for each customer who received goods on credit.

RECORDING BUSINESS TRANSACTIONS

Although computerized systems are invariably used for the recording of transactions the same principles are applied as for handwritten ledgers. Each page of the ledger would represent an account. The half of the page on the left-hand side is called the debit side. The half of the page on the right-hand side is called the credit side. A basic account can be drawn up as follows:

Name of the account

	Debit			Credit	
Date	Details of transaction	Amount	Date	Details of transaction	Amount

The next stage is to know the rules for the debit and credit transactions that are entered into by an organization.

RECORDING ASSETS AND LIABILITIES

The rules for recording transactions concerning assets and liabilities are a key component of successful bookkeeping. Remember with all accounts the debit side is the left hand and the credit side is the right hand. The following rules are simple but must be applied meticulously:

- To show an increase in an asset account, debit the account.
- To show a decrease in an asset account, credit the account.
- To show an increase in a capital or liability account, credit the account.
- To show a decrease in a capital or liability account, debit the account.

An asset is something that the business owns or over which it has control and will provide economic benefits such as premises, machinery and goods it will sell. A liability is where the organization owes a sum of money. Capital is invested in the business by the owner. In larger companies the term 'equity' is used for 'capital'.

Example

April 1

The owner invests £6000 in the business

The bank lends £4000 to the business

The accounts will look as follows when we apply our rules for capital, assets and liabilities. The entries will each refer to the other account.

Capital account

		£			£
			1 April	Cash account	6,000

Loan account

		£			£
			1 April	Cash account	4,000

Cash account

		£			£
1 April	Capital account	6,000			
1 April	Loan account	4,000			

The above entries show that the organization has £10,000 cash. It received £6000 from the owner and this forms the Capital of the business. It has also received £4000 from the bank and has presumably given a commitment that it will repay it plus interest at some agreed future date.

On 2 April, the organization decides to purchase machinery for £4000. The capital and loan accounts do not change as there have been no transactions with the owner or the bank. However, the cash account will change as cash is being paid and we need a new account to represent the machinery that has been purchased.

We have given cash (which is an asset), so that is a credit entry as we are showing a decrease in the asset of cash. We have received another asset in the form of machinery and that is a debit entry as we are showing an increase in an asset. Only the accounts affected by the transactions are shown below.

Cash account

		£			£
1 April	Capital account	6,000	2 April	Machinery account	4,000
1 April	Loan account	4,000			

Machinery account

		£			£
2 April	Cash account	4,000			

The above example can be continued until we have hundreds if not thousands of entries. With asset, capital and liability accounts the same principles apply for every transaction.

Asset account

Capital account

Liability account

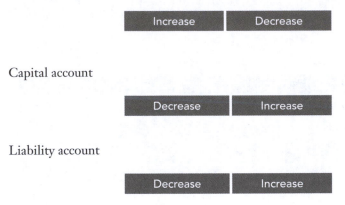

RECORDING REVENUE AND EXPENSES

The double-entry bookkeeping rules for recording transactions involving revenues and expenses are as follows:

- To show an increase in an expense account, debit the account.
- To show a decrease in an expense account, credit the account.
- To show an increase in a revenue account, credit the account.
- To show a decrease in a revenue account, debit the account.

An increase in a revenue account occurs when the company makes a sale or provides a service which is a credit to the revenue account. An increase in an expense account occurs when a company incurs expenses and this will be a debit entry.

We will take the cash account from above and open a revenue account and an expense account for the three following entries:

April 3 the company buys materials for £3000 cash.

April 4 the company sells materials for £4000 cash.

April 4 insurance is paid of £2000.

Cash account

		£			£
1 April	Capital account	6,000	2 April	Machinery account	4,000
1 April	Loan account	4,000	3 April	Purchases account	3,000
4 April	Revenue account	4,000	4 April	Insurance account	2,000

Purchases account

		£			£
3 April	Cash account	3,000			

Revenue account

		£			£
			4 April	Cash account	4,000

Insurance account

		£			£
4 April	Cash account	2,000			

We have only made a few entries and you can imagine how time consuming and tedious the work of double-entry bookkeeping can be. The advent of computerized systems has been a boon. We will complete this brief introduction to entering transactions into the accounts by looking at issues regarding the purchases and sales of goods.

PURCHASES, SALES AND INVENTORY

Purchases are recorded as a debit entry in the purchases account and a credit entry to the cash account. When the business sells the goods they are not shown as a credit entry in the purchases account for two reasons. First, the purchases account records what the goods cost. The goods will not be sold at the price for which they were purchased, as the business adds a mark-up in order to make a profit. The second reason is that at the end of a financial period it is likely there will be some unsold goods remaining, that is, closing stock or inventory. This is a major factor to be accounted for and will be explained in detail in Chapters 6 and 7.

As this is a new business, we will not use an inventory account until the end of the financial period. Instead, the purchases and sales of goods have been recorded in separate accounts, named the *purchases account* and the *sales account*, respectively.

To account for the closing inventory properly, the business must carry out a physical count and a valuation at the end of the financial period. Some businesses use a manual count of closing inventory; others operate a computerized control system which allows up-to-date inventory figures to be read off at any time. If there is a considerable amount of inventory, it is normal to carry out statistical testing as evidence that the computerized records are accurate.

We will come back to our inventory figure at the year-end when we discuss the Trial Balance later in this chapter. You will appreciate that inventory is an asset and if we have some remaining at the year-end there must be a debit to the inventory account.

CREDIT TRANSACTIONS

All the transactions in the examples so far have been for cash. If there are credit transactions, accounts must be opened in the name of the customer or the supplier. If a customer (a debtor) owes us money this is an asset account (accounts receivable) and if we owe supplier (creditor) money this will be a liability account (accounts payable).

At the end of the financial period, all the accounts of those customers still owing us money will be aggregated into one Accounts Receivable account. Similarly, all the accounts of the individual suppliers to which the business still owes money will be aggregated into one Accounts Payable account.

We will use the Purchases Account and the Revenue Account above to illustrate credit transactions but credit transactions can apply to many transactions, such as the acquisition of machinery. In the example, for simplicity, we will use accounts for Accounts Receivable and Accounts Payable and not open accounts in the name of individuals. The transactions are:

April 5 20 kilos materials are purchased for £4000 on credit.

April 6 The 20 kilos of materials are sold for £6000 on credit.

The entries are (remember a debit and credit for each transaction):

Revenue account

		£			£
			4 April	Cash account	4,000
			5 April	Accounts receivable account	6,000

Purchases account

		£			£
3 April	Cash account	3,000			
5 April	Accounts payable account	4,000			

Accounts receivable account

		£			£
5 April	Revenue account	6,000			

Accounts payable account

		£			£
			5 April	Purchases account	4,000

In the next section we are going to explain how accounts are 'balanced' or 'closed'. Before we end this section we will summarize the rules on double entry (Table 4.1).

To show an increase in an account	
Debit	Credit
Purchases	Revenue (Sales)
Assets	Liabilities
Expenses	Capital
To show a decrease in an account the above columns are reversed	

Table 4.1 Rules of double entry

BALANCING ACCOUNTS

Periodically, and at least at the end of a financial period, a company closes or balances its accounts. The rules for this are straightforward and we will illustrate this by using some of the accounts above. The date we are closing the accounts is 6 April.

1. If the account contains entries on each side which are equal to one another, they can be double underlined to close the account for that financial period. This means that there is no outstanding balance on this account at the end of the period. The accounts most likely to be closed are where goods were either sold or bought on credit and the outstanding amount has been paid in full before the end of the financial period.

2. If the account contains only one entry, insert the balancing figure on the opposite side and carry this down to the same side as the original entry to start the next period. The term 'carried down' is often abbreviated to c/d; 'brought down' is abbreviated to b/d. The Accounts Receivable below demonstrates this transaction. The balance shows that we are still owed £6000 on 7 April.

Accounts receivable account

		£			£
5 April	Revenue account	6,000	6 April	Balance c/d	6,000
7 April	Balance b/d	6,000			

3. If the account contains a number of entries, add up both sides. If both sides are the same, insert the totals and double underline them. This means that there is no outstanding balance on this account. This is the same action as number 1.

4. If both sides do not agree, first insert the balancing figure on the side with the lower amount and then insert the totals, which should now be equal, and double underline them. Complete the entry by carrying down the balancing figure on the opposite side as the opening balance for the new financial period. The Cash Account below demonstrates this action. The account shows that we should have £5000 in Cash on 7 April.

Cash account

		£			£
April 1	Capital account	6,000	April 3	Machinery	4,000
April 1	Loan account	4,000	April 3	Purchases account	3,000
April 4	Revenue account	4,000	April 4	Insurance account	2,000
			April 6	Balance c/d	5.000
		14,000			14,000
April 7	Balance b/d	5,000			

For every debit entry we are making a credit entry and vice versa. The list of debit balances and credit balances, therefore, should be equal. This process of adding and comparing the two lists of account balances is known as preparing a Trial Balance.

THE TRIAL BALANCE

A Trial Balance is a list of all the closing balances on the accounts of an organization with debit balances in one column and credit balances in the other. If the double-entry bookkeeping has been done properly, the two totals should agree. The outstanding balances on the above account are shown as a Trial Balance.

Trial Balance as on 7 April

	Debit	Credit
	£	£
Capital		6,000
Loan		4,000
Revenue		10,000
Purchases	7,000	
Accounts receivable	6,000	
Accounts payable		4,000
Insurance	2,000	

	Debit	Credit
	£	£
Machinery	4,000	
Cash	5,000	
	24,000	24,000

(Continued)

Looking at the two columns, you will see that the debit column is a list of all the expenses (for example, purchases), which will appear on the Income Statement, and assets (for example, machinery), which will appear on the Balance Sheet. The credit column is a list of the capital and the liabilities which will appear on the Balance Sheet and the sales or revenues which will appear on the Income Statement.

The only figure still missing is the closing inventory. The organization has purchased goods but has not sold them in the financial period. The assumption is that this closing inventory at the end of this financial period will form the opening inventory for the next period.

On 6 April at close of business, the inventory is counted and valued at £1000. As this is an asset we would have to debit the Inventory Account. The credit entry goes to the Profit and Loss Account as that is really a part of the double-entry system. Many companies have now switched to using the term 'Income Statement' instead of 'Profit and Loss Account' but the principles are the same.

To complete our explanation of the procedure we will give a simple explanation of how the Profit and Loss Account and Balance Sheet are constructed from the Trial Balance. The purpose of the profit and loss account is to calculate the profit or loss for the financial period. This is done by deducting all the expenses incurred from the revenue generated. This is a matching process. The Balance Sheet shows at the end of the financial period the assets, liabilities and the capital invested by the owners of the organization. The sum of all the assets should agree with the sum of all the liabilities and capital. In other words, the Balance Sheet balances.

We can now draw up our Profit and Loss Account, putting in our closing inventory amount. This is a credit amount and is shown as a deduction from the purchases. This gives an amount which is referred to as the Cost of Sales. This is the amount paid for the goods which were actually sold in the financial period. Needless to say, we can only make a profit on the goods we sell.

As the Profit and Loss Account is part of the double-entry bookkeeping system, we completely close the accounts involved, for example, revenue, purchases, expenses by either debiting them or crediting them. The corresponding debit or credit entry is to the Profit and Loss Account. In other words, those accounts that reflect the financial performance of the business over a period are closed completely when the period is ended.

When you are preparing the financial statements from the Trial Balance it is helpful to tick every figure on the Trial Balance. Every amount should be ticked once and once only.

And now the double-sided profit and loss account:

Profit and loss account for the period to 6 April:

	£		£
Purchases	7,000	Revenue	10,000
Deduct closing inventory	1,000		
Cost of sales	6,000		
Insurance	2,000		
Total costs	8,000		
Net profit	2,000		
	10,000		10,000

You will rarely see a published profit and loss account in the above horizontal format. Usually the vertical format as shown below is used.

Income Statement for the period to April 6:

	£	£
Revenue		10,000
Purchases	7,000	
Less closing inventory	1,000	6,000
Gross profit		4,000
Insurance		2,000
Net profit		2,000

We can now prepare the Balance Sheet ticking the remaining amounts on the Trial Balance. There are three things to bear in mind:

1. The Profit and Loss Account is really an account and part of the double entry. It has a net profit and this amount is a credit balance and will be shown on the Balance Sheet as retained profit. In the accounts of large companies the term 'Income Statement' will be used and normally it is shown in a vertical format.

2. The closing inventory was not on the Trial Balance but was an additional note. You have ticked the figure once when it was used on the Profit and Loss Account but you can tick it again as it will be used on the Balance Sheet.

3. The Balance Sheet is not part of the double-entry bookkeeping system. It is a list of the 'balances' at the end of the financial period and those balances will be carried forward to the start of the next financial period. It can be thought of as a 'snapshot' of the financial condition of the business at one point in time.

Balance Sheet as 6 April

	£	£
Non-current assets		
Machinery		4,000
Current assets		
Inventory	1,000	
Accounts receivable	6,000	
Cash	5,000	12,000
Total assets		16,000
Capital		6,000
Retained profit		2,000
Loan		4,000
Accounts payable		4,000
Capital and liabilities		16,000

This is only a simple example which demonstrates how the recording of transactions by using double entry has the following advantages.

- It is a logical system and for every debit there must be a credit and vice versa.
- A full record of all transactions is maintained.
- The Trial Balance demonstrates that you have maintained the system properly, although there are errors that can arise that are not shown by the Trial Balance.
- If the Trial Balance does not balance you know you have made a mistake in your original double-entry bookkeeping.
- The system provides a Profit and Loss Account which shows the profit or loss for the financial period.
- The system shows the financial condition of the business at a specific date – the end of the financial period.

At this stage use caution. The Balance Sheet is exactly what it purports to be: a list of the historical costs that were entered into our records when the transaction was recognized. As we work through later chapters you will find that we have moved away from that concept and we now have a Statement of Financial Position that has a mix of historic costs and current values.

The mechanics of recording transactions by using the double-entry system of bookkeeping should cause you few problems and we do not intend to provide further examples in this book. However, for lecturers and students who wish to pursue the topic further, additional examples and questions are given on the companion website.

THE MAIN FINANCIAL STATEMENTS

The above example demonstrated the recording of business transactions and the compilation of financial statements that could be disclosed to a third party. If we look at present practices and regulatory requirements, a complete set of annual financial statements for a large company comprises:

1. A Statement of Cash Flow which shows from where the entity received cash and how it has used it. The statement provides summative information on all inflows of cash received by a company from its ongoing operations as well as external investment sources. It also shows cash outflows for business activities as well as investments. The statement is the main topic in Chapter 5.

2. A Profit and Loss Account for larger companies now expanded and usually referred to as a Statement of Comprehensive Income incorporating an Income Statement. This shows how well or poorly the entity has performed financially over a period of time. The main elements of the Income Statement will be the revenue that has been received over that period of time and the expenses that have been incurred in generating that revenue. The statement of comprehensive income is discussed fully in Chapter 6.

3. A Balance Sheet which is also known as a Statement of Financial Position. This is like a financial snapshot of the business entity at one point in time and shows its financial position at the end of a financial period. The Statement of Financial Position will be dated on the very last day of the financial period. The main elements of the Statement of Financial Position are the assets that the company has, the investment by the shareholders and the liabilities of the company. The statement of financial position is the main topic in Chapter 7.

4. A statement of changes in equity which shows certain transactions that directly affect shareholders as it discloses the composition of equity and how it has changed over the financial period.

The amount of new share capital issued.

The amount of dividend paid during the year to shareholders.

The amount by which property, plant and equipment is revalued.

The amount of net income earned during the year.

The amount of net income retained during the year.

Any movement in the unrealized loss or gain reserve and reserve for changes in foreign exchange gain or loss.

5. Notes to the financial statements that explain an entity's accounting policies and important matters relating to the other financial statements. The notes are critical to understanding how a company accounts for economic transactions and events and will take several pages of a company's Annual Financial Report

Even for modest-sized businesses, a complete set of annual financial statements will be well over 50 pages and more for larger entities. Companies listed on the Stock Exchange include a substantial volume of information and can be over 200 pages in length. In Chapter 8 we discuss the Annual Financial Report.

In addition to the regulatory disclosures which are required, companies use the Annual Report as a promotional document. There are photographs, information on products and services and news of the company's charitable and environmental efforts. If we look at the entire document, a large part of it will be information that is voluntarily provided and is not governed by any regulations.

Many companies have the Annual Financial Report, and much more, on their website. We recommend that you obtain a copy of the published financial statements of a company that interests you. It is preferable to choose a company that is listed on a stock exchange as this should comply fully with GAAP.

Discussion point

Do you consider that the Annual Report of a company should contain only the financial information legally required or is it acceptable for companies to include other corporate information?

IAS 37 PROVISIONS

IAS 37 *Provisions, Contingent Liabilities and Contingent Assets* was first issued in 1998 and last revised in 2005. In this section we are limiting our discussions to provisions. The purpose of the standard is to ensure that appropriate recognition criteria and measurement methods are used in the creation of provisions.

> ### Definition – Provision
>
> A provision is a liability of uncertain timing or amount.

Prior to the issue of this standard there was scope for companies to manipulate the published profit for the year. If a company had a very profitable year, but did not wish to declare this, it could reduce the profit by charging to the Income Statement a 'provision'. This was an amount put aside as a fund to pay for future events. Examples could be the major maintenance of machinery that usually took place every two years, the repainting of the factory or a proposed restructuring of the company.

The provision reduced the current year's profits and if, in following years, profits declined for some reason, the company could release these provisions to increase their profits instead of using them for the declared purpose.

As far as the users of the financial statements were concerned, the company was reporting a steady profit every year. A more accurate record may have shown that the company had moved from high profits to low profits, but was obscuring this by the release of provisions. The use of provisions in this way was well known and they were often referred to as 'Big bath provisions' or 'Cookie jar provisions' because companies were using them to sweeten their profits and clean up any messes they did not like. The result was that users were being misled, and IAS 37 attempts to bring order into a somewhat chaotic practice.

Under the standard certain criteria must be met to create a provision. There must be:

- A present obligation (legal or constructive);
- It must have arisen as a result of a past event;
- Payment is probable in order to settle the obligation;
- The amount can be estimated reliably.

Present obligation

The key to this criterion is that there must be an obligation which cannot be avoided. The standard defines two types of obligations: legal and constructive. A legal obligation is possibly the easiest to identify and could:

- be contractual; or
- arising due to legislation; or
- result from some other operation of law.

A constructive obligation arises from a company's own policies and practices which can lead others to conclude that, in certain circumstances, the company will act in a certain way. This includes those circumstances where past practice leads third parties to reasonably assume that the entity will settle the obligation (e.g. a sale or return policy by a retailer).

Past events

A company cannot make a provision for an event it considers may take place in the future. For example, businesses cannot make provisions this year for suspected future operating losses. A more common occurrence is routine maintenance. For example, a company may carry out routine maintenance costing £120,000 every three years. It cannot charge to the Income Statement provisions of $40,000 in each of the first two years as there is no certainty that the company will carry out the maintenance in Year 3.

However, there can be a valid reason for making a provision for maintenance as illustrated in the following example from easyJet.

LINK TO PRACTICE

Easyjet plc

easyJet incurs liabilities for maintenance costs in respect of aircraft leased under operating leases during the term of the lease. These arise from legal and constructive contractual obligations relating to the condition of the aircraft when it is returned to the lessor. To discharge these obligations, easyJet will also normally need to carry out one heavy maintenance check on each of the engines and the airframe during the lease term. A charge is made in the income statement based on hours or cycles flown to provide for the cost of these obligations.

£ http://corporate.easyjet.com/ /media/Files/E/Easyjet-Plc-V2/pdf/investors/ result-center-investor/annual-report-2012.pdf

EasyJet can make the provision towards future maintenance as there is a legal obligation to carry out the maintenance.

Payment is probable

The payment will involve an outflow of economic resources and it is more likely than not that the company will have to make this payment. The phrase 'more likely than not' can cause a few headaches but can arise in legal cases that last several years before there is a judgement. The following example is from Smith and Nephew.

In such cases it is normal for the company to depend on legal advice on their probability of winning the case. One assumes that Smith and Nephew had received legal advice that they were likely to lose this case and therefore made a provision.

Amount can be estimated reliably

Reliably does not mean precisely. The definition states that a provision is uncertain in amount or timing. The amount recognized as a provision should be the best estimate of the expenditure required to settle the present obligation at the Balance Sheet date. A business should assess the risks and uncertainties that may operate in reaching their best estimate and any material future cash flows should be discounted to present values.

Examples of provisions allowed under the standard include:

- warranty obligations,
- a retailer's policy on refunds to customers,
- obligation to clean up contaminated land,
- onerous contracts,
- company restructuring.

Definition – Onerous contracts

An onerous contract is where the company has unavoidable costs in meeting its obligations and these exceed the economic benefits that the company expects to receive.

Onerous contracts are reasonably common. Companies enter into many contracts and sometimes these can only be cancelled by a company continuing to make payments. An example is where a company has entered into a non-cancellable ten-year lease to occupy retail premises. After six years the company decides that it wishes to move to a more prestigious location. As the lease is non-cancellable, the company will still have to make the lease payments until the end of the contract. In these circumstances, the company would make a provision for the outstanding amounts to be paid under the lease agreement.

Company restructuring

One area where the use of provisions was blatantly abused was when company restructuring was the claimed reason. If a company wished to hold back some of its profits in a particular year, it was possible, prior to IAS 37, to claim that it intended to carry out restructuring in the following year and include a provision for this. Such provisions frequently were bloated with every receivable cost and, for this reason, were known as "big bath" provisions. If in the following year profits were low, some of the overstuffed provision could be released to the Income Statement to lift profits.

However, a company may decide that it has to make substantial changes to its organization. This could be because of an economic downturn and could result in job losses. The company may decide in the current financial year that it will restructure but the actual event, and the costs arising from it, will take place in the next financial year. If the company can make a reliable estimate of the costs to be incurred, it can make a provision. To prevent repetition of the previous abuses the standard lays down certain examples which are considered restructuring.

- Sale or termination of a line of business;
- The closure of a business location in a country or region or the relocation of business activities from one country;
- Changes in management structure, for example, eliminating a layer of management; or
- Fundamental reorganizations that have a material effect on the nature and focus of the business operations.

In the above circumstances a company can make a provision as long as it has a constructive obligation. We observed in the beginning of this section that a company can make a provision for a legal or constructive obligation. Assuming there is no legal reason for the reconstructing a company must demonstrate a constructive obligation by fulfilling two criteria:

- It must have a detailed formal plan, and
- It must be communicated to those affected prior to the restructuring.

A detailed formal plan must contain at the minimum the following information:

- The business or part of a business concerned;
- The principal locations affected;
- The location, function and approximate number of employees who will be compensated for terminating their services;
- The expenditure that will be undertaken; and
- When the plan will be implemented.

Although a restructuring plan is usually designed at a senior management level and often requires board approval, it does not make the plan a constructive obligation. It is essential that the plan is communicated to those who are going to be affected prior to the restructuring. The disclosure may either be directly to those affected by the plan, for example employees and suppliers, or a public announcement can be made giving details of the plan.

There are several conditions in the standard restricting the use of provisions. An important topic is where a provision is no longer required. A company may have in good faith made a provision but subsequently discovers that it is not needed. Companies should make an annual review of provisions and if the provisions are no longer required it should be reversed to income. They are not able to use a provision made for one eventuality that did not occur as expected for another eventuality that was not predicted. A provision can be applied only to the expenditure for which the provision was originally recognized.

Discussion point

Do you consider that allowing companies to make provisions discloses useful information or should provisions be banned entirely and expenses only shown in the financial statement when they actually occur?

IAS 10 EVENTS AFTER THE REPORTING PERIOD

IAS 10 *Events after the Reporting Period* was reissued in December 2003 and applies to annual periods beginning on or after 1 January 2005. Its purpose is to set out the requirements for events which occur after the end of the reporting period, but before the authorization of the financial statements. Depending on the nature of the event, either the financial statements should be adjusted or the event should be disclosed as a note to the accounts.

Listed companies have four months to file their accounts with the stock exchange but many will do it much quicker. However there is bound to be a delay between the date on the financial statements and the date they are authorized by the board of directors and subsequently filed. For example, a company that has financial statements for the year to 31 December 2012 may not authorize them until the end of March 2013 or even later.

There are many reasons for this delay. First, if the end of the year is 31 December, it requires considerable work by the accountants to prepare financial statements. Secondly, companies may not have all the available information and must make some estimates. Finally, and importantly, the financial statements will have to be approved by the auditors before the board of directors authorizes that they can be made publicly available.

In that period between the end of the financial period and the authorization by the company's Board of Directors further significant information may become available. Some of this will refer to events that occurred in the previous year. Items that were initially estimates will now have the actual figures and some assumptions will be supported by facts. Other information may be significant but refers to events after the end of the reporting period but before the authorization of the financial statements.

These events may be favourable or unfavourable as far as the financial performance and position of the company is concerned. However, without this information, the user of the financial statements may not obtain a full understanding of the position and performance of the business.

The problem arises on how best to account for this additional information and timing becomes a critical criterion. For example, a company with the year end 31 December 2012 owns a factory which is shown at a value of £1.5 million in its financial statements. The board meeting to authorize the financial statements takes place on 10 April 2013.

One scenario is that on 22 December there is a major fire. The factory is not insured and at the end of February an assessor states that the factory is now valued at £1.2 million. Another scenario is that the fire takes place on 15 January 2013 with the assessor making the same valuation. The dilemma facing the board is how to treat these events. There are several potential avenues for the fire on 22 December as follows:

- The valuation of £1.5 million was estimated on information available at that time. The assessor's valuation did not come until after the year end and should be ignored.

- The amount in the financial statements should be changed to £1.2 million.

- A note should be given in the accounts informing the shareholders of the event.

If the fire had taken place on 15 January, after the year end, there is an argument that the financial statements for 2012 are correct and no action needs to be taken.

Discussion point

What do you consider to be the most appropriate action to be taken by the board in both these circumstances?

We have two similar but, from the point of timing, different situations. In the first the board receives new information about conditions in the Balance Sheet date and in the second receives information about events after the Balance Sheet date but before the financial statements are authorized. The standard divides these events into adjusting events and non-adjusting events. The accounting treatment of each differs.

Adjusting events

Adjusting events give new evidence on conditions as on the date of the Balance Sheet. Where we have adjusting events, the financial statements must be changed to show this new information before they can be authorized. With the factory fire on 22 December, evidence has become available which reveals the original valuation to be incorrect. The financial statements must be restated before they can be authorized. Examples of adjusting events are:

- Discovery of fraud or errors.

- Information about the value or recoverability of an asset at the year end.

- Settlement of an outstanding court case, that is, a case that was in court before the year end has been settled after the year end.

Non-adjusting events

Non-adjusting events do not provide new evidence on the conditions as on the Balance Sheet date. Non-adjusting events occur after the year end of the company but before the financial statements are authorized. The events have no impact on the Balance Sheet on the date it was drawn up but are of such significance that the users should be informed.

In the above example, the factory has been correctly valued at the year-end but is later destroyed by fire but before the authorization date. The financial statements are correct as at the year-end and do not have to be restated. However, a non-adjusting event has occurred that is of significant importance and disclosure should be made. A company would include this information in its Notes to the Accounts in its Annual Report. Examples of non-adjusting events are:

- Fire after the Balance Sheet date destroying or damaging non-current assets.
- Announcements of a major restructuring plan.
- Major purchases of items such as property plant and equipment.
- Purchase of another company.
- Major disposal of property plant and equipment.

The example of a note explaining the nature of a provision is taken from the J Sainsbury Annual Report.

LINK TO PRACTICE

J Sainsbury

On 7 May 2013, the Group signed a share purchase agreement with Lloyds Banking Group to purchase the remaining 50 per cent of Sainsbury's Bank and take sole ownership. The Group intends to fund the future consideration from internal resources. The transaction, subject to regulatory approval, is expected to complete in January 2014.

http://annualreport2013.j-Sainsbury.co.uk/media/30349/
Notes%20to%20the%20Financial%20Statements.pdf#page=24

In determining the appropriate classification of the event, it is essential to take all the surrounding circumstances into account. For example, the reduction in value of a property after the Balance Sheet date but before the authorization date would normally be considered a non-adjusting event. However, information received after the Balance Sheet date that demonstrated that the property had, in fact, lost its value before the Balance Sheet date is an adjusting event.

Discussion point

As non-adjusting events occur after the end of the financial period, do you consider that it is useful for companies to disclose them or is it better to focus solely on events during the financial period?

The standard also requires that an entity should not prepare financial statements on a going concern basis if events occur between the Balance Sheet date and the date of authorization that indicate that the entity is not a going concern. Entities should disclose the authorization date for financial statements. It is essential that users know this date as the financial statements and disclosures will not report any events occurring after the authorization date.

The critical aspect of this standard is the timing of the event and the date of authorization of the financial statements. The standard offers the following guidance:

1. An entity may have to submit its financial statements for approval after the financial statements have been issued. It is usual for the board to authorize the financial statements for issue prior to submitting them to the shareholders. The date of issue will be the date of authorization and not the later date when they are submitted to the shareholders for approval.

2. The management of an entity may have to issue its financial statements to a supervisory board (made up solely of non-executive) for approval. The financial statements are authorized when the board issues them for issue to the supervisory board.

The classification of events is shown in Figure 4.1.

CONCLUSIONS

Record keeping is one of the stages of accounting, but is far less important than some would suggest. Bookkeeping is a simple task and mostly conducted on computerized systems nowadays. Numbers are an essential element of accounting but far more important are concepts.

The end process of recording is the construction of an Income Statement and a Balance Sheet.

The Income Statement is explained more thoroughly in Chapter 6 and the Balance Sheet or Statement of Financial Position in Chapter 7.

In this chapter we have introduced some of the concepts concerned with recognition and measurement. The major problems in accounting are the recognition and measurement of economic events and transactions. Two circumstances which have caused problems in the past have been the creation of 'provisions' and events which occur after the end of the financial period. The standards which have been issued have appeared to address the problems.

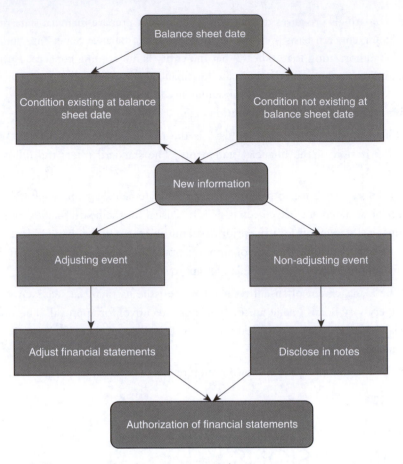

Figure 4.1 IAS 10 Events after the reporting period

CASE STUDY WORDAL PLC.

The Accountant for Wordal plc., an international company, is completing the financial statements to 31 December 2012. The board meeting to authorize the financial statements is on 15 March 2013 and the following problems are outstanding. Advise the accountant as to the actions which should be taken and the reasons.

1. In the month of November 2012, the company caused environmental damage in contravention of the current legislation. In December, the senior surveyor estimates that it will cost approximately £750,000 to remedy. The work to remedy the damage is scheduled to commence on 5 March 2013.

2. In October Wordal learns of an Indian company developing new technology. It considers it must invest the £3.5 million required to stay in

front of its competitors. Negotiations have taken place with the Indian company, and subject to some changes in the agreement, Wordal is planning to invest in the technology in April 2013.

3. The board approves on 1 November 2012 to close permanently one of its factories in Mexico and another in India. Because of the timing and logistical issues, the board was unable to communicate its decision before 31 December 2012 to any of those affected in India. However, extensive discussions had been conducted with all those affected in Mexico.

4. In February 2013, it was discovered that fraud had been committed at one of the divisions throughout the 2012 year and the figure for revenues were overstated by 35 per cent.

5. Early in January 2013, a heavy storm caused extensive damage to its Head Office. A surveyor has examined the damage and estimated that the cost of repairs will be in the region of £500,000.

CHAPTER 5
THE STATEMENT OF CASH FLOWS

LEARNING OBJECTIVES

At the end of this chapter you should be able to:

- Explain the importance of cash both in managing a business and understanding its financial operations.
- Construct a cash flow forecast and explain its various uses.
- Summarize the main requirements of IAS 7 The Statement of Cash Flows
- Differentiate between the direct and indirect methods in calculating cash from operating activities.
- Identify and calculate the adjustments to be made to operating profit to arrive at the cash figure.

EXECUTIVE SUMMARY

Cash is a scarce resource and, in addition to recording cash an organization will monitor and manage the flow of cash flow in and out. If in a financial period the cash flows in are greater than the cash flows out there will be a cash surplus. If the cash flows out are higher there will be a cash deficit.

Cash surpluses and deficits must not be referred to as profit or loss. The cash flow statement tells us about cash. The Income Statement which is discussed in Chapter 6 uses the accruals concepts and shows profit or loss.

Organizations use forecasts of cash movements to manage their finance strategy. If the forecast shows a cash surplus, ways must be found to use this money. It may be making investments, refurbishing a building, purchasing machinery or acquiring another company. If the predictions show a cash deficit, the possibility of loans will be examined but it may be possible to change the timing of cash movements or increase positive cash flows by increasing revenues or decrease cash flows out by cutting costs.

Because of the importance of cash to the well-being of an organization external parties are very interested in such information. IAS 7 *Statement of Cash Flows* was issued by the IASB in 1977 to meet the needs of users. It was retitled Statement of cash flows in 2007 and minor amendments made in 2009.

The objective of IAS 7 is to require the presentation of information about the historical changes in cash and cash equivalents of an entity classifying cash flows during the period according to operating, investing and financing activities. The standard does not require companies to issue cash flow forecasts.

In addition to the case study (Bethan Harrow) at the end of this chapter, additional case studies are given on the companion website.

CONCEPTUAL AND PRACTICAL ISSUES

In calculating profit the accruals concept is used. Transactions and other events are recognized as they occur and not when cash or any other consideration such as cheques are given or received. These transactions and events are recorded in the accounting records when they occur and not when payment is made or received.

In some instances the actual transaction and the payment for it occur at the same time. You go into a store and buy a bottle of milk and pay for it immediately at the check-out. This is recorded as a sales transaction and the organization has received the cash.

Compare this to a retailer who offers credit. In December the retailer buys goods or £8000 and sells them for £10,000. This will be recorded in the accounts and a profit on the transaction, ignoring other costs is £2000. However, if the customers do not pay until the following March then there may be a substantial lack of cash in the business. This depends, of course, on whether the retailer has paid for the goods in the first place.

Using the above example, let us take three scenarios where there is a difference in the timing of the cash movements.

A. The retailer and the customer have paid for the goods in the same financial period.

B. The retailer has not yet paid the supplier for the goods but the customer has paid for the goods.

C. The retailer has paid the supplier for the goods but the customer has not yet paid.

These three positions are shown below from the view of the retailer.

The cash position

	Scenario A	Scenario B	Scenario B
Cash from customers	£10,000	£10,000	–
Cash paid to suppliers	£8,000	–	£8,000
Cash surplus/(deficit)	£2,000	£10,000	(£8,000)

In all three situations, the retailer will record the same profit of £2000 in the financial period. The cash position is very different and therefore the manager of a business must closely monitor the cash position in the company separate from the calculation of the profit. The monitoring and control of cash is critical in a business.

Historically, companies were only required to publish Income Statements and Balance Sheets. It became recognized that cash is interesting and useful information for those who are external to the business. They want to get an overview of where the cash came from, how it is spent, and where any cash surplus is invested. The requirements for cash disclosures are contained in IAS 7 and this is discussed later in the chapter.

Definition – Cash flow statement

A statement showing the timing and amounts of cash inflows and outflows of a business over a financial period. The statement may show actual cash flows in the past or predictions of future cash flows.

RECORDING CASH

In Chapter 4 we introduced Cash Accounts as part of the bookkeeping system in a business. With normal record keeping, organizations have a cash account as part of double-entry bookkeeping. A large company may have several types of cash accounts and may also maintain accounts for transactions with any banks with which they have dealings. In this book we use the term 'cash accounts' to mean any type of cash or bank record that is maintained by the business.

In recording cash we are dealing with present transactions and building an historical bookkeeping record. This will allow the monitoring and control of movements of cash.

Where actual cash is received as notes and coins, security is always an issue. At regular intervals, possibly daily, it is essential that there is a reconciliation of the physical amount of cash held, if any, and the amount shown in the records. Differences, which must be investigated, can arise for the following reasons:

- Incorrect recording of the amount received or paid.

- Theft or loss of cash.

- Incorrect additions.

- Omission of entries in the records either through error or by intent.

A company may hold a certain amount of cash, but it is usual practice to pay cash into the bank as soon as possible. The company will maintain in its own records of all deposits into the bank account and any payments made from the bank account.

A Bank Reconciliation must be made regularly to ensure that the records made by the company agree with the bank statements. Differences may arise because errors have been made either by the bank or in the company's own records. These should be corrected immediately.

Sometimes items may be shown in the company's records and not the banks or vice versa. One example is a cheque has been received by the company and entered into its records but is subsequently dishonoured and not shown in the bank statement. Also entries may have appeared on the bank statement such as bank charges, direct debits and cash withdrawals and the company has failed to record these.

The main reason for company records and bank statements not agreeing is one of timing. For example, a cheque may have been sent by the company and entered into its records but the recipient has not yet paid it into its bank account. Alternatively, the company has immediately recorded cheques that have been received but there has been a slight delay in recording these on the bank statement. A bank reconciliation should resolve these differences. A simple example follows.

Fred Smith maintains a cash book for his small business. He receives some cash payments but the majority are made by cheque. He makes a few small cash payments on a daily basis but for any significant amounts he issues a cheque. On the 31 March the bank statement shows a balance of £5420 and his cash book a balance of £ 4540.

Bank reconciliation as at 31 March 2013

	£
Balance shown on the bank statement	5,420
Add deposits into bank but not yet cleared	1,040
	6,460
Less cheques not yet presented by recipients	1,920
Balance as shown in cash book	4,540

The reconciliation shows that the reasons his cash book and his bank statement were as follows

- Fred had paid some cheques he had received into the bank. These deposits had not been cleared by the bank and therefore did not appear on the bank statement.
- Fred had issued cheques to various people who had not yet paid them into their own banks.

With the advent of electronic banking, automated payments, sophisticated cash registers, the need for bank reconciliations has diminished. However, many small business transactions are still made in cash and this is an obvious area for fraud.

Although detailed records must be maintained, management usually monitor cash by regular summaries of movements over a period of time and the current cash position. These summaries are not required by any regulations but businesses will construct one that meets their needs. This allows management to consider its cash performance in the past and their current financial position.

FORECASTING CASH

Good management must ensure that funds are available for future activities otherwise the business may go bankrupt. If there appears to be a future, but temporary, shortage of cash the business may seek a bank loan. In this case the bank will require the company to submit a credible cash flow forecast. On a more optimistic note, there may be predicted a substantial cash surplus in which case the company must determine what to do with the funds.

The cash flow forecast is a planning document enabling the company to make decisions about its future activities and how they will be financed. Control is maintained by comparing the actual cash flows on a regular basis with the original forecasted cash flows. It is important to emphasize that a company's cash flow forecast will not be published and is usually regarded as a confidential document within the company.

Although a company will draft its own format for a cash flow forecast, there are some basic ingredients. The objective of the document is to record the amount and timing of cash movements. The cash coming into the business is known as cash inflow and the cash going out is known as a cash outflow. If more cash comes in than goes out, the difference is known as a cash surplus. If more cash goes out than comes in then the difference is known as a cash deficit.

A Cash Flow Forecast is usually drawn up and maintained in the form of a spread sheet with the following format or one similar:

- A heading that gives the financial period to which the cash flow forecast refers. This could be a month, a year or even longer. For example, a construction company with a long-term project may have a cash flow forecast for two or three years showing the expected cash outflows and the dates when stage payments are made by the client.

- The columns should be labelled with the days/weeks/months to which they relate. The final column is a total for each row.

- The top section of rows will show the cash inflows, for example, payments made to the company. The number and category of items is decided by the company. This subsection will be totalled.

- A lower section of rows will show the expected cash outflows and will be subtotalled. Once again the number and categories of items is decided by the company.

- For each column the subtotal of cash outflows is deducted from the subtotal of cash inflows, to give the cash surplus or deficit for that particular period.

- The final row is the sequential addition of each column to give the cumulative cash position at the end of each period.

We give below a cash flow forecast for an individual decision. This exemplifies all the points we have made without causing confusion with too much detail.

Worked example – An individual decision

Emma Wang has been working for several years and has managed to save £8000. Her employer has introduced a scheme where an individual can take an unpaid sabbatical for a period not exceeding three months. Their position in the company is held open for their return.

Emma is contemplating three months unpaid leave to travel to the Far East and pursue her hobby of wild life photography. She calculates the travel cost at £6000 which must be paid before she leaves. Accommodation she decides will be £450 to be paid at the beginning of each month. Food costing £400 per month will be paid on a daily basis. She has decided to purchase her photography supplies before she leaves and that will cost £500. Finally, she decides that she should have £1000 in case of emergencies.

Emma does a rough calculation of the total cost of her sabbatical.

Travel	£6,000
Accommodation	£1,350
Food	£1,200
Photography supplies	£500
Emergencies	£1,000
Total	£10,050

Emma is very cautious and is uncertain whether the £1000 for emergencies will be sufficient. She considers it would be prudent to save a further £2500 (an extra to £450) instead of £2050 add to her savings of £8000. She will then be confident that she will not run out of money.

Her trip is planned for six months' time so she constructs a cash flow forecast to determine whether she will have a total of £10,500.

After tax she receives £2500 per month salary. She anticipates that she will receive a salary increase to £3000 from 1 April. Her estimated expenditure is:

- Rent £800 per month, payable monthly at the start of each month.
- Electricity £720 every three months, payable at the end of each three months.
- Daily travel to and from work £50 per week.
- Photo supplies £120 per month.
- General living expenses are £480 per month.
- Food is estimated at £600 per month

SOLUTION

Emma Wang Cash flow forecast January to June (£)

	January	February	March	April	May	June	Total
Cash inflows:							
Salary	2,500	2,500	2,500	3,000	3,000	3,000	16,500
Total inflows (A)	2,500	2,500	2,500	3,000	3,000	3,000	16,500

Cash outflows:							
Rent	800	800	800	800	800	800	4,800
Electricity	–	–	720	–	–	720	1,440
Travel	200	200	200	200	200	200	1,200
Photo supplies	120	120	120	120	120	120	720
General	480	480	480	480	480	480	2,880
Food	600	600	600	600	600	600	3,600
Total outflows (B)	2,200	2,200	2,920	2,200	2,200	2,920	14,640
Net cash flow (A–B)	300	300	(420)	800	800	80	1,860
Cumulative cash	300	600	180	980	1,780	1,860	

If Emma wishes to save an additional £2500 over the next six months she is not going to make it. But she does have the following options:

- Take a part-time job.
- Try to get a loan from the bank to cover the shortfall.
- If the food bill is mainly eating out, she could cook at home.
- Reduce the monthly amount spent on photo supplies.
- Look closely at the expenses that fall under the 'General' heading.
- Move into cheaper accommodation.
- Plan for a less expensive trip.

Unfortunately, she also has some problems she has not addressed:

- How certain is she that she will have the anticipated salary increase?
- Will she have to pay her rent when she is absent?
- Are there any other payments at home she must continue to make on a regular basis?
- Does she need travel insurance?
- Is there likely to be a change in currency exchange rates?
- Will any of the costs increase before she makes the trip?

Before she makes a final decision, Emma could run her spread sheet again, assuming it is on her computer and conduct a simple sensitivity analysis. This involves using different estimates for some of her predictions. For example, her salary increase may only be £300, her food costs may only be £500 per month and there may be an opportunity to cut back on travel costs.

The advantage of the cash flow forecast is that Emma now has the opportunity to plan and control her expenditure to meet her target. It is important that she does control the spending by checking each month the amount of cash that actually went out compared to the amount she had planned.

> ### Definition sensitivity analysis
>
> This is a technique of altering assumptions or predictions when making decisions.

The above example demonstrates that a simple cash flow will require a substantial amount of work. Data has to be collected and assumptions made but there is a framework in which to do it. Although the numerous transactions and the detailed data make cash flow forecasts for companies more complex, the document is essential for determining management strategy.

If there is a prediction of a future cash surplus, the company has to determine the best way in which it could be used. This could include:

- Investing the funds.
- Expanding the current business.
- Carrying out renovations.
- Acquiring another business.

In the case of a possible future cash deficit, the strategies include:

- Obtain a loan.
- Increase cash coming in from normal trading.
- Reduce cash going out for operating expenses.
- Sell some of the assets.
- Go bankrupt.

The predictions and control of cash flow have an important impact on operations. An attempt to reduce the flow of cash out may involve making substantial cuts to expenses. To increase cash flows coming in could entail increasing the price of products or increasing the number of products sold.

The cash flow forecast is an essential document that allows companies to manage their cash flows. Companies will also monitor their performance by comparing what actually happens against their predictions. By comparing the two statements as they progress through the financial period the company can ascertain whether the strategies it adopts to prevent a cash deficit are working. These are not just cash strategies but also impact on the Income Statement and the Balance Sheet. Another example will illustrate these issues.

Worked example – Lakeside Products

LAKESIDE PRODUCTS

Lakeside Products have been in business for several years. As a small company they have not been concerned too much about financial planning but 2012 was a tough year. They reached the year end with cash in the bank of £10,000. They are owed £15,000 from the sales made in December 2012 which they will receive in January. The main problem is that they have to purchase some new equipment in 2013 which will cost £20,000. This equipment is required urgently to meet the anticipated increased sales.

They have estimated their purchase of goods costs and credit sales for the first four months of 2013 as follows

	January	February	March	April
Sales	£16,000	£20,000	£20,000	£25,000
Purchase costs	£8,000	£10,000	£10,000	£12,500

They have to pay the purchase costs in the month they are incurred. They are not too confident about the full costs of running the business but in 2012 it averaged £6000 per month. That amount was increasing towards the end of the year.

It is simple to draw up a cash flow forecast on the very basic information given. The cash for sales is not received until the month following the month of sales. The company has £10,000 in the bank to commence the period thus the cash brought forward of that amount is shown as the first entry in the cash brought forward row. The cash surplus for the four months is £6500 which means the company has cash in the bank of £16,500.

LAKESIDE PRODUCTS

Cash flow forecast January to April 2013:

	January	February	March	April	Total
Credit sales	$15,000	£16,000	£20,000	£20,000	£71,000
Purchases	£8,000	£10,000	£10,000	£12,500	£40,500
Operating costs	£6,000	£6,000	£6,000	£6,000	£24,000
Cash surplus/(deficit)	£1,000	0	£4,000	£1,500	£6,500
Cash b/f	£10,000	£11,000	£11,000	£15,000	
Cash c/f	£11,000	£11,000	£15,000	£16,500	

The questions the company has are:

Can they afford to purchase the equipment?

When can they afford to buy it?

Is it worthwhile getting a bank loan?

When could they afford to pay back the loan?

Discussion point

Assuming that the April trading figures are likely to continue for the remainder of the year, what advice would you give the company?

DETERMINING FUTURE FUNDING

As demonstrated in the above example, the cash flow forecast is used in continuing businesses to ensure that sufficient cash is being generated at the right time to ensure continuity of operations. It is also essential if a business wishes to start a new venture or individuals are contemplating starting a new business. The cash flow forecast will allow them to:

- calculate the amount of capital (cash) they need to start the business;
- ensure the repayment of a loan and interest;
- determine if the proposed business will generate sufficient cash to remain in successful operation;
- decide on the timing of cash inflows and outflows – as a general rule in a business, you want the cash to come in as quickly as possible, but go out as slowly as possible.

New businesses or those aiming at some form of expansion or other developments will usually require external funding. A cash flow forecast allows the prediction of the amount required and when. A bank or any other lender will also require a cash flow forecast to ascertain whether there is sufficient cash generated for interest payments to be made and when their loan will be paid back.

Worked example – the funding decision

Two friends wish to open their own business manufacturing garden tools. They plan to commence the business on 1 January and wish to calculate the amount of funding they will require to make the business viable. Their predictions on cash movements are as follows:

Equipment will cost £80,000 and will be purchased and paid for on 1 January.

- Factory rent will be £2000 per month, payable monthly at the start of each month.

- Costs to run a small workshop are estimated at £4000 per month, payable monthly during the month in which they are incurred.
- Sales are estimated at £24,000 per month for the first three months, then increasing to £30,000 per month from April onwards. Customers are allowed two months in which to make their payments, thus with goods sold in January cash will not be received until the end of March.
- The cost of the materials will be £8000 per month for the first three months and then £10,000 per month. Suppliers have agreed to allow one month's credit.
- The bank has provisionally agreed to grant them a loan of up to £40,000 from 1 January as long as the brothers match this with their own money. Interest will be charged at 5 per cent each year calculated and charged to their bank account at the end of each six months. The loan must be repaid at the end of five years.

To determine how much cash they need to invest to commence the business they prepare a cash flow forecast.

Cash flow forecast for the six months ending June 30 (£000):

	January	February	March	April	May	June	Total
Cash inflows							
Loans	40						40
Sales	-	-	24	24	24	30	102
Total inflows	40	-	24	24	24	30	142
Cash outflows							
Equipment	80	-	-	-	-	-	80
Rent	2	2	2	2	2	2	12
Workshop costs	4	4	4	4	4	4	24
Materials	-	8	8	8	10	10	44
Interest on loan						1	1
Total outflows	86	14	14	14	16	17	161
Difference Inflows/outflows	(46)	(14)	10	10	8	13	(19)
Cumulative cash flows	(46)	(60)	(50)	(40)	(32)	(19)	

The above cash flow forecast predicts that the business will have a cash deficit of £60,000 at the end of February so the brothers must expect to invest that amount.

If the forecast is correct the business will start enjoying a monthly cash surplus for the month of March and for following months. If the business continued at the same level in July, by the end of August the cumulative cash deficit will have been cleared.

Confirmation of these calculations is given by just taking the monthly sums of cash in and out, ignoring the opening bank loan of £40,000.

Total cash in from sales	£102,000
Total cash out	£161,000
Cash deficit at 30 June	£59,000

Total Cash deficit is £40,000 owed to the bank and a cumulative operating cash deficit of £19,000.

As with Emma Wang, the results of the cash flow forecast lead on to other questions and decisions. It would be advisable to conduct a sensitivity analysis by rerunning the spread sheet and adjusting some of their predictions. Sales may be 5 per cent lower than they predicted and their material cost 5 percent higher. The friends may also wish to make the assumption that they will receive some personal reimbursement for their work.

One major issue to resolve is the terms of the loan with the bank. If the business goes well, the friends may well be in a position to repay the loan within 12 months. Will the bank permit this or is there a penalty for early repayments? The bank may also be seeking some form of security for the loan such as a lien on the equipment or on the private residences of the friends.

Cash flow forecasts are an indispensable tool in managing a business. The keying of numbers into a spread sheet is only a small part of the technique. The strength of the technique relies on realistic predictions and the ability to identify the questions that arise and make sound decisions.

IAS 7 STATEMENT OF CASH FLOWS

In the previous section we discussed cash flow statements that summarize the past and cash flow forecasts that predict the future as management documents. We explained that, as the Income Statement uses the accruals concept, it is essential for those managers running the business to know the cash position. Equally, the cash flow information is helpful to users of financial statements. Stakeholders want to know how a company generates and spends cash to answer such questions as:

- Can the company generate enough cash to pay its bills, including debt payments?
- Can the company generate cash in order to earn a sufficient return on investment and pay dividends?
- Can the company generate enough cash to avoid bankruptcy?

The user can assess both the changes in net assets and the financial structure of the business by evaluating cash flow information in the context of the Statement of Comprehensive Income and Statement of Financial Position. This gives control over the amounts and timings of cash flows for adapting to changing circumstances and opportunities can also be assessed.

There are persuasive arguments why a cash flow is valuable to users.

- Cash is crucial for survival. Companies can go bankrupt even when they are making a profit.

- Cash is more understandable than profit which is calculated on the accruals basis which may not be familiar to the financially unsophisticated user.

- Cash is less subjective than profit for forecasting because Income Statements contain several non-cash entries such as depreciation and provisions. These are based on the judgement of the company.

- Loan repayments depend on cash availability so lenders can assess whether the company is likely to repay its loans.

- Cash satisfies the stewardship function as managers are responsible for safeguarding the assets of the company.

- Cash can be objectively verified by independent auditors who can physically count the cash or request a bank to confirm the amounts held in the name of the company.

- Inter-company comparison improved because cash is a definite figure regardless of the accounting regulations and practices that might be used.

IAS 7 *Statement of Cash Flows* was issued by the IASB in 1977 to meet the needs of users. It was retitled Statement of cash flows in 2007 and minor amendments made in 2009. The objective of IAS 7 is to require the presentation of information about the historical changes in cash and cash equivalents of an entity classifying cash flows during the period according to operating, investing, and financing activities.

The information enables users to assess the entity's ability to generate cash and cash equivalents and to use those cash flows. IAS 7 includes an example of a cash flow statement for all entities other than financial institutions. An example of a cash flow statement specifically for a financial institution is also illustrated in the standard.

Definition – Cash equivalents

These are short-term, highly liquid investments that are readily convertible to known amounts of cash and which are subject to an insignificant risk of changes in value.

Cash equivalent is a term introduced by the standard. Businesses, if they have a cash surplus, wish to invest it to earn interest. They can do this through a long-term investment where they commit to leave their funds, without making any withdrawals, for an extended period of time. A business may also decide to put part or all of its surplus funds in a short-term investment, possibly something that will mature in less than three months.

For example, if you had deposited money in an account with a bank which had to stay there for six months, this would not be a cash equivalent. Deposits tied up for a specific period are known as time deposits or fixed deposits. As a general rule, three months from the date of making the investment is regarded as short term.

Under the standard short-term investments are regarded as the equivalent of cash. The standard states that cash and cash equivalents are:

- cash on hand and deposits that can be withdrawn immediately in cash without suffering any penalties;
- short-term, highly liquid investments that are readily convertible to a known amount of cash and that are subject to an insignificant risk of changes in value;
- bank overdrafts that are repayable on demand and are an integral part of cash;
- equity investments if they are in substance a cash equivalent (e.g. preferred shares acquired within three months of their specified redemption date).

The standard distinguishes between cash equivalents and equity investments. If you have made an investment in a specific number of share of another company (known as an equity investment), the current amount of your investment is uncertain. Shares are liable to change their value, even in a few days, and therefore the amount is not capable of being converted into known amounts of cash with an insignificant risk of changes in value.

THE STRUCTURE OF THE STATEMENT OF CASH FLOWS

The standard requires the statement to classify the cash flows under three main activities: operating, investing and financing. The first main heading is *Cash flows from operating activities*. It is also the only main classification where the standard allows two different methods for presenting the information

Examples of cash flows from operating activities are:

- Cash receipts from sale of goods and services.
- Cash receipts from royalties, commissions.

- Cash payments to employees.
- Cash payments to suppliers of goods and services.

Under IAS 7 Cash *flows from operating activities* can be drawn up using either the direct method or the indirect method. The direct method is the one most preferred by the IASB and this shows each major class of gross cash receipts and gross cash payment. The indirect method, which is permitted by the IASB and most companies use, adjusts the net profit or loss for the effects of non-cash transactions.

Both methods will give a figure for the cash flow from operation activities. The direct method, however, provides the detail of the cash flows that make up the total of cash flows from operating activities. The indirect method makes adjustments to the net profit or loss for the period (e.g. adding back depreciation) to arrive at the total cash flow figure.

If a company chooses to use the direct method it will normally have the following main headings in its cash flow statement. We have inserted amounts so that you can see what are the deduction and additions.

Cash flows from operating activities:

	£000
Cash collected from customers	800
Interest and dividends received	50
Cash paid for operating expenses, such as employee salaries and wages	(250)
Cash paid to suppliers	(150)
Cash for other operating expenses	(100)
Interest paid	(50)
Taxes paid	(50)
Net cash flow from operating activities	250

You may not find all of these separate headings on a published cash flow or you may find more detail. It will depend on the cash activities of the company. The important point is that all of the above represents movements of cash that are related to the operating activities of the company. Under the indirect method we are still using the main heading of *Cash flows from operating activities* but we will not give cash movements but adjust the net income figure from the Income Statement by non-cash movements.

Below we give a worked example but it is useful to remind you of the types of adjustments you have to make and why.

Cash from customers (Accounts Receivable)

In the above extract we show the actual cash received from customers but in the Income Statement, using the accruals concept, we show the total amount of revenue regardless whether cash has been received. This total amount shows not only the cash received but the amount still owing to the company because the customers have not yet paid. If our Income Statement shows total revenue for the period of £25,000 but we know that customers still owe £3000 the amount of cash we have received for the period is £22,000.

Cash paid to suppliers (Accounts Payable)

The Income Statement shows the total amount paid to suppliers on an accruals basis. Let us assume it is £60,000 for the financial period. If the company still owes suppliers £8000 for the period, the total amount of cash actually paid will be:

Amount according to the Income Statement	£60,000
Deduct cash not yet paid for period	£8,000
Amount of cash paid to suppliers in the period	£52,000

Depreciation

In Chapter 7 we explain depreciation but we will look briefly at the impact on the Income Statement and the Cash Flow Statement when a company purchases an asset such as machinery. The entire concept is that when an asset is purchased the amount of the payment is entered on the cash flow statement. As the machinery is expected to last several years it would not be reasonable to match the full cost on the Income Statement for one year. The full cost is therefore spread on the Income Statement over the years which the machinery is expected to last. The following example demonstrates this.

A company purchases a machine for cash costing £40,000 in 2012. This will be an outflow of cash in the period in which the transaction takes place. The company expects the machine to last eight years before it needs replacing. We have the position that there is an outflow of cash, which occurs once in 2012 but the company will benefit from it for eight years.

Instead of charging the full cost of £40,000 to the Income Statement in 2012 the company shares the cost over the eight years it will benefit from its use. One practical way to do this is to charge £5,000 to the Income Statement annually and after eight years the full cost of £40,000 will have been charged.

Definition – Depreciation

A portion of the full cost of an asset which it is considered has been 'used up' during the financial period. It is an annual charge to the Income Statement and reduces the carrying value on the balance sheet.

We now demonstrate a simple example of adjusting the profit figure by non-cash items to calculate the cash flow using the indirect method, but there is a final complication. Companies have continuing operations and their activities go from year to year with a balance sheet constructed at the end of each year.

To calculate the amount of cash not collected from customers for the year, we must take the amount for accounts receivable at the beginning of the year and deduct this from the amount at the end of the year. The difference will show the amount of cash we did not receive during the year.

Similarly with cash paid to suppliers. We must take the amount for accounts payable shown on our balance sheet at the end of the year and deduct the amount at the beginning of the year. Let us put all this together into one example.

Mutterson plc. has the following information:

	£000
Net earnings as shown on the Income Statement	600
Depreciation charged in income statement	100
Accounts receivable at beginning of year	250
Accounts receivable at end of year	350
Accounts payable at beginning of year	200
Accounts payable at end of year	320

Below we show the calculation for calculating the net cash flow from operating activities using the indirect method.

Cash flow from operating activities – Indirect method

	£000
Net earnings as shown on the Income Statement	600
Adjustments for	
Add depreciation	100
Increase in accounts receivable	(100)
Increase in accounts payable	120
Net cash flow from operating activities	720

Comments

1. The net income of £600,000 has been calculated on an accruals basis. It does not represent movements of cash.

2. On the Income Statement, depreciation is shown a deduction from revenue but it is not a cash item. The full amount of cash paid for the item would have

been shown on the Cash Flow Statement in the period that the transaction took place. As the depreciation is a non-cash item it must be added back to the net income for the year.

3. The revenue on the Income Statement was on an accruals basis. Our accounts receivable has increased by £100,000 in the year and this represents the cash we did not receive. Our amount of revenue stated on an accruals basis is therefore higher than the amount of cash we received by £100,000. If the revenue is higher, the net income is higher. We must therefore reduce the net income by £100,000 to adjust for the cash we did not receive.

4. On the Income Statement the purchase of goods and materials was shown on an accruals basis. This amount would be deducted from the revenue to arrive at the net income. However, the accounts payable has increased by £120,000. On the Income Statement we have therefore deducted £120,000 more that we paid in cash. The net income must therefore be increased by £120,000 to calculate the cash figure.

Although we have stated that the majority of companies use the indirect method, there are examples of companies using the direct method.

THE MAIN HEADINGS

We have examined in detail the heading *Cash flows from operating activities*, but the standard requires the total cash flows to be classified under the following three main headings:

- Cash flows from operating activities.

The main revenue-producing activities of the enterprise, for example, cash received from customers and cash paid to suppliers and employees.

- Cash flows from investing activities.

The acquisition and disposal of long-term assets and other investments that are not considered to be cash equivalents, for example, acquisition of plant and equipment.

- Cash flows from financing activities.

Activities that alter the equity capital and borrowing structure of the enterprise, for example, cash from issuing shares

The types of disclosures under the other two headings are:

Cash flows from investing activities

Purchase of a subsidiary company

Purchase of property plant and equipment

Capitalized development costs

Cash payments to construct property plant and equipment

Proceeds from sale of property, plant and equipment

Proceeds from sale of intangible and any other non-current assets

Cash payments to acquire shares or debentures in other entities

Cash receipts from sales of shares or debentures in other entities

Cash flows out as loans made

Cash flows in from repayments of loans made

Interest received

Dividends received

Net cash used in investing activities

You will appreciate from the above that 'purchases' represent cash going out and 'receipts' and 'proceeds' represent cash coming in.

Cash flow from financing activities

Proceeds from issue of share capital

Proceeds from long-term borrowings

Payment of finance lease liabilities

Dividends paid

Interest and dividends can come under several headings and the standard states that interest and dividends received and paid may be classified as operating, investing or financing cash flows but must be treated consistently. Tax cash flows can also cause a problem and the standard states that these flows relating to income are normally classified as operating unless they can be specifically identified under another heading. There are also various regulations concerned with foreign currency cash flows.

Definition – Debenture

A long-term loan usually taken by an organization and repayable at a fixed date. Some debentures are irredeemable securities. Most debentures pay a fixed rate of interest which must be paid before a dividend is paid to shareholders.

In the example above we demonstrated the reconciliation between cash and net earnings for some of the main operating transactions. In Table 5.1 we summarize the different types of adjustments to be made to net earnings to calculate the cash movement.

Additions to net earnings	
Movement	Reason
Depreciation	It is deducted in the Income Statement to calculate profit but it is not cash
Decrease in inventory	Inventory has been sold that was acquired in a previous period so we have more cash than profit
Decrease in accounts receivable	Customers have paid from sales made in a previous period so we have more cash
Increase in accounts payable	We have not paid suppliers fully for this financial period so we have more cash
Deductions from net earnings	
Movement	Reason
Increase in inventory	We have purchased more inventory so we have less cash
Increase in accounts receivable	Not all customers have paid for the sales shown on the Income Statement
Decrease in accounts payable	We have paid more to suppliers than for the period's receipts of goods so we have less cash

Table 5.1 Adjusting net earnings to cash

COMPANY EXAMPLE – DIAGEO PLC.

Below we give the example from Diageo plc. Amounts were given for three years but we are showing only one year.

Consolidated statement of cash flows:

	Year ended 30	June 2011
£ million		£ million
Cash flow from operating activities		
Cash generated from operations		2,879
Interest received		213
Interest paid		(524)
Dividends paid to non-controlling interests		(112)

Taxation paid		(365)
Net cash from operating activities		2,091
Cash flows from investing activities		
Disposal of property, plant and equipment and computer software	47	
Purchase of property, plant and equipment and computer software	(419)	
Net disposal/ (purchase) of other investments	1	
Sale of businesses	34	
Acquisition of businesses	(117)	
Net cash outflow from investing activities		(454)
Cash flows from financing activities		
Proceeds from issue of share capital	1	
Net (purchase)/sale of own shares for share schemes	(9)	
Net (decrease)/increase in loans	(414)	
Equity dividends paid	(973)	
Net cash outflow from financing activities		(1,395)
Net increase in net cash and cash equivalents		242
Exchange differences		(68)
Net cash and cash equivalents at beginning of the year		1,398
Net cash and cash equivalents at end of the year		1,572
Net cash and cash equivalents consist of:		
Cash and cash equivalents		1,584
Bank overdrafts		(12)
		1,572

CONCLUSIONS

Cash is critical in an organization. It must be monitored and controlled. Management decision making also relies heavily on forecasts of cash flows. These can be used to amend payment and collection policies: seek funding before it is essential; plan the investment to make with cash surpluses; identify the amount of funding required to operate a business or start a new project.

IAS 7 Statement of Cash Flows has been in existence for many years and definitely removed a deficiency in the information given to users. Although there have been discussions on the appropriateness of the main headings and definitions of some of the items, generally it has been considered a good standard.

There is one major weakness in that it permits both the direct and indirect method for disclosing cash from operating activities. There are signs that this choice may be removed in the future but some companies are strongly opposed to the direct method.

RECOMMENDED READING

Hodge, F. D., Hopkins, P. E., Wood, D. A. (2010) 'The Effects of Financial Statement Proximity and Feedback on Cash Flow Forecasts'. *Contemporary Accounting Research*. Spring, Vol. 27 Issue 1, pp. 101–133.

Bradbury, Michael. (2011) 'Direct or Indirect Cash Flow Statements'. *Australian Accounting Review*. Vol. 21 Issue 2, pp. 124–130.

CASE STUDY BETHAN GREENWICH (1)

The following case study will also be used in Chapter 6, The Income Statement, and Chapter 7, The Statement of Financial Position. You should retain your workings on the Cash Flow Statement.

Bethan Greenwich has inherited £30,000 and intends to start her own business as a retailer selling kitchen items. The planned starting date for the business is 1 September 2013. Bethan is aware of the need for good planning and her initial draft is as follows:

1. Buy and pay for shop fittings costing £16,000 on 1 September. Buy and pay for additional shop fittings costing £8000 on 1 December. All shop fittings will be depreciated on a straight line basis from the commencement of the year in which it is purchased. She assumes that the life is 10 years and scrap value is zero.

2. Pay wages to an assistant at £2000 for the first three months and £3000 per month for the remainder of the financial year.

3. Selling and administration costs are £1200 for the first three months and £1,400 for the remainder of the financial year. They are payable when the costs are incurred.

4. Premises are rented at £7200 each year, payable quarterly in advance starting on 1 September 2013.

5. Selling price of goods is calculated at purchase price plus 50 per cent.

6. Customers pay for their goods in the month following receipt of the goods and suppliers are paid by James two months after the month of purchase – Customers buying in April will not pay until June.

Bethan is aware that she will have to stock her shop but has decided to do this gradually while she is trading. Her sales and purchases predicted for the first six months are:

	Sales (£000)	Purchases (£000)
September	12	30
October	16	24
November	20	20
December	24	20
January	24	20
February	<u>24</u>	<u>20</u>
	120	134

Complete the following template to show the flows of cash in and out of the company and the cash position at the end of the year.

Bethan Greenwich
Cash flow forecast

	Sept.	Oct.	Nov.	Dec.	Jan.	Feb.	Total
Cash in							
Capital							
Sales							
Total A							
Cash out							
Purchases							
Wages							
S&D							
Rent							

	Sept.	Oct.	Nov.	Dec.	Jan.	Feb.	Total
Equipment							
Total B							
Surplus/(deficit)							
Cash b/f							
Cash c/f							

CHAPTER 6
THE INCOME STATEMENT

LEARNING OBJECTIVES

At the end of this chapter you should be able to:

- Illustrate the difference between profit and cash.
- Construct a simple Function of Expenses Income Statement.
- Explain the importance of IAS 2 *Inventories* in arriving at gross profit.
- Apply recognition of revenue according to IAS 18 *Revenue*.
- Define the concept and purpose of the Statement of Comprehensive Income.

EXECUTIVE SUMMARY

The Income Statement complies with the accruals basis of accounting and the profit or loss is calculated by matching the expenses incurred in the financial period with the revenue generated. This raises issues, both of recognition and measurement, concerned with both the timing and value of transactions.

The two items that require particular attention are the closing inventory and the revenue. Closing inventory is critical to the validity of the Income Statement as the value placed on inventory can have a significant impact on the gross profit on the Income Statement. IAS 2 Inventories requires inventories to be measured at the lower of cost and net realizable value (NRV) and outlines acceptable methods of determining cost. The two main methods of measuring cost are First In First Out (FIFO) and Weighted Average.

It is essential to calculate the amount of the revenue and the financial period to which is belongs. IAS 18 details the accounting requirements as to when to recognize revenue from the sale of goods, rendering of services and for interest, royalties and dividends. Revenue is measured at the fair value of the consideration received or receivable and recognized when prescribed conditions are met, which depend on the nature of the revenue.

The Statement of Comprehensive Income was introduced by the IASB in 2007. It is an expansion in content of the previous statement which was known as an Income Statement, Profit and Loss Account or Earnings Statement. The Statement of Comprehensive Income has two parts to it: a statement income and a statement of other comprehensive income.

The Statement of Comprehensive Income shows the profit or loss as calculated under Income statement and contains components of other comprehensive income. It provides information on line items not shown in the Income Statement and which should be disclosed to inform fully the performance of the entity.

Fraud and corruption can sometimes be found when companies are calculating their profits. There is the temptation to enhance revenue and to adjust inventory amounts. We highlight at the end of the chapter some of the more interesting cases.

In addition to the case study (Bethan Greenwich) at the end of this chapter, additional case studies are given on the companion website.

CONCEPTUAL AND PRACTICAL ISSUES

The major conceptual issue is determining what is meant by the term 'income'. Essentially, there are two very different approaches.

1. Income is regarded as a measure of performance of an entity as a result of purposeful activities which generate revenue and incur costs. This view is sometimes referred to as current operating performance and is reflected in the profit and loss account, also referred to as the income or earnings statement. This is the financial statement which has been produced by entities and is explained in the first part of the chapter.

2. Income is regarded an enhancement of investor wealth. It is calculated by determining the difference between the amount invested in an entity and the total amount either distributed or available for distribution to the investors in the entity. This view is sometimes referred to as the all-inclusive approach and is reflected in the Comprehensive Income Statement. This statement was introduced in a revised IAS 1 *Presentation of Financial Statements* which was issued in 2007. We discuss this approach towards the end of the chapter.

The Income Statement, now regarded as the first part of the Statement of Comprehensive Income, is based on the accruals concept and its purpose is to show the amount of profit earned by a business in a specific period of time. The profit is calculated by taking the sales for the period and deducting the costs incurred in generating those sales, ignoring any cash movements. This is demonstrated in the following example.

Example 1

In the month of January an antiques dealer buys an old oil painting for £2000 in an auction. He pays for it immediately in cash. When he returns to his home he discovers the painting is quite valuable and he is able to sell it immediately for £5000 cash. Assuming that the antiques trader has no other business transactions In January, how much cash surplus will he have from this one transaction?

As he pays £2000 cash and receives £5000 so he must have a cash surplus of £3000.

Now imagine that he does not receive the cash for the painting in January but is promised that he will be paid in March. What would be his cash deficit at the end of January?

Once again, this is the simple transaction where you can easily calculate that he will have a cash deficit, that is, cash goes out but no cash comes in, of £2000 – the amount of cash that he has paid out.

Looking at the circumstances in No. 2, how much profit or loss will he make in the month of January?

We have purposely kept this example simple so you can calculate the amount in your head without worrying about drawing up a financial statement of any kind.

Before you do your calculation, we will remind you of the definition of the accruals assumption.

> ### Definition – Accruals assumption or concept
>
> Financial statements must be prepared on the accruals basis. Transactions and other events are recognized as they occur and not when cash or any other consideration such as cheques are given or received. These transactions and events must be recorded in the accounting records when they occur and not when payment is made or received.

If you apply the accruals assumption you will see that the profit amount is £3000, although there is a cash deficit of £2000. We have taken the amount that the trader has agreed to receive for the painting of £5000 and deducted from this the amount he paid of £2000. The trader may be concerned that he has a cash deficit but as far as the Income Statement is concerned he has made a profit.

The Income Statement shows the sales for a financial period and deducts the costs incurred in that period. The difference in the two amounts is either a profit or a loss. Unfortunately, it can be very difficult to determine the value of sales for financial periods and the costs incurred in generating them.

We can use a software development company with a year end at 31 December as an example. It signs a contract with a client to investigate their current software configurations, to develop a much more efficient system, install it, ensure that it is operational and carry out maintenance for the next five years. The work begins in October 2011, the new system built by November 2012 and installed and made operational by March 2013. The maintenance contract runs for the next five years. The agreed price is £1.4 million including the maintenance. What is the sales figure for 2011?

There is an answer to such problems and it is found in IAS 18 Revenue which we discuss later in the chapter. Because of the variety and nature of transactions, identification of revenue to the correct period is not always easy and IAS 18 addresses these issues.

The other, but less troubling issue is inventory. At its simplest, you can only make a profit on things that you sell. In most manufacturing and merchandising operations this means that at the end of a financial period there is a closing inventory and no profit can be attributed to that. The determination of the correct value of closing inventory is critical as it has an impact on the profit for the financial period as we demonstrate subsequently.

A SIMPLE INCOME STATEMENT

Continuing the theme of the antiques dealer, we look at the month of February. At the beginning of the month, the dealer buys 40 Victorian prints for £600 cash. He has a contact who will put each print in a suitable frame for £20 each and the dealer agrees to pay 50 per cent cash and the other 50 per cent in March.

By shrewd advertising, costing £40, and telephoning various contacts he is able to sell 25 of the prints at £60 each. At the end of February he is still waiting for three of these customers to pay him. He also attends an art fair at a cost of £50 but is able to sell another 10 painting there at £60 each. He keeps a record of the cash he pays out and receives and any money he is owed or owes at the end of the month. We will work through the calculations for February ignoring the transactions in January.

At the end of February the record is as follows:

Cash out	
Purchase of Victorian prints	£600
Advertising costs	£40
Art Fair entrance	£50
Framing	£400
Cash in	
Sell of prints	£1,920

In addition to these past cash movements, there is still some cash to come in and go out.

Customers to pay for three prints	£180
Debts to pay for Framing	£400
Telephone (not yet billed – estimated)	£45

In a more sophisticated business, the owner could use a computerized record keeping system. In the absence of this we will draw up the cash account. Following the dual nature of transactions there would also be the other accounts as described in Chapter I.

CASH ACCOUNT – FEBRUARY

		£			£
February	Sales	1,920	February	Purchase of prints	600
				Framing (50%)	400
				Advertising	40

		£			£
				Art Fair entrance	50
				Balance c/d	830
		1,920			1920
March 1	Balance b/d	830			

(Continued)

The cash account shows that at the end of February, the dealer should have a cash balance of £830 to continue business at the end of March. This is not the profit and the following Income Statement shows that position. We have added some details to clarify the calculations:

Income statement – February

	£	£
Revenue (35 × £60)		2,100
Purchases – prints	600	
Framing (40 × £20)	800	
	1,400	
Less closing inventory (5 × £35)	175	1,225
Gross profit		875
Advertising	40	
Art fair entrance	50	
Telephone (estimated)	45	135
Profit		740

The value of £35 for the closing inventory is the cost of the print (£15) and the £20.00 for framing

We can reconcile the cash position and the calculation for profit with a simple statement. We have started with the cash figure but you can start with the profit figure and reverse the adjustments. We explain in the notes below the statement the basis of the calculations.

Reconciliation of profit and cash:

Cash as shown on the Cash account	£830
Value of closing inventory (1)	£175
	£1005

Add the cash due from customers (2)	£180
	£1185
Deduct framing and telephone owed (3)	£445
Profit as shown on income statement	£740

Notes:

1. The closing inventory is value at the cost to the dealer. He hopes to sell it in the future at a profit.

2. On the Income Statement we entered the revenue using the accruals basis, that is as if every customer had paid. Three customers had not yet paid so our cash balance will be increased by £180 when payment is made.

3. We have not paid for 50 per cent of the framing and telephone but, using the accruals concept, we had shown these amounts as a deduction on the Income Statement. This means that our final cash will be £445 lower as the owner has to pay that amount.

The essential lesson from the above example is that the accruals assumption is applied to the Income Statement and that gives the figure of profit. The amount of cash surplus or deficit for the period, however, is likely to be significantly different from the profit figure.

The fact that the company is owed cash and owes its suppliers is very important. We will address these issues when we examine the Statement of Financial Position in Chapter 7. At this stage we need to discuss the requirements of the accounting standard in respect of the Income Statement.

IAS 1 PRESENTATION OF FINANCIAL STATEMENTS

IAS 1 was originally issued in 1975 but substantially revised in 2007. The objective of the standard is to prescribe the basis for presentation of general purpose financial statements, to ensure comparability both with the entity's financial statements of previous periods and with the financial statements of other entities.

The standard sets out the overall requirements for the presentation of financial statements, guidelines for their structure and minimum requirements for their content. Standards for recognizing, measuring and disclosing specific transactions are addressed in other Standards and Interpretations.

As we demonstrated in Chapter 4 the profit and loss account is part of the double entry bookkeeping system. There have been various additions to make the statement more informative and this can obscure the relationship with double entry bookkeeping. One weakness of the traditional profit and loss account was that some transactions could take place but their full importance was not always transparent as relevant information would appear on the balance sheet or may perhaps be shown as a note to the accounts. IAS 1 addresses this deficiency by requiring a Statement of Comprehensive Income for the financial period which discloses:

- profit or loss for the period attributable to non-controlling interests and owners of the parent; and
- total comprehensive income attributable to non-controlling interests and owners of the parent.

Definition – Non-controlling interests

This is the equity in a subsidiary not attributable, directly or indirectly, to a parent. It is the partial ownership of a company which does not give the shareholder the control of the company. Previously, the term 'minority interests' was used.

The Statement of Comprehensive Income can be presented in two ways. Either a single Statement of Comprehensive Income can be used or two statements. If two statements are presented, the first statement will give the different components of profit or loss and we will refer to this as the Income Statement. The second statement includes the profit or loss figure for the period shown in the Income Statement and discloses the other components of comprehensive income.

In presenting the Income Statement under IAS 1 a company can choose to use either the function of expense method or the nature of expense method. There are advantages and disadvantages for both methods and it is the responsibility of management to select the method which they consider provides the most relevant and reliable financial information.

With the nature of expense method, the expenses incurred by the company are shown according to their nature. For example purchase of materials, transport costs, employee benefits and advertising costs. The following shows the items that may appear on such a statement. There will be some terms you are unfamiliar with; these are discussed later.

Revenue	X
Other income	X
Changes in inventories of finished goods and work in progress	X
Raw materials and consumables used	X
Employee benefits expense	X

Depreciation and amortization expense	X
Other expenses	X
Total expenses	(X)
Profit before tax	X

With the function of expense method, sometimes known as the cost of sales method, expenses are classified according to their function, for example distribution and administration. As a minimum the company must disclose the cost of the goods that it has actually sold. In doing this the company will also show its gross profit and this can be relevant information to the users. The following example shows the items that may appear in such a statement.

Revenue	X
Cost of sales	(X)
Gross profit	X
Other income	X
Distribution costs	(X)
Administrative expenses	(X)
Other expenses	(X)
Profit before tax	X

The standard allows either presentation but most users would possibly find the function of expense method the most informative.

Discussion point

Do you consider it advisable and feasible to compel all companies to follow the function of expense method for the Income Statement?

A FUNCTION OF EXPENSE INCOME STATEMENT

The function of expense method requires the calculation for 'cost of sales' sometimes referred to as 'cost of goods sold'. In our earlier example of the antique dealer we demonstrated that at the end of a financial period a company will usually have goods that it has made or bought still unsold. These are known as the closing inventory or closing stock.

> ### Definition – Inventory
>
> The products or supplies held by a company at any one time. For a manufacturing company inventory could consist of raw materials required for production, items known as work in progress which are part way through the production process, and finished goods awaiting delivery to customers.

If some goods have not been sold in the financial period, then a profit on them has not been made. You can only make a profit on the goods that you sell in that financial period. To express this more formally, when inventories are sold, the carrying amount of those inventories must be recognized as an expense in the period in which the related revenue is recognized. The carrying amount is the value at which they are shown in the accounting records.

To carry out this matching exercise of goods bought and sold, accountants use a particular procedure that has the advantage of both giving them the costs of the goods actually sold but also acts as a check on the accounting records. The calculation also provides the gross profit figure which is very informative to the users of financial statements.

The following example explains the purchase of goods and their resale by the Medical Supplies Company over a three-month period. In this example the accruals assumption will be used and any movements of cash are ignored.

The Medical Supplies Company (MSC)

The Medical Supplies Company has a business in the Middle East. It imports specialized medical instruments from Germany at £8 each and sells them at £12 each. For the first three months of 2012 the number of instrument it purchases and sells is:

Month	Number purchased	Number sold
January	1,000	900
February	1,500	1,300
March	1,400	1,500

We will do the calculations for each month separately showing how we have arrived at the figures for closing inventory.

Calculation of gross profit for January:

	£	£
Revenue (900 instruments @ £12)		10,800
Cost of goods sold		

Purchases (1,000 instruments @ £8)	8,000	
Deduct closing inventory (100 instruments @ £8)	800	7,200
Gross profit		3,600

With this simple model it is easy to calculate that MSC makes a gross profit of £12 − £8 = £4 for each medical instrument. If it sells 900 medical instrument the gross profit must be £40 × 900 = £3600. The great advantage of the Cost of Sales calculation is that all the figures can be checked as follows:

1. There should be an invoice that MSC has received for the 1000 instruments it has purchased.

2. There should be a record that 1000 instruments were physically received by MSC in good condition.

3. There should be records that 900 instruments were purchased by customers. This record should also show whether payment was made at the time of purchase or whether the amount is still owed to MSC.

Although these paper records are crucial the critical factor is the inventory or stock taking at the end of the period. It is imperative to ensure that the closing inventory is physically in the company. On the last day of January, MSC can physically count the number of instruments it has remaining – it's closing inventory. If there are not 100 instruments but only 90 we can assume that 10 have been stolen, lost or so badly damaged they had to be scrapped.

If the number of instruments is not available it has an impact on the gross profit calculation. On our Income Statement we must use the value of the closing inventory that is actually present and not what our paper records may lead us to believe.

If MSC finds that it only has 90 instruments remaining its Cost of Gross Profit calculation would be as follows:

Calculation of gross profit for January (10 medical instruments missing):

	£	£
Revenue (900 instruments @ £12)		10,800
Cost of goods sold		
Purchases (1,000 instruments @ £8)	8,000	
Deduct closing inventory (90 instruments @ £8)	720	7,280
Gross profit		3,520

The gross profit has decreased by the £80 attributable to the missing medical instruments. The calculation of this amount of closing inventory is so critical that there is a standard, IAS 2 *Inventories*, which explains the correct procedures. Before we look at that standard, we will show the calculation for February and March assuming that at the end of January there are 100 instruments.

Calculation of gross profit for February:

	£	£
Revenue (1,300 instruments @ £12)		15,600
Cost of goods sold		
Opening inventory (100 instruments @£8)	800	
Purchases (1,500 instruments @ £8)	12,000	
	12,800	
Deduct closing inventory (300 instruments @ £8)	2,400	10,400
Gross profit		5,200

The explanation of these calculations is as follows:

1. At the beginning of February, MSC has the 100 instruments to sell that remain unsold in January. These may be sold in February.

2. An additional 1500 instruments were purchased, so there was now a total of 1600 instruments to be sold.

3. As 1300 instruments were sold there should be 300 instruments in closing inventory. In practice this is a number that has to be physically checked.

Calculation of gross profit for March:

	£	£
Revenue 1,500 instruments @ £12)		18,000
Cost of goods sold		
Opening inventory (300 instruments @£8)	2,400	
Purchases (1,400 instruments @ £8)	11,200	
	13,600	
Deduct closing inventory (200 instruments @ £8)	1,600	12,000
Gross profit		6,000

Once again, in the absence of information, we have calculated the closing inventory figure. The closing inventory amount for one month is the opening inventory amount for the following month.

In the simple example above, it is possible to calculate that the total gross profit should be the gross profit each medical instrument (£4) multiplied by the number of instruments sold. The gross profit is very important for users as it is a good measure of how well a company performs at buying and selling goods. We can express this performance in percentage terms by calculating the gross profit margin, also known as the gross profit ratio.

> ### Definition – Gross profit margin
>
> This is calculated by expressing the gross profit as a percentage of revenue and is a good measure of the performance of a company in buying and selling goods.
>
> $$\text{Gross profit margin} = \frac{\text{Gross profit}}{\text{Revenue}} \times 100$$

If we take the above formula and apply it to one medical instrument the gross profit margin is:

$$\frac{£4}{£12} = 33.3\%$$

If this gross profit margin is calculated for each of the three months it will always be 33.3 per cent as the company has been able to maintain its selling price, purchase costs and inventory control. If any of these factors had changed there would have a different gross profit margin and this could be a warning signal. If you calculate the gross profit margin for January, as if the medical instrument had been stolen, the answer is

$$\frac{£3,520}{£10,800} = 32.6\%$$

This may not appear to be a significant decline but it would be worrying for investors as it suggests that there are some issues the company needs to resolve.

In the above example, the calculations were based on the number of instruments and the original cost of each. The problem illustrated the impact on profit if the number of instruments was less than it should have been. The other side to the calculation is deciding on the value of the inventory. If we had decided that we would use either £7 or £9 per instrument to value our closing inventory there would have been a direct impact on our gross profit.

Because of the importance of the gross profit figure, there is a temptation for companies to manipulate their financial records to increase their gross profit. To achieve this they can either inflate the revenue figure or increase the closing inventory value. The company will show a more favourable profit figure than it should have been. At the end of this chapter we look at some cases that reveal how companies have misled users of financial statements by improper accounting.

It is also possible that because of the complexity of business companies may experience some difficulties in determining what the correct amount should be. To prevent these uncertainties IAS 2 sets out the procedures to follow for measuring inventories.

IAS 2 INVENTORIES

IAS 2 inventories was first issued in 1975 with a revised version on 2003. The objective of the standard is to establish the methods to be used for valuing most types of inventory. The standard requires inventories to be measured at the lower of cost and NRV and outlines acceptable methods of determining cost, including FIFO and weighted average cost.

With a manufacturing company, at the end of a financial period inventories will include several groups of items. There will be goods it has manufactured in the warehouse ready to go to customers. The production process will be in operation and there will be goods that are part completed known as work in progress. These items in the course of production present some accounting difficulties in measuring the value and this will be discussed in the Management Accounting part of the book. Finally, the company will have raw materials in its stores waiting to go to the production process. The example below is taken from the 2011 Annual Report of Rolls Royce Holdings plc.

LINK TO PRACTICE

Rolls Royce

11 Inventories

	2011	2010
	£m	£m
Raw materials	319	377
Work in progress	921	943
Long-term contracts work in progress	12	42
Finished goods	1,267	1,024

It is noticeable that the work in progress at £921,000,000 is almost three times the value of raw materials. This is a substantial sum of money to be tied up in the production process and requires a considerable amount of accounting work to arrive at this value.

The amount of funds a large company can have tied up in inventories can be significant. The following note from GlaxoSmithKline plc. demonstrates that for major companies the management of inventory is a key activity.

LINK TO PRACTICE

GlaxoSmithKline

Inventory of £3873 million has increased by £36 million during the year. The increase reflects higher vaccine stocks, principally *Cervarix* for the national HPV programme in Japan, partly offset by initiatives to reduce manufacturing cycle times and reduce stockholding days through more efficient use of inventory throughout the supply chain.

GlaxoSmithKline Annual Report 2011, p.61

At the end of the financial period a company has to put values on its closing inventories. Even if there is no intention to mislead the users, the method to carry out the calculation can give different answers and different figures of gross profit. The following simple example demonstrates the problem.

Worked example: Valuing closing inventories

In a two-month period, a manufacturer purchases the following raw materials:

January: 1000 tonnes at £5 per tonne

February: 400 tonnes at £6 per tonne

At the end of February the company has 600 tonnes of material in its store. It finds that the cost of the raw materials has fallen and in March the cost will be only £4 per tonne.

We know the quantity of the closing inventory but the value we place on it depends on which of the following assumptions we make.

1. We can assume that the 600 tonnes remaining were bought in January. In this case the value will be 600 tonnes × £5 per tonne = £3000.

2. We can assume that of the 600 tonnes, 400 were purchased in February and the other 200 tonnes remain from January. The value will be (400 × £6) + (200 × £5) = £3400.

3. We can take a raw average price and value the 600 tonnes at £5.50 per tonne = £3300.

4. We can take a weighted average price calculated as follows:
   1000 tonnes × £5 per tonne = £5000

$$\frac{400}{1400} \text{ tonnes} \times £6 \text{ per tonne} = \frac{£2400}{£7400}$$

Weighted average cost = £7400/1,400 = £5.29 per tonne
Closing inventory = 600 × £5.29 = £3174

5. Finally, we can assume that the value is the 600 tonnes at the current price in March and is £2400.

All of the above answers are 'correct' but users would have difficulty in comparing companies and there would be a loss of credibility in the profit figure if companies could use whichever method they wished whenever they chose. IAS 2 *Inventories* sets out the procedure for calculating the value of inventory to ensure that there is consistency in the approach that management uses. The standard is not designed to specifically prevent fraud.

A key principle in the standard is that inventories are required to be stated at the lower of cost and NRV. We will discuss NRV later but first we will look at what is included in the cost. It includes the following items:

- costs of purchase (including taxes, transport and handling) net of trade discounts received;
- costs of conversion (including fixed and variable manufacturing overheads); and
- other costs incurred in bringing the inventories to their present location and condition.

The phrase 'to their present location and condition' is very important and lays down the boundary beyond which further costs cannot be added. Cost cannot include:

- abnormal waste;
- storage costs;
- administrative overheads unrelated to production;
- selling costs;
- foreign exchange differences arising directly on the recent acquisition of inventories invoiced in a foreign currency;
- interest cost when inventories are purchased with deferred settlement terms.

The two main methods of valuing inventory are described below. We use the following data to demonstrate the calculations and the impact on closing inventory and gross profit.

A retailing company trades in luxury leather covers for ipads. The transactions for the first two months of the year are:

January: 200 covers purchased at £25 per cover

February 300 covers purchased at £28 per cover

February 400 covers sold for £40 per cover

First-in, first-out (FIFO)

This assumes that the first items purchased are the first items sold. This accords to good business practices where companies ensure that the oldest materials received are the first used. For our example the calculations for the first two months are:

> ### Definition – First-in, First-out
>
> This method assumes that items purchased or manufactured first are sold first. The result of this is that the value of inventory at period end is the most recently purchased or produced.

Income statement for two months:

	£	£
Revenue (400 covers at £40)		16,000
Purchases	13,400	
Deduct closing inventory (100 covers at £28)	2,800	10,600
Gross profit		5,400

An example of the FIFO method is taken from the 2011 Report of Associated British Foods

> ### LINK TO PRACTICE
>
> **Associated British Foods**
>
> Finished goods and work-in-progress are valued at factory cost, including appropriate overheads, on a first-in first-out basis. Raw materials and bought-in finished goods are valued at purchase price. All inventories are reduced to net realizable value where lower than cost.

Weighted average

> ### Definition – Weighted average
>
> This method calculates the average cost of items at the beginning of the period and the cost of similar items purchased or produced during the period.

Taking the above example but using the second method we need to calculate the weighted average of purchases on a continuing basis and using this figure the closing inventory. It is best shown in the form of a table.

Number of covers	Cost each cover	Total cost	Cumulative value	Weighted average cost each cover
200	£25	£5,000	£5,000	£25
300	£28	8,400	£13,400	£26.80

As the sale takes place at the end of February, the Income statement will be as follows.

Income statement for two months:

	£	£
Revenue (400 covers at £40)		16,000
Purchases	13,400	
Deduct closing inventory (100 covers at £26.80)	2,680	10,720
Gross profit		5,280

One problem is that the costs of purchasing goods may go down, or more importantly, the price at what you can sell them is lower than what you paid for them originally. This introduces the topic of net realizable value.

Definition – Net realizable value

Net realizable value (NRV) is the estimated sales value of the goods minus the additional costs likely to be incurred in completing production, if necessary, and any other costs necessary to make the sale.

The standard requires that a company should state its closing inventory at the lower of cost or NRV. The NRV can be lower than the original cost because:

- The inventories have been damaged while in store.
- The inventories have become obsolete.
- The selling prices have declined below the original cost.
- The cost of completing production or making the sale have increased.

Although a company may purchase or manufacture goods with the intention of selling them at a profit, this may not happen. Occasionally in some industries, or with certain goods, or in certain economic climates, the amount a company could achieve by selling its inventory is lower than what it cost them originally.

One example is where the goods are fashionable, such as certain clothes items. If the demand for these clothes falls, shops will have to lower their prices considerably to sell their goods. The selling price could even be lower than the cost to them. In this instance any closing inventory must be valued at the net realizable value. Electronics are another example where selling prices can drop dramatically as new advances are made.

The consequence of a change in the market is demonstrated by the following extract taken from a News release issued by the Canadian company Research in Motion on 2 December 2011.

LINK TO PRACTICE

Research In Motion

Research In Motion Limited (RIM) (Nasdaq: RIMM; TSX: RIM), a world leader in the mobile communications market, today announced that it would record a pre-tax provision in the third quarter of fiscal 2012 of approximately £485 million, £360 million after tax, related to its inventory valuation of BlackBerry PlayBook tablets. The charge is expected to be predominantly non-cash. All figures in this release are in US dollars and US GAAP, except where otherwise indicated.

As previously disclosed, RIM has a high level of BlackBerry PlayBook inventory. The Company now believes that an increase in promotional activity is required to drive sell-through to end customers. This is due to several factors, including recent shifts in the competitive dynamics of the tablet market and a delay in the release of the PlayBook OS 2.0 software. As a result, RIM will record a provision that reflects the current market environment and allows it to expand upon the aggressive level of promotional activity recently employed by the Company in order to drive PlayBook adoption around the world.

Although US standards are being applied, the message is clear. If you are not selling your products it impacts on your inventories and profits. Problems such as this should be disclosed to investors.

The standard stipulates that the difference between the cost and the NRV should be recognized as an expense in the period in which it occurs: in other words it must go to the first part of the statement of comprehensive income. Of course, it is possible that in a later period, the selling price that can be obtained for the goods increases above the original cost. In these circumstances, the original write down can be reversed in the income statement in the period in which it occurs.

Comparing FIFO and weighted average methods

We will now look at a slightly more complex example and compare the two methods. The information we have about a company is as follows:

Day 1 purchases 200 items at £10 each

Day 2 purchases 200 items at £12 each

Day 3 sells 250 items at £20 each

Day 4 purchases 100 items at £13 each

Once again we will use tables to illustrate the calculations.

FIFO example:

Day	Activity	Calculation	Inventory value £
1	Purchases	200 items @ £10 each	2000
2	Purchase	200 items @ 12 each	2400
	Balance		4400
3	Sales	200 items @ 10 each	(2000)
		50 items at £12 each	(600)
	Balance		1800
4	Purchases	100 items @ £13 each	1300
	Balance		3100

FIFO Income statement (days 1–4)

	£	£
Sales		5,000
Cost of goods sold		
Purchases	5,700	
Less closing inventory	3,100	2,600
Gross profit		2,400
FIFO Proof		
Sold 250 items @ £20 each	=	£5,000
Cost of 250 items		
200 @ £10 + 50 @ 12	=	£2,600
Gross profit		£2,400

Weighted average example:

Day	Activity	Calculation	Average cost each item	Inventory value £
1	Purchases	200 items @ £10 each		2,000
2	Purchases	200 items @ 12 each		2,400

	Balance	£4,400/400	£11	4,400
3	Sales	250 items @ 11 each		(2,750)
	Balance	£1,650/150	£11	1,650
4	Purchases	100 items @ £13 each		1,300
	Balance	£2,950/250	£11.80	2,950

Note that with the Weighted Average method the balance (carrying amount) of our inventory is calculated by taking the total amount and dividing by the number of items. It is this carrying amount per item that is used to calculate, the succeeding closing balance. Thus, at the end of Day 3 we have total inventory valued at £1650 (£11 for 150 items). To this we add our purchases that cost £1300 so the total balance for our inventory is £2950. This represents 250 items so the average cost per item is £11.80.

Weighted average income statement (days 1–4)

	£	£
Sales		5,000
Cost of goods sold		
Purchases	5,700	
Less closing inventory	2,950	2,750
Gross profit		2,250
Weighted average proof		
Sold 250 items @ £20 each	=	£5,000
Cost of 250 items		
250 @ £11 each	=	£2,750
Gross profit		£2,250

If we do a summary comparing the two methods the figures are as follows:

FIFO/Weighted average summary

Method	Purchase costs £	Closing inventory £	Cost of goods sold £	Gross profit £
FIFO	5,700	3,100	2,600	2,400
Weighted average	5,700	2,950	2,750	2,250

The main points to note are:

1. Under both methods the revenue amounts are exactly the same.

2. Under both methods the costs of purchases are the same.

3. It is the closing inventory, cost of sales and gross profits that are different.

Given that we have different amounts, the question arises as to which is the correct method. The answer is that they are both correct as they are both permitted under the standard. However, once a company has determined the policy which it will use it must continue to use it. This complies with the consistency assumption that we explained in Chapter 3. In the long term, the differences in reported profit will even out but is it essential that the users appreciate which method is being applied.

In some industries there may be difficulties in ascertaining the cost or the internal accounting system may not capture the cost. The standard makes particular provisions for these. In particular it refers to the retail industry where it is the practice to reduce the sales value of inventory by the percentage gross margin to arrive at an approximation of cost. This method is acceptable. The following example is from the 2012 Marks and Spencer Group plc. Annual report and financial statements:

LINK TO PRACTICE

Marks and Spencer

Inventories are valued at the lower of cost and net realizable value using the retail method, which is computed on the basis of selling price less the appropriate trading margin. All inventories are finished goods.

IAS 18 REVENUE

Definition – Revenue

Revenue arises from the sale of goods, the provision of services and the use of assets yielding interest, royalties and dividends. It is the gross inflow of economic benefits, for example, cash, receivables and other assets arising from the ordinary operating activities of an enterprise

IAS 18 was issued in 1982. The objective of IAS 18 is to prescribe the accounting treatment for revenue arising from certain types of transactions and events. In some countries, revenue is referred to as sales or turnover but the IASB uses the term 'revenue'.

For accounting purpose we need to know the revenue from the transaction, that is, the sale of goods or services and the financial period in which it took place. This will enable to apply the matching and accruals concepts and allocate to the Income Statement the expenses relevant to the revenue to produce the appropriate amount of profit for the financial period.

IAS 18 defines identifies two criteria for the recognition of revenue.

1. It is highly likely that future economic benefits will flow to the business, and

2. that these benefits can be measured reliably.

The standard defines the circumstances when these two criteria are satisfied and provides guidance on the practical application of the criteria. Taking the first criterion, which is one of recognition, the standard separates revenue from the sale of goods and revenue from the provision of services.

Revenue from the sale of goods should only be recognized when:

- the seller has transferred to the buyer the significant risks and rewards of ownership;

- the seller retains neither continuing managerial involvement to the degree usually associated with ownership nor effective control over the goods sold;

- the amount of revenue can be measured reliably;

- it is probable that the economic benefits associated with the transaction will flow to the seller;

- the costs incurred or to be incurred in respect of the transaction can be measured reliably.

Revenue from the provision of services should be recognized when:

- the amount of revenue can be measured reliably;

- it is probable that the economic benefits will flow to the seller;

- the stage of completion at the balance sheet date can be measured reliably;

- the costs incurred, or to be incurred, in respect of the transaction can be measured reliably.

If these criteria cannot be met, a cost-recovery basis should be used with revenue being recognized only to the extent that the recoverable expenses are recognized. Although the criteria for recognition are detailed in the standard there are complications in practice. These issues can be resolved but revenue recognition can require adjustments.

The following example illustrates some of the issues in identifying the amount of revenue for a specific period. Smith and Nephew plcs develops advanced medical devices for healthcare professionals around the world. The following note is from page 91 of the Annual Report and Accounts of Smith and Nephew plc.

Revenue from interest, royalties and dividends, assuming that these are probable economic benefits that will flow to the business and the amount of revenue can be measured reliably, are recognized as follows:

- revenue interest: on a time proportion basis that takes into account the effective yield;
- royalties: on an accruals basis in accordance with the substance of the relevant agreement;
- dividends: when the shareholders' rights to receive payment are established.

Discussion point

If allocating revenue to the correct period causes so many problems, would it not be preferable to revert to a purely cash basis?

Revenue should be measured at the fair value of the consideration that is received or receivable for the goods or services. That sometimes needs careful adjustment. To attract customers to purchase large ticket items, such as furniture, some retailers will allow customers to take the goods immediately but not pay for two years and it appears that the customers do not have to pay the interest. However, under the standard the company should separately report the interest element from the cash received for the sale of goods.

Although in practice, the recognition and measurement of revenue can cause problems, at this stage of your studies you should have few difficulties if your remember two important points:

1. We are using the accruals assumption. In other words you ignore cash.

2. You are calculating the revenue generated in a specific financial period. This means that sometimes you will have to allocate the revenue over the periods that will benefit from it.

The following two examples should help you to understand these points.

Worked example – Allocating revenue to the financial period

A language tuition centre commences business on 1 July 2012 and has a year end at 31 March 2013. It has 200 members signed in for 12 months membership. The membership fee for each customer is £2000 and they are expected to pay the full amount on 1 July. One hundred and fifty customers pay the full amount immediately but 50 have managed to negotiate a deal whereby they pay one half on the 1 July 2012, one quarter on 1 March 2012 and the final balance of £500 on 30 June 2013.

As we are concerned with the Income Statement for the nine-month period to 31 March 2013, and we are using the accruals concept. When the payment is finally made is of no importance. The calculations for revenue recognition ignore the timing of payments.

The fee is £2000 for 12 months but by 31 March 2013 only nine months of the membership will have expired. The amount of revenue to be shown on the Income Statement is £2000/ 12 months × 9 months × 200 members = £300,000. The remaining £100,000 will be shown as revenue in the financial statement for the year ended 31 March 2013 together with the additional revenue for the year ended 31 March 2014.

Worked example maintenance contract

Techno Ltd sales and maintains computerized systems. In the year ended 31 December 2012 it sold equipment to a client for £750,000. It also enters into an agreement with them for the maintenance of the equipment for a five-year period starting in 2012. The company charges a fee of £250,000 for the five-year contract. Under the agreement, the hospital must pay the full amount of £1,000,000 for the equipment and maintenance as soon as the system is installed.

As the system was installed in 2012 Techno Ltd can recognize the sale of £750,000 in that year. Although the hospital has agreed to pay for the maintenance contract up front, it is for a five-year period. Techno can only recognize one–fifth, that is, £50,000 of the total amount. The remaining £200,000 will be recognized at £50,000 each year for the life of the contract.

A joint project by the FASB and the IASB intends to result in the publication of a revised IFRS in 2013. The project has the main objectives of:

- removing inconsistencies and weaknesses in existing revenue recognition standards by providing clear principles for revenue recognition in a robust framework;

- providing a single revenue recognition model which will improve comparability over a range of industries, companies and geographical boundaries; and

- simplifying the preparation of financial statements by reducing the number of requirements to which preparers must refer.

The core principle of their approach is that an entity recognizes revenue from contracts with customers when it transfers promised goods or services to the customer. The amount of revenue recognized would be the amount of consideration promised by the customer in exchange for the transferred goods or services. Given the present uncertain relationship between the FASB and the IASB it is uncertain when this project will be completed.

STATEMENT OF COMPREHENSIVE INCOME

The Statement of Comprehensive Income is concerned with changes in the wealth of investors. Two simple examples will demonstrate the concept and the difference with Income as a measure of the outcome from productive activities.

Example 1

A speculator believes that some apartment buildings in a depressed area will increase in value as the land will be required for erecting prestigious office buildings in the future. He purchases the buildings for £1.5 million and at the end of the year his profit from letting the apartments is £50,000. However, as he hoped, the land is now valued at £1.8 million. This will not appear on his Income Statement as that profit has not been realized because he has not sold the land.

Example 2

A UK entity has surplus funds of £500,000 which it has invested for 12 months in a foreign country at a high interest rate of 10 per cent and it is receiving the interest regularly each quarter. However, the reason for the high rate is that the foreign currency is very weak. If the UK entity were to convert its investment into GB pounds at the end of the year it would receive only £420,000.

In both these scenarios a single income statement would not give a complete picture. It would correctly show the profit from the apartments in Example 1 and the interest received in Example 2 as both of these have been realized. However, the Income Statement would not show the changes in the value of the assets of the land which has increased and the invested funds which have decreased. The readers of the Income Statement may therefore be misled as to the possible financial performance of the organizations.

The accounting bodies are attempting to resolve such issues but they are problematic. The Statement of Comprehensive Income, a joint project by the FASB and the IASB, would appear to be addressing the issues but it has been severely criticized.

The thinking for the IASB and FASB requiring a Statement of Comprehensive Income can be traced back to is a definition of income by Hicks in 1946. He posited that income is 'the amount an individual can consume and expect to be as well off at the end of a week as he was at its beginning' and elaborated on this theme (Hicks, 1946, pp.171–178). He was referring to individuals and there is considerable debate on how his work should be interpreted and applied, if at all, to the modern corporation.

The criticisms have been fierce and Bromwich et al. (2010, p.348) argue that the IASB and the FASB 'have selectively picked from, misquoted, misunderstood and misapplied Hicksian concepts of income'.

A commentary on their article by Clarke (2010) endorses their view and traces the history of the misunderstandings.

Whatever the criticisms, the Statement of Comprehensive Income is now required. An entity has a choice of presenting a single statement of comprehensive income or two statements. If the latter is chosen the company must disclose:

- an income statement displaying components of profit or loss; and
- a statement of comprehensive income that begins with profit or loss (bottom line of the income statement) and displays components of other comprehensive income.

Taking option 2, the statement starts with the profit or loss as calculated under an Income statement and contains components of other comprehensive income. It provides information on line items not shown in the Income Statement that need to be disclosed to inform fully users of financial statements of the total performance of the entity. These items include:

- changes in revaluation surplus on tangible and intangible assets.
- actuarial gains and losses on defined benefit plans.
- gains and losses arising from translating the financial statements of a foreign operation.

- gains and losses from investments in equity instruments measured at fair value through other comprehensive income.
- the effective portion of gains and losses on hedging instruments in a cash flow hedge.

The following example of a single statement, using the function of expense method, is taken from Henry Boot plc.

	2012 £'000	2011 £'000
Revenue	103,147	114,583
Cost of sales	(75,607)	(78,783)
Gross profit	27,540	35,800
Other income	28	25
Administrative expenses	(13,286)	(13,420)
Pension expenses	(1,956)	(1,657)
	12,326	20,748
Increase/(decrease) in fair value of investment properties	1,346	(4,275)
Profit on sale of investment properties	1,032	19
(Loss)/profit on sale of assets held for sale	(11)	390
Operating profit	14,693	16,882
Finance income	633	795
Finance costs	(1,415)	(1,595)
Share of (loss)/profit of joint ventures	(8)	30
Profit before tax	13,903	16,112
Tax	(2,452)	(5,323)
Profit for the year from continuing operations	11,451	10,789
Other comprehensive income:		
Revaluation of Group occupied property	(35)	–
Deferred tax on property revaluations	102	60
Actuarial loss on defined benefit pension scheme	(10,687)	(9,902)
Deferred tax on actuarial loss	2,079	2,155
Movement in fair value of cash flow hedge	169	184
Deferred tax on cash flow hedge	(51)	(54)
Other comprehensive expense for the year	(8,423)	(7,557)
Total comprehensive income for the year	3,028	3,232

Profit for the year attributable to:		
Owners of the Parent Company	9,533	8,934
Non-controlling interests	1,918	1,855
	11,451	10,789
Total comprehensive income attributable to:		
Owners of the Parent Company	1,064	1,327
Non-controlling interests	1,964	1,905
	3,028	3,232

Source: http://annualreports.henryboot.co.uk/2012/public_html/financial-statements/consolidated_statement_of_comprehensive_income/

FRAUD AND MANIPULATIONS

Closing inventory valuations and revenue recognition offers opportunities for the unscrupulous to manipulate their profit figures. Fraudulent practices can be found in all countries and are used by both large and small organizations. For example, the small business may wish to reduce its profit to lower the tax it has to pay and the large organization may wish to inflate its profit to increase its share price on the markets.

In this section, we have drawn from US cases as these are well documented by the Securities and Exchange Commission in the United States and usually involve very large amounts.

Possibly, the most publicized fraud was the Great Salad Oil Swindle. To carry out such a scheme you only need to know that oil floats on top of water. The perpetrator, Tino DeAngelis, rented a petroleum tank farm in New Jersey. He was able to convince auditors, investors and investment bankers that the tanks contained over $100 million in valuable vegetable oil. Indeed independent auditors could easily check this claim using dipsticks that the tanks were full. Unfortunately, the tanks were mainly filled with sea water with a little vegetable oil floating on the surface to give a positive reading on the dipstick.

Another major case was the *Securities and Exchange Commission v. Bristol-Myers Squibb Company*, Civil Action No. 04–3680 (D.N.J.) (Filed, 4 August 2004) (Hochberg, J.). The allegation by the SEC was that, from the first quarter of 2000 through the fourth quarter of 2001, Bristol-Myers engaged in a fraudulent scheme to overstate its sales and earnings. The purpose of this was to make it appear that the company had met or exceeded financial projections set by the Company's officers ('targets') and earnings estimates established by Wall Street securities analysts.

There were two main methods used by Bristol-Myers. The first was stuffing its distribution channels with excess inventory near the end of every quarter in amounts sufficient to meet sales and earnings targets set by officers. In other words, the company was moving closing inventory from its own premises to distributors to make it appear as sales. Secondly, the company improperly recognized about £1.5 billion in revenue from consignment-like sales associated with the channel-stuffing in violation of generally accepted accounting principles.

At no time during 2000 or 2001, did Bristol-Myers disclose that: (1) it was artificially inflating its results through channel-stuffing; (2) channel-stuffing was contributing to a build-up in wholesaler inventory levels; (3) the build-up in wholesaler inventory posed a risk to Bristol-Myers' future sales and earnings; or (4) the Company was using improper accounting, including 'cookie jar' reserves, to further inflate its results. In March 2003, Bristol-Myers restated its prior financial statements and disclosed its channel-stuffing activities and improper accounting.

The next case exemplifies the comments we made earlier about recognizing in which financial period the revenue was actually earned. In 2002 the SEC alleged that between 1997 and 2000 Xerox employed several 'accounting manoeuvres', to enhance its reported profits. The most significant was a change in which Xerox recorded revenue from copy machine leases – recognizing a 'sale' when a lease contract was signed, instead of recognizing revenue over the entire length of the contract. The amount of total revenue was not in dispute but the financial periods to which it should be allocated. At issue was when the revenue was recognized, not the validity of the revenue. In response to the SEC's complaint, Xerox Corporation neither admitted nor denied wrongdoing. However, it agreed to pay a $10 million penalty and to restate its financial results for the years 1997 through 2000.

Valuation of inventory is a fruitful area for fraud. The following example, brought by the SEC in 2011, highlights the issue of valuing inventory. Point Blank Solutions formerly DHB Industries was a supplier to the US military. Unfortunately for Point Blank Solutions the US Army changed its specifications for hard armour plates for use in protective clothing. This meant that approximately $12.5 million of hard armour plates became obsolete. An additional $4.5 million of inventory became obsolete due to other changes including the discontinuation of certain vest fabrics and colours. The SEC claimed that the company failed to report that its inventory was obsolete and started overvaluing inventory in 2003. Two years later, the books were carrying inventory that was overvalued by $33 million.

For those interested, the SEC website contains many examples of revenue and inventory fraud. Frequently, these manipulations are not detected for many years. The user of financial statements must be diligent and be alert to such factors as:

1. A significant change in trends in sales or inventories over a period of time.

2. Increases in revenue figures when the general market is stagnant or declining.

3. Closing inventory values increasing faster than revenues.

4. Decreases in inventory turnover, that is, the amount of inventory held in relationship to the level of sales in the financial period.

5. Inventory increasing as a percentage of total assets.

6. Changes in the gross profit margin.

CONCLUSIONS

In many respects the Income Statement is a straight forward financial document. Its purpose is to calculate the profit or loss for a financial period by matching costs against the revenue generated. Two major issues which require a careful watch are the valuation of closing inventories and revenue recognition.

The main concern with an Income Statement or Profit and Loss account is that it fails to show all the transactions and events that impact on a company's wealth. The Statement of Comprehensive Income, introduced by the revised IAS 1, attempts to address that. However, the concept employed of 'income' has been severely criticized.

IAS 2 Inventories has been working successfully for many years and there appears to be no reason for the standard setters to make any changes. Although IAS 18 Revenue causes few problems it does not fit easily into the Conceptual Framework which is being developed. The standard setters are part way through introducing changes but these have been criticized. If the FASB/IASB relationship is at an end, the suggestion of amendments may be modified.

Financial fraud is a continuing problem. The cases cited in the chapter did not occur because of the weaknesses in accounting standards but because some people wish to commit fraud.

RECOMMENDED READING

Beaubien, Louis (2011) 'Recognising Revenue', *CMA Magazine* September/October, Vol. 85 Issue 5, pp. 15–16.

Reidy, Mari and Theobald, Jonathan (2011) 'Financial Reporting Fraud: Prevention Starts at the Top', *Financial Executive* November, pp. 47–50.

Doig, Alan (2012) *Fraud. The Counter Fraud Practitioner's Handbook*, Gower.

CASE STUDY BETHAN GREENWICH (2)

If you have completed the cash flow statement correctly your answer should correspond with the following. We have shown the first and sixth month and the position at the end of the full period.

	September	February	Total
Capital	30.0		30.0
Sales		24.0	96.0
Total (A)	30.0	24.0	126.0
Purchases		20.0	94.0
Wages	2.0	3.0	15.0
S&D	1.2	1.4	7.8
Rent	1.8	–	3.6
Equipment	16.0	–	24.0
Total (B)	21.0	24.4	144.4
Net CF	9.0	(0.4)	18.4

For the next stage you need to complete the Income Statement. The points to look out for are:

1. The Income Statement is drawn up using the accruals concept.

2. Not all the goods have been sold so you will have to calculate the closing inventory using the information that the selling price of goods is calculated at purchase price plus 50 per cent.

3. Depreciation must be charged.

CHAPTER 7
THE STATEMENT OF FINANCIAL POSITION

LEARNING OBJECTIVES

At the end of this chapter you should be able to:

- Explain the accounting equation and its relevance to the balance sheet.

- Construct a balance sheet in horizontal and vertical format.

- Summarize the requirements of IAS 16 Property, Plant and Equipment and discuss the concept of depreciation.

- Explain the capitalization of interest required under IAS 23 Borrowing Costs.

- Identify the different types of intangible assets with specific reference to goodwill.

EXECUTIVE SUMMARY

The Statement of Financial Position or Balance Sheet is regulated by several related standards. The two main standards dealing with assets are IAS 16 and IAS 38 and these have some connections. The issue which causes the greatest problems is the treatment of intangible assets, particularly goodwill.

IAS 16 *Property, Plant and Equipment* outlines the accounting treatment for most types of property, plant and equipment. Property, plant and equipment is initially measured at its cost, subsequently measured either using a cost or revaluation model. The asset must be depreciated so its depreciable amount is allocated on a systematic basis over its useful economic life.

IAS 16 is impacted by IAS 23 *Borrowing Costs* which requires that borrowing costs directly attributable to the acquisition, construction or production of a 'qualifying asset' (one that necessarily takes a substantial period of time to get ready for its intended use or sale) are included in the cost of the asset. Other borrowing costs are recognized as an expense.

Intangible assets are covered by IAS 38. This standard sets out the accounting requirements for intangible assets, which are non-monetary assets which are without physical substance and identifiable (either being separable or arising from contractual or other legal rights). Intangible assets meeting the relevant recognition criteria are initially measured at cost, subsequently measured at cost or using the revaluation model, and amortized on a systematic basis over their useful lives (unless the asset has an indefinite useful life, in which case it is not amortized).

IAS 36 *Impairment of Assets* applies to property, plant and equipment as well as intangible assets. The standard seeks to ensure an entity's assets are not carried at more than their recoverable amount (i.e. the higher of fair value less costs to sell and value in use). With the exception of goodwill and certain intangible assets for which an annual impairment test is required, entities are required to conduct impairment tests where there is an indication of impairment of an asset.

Goodwill is an intangible asset but is still conceptually challenging both in regard to recognition and measurement. Under the present accounting standards we cannot recognize internally generated goodwill but we can when goodwill is purchased as part of an acquisition. IAS 36 attempts to restrict the recognition and measurement of goodwill by requiring it is tested annually for impairment.

Financial instruments are regulated by two recently issued standards. IFRS 7 Financial Instruments: Disclosure which was issued in 2005. The standard requires that entities disclose information about the significance of financial instruments to an entity, and the nature and extent of risks arising from those financial instruments, both in qualitative and quantitative terms.

IFRS 9 *Financial Instruments* was issued in 2009 and applies to annual financial periods beginning on or after 1 January 2015. The objective of IFRS 9 is to establish the recognition and measurement requirements for financial instruments and some contracts to buy or sell non-financial items.

In addition to the case study (Bethan Greenwich) at the end of this chapter, additional case studies are given on the companion website.

CONCEPTUAL AND PRACTICAL ISSUES

Chapter 4 explained the principles of double entry for keeping records. When a transaction takes place there are always two entries in the books of account. One on the left-hand side of an account: the debit entry, and on the right-hand side of another account: the credit entry.

At the end of the financial period, all the accounts will be balanced. Most accounts will have either a debit or credit balance. The balance on the sales account and all those expense accounts reflecting the costs of generating the sales will be transferred to the profit and loss account, that is, Income Statement to show the profit or loss for the period. All the remaining balances, being the asset and liability accounts, will be shown on the Balance Sheet: a financial statement which shows a list of all the outstanding balances.

The basis of the Balance Sheet is the accounting equation. Underpinning the equation is the concept that the business is separate from its owners. When a business is first established, it has nothing. The owners of the business will invest money in it, known as capital or equity, so that the business can, in turn, acquire or control those items it requires to operate the business such as machinery, premises and materials. These are known as assets. It may be the owners do not have sufficient funds to make the business fully operational so it will have to borrow funds from other sources such as a bank to acquire assets.

The relationship between the assets, capital and other liabilities in the business forms what is known as the *accounting equation* which is stated thus:

$$Assets = Capital + Liabilities$$

The mechanics of the accounting equation are simple but it is the definitions of assets and liabilities which cause the problems. At one time it was possible to refer to assets as 'things which the business owns'. Life has become more complicated and the formal definition in IAS 1 *Presentation of Financial Statements*, is

The definition recognizes that a business may not own an asset but may have entered into an agreement with another party that it can use or has control of an asset. This control will arise from an event in the past, such as entering into a formal agreement. However, as we discuss later in the chapter, even the above definition does not appear satisfactory to encompass all financial arrangements.

The other key requirement of the definition is that future economic benefits are expected to flow to the enterprise. A business will acquire control of premises, machinery, equipment, vehicles and other assets in the expectation that they will generate future benefits. This may be cash or other benefits. For example, the purchase of improved machine may lead to a reduction in manufacturing costs.

Assets are classified into current and non-current assets and the standard requires these to be shown separately on the Balance Sheet. We have already seen examples of non-current assets such as premises, machinery and equipment. These are items which will last a long time and are used for business operations. It is not intended that they will be immediately resold in the short term. Sometimes the terms fixed and long-lived assets are used to refer to non-current assets.

The standard does not define non-current assets but states that if an asset does not fall under the definition of a current asset it must be non-current. We need to look at the characteristics of a current asset and the standard states that it is an asset which meets any one or more of the following criteria:

- It is expected to be sold or used in the entity's normal operating cycle. For example, raw materials will be used in production; goods will be bought and resold at a profit.

- It is held primarily for the purposes of trading.

- It is expected to be realized within 12 months after the balance sheet date. For example, money owing to the company will be paid.

- It is cash.

The definition of a liability is expressed in the same terms as an asset. There has been a past event and this will result in an outflow of resources in the future. The formal definition is given below and should not cause any problems.

The standard categorizes liabilities into current and non-current. It defines what it means by current liabilities and all other liabilities are non-current. A liability is current when it satisfies *any* one or more of the following criteria:

- It is expected to be settled in the entity's normal operating cycle.
- It is held primarily for the purposes of trading.
- It is due to be settled within 12 months of the balance sheet date.
- The entity does not have an unconditional right to defer settlement of the liability for at least 12 months after the balance sheet date.

Usually you will find that companies owe money to suppliers (accounts payable), may owe the tax, and could have an overdraft.

THE ACCOUNTING EQUATION

As explained above, the Balance Sheet derives from the accounting equation which is Assets = Liabilities + Capital. This can also be shown as Capital = Assets – Liabilities. The application of the equation can be illustrated in the following simple example.

Two friends decide to open a business selling health foods. They have found premises which cost £500,000 and the cost of the equipment is £200,000. The bank agrees to loan the business £250,000 on the understanding that the friends can provide the balance required from their own funds.

Applying the accounting equation we have:

$$\text{Assets} = \text{Capital} + \text{Liabilities}$$
$$(\pounds500,000 + \pounds200,000) = (?) \quad (\pounds250,000)$$

The friends must therefore find £450,000 from their own resources for the health shop to open. This information would be presented formally as a Statement of Financial Position or Balance Sheet as follows.

Balance Sheet on Day 1:

	£		£
Assets		Capital	450,000
Premises	500,000	Liabilities	250,000
Equipment	200,000	–	
	700,000		700,000

The mechanics of the statement are simple but the difficulty arises in defining and deciding what are assets and liabilities. At this stage we will give some brief examples of assets and liabilities found on most balance sheets.

NON-CURRENT ASSETS

Examples are premises, machinery, vehicles and fixtures. These should be listed in their separate classes.

CURRENT ASSETS

Inventory, accounts receivable or debtors representing money owed to the business. Bank or cash

NON-CURRENT LIABILITIES

Long-term loans.

CURRENT LIABILITIES

Accounts payable or creditors representing money owed by the business to others. Bank overdraft.

Capital or equity will appear separately on the right-hand side of the balance sheet as this is the amount which the business owes to the owners and investors. Any profit which is shown on the Income Statement must be listed on the balance sheet. This amount belongs to the owners but it may be held in the business to help expansion or as part of strategy. It is normally shown as Retained Profits under the Capital heading.

WORKED EXAMPLE – BEN ROGERS

The following example for Ben Rogers explains the points made above and demonstrates how a balance sheet changes. Ben has opened a small trading company. We illustrate how the daily transactions would appear on the Balance Sheet, although such a statement would not be drawn up on a daily basis but at the end of the financial period. The transactions would initially be made in the books of account.

We use the accounting equation for our format but at the end we demonstrate a 'vertical' form of balance sheet.

On Day 1 Ben Rogers opens a business with £20,000 as his capital.

On the first day fixtures are purchased for £11,000 and goods for resale for £7000.

Ben Rogers

Balance Sheet on Day 1:

	£		£
Non-current assets		Capital	20,000
Fixtures	11,000		
Current assets			
Inventory	7,000		
Cash	2,000		
	20,000		20,000

Comment

1 Ben invested £20,000 into the business and that is the Capital.
2 The business uses £18,000 of the capital invested to purchase fixtures and goods for sale.
3 The remaining cash unspent is an asset which the business has and appears on the balance sheet.

On day 2, the business buys a further £2000 of goods but on credit.

Ben Rogers

Balance Sheet on Day 2:

	£		£
Non-current assets		Capital	20,000
Fixtures	11,000		
Current assets		Current liabilities	
Inventory	9,000	Accounts payable	2,000
Cash	2,000		
	22,000		22,000

Comment

1. The rule is the balance sheet must always balance. The increase in the current asset of inventory is matched by accounts payable or creditors.

2. The amount for goods is now increased to £9000 to give a total of assets of £22,000.

3. The business now owes £2000 to its suppliers and this appears on the right-hand side of the balance sheet as a liability.

4. If we were carrying out a financial audit of Ben's business on Day 2 we would want to ensure that the business had inventories to the value of £9000 and had cash of £2000. We would also make certain the business had a liability of £2000.

On day 3 the business sells for £6000 cash, goods it had purchased for £4000.

Ben Rogers

Balance Sheet on Day 3:

£			
Non-current assets		Capital	20,000
Fixtures	11,000	Profit retained	2,000
Current assets			
Inventories	5,000		
Cash	8,000	Accounts payable	2,000
	24,000		24,000

COMMENTS

1. These transactions introduce some new concepts but as long as you apply the accounting equation they should cause few difficulties.

2. The business has sold goods which cost £4000. The amounts shown for inventory on the balance sheet is decreased by £4000 – the value of the goods which the business now owns.

3. Customers paid cash of £6000 increasing the amount of cash held to £8000.

4. The difference of £2000 between the cost of the goods and what they were sold for is profit. This belongs to the owner of the business. The business owes this amount to Ben Rogers and it is shown as Profit Retained.

5. If the business pays the profit to Ben the Profit retained amount would disappear and the cash held would reduce by £2000 – the balance sheet still balances.

6. The amount of capital paid into the business will always appear separately and remain at the same amount unless more capital is introduced or withdrawn.

With companies where shares have been issued to investors, the heading used is 'Equity'. The amount shown will remain the same unless more equity is issued to investors. If a company has issued 50,000 shares at a price of £1 per share it shows its total equity at £50,000. This is known as the 'face' value or 'par' value of the share.

With companies which are listed on the stock exchange their share prices can change daily and this is public information. These changes are not reflected in the Equity amount on the balance sheet and it remains at par value.

Definition – Par value

Also known as the face value or nominal value, this is the nominal price of the share or equity, that is, the price shown on the share. Usually the market price will be higher than this and the share is known as being above par value.

Of course, a company after several years may decide to issue 1000 more shares when the market price is high, let us say £1.50. The company will issue these new shares at the higher price. The par value of the shares is still £1 and the amount added to equity in the balance sheet will be £1000. The difference of 50 pence per share between the par value and the market price is shown separately as £500 in a share premium account.

The simple presentation we have shown above is known as a 'horizontal' format and is perfectly acceptable. However, it is more common now to use a 'vertical' format. This applies the same principles as the horizontal format but the structure of the presentation of the information differs. It is less easy to immediately identify the application of the accounting equation, but the information may be better understood by the user.

Below we have taken the horizontal format for Ben Rogers for day 3 and changed it to the vertical format.

Ben Rogers

Balance Sheet on Day 3:

	£	£
Non-current assets		
Fixtures		11,000
Current assets		
Inventories	5,000	
Cash	8,000	13,000
		24,000
Current liabilities		
Accounts payable		2,000
Capital and reserves		
Capital	20,000	
Retained profits	2,000	22,000
		24,000

Sometimes a company may reorder the vertical above format shown above to emphasize the amount of working capital. In this instance the current liabilities would be deducted from current assets to show the amount of working capital. This must not be confused with the Capital invested by the owner and a formal definition is below.

Definition – Working capital

The amount of funding required for the organization's day-to-day operations. It is the sum of current assets minus the sum of current liabilities.

A Balance Sheet presented in such a way is below.

Ben Rogers

Balance Sheet on Day 3

	£	£
Non-current assets		
Fixtures		11,000
Current assets		
Inventories	5,000	
Cash`	8,000	
	13,000	
Less current liabilities		
Accounts payable	2,000	11,000
		22,000
Capital and reserves		
Capital		20,000
Retained profits		2,000
		22,000

DEPRECIATION

In the examples we have discussed so far, the business has purchased a non-current asset and we have shown the cash paid in the cash flow statement. The non current assets will not last forever but will be 'used up'. Machinery, equipment and vehicles will need replacing after a number of years and even buildings will not last forever. We briefly discussed this topic in the previous chapter but we will expand on it because of its importance in understanding the Balance Sheet and the Income Statement.

The total amount companies spend on non-current assets is usually substantial so it is important they are entered into the balance sheet correctly. To ensure this is done will also involve an entry in the Income Statement.

As a business has the use of the non-current asset to generate profit for several years it is logical some form of charge appears in the Income Statement while the asset is used. It would not be reasonable to enter the cash amount paid for the asset in the year it was purchased. The asset will continue to generate profit for several years, although it is gradually wearing out.

To 'spread' the total cost over the economic life of the asset a depreciation charge is made annually to the Income Statement. This has the effect of reducing the carrying amount on the balance sheet by the same amount. At the end of its economic life the asset will have a carrying value of nil and be derecognized.

Definition – Depreciation

Depreciation is the allocation of the original cost of a non-current asset to the Income Statements over its useful economic life.

Below is a simple example of the purchase of an asset and the calculation of depreciation over the life of the asset and the amount shown on the balance sheet each year.

DEPRECIATION EXAMPLE

A business purchases some equipment for £10,000 on 1 January. The anticipated useful economic life of the asset is ten years and at the end of that time it can be sold for the scrap value of £1000.

To calculate the annual amount of depreciation to be charged to the Income Statement we use the formula:

$$\text{Annual depreciation charge} = \frac{\text{Original cost} - \text{residual value } £10,000 - £1,000}{\text{Life of asset 10 years}}$$

$$= £900 \text{ each year}$$

The annual depreciation charge has an impact on the Income Statement and on the Balance Sheet as follows:

	Charge to income statement	Balance sheet carrying amount
Original cost		£10,000
End of year 1	£900	£9,100
End of year 2	£900	£8,200
End of year 3	£900	£7,300
Years 4–9	£5,4000 (£900 × 6 years)	£1,900
Year 10	£900	£1,000

At the end of year 10 the non-current asset is £1000. It will be disposed of as scrap and nothing will appear on the balance sheet. The cash flow statement will have shown a cash outflow of £10,000 when the asset was originally purchased. The income statement has been charged each year with the £900 use it has made of the asset.

A word of caution: the application of depreciation is not intended as a method of valuation. The balance sheet at the end of year 2 shows £8200 but that is not necessarily the value of the asset. It is merely the part of the original cost of the asset which remains to be charged to the Income Statement.

The use of the depreciation method involves predictions on the life of the asset and assumptions on what the scrap value is in ten years' time. Depreciation is an estimate which allows us to make a charge to the income statement annually and also show on the balance sheet how much of the original cost of the asset still has to be depreciated.

Sometimes the terms carrying value or written down value are used to refer to the amount of the non-current asset appearing on the balance sheet. Both of these terms are misleading as we are not trying to show what the current value or market price of the asset is. It is more precise to use the term 'carrying amount' or 'written down amount'.

To make certain you understand the treatment of depreciation and to refresh your memory on the three financial statements and their interrelationship, we demonstrate another example of a small business. We are using examples of small businesses to keep the figures simple but exactly the same methods and principles are used by large businesses.

WORKED EXAMPLE – JAI DEWAR

Jai Dewar establishes a part-time business importing herbs from abroad and selling to shops and restaurants. He establishes contact with suppliers and agrees a purchase price of £15 per kilo. Payments to the suppliers must be in cash as he has no credit history. Jai estimates he can sell the herbs at £30 per kilo but his customers will demand one month's credit so he will not receive the cash until the month following the sale.

Jai decides an investment of £9000 is sufficient to fund the business. He rents storage space in a warehouse at £100 per month and a van to make deliveries which costs £4000. He hopes the van will last for five years but have no scrap value. Tax and insurance will be £1600, paid in advance, and estimated monthly running costs of £250.

Jai decides to charge depreciation on a straight line basis, that is, the same amount each year.

Jai commences trading in January 2012. For the first three months the purchases and sales are

	Purchases kilos	Sales kilos
January	200	200
February	300	250
March	300	320

We are now going to prepare the three financial statements. It is possible to do this by using double entry and making an account for each type of transaction. This is very tedious and we can easily draw up the financial statements from the information given. This also has the advantage of demonstrating how the three financial statements are related.

Jai Dewar

Cash flow statement

January to March 2012

Item	January £	February £	March £	Total £
Capital invested	9,000			9,000
Sales	–	6,000	7,500	13,500
Sub-total A		6,000	7,500	22,500
Van purchase	4,000			4,000
Tax/insurance	1,600			1,600
Running costs	250	250	250	750
Storage space	100	100	100	300
Purchases	3,000	4,500	4,500	12,000
Subtotal B	8,950	4,850	4,850	18,650
Balance (A–B)	50	1,150	2,650	3,850
Cumulative	50	1,200	3,850	

COMMENTS

1. We have recorded cash movements only.

2. A cumulative cash row has been calculated as this is useful information and also provides a check on accuracy by comparing with the final balance shown in the last column.

The Income Statement, using the accruals concept, is shown below with the transactions entered into irrespective of any cash movements.

Jai Dewar

Income Statement January to March 2012

	£	£
Sales (770 kilos × £30)		23,100
Purchases (800 kilos × £15)	12,000	
Less closing inventory (30 kilos × £15)	450	11,550
Gross profit		11,550
Less expenses		
Depreciation on van	200	
Tax and insurance	400	
Running costs (3 months × £250)	750	
Storage costs (3 months × £100)	300	1,650
Net profit		9,900

COMMENTS

1. Depreciation on van is for three months only. The calculation is £4,000/5 = £800 annual depreciation.

2. A count of the inventory would take place to ensure the closing inventory figure is correct. You sometimes see in retail stores that certain sections are closed for 'stock-taking'.

3. The tax and insurance are for three months only.

Finally, we can complete the balance sheet. We have shown how we have calculated the amounts from the cash flow statement and income statement. We have shown more detail than would normally be shown on the face of the balance sheet so you can follow the calculations.

Jai Dewar

Balance sheet at as 31 March 2012

	£	£
Non-current assets		
Van at cost	4,000	

	£	£
Less depreciation (for 3 months only)	<u>200</u>	3,800
Current assets		
Inventory (30 kilos at £15)	450	
Accounts receivable	9,600	
Amounts prepaid (tax and insurance)	1,200	
Cash (closing amount on cash flow statement	<u>3,850</u>	<u>15,100</u>
Total assets		<u>18,900</u>
Capital (from cash flow statement)		9,000
Net profit (from Income Statement)		<u>9,900</u>
		<u>18, 900</u>

COMMENTS

1. The amount for closing inventory is as shown on the Income Statement.

2. Accounts receivable are sales (£23,100) as shown on Income Statement deducting the cash received (£13,500) from the cash flow statement.

3. The amounts of tax and insurance prepaid are calculated as follows. On the cash flow statement an amount of £1600 is shown for the annual payment. However, the Income Statement is only for three months so we show the amount of £400 only in the Income Statement. The difference of £1200 is an asset as it is an amount paid in advance for the full year. On the Cash flow statement for April to June no tax and insurance would be shown but the Income Statement would show £400 for the three-month financial period. On the balance sheet at the end of June the amount prepaid would be reduced to £800.

In the above example we have concentrated on the mechanics of the statement and emphasizing the relationship of the three statements. There are of course several business issues to address such as:

1. Can Jai now arrange credit with suppliers as he has a successful record?

2. Is he confident his customers will all pay him?

3. Will the herbs in storage spoil if they are held for any time?

4. Although he has made £9900 net profit the business has only £3850 cash so he cannot be paid the profit. Is he happy with that position?

5. Is it a worthwhile venture?

> ### Discussion point
>
> What do you consider Jai's business will look like at the end of the year if he continues the same level of activity?

IAS 16 PROPERTY PLANT AND EQUIPMENT

IAS 16 was issued in 1982 and the objective of the standard is to set out the accounting treatment for most types of property, plant and equipment. One particular feature of the standard is that recognition should be originally at cost but subsequently may be carried at either cost or a revalued amount. The revalued amount arises where a company considers the carrying amount of an asset shown in the Balance Sheet is misleading.

Whether cost or revalued amount, the accumulated depreciation and any accumulated impairment losses should be deducted from the asset. In practice the great majority of companies use cost but it is important to remember revaluation of the non-current assets is an option.

Costs include:

- costs incurred initially to acquire or construct an item of property, plant and equipment to bring it to working condition for its intended use; and
- costs incurred subsequently due to additions to the original property, plant and equipment or to replace part of it or to service it. Routine servicing should be charged to the income statement as an operating expense but if the asset is improved so that additional economic benefits will flow, the additional costs can be recognized as part of the asset.

As a general rule, costs which add to the value of the finished asset may be added to the original cost and shown on the balance sheet. In addition, costs which are unavoidably incurred in purchasing, installing or preparing an asset may be included as cost.

Examples of costs which are normally recognized for each class of asset are as follows:

- Land – purchase price, legal fees and preparation of land for intended use.
- Buildings – purchase price and costs incurred in putting the buildings in a condition for use.
- Plant and machinery – purchase price, transport and installation costs.

Abnormal costs such as rectifying installation errors, design errors, wastage and idle capacity should not be considered as a part of the original cost of the asset but should be treated as an expense in the Income statement.

The standard states that property plant and equipment should be depreciated on a systematic basis over the asset's useful economic life. Depreciation applies to both the cost and revalued bases for assets. The depreciation charge commences when the asset is available for use and continues until the asset is derecognized regardless of periods of idleness.

The previous section explained the application of the straight line method of depreciation. There are several depreciation methods with two main methods: the straight line method being one and the reducing balance method being the other.

This latter method of depreciation uses a set percentage rate annually over the life of the asset. This results in the amount of depreciation being charged each year decreasing. Some prefer this method as it is argued that as the asset ages it becomes less productive and costs more in repairs. Therefore the depreciation charge is decreasing as the charge for repairs is increasing thus, one hopes, resulting in the total of the two charges being similar over the years.

To apply the reducing balance method the depreciation is calculated by applying the set percentage rate to the cost of the asset in the first year. In subsequent years, the depreciation rate is applied to the carrying amount of the asset in the preceding year.

The following example illustrates the reducing balance method and the straight line method. The approximate rate of depreciation required for the reducing balance method is 33 per cent. We have rounded the amounts to the nearest £10. The asset cost is £10,000; it has a life of four years and will be sold for scrap for £2000 at the end of its useful economic life (Table 7.1).

Depreciation method	Reducing balance method		Straight line method	
	Annual depreciation charge to Income Statement £	Written down amount Shown on balance sheet £	Annual depreciation charge £	Written down amount £
Original cost 1 January 2012		10,000		10,000
Depreciation to 31 December 2012	3,300	6,700	2,000	8,000
Depreciation to 31 December 2013	2,210	4,490	2,000	6,000
Depreciation to 31 December 2014	1,480	3,010	2,000	4,000
Depreciation to 31 December 2015	990	2,020	2,000	2,000

Table 7.1 Comparison of depreciation methods

The reducing balance method leads to a substantial charge for depreciation in the early years and lower in later years compared to the straight line method. Similarly the written down amount on the balance sheets vary. The method of depreciation will result in different profits for the year. To comply with the consistency concept, once chosen the same method of depreciation should be used every year, unless there is good reason to change it.

The depreciation charges above have been calculated on using estimates on the useful economic life and the residual values. The predicted residual value is usually an insignificant amount and is unlikely to change our calculations. However, the estimate of the useful life may change considerably as time passes. The following example demonstrates the impact which this can have on the company's financial statements.

EXAMPLE – CHANGE IN USEFUL LIFE

A non-current asset with a useful life of ten years and no residual value is acquired for £200,000. The annual depreciation charge is £20,000 and at the end of Year 4, the carrying amount is £120,000. The remaining useful life is revised from six years to four years.

Original cost of asset	£200,000
Cumulative depreciation charge at end of year 4 (£20,000 × 4)	£80,000
Carrying amount at end of year 4	£120,000

$$\text{New depreciation charge} = \frac{£120,000}{4 \text{ years}} = £30,000 \text{ each year}$$

This revision of the useful life in of the asset increases the depreciation charge in the Income Statement by £10,000.

Under IAS 16, after the initial recognition and measurement on the acquisition of an asset, a company may decide to revalue it. A revaluation can be either an increase or decrease in the value of the asset. Few companies use the option in IAS 16 to revalue some of their assets but where they choose to do so they must follow the following regulations:

- revaluations should be carried out regularly, so that the carrying amount of an asset does not differ materially from its fair value at the balance sheet date;
- the entire class of assets to which that asset belongs to should be revalued;
- depreciation is charged in the same way as under the cost basis;
- increases in revaluation value should be credited to equity under the heading 'revaluation surplus' unless it represents the reversal of a revaluation decrease of the same asset previously recognized as an expense, in which case it should be recognized as income;

- decreases as a result of a revaluation should be recognized as an expense to the extent it exceeds any amount previously credited to the revaluation surplus relating to the same asset;
- disposal of revalued assets can lead to a revaluation surplus which may be either transferred directly to retained earnings or it may be left in equity under the heading 'revaluation surplus'.

The requirement to review revaluations regularly can be interpreted as meaning annually or at least when there are indications that there have been changes in the prices in the market. Each class of assets must be revalued to prevent what is known as 'cherry picking', that is, the revaluation of only those particular assets in a class which have increased in value and excluding those in a class which have not increased in value.

Discussion point

Do you consider companies should be compelled to revalue their assets to make the financial statements more useful?

After the initial recognition and measurement of the asset, the final stage comes of derecognition either at the end of the life of the asset or it is disposed of for some other reason. The standard states that the carrying amount of an item of property, plant and equipment shall be derecognized on disposal or when no future economic benefits are expected from its use or disposal. The gain or loss arising from the derecognition goes to profit or loss when the item is derecognized. Although the company may sell the unwanted asset, gains on the derecognition cannot be classified as revenue on the Income Statement.

Definition – Derecognition

The removal from the balance sheet of assets and liabilities which had previously been recognized in the financial statements of an organization.

IAS 23 BORROWING COSTS

IAS 23 was first issued in 1984 and revised in 2007. The objective of the standard is to establish that borrowing costs directly attributable to the acquisition, construction or production of a 'qualifying asset' (one which necessarily takes a substantial period of time to get ready for its intended use or sale) are included in the cost of the asset. Other borrowing costs are recognized as an expense.

Some companies will purchase their non-current asset and some companies may construct their own and borrow money to do so. The question arises whether the interest on the borrowings can be considered as part of constructing the asset and thus goes on the Balance Sheet or, as with other interest payments go to the Income Statement.

If the borrowings are considered as an expense on the Balance Sheet this will decrease profits. If the interest is considered as part of the asset it goes to the balance sheet.

Discussion point

Do you consider that borrowings are an interest charge to the Income Statement or part of the cost of the asset and should go to the Balance Sheet?

For several years there was no guidance on this issue and a company could select its own policy. For the user his could be confusing. Since the 2007 revision, IAS 23 now states that borrowing costs which are directly attributing to the acquisition, construction or production of a qualifying asset should be capitalized as part of the cost of the asset. The amount of borrowing costs on the balance sheet can be significant as shown in the following extract.

LINK TO PRACTICE

Kingfisher

The amount of borrowing costs capitalized in property, plant and equipment in the year has been £1m (2011/12: £1m). The cumulative total of borrowing costs included at the balance sheet date, net of depreciation, is £27m (2011/12: £26m).

http://www.kingfisher.com/files/reports/annual_report_2013/files/pdf/
annual_report_2013.pdf

Borrowings may include:

- Interest on bank overdrafts and borrowings.
- Amortization of discounts or premiums on borrowings.

- Amortization of ancillary costs incurred in the arrangement of borrowings.

- Finance charges on finance leases.

- Exchange differences on foreign currency borrowings where they are regarded as an adjustment to interest costs.

Definition – Qualifying asset

A qualifying asset is an asset which necessarily takes a substantial period of time to get ready for its intended use or sale.

Examples of qualifying assets include manufacturing plants, power generation facilities and investment properties. Inventories which require a substantial period of time to bring to a saleable condition but not inventories which are manufactured on a routine basis or produced in large quantities on a repetitive basis over a short period of time.

There are restrictions on the amount which a company can capitalize. The general philosophy is only those borrowing costs which are incurred during construction can be capitalized.

- Costs eligible for capitalization are the actual costs incurred less any income earned on the temporary investment of funds borrowed specifically.

- Capitalization commences when expenditures and borrowing costs are being incurred and activities which are necessary to prepare the asset for its intended use or sale are in progress.

For example, a company may receive the loan on 1 January but because of technical difficulties construction does not start until 1 March. The interest for January and February cannot be capitalized.

- Capitalization ceases when substantially all of the activities are complete.

- Capitalization must be suspended during periods where active development is interrupted.

- Where construction is completed in stages, capitalization should cease when substantially all of the necessary preparatory activities are complete.

Definition – Borrowing costs

Borrowing costs directly attributable to the acquisition or construction of qualifying assets are capitalized. Qualifying assets are those which necessarily take a substantial period of time to prepare for their intended use. All other borrowing costs are recognized in the Group Income Statement in finance costs, excluding those arising from financial services, in the period in which they occur.

IAS 38 INTANGIBLE ASSETS

IAS 38 was issued in 1998 and revised in 2004. The objective of the standard is to set out the accounting requirements for intangible assets. These are defined as assets which are without physical substance and identifiable (either being separable or arising from contractual or other legal rights).

Increasingly, companies have found their most important assets for generating future benefits are not physical assets such as buildings and machinery but assets which have no physical substance. For example, every cab in New York City has to purchase a license in the form of a medallion to display. The city strictly limits the number of licences which are issued and the cost of a license in auction can be over $1 million. The possible value of a pair of peak time slots at London Heathrow is between £25 and £30 million (Deloittes undated). Other examples of intangible assets are:

Examples of intangible assets

Fishing quotas
Airline landing slots
Taxi licences
Patents
Trademarks
Customer databases
Brand names
Computer software

There are other items not on the list which are definitely a benefit to the company. Possibly the main one is the 'reputation' of the company. This may be due to highly trained employees, excellent products and a high degree of customer satisfaction. These are difficult to measure so are not on the balance sheet but we will return to this discussion when we discuss brands later in the chapter.

For an intangible asset to be recognized it must be identifiable and there should be reliable measurement. This means they must be capable of being separated from the rest of the company and can be sold, licensed, rented or exchanged either individually or together with a related item. The intangible asset can also be identifiable because it arises from contractual or legal rights even if those rights are not separable from the business.

Recognizing and measuring the intangible asset will depend on how it has been identified. Some intangible assets will have been purchased by the company from another company. The recognition is evident through the purchase and the measurement of the asset is by the price paid.

Some intangible can be internally generated, in other words the company has developed the intangible asset itself. For example, a drinks company may have developed a new 'energy' drink or a company may have developed software for controlling its operations. The standard is more restrictive in its approach to internally generated intangible assets than those which have been purchased.

The standard separates the requirements for acquired and internally generated assets below.

ACQUIRED INTANGIBLE ASSETS

There are three situations where acquisition has taken place:

1. The company has acquired the asset with a single transaction and paid for it.

2. The company acquires an asset by exchanging another for it. In these circumstances, the asset is measured at fair value. Where this is not possible, the asset acquired is measured at the carrying amount of the asset given up.

3. The third situation is where the intangible asset is acquired in the course of taking over another business: a business combination. In these circumstances the intangible asset should be recognized at fair value which is the amount for which an asset could be exchanged between knowledgeable, willing parties in an arm's length transaction.

After initial recognition a company has a choice of measurement methods. An intangible asset may be carried in the balance sheet at either:

- cost less any accumulated amortization and impairment losses; or
- a revalued amount (based on fair value) less any subsequent amortization and any accumulated impairment losses. This method cannot be used at initial recognition.

Cost should be easy to identify from the transaction itself. The standard specifies those components of cost which can be recognized. There are certain items which cannot be included in the original cost and these are:

- Administration costs.
- Costs of introducing new products or services.
- Costs of conducting new business.

- Costs incurred while waiting to use the asset.
- Initial operating losses from operation.

Having placed the asset on the balance sheet, the issue arises as to how it should be treated. The choices are:

- It can stay on the Balance Sheet until some event occurs which makes it no longer an asset, that is, able to generate future benefits.
- It can be depreciated, as with tangible assets, over its useful economic life.
- It can be depreciated over an arbitrary period of time established by the standard setters.

Over the years and in different countries various approaches have been adopted. Depreciation over an arbitrary period of time has possibly been the most popular. IAS 38 establishes an alternative approach which seems to be effective. Two different situations are identified and the approach required for each one.

1. The standard requires that where the intangible assets are similar to tangible assets they need to be depreciated. The term 'amortization' is generally used.

2. The IASB argues that no intangible asset can have an infinite life. If a company is unable to estimate the useful economic life the standard requires that the asset must be tested for impairment annually. To do this the requirements of IAS 36 Impairment of Assets must be applied. This is discussed in the next section.

A useful example of intangible assets and the company's view on their expected economic life is given in the following extract from the annual report of Rentokil.

LINK TO PRACTICE

Rentokil

The estimated useful economic lives of intangible assets are as follows:

    Customer lists and relationships: 5–16 years

    Brands and patents: 2–15 years

    Reacquired franchise rights: 3–5 years

    Computer software: 3–5 years

The following are the main categories of intangible assets:

(a) Customer lists and relationships

Customer lists and portfolios acquired as part of a business combination are initially measured at fair value and amortized on a straight-line basis over their useful economic lives. Separate values are not attributed to internally generated customer lists or relationships.

(b) Brands and patents

Brands and patents acquired as part of a business combination are initially measured at fair value and amortized on a straight-line basis over their useful economic lives. Expenditure incurred to develop, maintain and renew brands and patents internally is recognized as an expense in the period incurred. Separate values are not attributed to internally generated brands and

(c) Reacquired franchise rights

Reacquired franchise rights acquired as part of a business combination in City Link represents the benefit to the group from the right to operate in certain geographical regions. These are initially measured at fair value and amortized on a straight-line basis over the remaining contractual period of the franchise agreements which terminated on 25 October 2010.

(d) Computer software

Acquired computer software licences are capitalized on the basis of the costs incurred to acquire and bring into use the specific software and are amortized over their estimated useful lives.

Costs associated with maintaining computer software programs are recognized as an expense as incurred. Costs that are directly associated with the production of identifiable and unique software products controlled by the group, and that will probably generate economic benefits exceeding costs beyond one year, are recognized as intangible assets. Direct costs include the software development, employee costs and an appropriate portion of relevant overheads.

Computer software development costs recognized as assets are amortized over their estimated useful lives

(e) Research and development

Research expenditure is recognized as an expense as incurred. Costs incurred on development projects (relating to the design and testing of new or improved products) are recognized as intangible assets when it is probable that the project will be a success considering its commercial and technological feasibility and only if the cost can be measured reliably.

Other development expenditure is recognized as an expense as incurred. Development costs previously recognized as an expense are not recognized as an asset in a subsequent period. Development costs that have been capitalized are amortized from the date the product is available for use on a straight-line basis over the expected benefit

http://www.rentokil-initial.com/annualreport2011/pdfs/
Acounting_policies.pdf

The above example illustrates the expected economic life of intangible assets, the treatment of subsequent costs and differences between acquired and internally generated assets. We discuss internally generated assets in the next section.

INTERNALLY GENERATED INTANGIBLE ASSETS

The standard setters are very reluctant to allow companies to recognize internally generated intangible assets and they set out specific criteria for the recognition of internally generated assets. Certain internally generated assets cannot be recognized as intangible assets, including internally generated goodwill, brands and publishing titles.

Although these particular intangibles should not be recognized if internally generated, they may meet the general recognition criteria if purchased by another company. A similar asset may, therefore, be recognized on the balance sheet if purchased but must be charged to the Income Statement if internally generated. The result of this regulation is you can examine the financial statements of companies and some very famous brands and publishing titles will only appear on a balance sheet if they have been acquired externally.

Discussion point

Do you consider it reasonable that some internally generated intangible assets cannot be recognized on the Balance Sheet but can be if they are purchased?

One asset which has caused the greatest discussion is goodwill. Lord MacNaughten in the case of Commissioners of the Inland Revenue v Muller and Co. declared that goodwill

> is a thing very easy to describe, very difficult to define. It is the benefit and advantage of the good name, reputation and connection of the business. It is the attractive force which brings in custom. It is the one thing which distinguishes an old established business from a new business at its first start.

This ephemeral nature of goodwill has been the basis of many legal cases and judges have delighted in drawing zoological comparisons to explain the problems. In the 1934 case of Whiteman Smith Motor Company v Chaplin four types of customers were identified.

- The dog that stays faithful to the person and not the location.
- The cat that stays faithful to the location and not the person.

- The rabbit who is a customer because the premises are close and for no other reason.

- The rat that is casual and is attracted to neither person nor location.

Most acquirers assume they are going to have cat customers that will stay with the business. Unfortunately, the world if full of dogs, rats and rabbits.

A company can acquire goodwill and, under the standard, this will be shown on its balance sheet. We will give a very simple example. Imagine that a very large company purchases a smaller but highly successful smaller company. Because it is so successful the large company is willing to pay a very good price for it. Let us assume it is one million pounds. The purchase is successful and the large company calculates the fair value of the tangible assets it has acquired.

It calculates the fair value to be £750,000. As the purchase price was £1 million the large company paid an extra £250,000. It is assumed this payment is for the goodwill. This does not appear on the Balance Sheet of the smaller company as they generated it internally. However, as the large company acquired the goodwill, it will appear on their Balance Sheet. The amounts of goodwill a company has acquired can be substantial and below is an extract from the notes of the 2011 Annual Report of the WPP Group.

LINK TO PRACTICE

WPP Group

Intangible assets comprise goodwill, certain acquired separable corporate brand names, acquired customer relationships, acquired proprietary tools and capitalised computer software not integral to a related item of hardware.

Goodwill represents the excess of fair value attributed to investments in businesses or subsidiary undertakings over the fair value of the underlying net assets, including intangible assets, at the date of their acquisition.

12. Intangible assets

Goodwill

The movements in 2011 and 2010 were as follows:

	£m
	Cost:
1 January 2010	9,246.8
Additions	164.3
Revision of earnout estimates	82.0

	£m
Exchange adjustments	185.7
31 December 2010	**9,678.8**
Additions1	434.6
Revision of earnout estimates	25.9
Exchange adjustments	(150.8)
31 December 2011	**9,988.5**
Accumulated impairment losses and writedowns:	
1 January 2010	549.3
Impairment losses for the year	8.3
Exchange adjustments	14.9
31 December 2010	**572.5**
Exchange adjustments	(14.8)
31 December 2011	**557.7**
	Net book value:
31 December 2011	9,430.8
31 December 2010	9,106.3
1 January 2010	8,697.5

(continued)

There is some scope in IAS 38 for companies to put their development costs but not research on their balance sheet as an intangible asset. The conditions allowing a company to do this are very restrictive and 'research' itself cannot be capitalized. This means these activities must be divided into a research phase and a development phase. Expenditure on research must be charged to the Income Statement in the financial period in which it occurs and includes such costs as:

- The pursuit of new knowledge.
- The search for, or evaluation, and selection of applications of research.
- The search for such items as alternative materials, products and systems.
- The pursuit of possible alternatives for improved such items as materials, products and systems.

The restrictions on the capitalization of research are so restrictive it is better to look at the criteria which must be met in order to capitalize development costs. To be able to put the development costs on the balance sheet as an intangible asset a company must separate the research and development phase. The expenditure for the development phase can only be capitalized if the following can be demonstrated:

- The technical feasibility of completing the asset so it will be ready for sale or use.
- The intention to complete the asset and sell it or use it.
- The ability to use or sell the asset.
- That the asset will generate future economic benefits for the company.
- The availability of sufficient technical, financial and other resources to complete the development of the asset.
- The ability to be able to measure reliably the costs of development.

For some companies the transition from a research phase to a development phase may be difficult to identify. There is also the issue that in some industries many research projects are started but abandoned as the results are not looking promising. A project will often start as research and, if unsuccessful, will be terminated.

If the research is successful the project will enter into a development phase. Usually a business plan is required for the company to go back and capitalize the development costs.

IAS 36 IMPAIRMENT OF ASSETS

IAS 36 was issued in 1998 and revised in 2004. The objective of the standard is to ensure that an entity's assets are not carried at more than their recoverable amount. The recoverable amount is defined as the higher of fair value less costs to sell and value in use. This section will explain these terms.

The recoverable amount is the greater of the asset's net selling price and its value in use. Without knowledge of the proper carrying value of assets, users can be misled on the financial strength of the entity and its financial performance. IAS 36 addresses this issue and it applies to:

- Property, plant and equipment.
- Intangible assets and goodwill.
- Investment property carried at cost.
- Subsidiaries, associates and joint ventures.

IAS 36 describes the procedures to be followed to ensure that an asset is not carried at greater than its recoverable amount. The standard also explains the accounting treatment for impairment loss. Entities may find the requirement to write off impairment losses in the financial period they occur has a significant negative effect on earnings and associated performance ratios.

Companies must assess annually whether there has been an indication of impairment of all its assets. This could involve a considerable amount of work but the key word is 'indication'. Looking at the first stage of assessing indications of impairment, companies should carry out a review of its assets at the end of each year. The external indications of a possible impairment are:

- An abnormal fall in the asset's market value.
- A significant change in the technological, market, legal or economic environment of the business in which the assets are used.
- An increase in market interest rates or market rates of return on investments likely to affect the discount rates in calculating the value in use of the assets.
- The carrying value of the net assets being more than its market capitalization.

The internal indications of impairment are:

- Evidence of obsolescence or physical damage.
- Adverse changes in the use to which the asset is put.
- The asset's economic performance.

If there are no indications of impairment, the company need take no action.

In addition to the indication assessment there are certain assets which entities must conduct a full impairment assessment. The assets for the full test are:

- Intangible assets with indefinite lives.
- Intangible assets not ready for use.
- Goodwill arising through a business combination.

With the above three classes of assets, the company must make an estimate of the recoverable amount of the assets. It must also do the same with those assets where there are indications of impairment.

The recoverable amount is compared to the carrying amount of the asset on the Balance Sheet. If the carrying amount on the balance sheet is higher than the recoverable amount the asset is impaired. The amount of the impairment must be charged to the Income Statement and the carrying amount on the Balance Sheet reduced.

The recoverable amount is the higher of fair value and value in use. Fair value is the amount expected to be received if the assets were to be sold. This can be sometimes difficult to assess in practice.

The two steps a company would take in arriving at the value in use of an asset are:

▪ Estimate the future cash flows which a company anticipated over the remaining life of the asset. This is the cash flow forecast for the one asset. The company has to determine the cash inflows and cash outflows for which asset to find the cash surplus or deficit each year for its remaining years of use.

▪ The next stage is to calculate the present value of those cash surpluses and deficits. To do this a company will apply a discount rate to those cash flows and calculate the present value of those future cash amounts.

Although the amount of work required identifying the various elements, the principles are simple. The recoverable amount is either the estimated amount to be received if the asset is sold (fair value) or the discounted future cash flows if the asset is retained (value in use). The business logic is that you would choose the highest of fair value or value in use. For example you believe you could sell an asset for £8000 but if you retain it the total amount of the discounted future cash flows is only £6000. The rational decision is to sell the asset and the recoverable amount is the fair value.

Discussion point

How feasible in practice do you consider the methods for calculating the recoverable amount?

You can have the situation where you could sell the asset for only £6000 but if you retain it the value in use is £8000. This is the recoverable amount and it would be a sensible decision to retain the asset. The £8000 is the recoverable amount of the asset and, if this is lower than the carrying amount on the Balance Sheet, the asset is impaired. In Figure 7.1 we have assumed the carrying amount on the balance sheet of the asset is £10,000 and the asset value is impaired.

The following is an example of a company which has carried out this procedure and compared the value in use of the asset, in this case retail stores, to the carrying amount shown in the balance sheet.

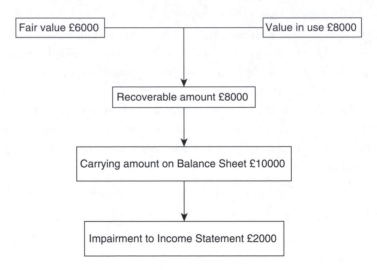

Figure 7.1 Calculating impairment

Wherever possible, the calculation of the recoverable amounts should be determined for individual assets, as in the above example from Burberry. However, there may be several assets which are linked together to form the production activity. If it is impossible to determine the recoverable amount for an individual asset, the recoverable amount for the asset's cash-generating unit (CGU) should be identified and used.

A CGU is the smallest identifiable group of assets which generates cash inflows from continuing use, and are largely independent of the cash inflows from other assets or groups of assets. Mostly the assets will be tangible noncurrent assets such as property, plant and equipment. It is possible the CGU will also include goodwill which has been acquired.

Where there is acquired goodwill it requires specific accounting treatment. The amount of goodwill on the balance sheet should be allocated to each of the CGUs or groups of CGUs which are expected to derive benefit. It may be the goodwill can only be identified with one CGU.

Having identified the CGU, including goodwill where appropriate, the company must then calculate the fair value and the value in use. If the recoverable amount of the CGU is higher than the carrying amount of the CGU as shown in the balance sheet, the unit and the goodwill allocated to the unit is not impaired. If the carrying amount exceeds the recoverable amount, the CGU is impaired by the amount of the difference and the company must recognize this impairment loss by writing the loss as an expense in the Income Statement and reducing the carrying amount on the balance sheet.

Where acquired goodwill is involved, the procedure is as follows:

1. The loss is first charged against the goodwill allocated to the CGU;

2. If the goodwill is insufficient to absorb the loss, then the loss will be allocated over other assets in proportion to the carrying amount of each asset.

ILLUSTRATIVE EXAMPLE: IMPAIRMENT OF A CGU

A cash generation unit to which acquired goodwill has been allocated has the following assets.

	£000
Property	90
Machinery	60
Acquired goodwill	30
Carrying amount of CGU	180

An analysis shows the recoverable amount for the CGU is £135,000. The CGU is therefore impaired and an amount of £45,000 must be charged to the Income Statement and the carrying amount of the assets reduced in the balance sheet by the same amount.

The standard requires that first goodwill must be written off completely and any remaining impairment loss must be borne by the remaining assets in proportion to their carrying amount. Table 7.2 shows these calculations.

	Pre-impairment £000	Amount written off £000	Post impairment £000
Goodwill	30	30	–
Property	90	9	81
Machinery	60	6	54
	180	45	135

Table 7.2 Applying impairment loss

Once the goodwill is written off completely, the impaired amount remaining of £15,000 is written off against the pre-impairment amounts for property and machinery in proportion to their carrying amount:

$$\text{Property } £15,000 \times \frac{£90,000}{£150,000} = £9,000$$

$$\text{Machinery } £15,000 \times \frac{£60,000}{£150,000} = £6,000$$

It is possible in future years the asset is no longer impaired because of changes in the markets or the economy. In these circumstances a company can reverse the impairment but there are two rules.

1. Impairment for goodwill cannot be reversed.

2. The reversal on other assets is limited to their original carrying value. In other words you cannot increase to a higher value.

We will use the above to demonstrate the application of these rules if the recoverable amount was found to be £175,000.

Reversing impairment loss

	Pre-impairment £000	Post impairment £000	Reversal £000	Post reversal £000
Goodwill	30	–	–	–
Property	90	81	9	90
Machinery	60	54	6	60
	1800	135	15	150

Note that the amount of the goodwill has not been reversed. Although the new recoverable amount of the CGU is £175,000, the goodwill is not reversed so the total recoverable amount is now £150,000.

FINANCIAL INSTRUMENTS

The accounting regulations for financial instruments and the most recently issued standards are:

IFRS 7 *Financial Instruments*: *Disclosure* was issued in 2005. The standard requires that entities disclose information about the significance of financial instruments to an entity, and the nature and extent of risks arising from those financial instruments, both in qualitative and quantitative terms. Specific disclosures are required in relation to transferred financial assets and a number of other matters.

IFRS 9 *Financial Instruments* was issued in 2009 and applies to annual financial periods beginning on or after 1 January 2015. The standard is a complete replacement for IAS 39 *Financial Instruments: Recognition and Measurement*. The objective of IFRS 9 is to establish the recognition and measurement requirements for financial instruments and some contracts to buy or sell non-financial items.

The proper accounting treatment for financial instruments has been a controversial topic for many years. It is impossible to understand the standard without a basic understanding of the transactions involving financial instruments.

> **Definition – financial instruments**
>
> Any contract which gives rise to a financial asset of one entity and a financial liability or equity instrument of another entity.

Financial markets are used by companies to raise finance. External financial markets can be considered short term, less than a year, or long term. Short-term financial markets are often called money markets. Long-term financial markets are called capital markets, and include the equity market, the debt market which includes borrowing from other firms, and the bank market. Multinational companies which used to raise equity capital solely from sources within their own country now look to other countries for potential shareholders and this is known as cross border financing.

There are several types of risk associated with using financial markets. There is interest rate risk from making investments or taking out loans or exchange rate risk through international trade. It is impossible to eliminate risk completely but companies can attempt to reduce it by hedging the risk.

Definition – Hedging

Hedging is reducing risk by taking action now to reduce the possibility of future losses, usually with the possibility of not enjoying any future gains.

An example of hedging is where a company knows it has to purchase supplies of materials in three months' time. The materials, for example agricultural crops may not be ready or the company may not wish to hold the materials until they are needed. There is a risk that the price of materials will increase before the end of the three months.

The company can enter into an agreement now to purchase the goods in three months' time but at a current price. The company avoids the risk of the prices increasing in three months' time when it requires the materials. It also loses the opportunity to make a gain if the price decreases in three months' time.

Contracts are used for trading in derivatives. These are commonly traded among financial institutions, individual investors, fund managers, corporations and private companies. The trades are conducted at either a physical location such as an Exchange or remotely in what is termed the over-the-counter market.

Definition derivatives

A derivative is a complex financial instrument whose value depends on (or is derived from) the value of another basic underlying variable or asset.

The four main types of derivatives are forward contracts, future contracts, options and swaps.

FORWARD CONTRACT

The example discussed above is a forward contract. It is an agreement to buy or sell an asset at a certain future time for a certain price. These are the simplest form of derivative and are traded in the over-the-counter market. One of the parties in a forward contract agrees to buy the underlying asset on a future specified date for a certain specified price. The other party agrees to sell the asset on the agreed date for the agreed price. The price at which the parties agree to transact in the future is called the delivery price. No money changes hands at the time the parties enter into a forward contract.

Once forward contracts are agreed, they can be traded between investors, typically on the over-the-counter market. A company in the United States expects a large payment in Canadian dollars in three months' time. It will need to convert this payment in Canadian dollars into US dollars and there is the risk that the exchange rate will be unfavourable. The company will therefore attempt to hedge this exchange risk by entering into a forward contract.

FUTURES CONTRACT

A futures contract is very similar to a forward contract. The main difference is that futures contracts are traded on an exchange which sets rules for trading. This simplifies the trading process and helps the market achieve higher liquidity. Futures contracts are traded on a variety of commodities, including live cattle, sugar, wool, lumber, copper, gold, tin and aluminium. They are also traded on a wide array of financial assets, including stock indices, currencies and Treasury bonds.

OPTIONS

There are two types of options. In contrast to forwards and futures, options give the owner the right, but not the obligation, to transact. The owner therefore will only transact if it is profitable to do so. The price at which the parties transact in the future is called the strike price. When the transaction takes place, the owner of the option exercises the option.

SWAPS

A swap is simply an agreement between two parties to exchange cash flows in the future. The agreement defines the dates when the cash flows are exchanged and the manner in which amounts are calculated. Swaps typically lead to cash flow exchanges on several future dates. There are interest rate swaps where a floating-rate loan is exchanged for a fixed-rate loan by agreeing to pay a fixed payment in return for a variable payment. Similarly, currency swaps can be used to transform borrowings in one currency to borrowings in another currency, by agreeing to make a payment in one currency in return for a payment in another currency.

The definition of financial instruments states that there must be a contract and this gives rise to financial assets, financial liabilities and equity which appear on a balance sheet. The definition of a financial instrument is also two-sided: the contract must always give rise to a financial asset of one party, with a corresponding financial liability or equity instrument of another party.

If we look in detail by what is meant by equity, financial assets and financial liabilities, it will help to explain the types of transactions taking place.

FINANCIAL ASSETS

Examples of financial assets are:

- Cash.

- Equity instrument of another entity (e.g. investment in another entity's shares).

- Receivables and loans to another entity.

- Investments in bonds and other debt instruments issued by other entity.

- Derivative financial assets.

The following assets are NOT financial assets:

- Inventories.

- Property plant and equipment.

- Leased assets.

- Intangible assets.

- Prepaid expenses.

Financial liabilities are slightly more complex and include a contractual obligation to deliver cash or another financial asset to another entity or to exchange financial assets or financial liabilities with another entity under conditions which are potentially unfavourable to the entity; or a contract which will or may be settled in the entity's own equity instruments and is not classified as an equity instrument of the entity. Examples of financial liabilities are:

- Trades payable.

- Loans from other entities.

- Bonds and other debt instruments issued by the entity.

- Derivative financial liabilities.

- Preference shares which are redeemable at a specified date and for a specified amount.

- Obligations to issue own shares worth a fixed amount of cash.

Care must be taken with the last example as it emphasizes shares worth a fixed amount. Normally shares fluctuate in price so if you enter into a contract which specifies the number of shares the price will not be known until the contract is completed. You can enter into a contract where the amount is known but not the number of shares. For example, a company enters into a contract in 2012 which entails issuing its own shares in January 2018 to the value of £800,000. This is a financial liability as the number of shares is variable but the amount is fixed.

The following examples are NOT financial liabilities:

- Warranty obligations.

- Income tax liabilities.

- Constructive obligations.

> ## Definition – Equity
>
> A contract which evidences a residual interest in the assets of an entity after deducting all of its liabilities. If we put this in the terms of the accounting equation then Assets – Liabilities = Capital (Equity).

Examples of equity are:

- Ordinary shares.

- Preference shares (non-redeemable and discretionary dividend).

- Warrants or written call options (allow the holder to purchase ordinary shares for a fixed amount of cash).

The main standard for financial instruments was *Financial Instruments: Recognition and Measurement issued in 1998*. This is to be replaced by IFRS 9 Financial instruments issued in 2009. The IASB published new requirements for classifying and measuring financial instruments in IFRS 9 Financial Instruments issued in October 2010. A new Exposure Draft was issued in 2011 with limited amendments being made to IFRS 9 which will become operational in 2015.

The IASB issued the limited amendments because of:

- the interaction between the classification and measurement of financial assets and the accounting for insurance contract liabilities;

- the clarification of a narrow range of application questions, such as the amount/frequency of sales which would be consistent with a 'hold to collect' business model and how to apply the contractual cash flow characteristics assessment when there is an interest rate mismatch or the interest rate is leveraged; and

- the reduction of key differences between the IASB's requirements for classification and measurement of financial instruments and the tentative classification and measurement model considered by the US Financial Accounting Standards Board (FASB).

The main characteristics of IFRS 9 are:

- It is principle and not rule based.

- The classification depends on the business model and nature of cash flows.

- There are only two measurement bases.

- There is one impairment model.

The new IFRS 9 should simplify present requirements but it does not come into effect until 2015. As discussed in the last chapter, the rapprochement with the FASB appears to be fading and there may be differences in approach to accounting for financial instruments between the US and International standards by 2015.

CONCLUSIONS

The Statement of Financial Position, or Balance Sheet, is regulated by several standards. Although most are not technically challenging, there remain controversial issues.

Under IAS 23 companies are now obliged to capitalize borrowing costs on qualifying assets, although some continue to argue that it should be charged to the Income Statement as an expense.

Goodwill has been a debated topic for many years and will continue to be so. Purchased goodwill can be recognized, the argument by the standard setters being that it was paid for as part of an acquisition and it gives a reliable measurement. A safety net has been put in place by companies having to test goodwill for impairment annually.

Accounting for financial instruments was a major topic for discussion during the 2008 recession. Some claimed that the accounting treatment was deficient and contributed to the recession by producing misleading figures. The two new standards which have been issued have not been tested at the time of writing this chapter and it will be interesting to see the results of their application.

RECOMMENDED READING

Chalmers, Keryn G., Godfrey, Jayne M., Webster, John C. (2011) 'Does an impairment regime better reflect the underlying economic attributes of goodwill?' *Accounting & Finance*, Sep, Vol. 51 Issue 3, p. 634–660.

Pashang, Hossein, Fihn, Glenn. (2011) 'Understanding the phenomenon of goodwill'. *Review of Business Research*, Vol. 11 Issue 2, p. 137–145.

Hunter, L., Webster, E., Wyatte, A. (2012) 'Accounting for expenditures on intangibles'. *Abacus*, Mar, Vol. 48 Issue 1, p. 104–145.

CASE STUDY BETHAN GREENWICH (3)

If you have completed the Income Statement correctly in Chapter 6, your answer should correspond with the following.

Income Statement for the six months ending 28 February 2014:

	$'000	$'000
Sales		120.0
Less cost of sales:		
Purchases	134.0	
Less closing inventory	<u>54.0</u>	<u>80.0</u>
Gross profit		40.0
Less expenses:		
Wages	15.0	
Selling & distribution (S&D)	7.8	
Rent	3.6	
Depreciation	<u>1.0</u>	<u>27.4</u>
Net profit		<u>12.6</u>

The final stage is to complete the Balance Sheet at 28 February 2014. This is done by using the Cash Flow Statement and the Income Statement in combination. The main points to note are:

1) Remember to deduct depreciation as shown in the Income Statement from the original cost of the assets.

2) Closing inventory as shown in your Income Statement will appear as a current asset on the balance sheet.

3) The final cash balance shown on the cash flow statement will appear on the Balance Sheet.

4) The profit shown on the Income Statement will be shown on the Balance Sheet under Capital.

5) Accounts receivable and payable are calculated by taking the accruals amount on the Income Statement and deducting the cash movement on the Cash Flow Statement.

CHAPTER 8
CORPORATE RELATIONSHIPS

LEARNING OBJECTIVES

At the end of this chapter you should be able to:

- Describe the types of business relationships that a company may enter into.
- Summarize the information contained in a company's Annual Report and Accounts.
- Explain consolidated financial statements and the adjustments that are required.
- Demonstrate the calculations when there is an acquisition of a business by another.
- Discuss the nature and accounting treatment for goodwill.
- Explain the characteristics of joint ventures or joint operations.

EXECUTIVE SUMMARY

Companies that have their shares quoted on the stock exchange are required to meet certain legal and stock exchange requirements. Such companies must make publicly available their financial statements for the half year (interim accounts) and for the full financial year (the annual report and accounts).

The printed Annual Report and Accounts can easily be obtained by contacting the company and these documents are at least 100 pages in length. Not all the information is financial and the document is used to promote the company. In addition, companies have websites and these contain voluminous quantities of information of interest to investors and others.

Public companies are very large enterprises that will have entered into relationships with other companies. When users scrutinize the financial statements of companies they are entitled to believe that all the transactions reflected in those statements have been conducted 'at arm's length'. This may not be the case and the relationships may have an impact on their business dealings and affect their financial statements.

To ensure that users are aware of the possible consequences of these relationships several standards have been developed. Figure 8.1 illustrates the possible relationships and the appropriate standard.

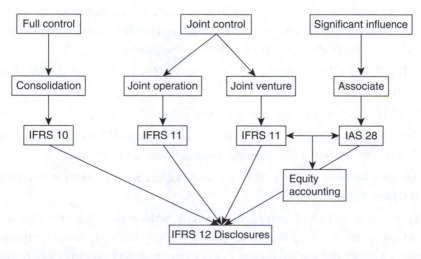

Figure 8.1 Corporate relationships and accounting standards

CONCEPTUAL AND PRACTICAL ISSUES

The IASB's *Framework for the Preparation and Presentation of Financial Statements* defines the reporting entity in one sentence with no further explanation. It is clearly important that there is some understanding of what is a reporting entity so that we can establish the boundaries within which business activities are conducted and should be reported, and those activities which fall outside those boundaries.

The IASB's present view is that a *reporting entity* should not be limited to business activities that are structured as separate legal entities. Using a broad definition, a reporting entity could be described as being a circumscribed area of business activity of interest to present and potential, investors and creditors. This would include, for example, a sole proprietor, branch, corporation, trading trust, or partnership.

This position presents some difficulties. There are many types of relationships in the business world. One company may own another company completely or to a large extent. Two or more companies may act together on a particular joint venture. For good operational reasons a company may invest in another business.

The requirements for reporting these relationships, and by default, sketching some boundaries have been contained in several standards. There have been several revisions to these standards and in 2011 the IASB issued a package of new relationship standards that come into effect in 2013. The package and amendments include:

- IFRS 10 'Consolidated Financial Statements' which establishes a single, control-based model for assessing control by one entity of another and determining the scope of consolidation. It replaces the corresponding requirements of both IAS 27 'Consolidated and Separate Financial Statements'.

- IFRS 11 'Joint Arrangements', which replaces IAS 31 'Interests in Joint Ventures'.

- IFRS 12 'Disclosure of Interests in Other Entities'.

- An amended version of IAS 27, which is renamed IAS 27 'Separate Financial Statements' and now addresses only separate financial statements.

- An amended version of IAS 28, now renamed IAS 28 'Investments in Associates and Joint Ventures'.

A most important part of each of the standards is the explanation of the types of relationship and how they may be identified. Possibly the most complex arrangements are where there is full control in the relationship and consolidated financial statements are required. This topic will take up the major part of this chapter.

A relevant standard to our discussions is IFRS 3 Business Combinations. A revised version of IFRS 3 was issued in January 2008 and applies to business combinations occurring in an entity's first annual period beginning on or after 1 July 2009. A business combination is a transaction or event in which an acquirer obtains control of one or more businesses. The issue is how we account for that acquisition at the date it takes place.

THE PUBLISHED REPORT AND ACCOUNTS

Companies listed on the Stock Exchange are required to issue an annual report and accounts and an interim report at the six month interval which is public information. Other terms are used for the document, the most common being annual accounts, annual financial statements and annual financial report. Copies of these reports can be easily obtained from the company or they are available on the company's website.

As well as the annual document, listed companies must also publish semi-annual statements (interims) and an announcement (prelims) of the main figures prior to the annual documents. Limited companies not listed on the Stock Exchange are also required to produce annual accounts, although the amount of information to be disclosed is considerably less than public companies.

Once prepared, a copy of the accounts must be sent to the Registrar of Companies, who maintains a separate file for every company. The Registrar's files may be inspected for a nominal fee by any member of the public.

It is the responsibility of the company's directors to produce accounts which show a true and fair view of the company's results for the period and its financial position at the end of the period. The requirement that the accounts show a true and fair view is critical.

The board approves the accounts by the signature of one director on the balance sheet. Once this has been done, and the auditors have completed their report, the accounts are presented to the members of the company in general meeting. When the members have adopted the accounts they are sent to the Registrar for filing.

Our focus in this chapter is the annual reports of public companies, although we discuss interim reports as these present some interesting conceptual issues. We extract examples from the Annual Report and Accounts 2012 of Diageo plc. (http://www.diageo.com/en-row/investor/Pages/Financial-Results.aspx). Diageo is the world's leading premium drinks business with brands that include Johnnie Walker, Crown Royal, J&B, Windsor, Buchanan's and Bushmills whiskies,

Smirnoff, Ciroc and Ketel One vodkas, Baileys, Captain Morgan, Jose Cuervo, Tanqueray and Guinness

Approximately 80 per cent of total production is undertaken in Diageo production areas located in Australia, Canada, Cameroon, Ghana, Ireland, Jamaica, Kenya, Nigeria, Uganda, the United Kingdom (most importantly Scotland) and the United States. The remaining 20 per cent of output is produced in many countries by joint-venture businesses or under contract with commercial partners.

Diageo's Annual Report contains 196 pages. The main sections with the approximate number of pages are shown below. We have expanded the details of the Financial Statements pages to illustrate the types of information they cover.

Company example – Diageo plc.

Performance summary
Business Description
Business Review
Governance

Financial Statements

The consolidated financial statements cover only six pages but are supported by over 50 pages of notes giving considerable detail. The consolidated statements refer to the results of the group of companies comprising Diageo plc. and Diageo also includes the company balance sheet as it is required to do so. In this chapter we will discuss the consolidated statements. In addition to 2012, the accounts show comparative results for the previous two years but we have omitted these. We discuss the main items following the example.

Company example Diageo plc. consolidated income statement

Notes		Year ended 30 June 2012 £million
Sales	2	14,594
Excise duties	3	(3,832)
Net sales	2	10,762
Cost of sales	3,5	(4,259)
Gross profit		6,503
Marketing	3	(1,691)
Other operating expenses	3,5	(1,654)
Operating profit	2	3,158
Sale of businesses	5	147
Interest receivable	6	262
Interest payable	6	(644)
Other finance income	6	8
Other finance charges	6	(23)
Share of associates' profits after tax	7	213
Profit before taxation		3,121
Taxation	8	(1,038)
Profit from continuing operations		2,083
Discontinued operations	9	(11)
Profit for the year		2,072
Attributable to		
Equity shareholders of the company		1,942
Non-controlling interests		130
		2,072

The Notes column refers to the note on the pages following the statement. The notes give considerably more information than contained on the face of the statement.

- Operating profit is before interest and finance. This figure is regarded by many as a key indicator of the success or otherwise of the business activities before consideration of the funding issues.

- The share of associates' profits after tax is discussed later in this chapter.

- Taxation is a complex area. The amount of taxation actually paid is likely to be lower than the amount showing in the Income Statement of a company.

- Profit for the year is similar to the net profit in the simpler examples that we explained in earlier chapters. The amount of profit attributable to equity shareholders is shown and in this chapter we explain non-controlling interests.

At the bottom of the page is given separately the calculation of earnings per share and we explain these in the following chapter.

Company example – Diageo plc. 2012

Consolidated statement of comprehensive income

	Year ended 30 June 2012 £million
Other comprehensive income	
Exchange differences on translation of foreign operations excluding borrowings – group	(74)
– associates and non-controlling interests*	(222)
Exchange differences on borrowings and derivative net investment hedges	210
Effective portion of changes in fair value of cash flow hedges	
– gains/(losses) taken to other comprehensive income	29
– transferred to income statement	(15)
Hyperinflation adjustment	3
Net actuarial (loss)/gain on post employment plans	(495)
Tax on other comprehensive income	103
Other comprehensive (loss)/income, net of tax, for the year	(461)
Profit for the year	2,072
Total comprehensive income for the year	1,611

Attributable to:	
Equity shareholders of the parent company	1,463
Non-controlling interests	148
Total comprehensive income for the year	1,611

We explained the comprehensive income statement in the previous chapter and the above example illustrates the many items that may be included. The sixth item from the bottom is the profit for the year shown on the consolidated income statement.

The presentation of the balance sheet follows the accounting equation Assets – Liabilities = Net Assets = Capital. There are many lines of detail so we show only the main headings but the detail for the Capital or Equity. There are also voluminous notes to support the balance sheet.

Company example – Diageo plc. 2012 Consolidated Balance Sheet

	£million
Non-current assets	15,097
Current assets	7,253
Total assets	22,350
Current liabilities	(4,784)
Non-current liabilities	(10,755)
Total liabilities	(15,559)
Net Assets	6,811
Equity	
Called up share capital	797
Share premium	1,344
Other reserves	3,213
Retained earnings	234
Equity attributable to equity shareholders of the parent company	5,588
Non-controlling interests	1,223
Total equity	6,811

We have not included the Consolidated Statement of Cash Flows as this was discussed in Chapter 5.

Interim reports covering a six-month period are required by the Stock Exchange. IAS 34 Interim Financial Reporting was issued in June 1998 and outlines the recognition, measurement and disclosure requirements for interim reports. The standard applies when an entity prepares an interim financial report, but does not prescribe which entities should publish interim financial reports, how frequently, or how soon after the end of an interim period.

The conceptual issue in respect of interim reports is whether they should use the discrete or integral approach. Remember that the Income Statement is on an accruals basis and not cash.

With an integral approach the six-month period is treated as part of the longer period. This approach recognizes that profits are earned unequally during the year and attempts to match planned costs on a basis relating to the year as a whole. For example, if in the first six months the annual maintenance costs are incurred, only half would be allocated to the first six months. Similarly, a big sales promotion in the first six months could be divided into two on the argument that the entire year benefits from the promotion.

With the discrete approach each six months is treated as a self-contained accounting period with costs and revenues being matched in each period. Using the discrete approach, the promotion costs in the example above would be charged in their entirety to the first interim period.

The criticisms of both approaches have been discussed by Hussey and Woolfe (1994). They recommended that the discrete method should be applied to interim reports but an accounting standard should identify the circumstances where departures from this would be acceptable. IAS 34 states that measurements for interim reporting purposes should be made on a year-to-date basis, so that the frequency of the entity's reporting does not affect the measurement of its annual results. In addition it emphasizes the following important issues:

- Revenues that are received seasonally, cyclically or occasionally within a financial year should not be anticipated or deferred as of the interim date, if anticipation or deferral would not be appropriate at the end of the financial year.

- Costs that are incurred unevenly during a financial year should be anticipated or deferred for interim reporting purposes if, and only if, it is also appropriate to anticipate or defer that type of cost at the end of the financial year.

- Income tax expense should be recognized based on the best estimate of the weighted average annual effective income tax rate expected for the full financial year.

Discussion point

Do you consider that the discrete or interim approach should be used for interim reports?

IAS 27 SEPARATE FINANCIAL STATEMENTS

IAS 27 was first issued in 1989 under the title IAS 27 *Consolidated Financial Statements and Accounting for Investments in Subsidiaries*. In 2003 it was revised and issued as *Consolidated and Separate Financial Statements*. In 2011 it was reissued as IAS 27 *Separate Financial Statements* (as amended in 2011) and becomes effective in 2013. The consolidation requirements that previously formed part of the original IAS 27 have been revised and are now contained in IFRS 10 *Consolidated Financial Statements* which we discuss later in this chapter.

The present standard sets out the accounting and disclosure requirements for separate financial statements. These are the financial statements prepared by a parent, or an investor in a joint venture or associate, where those investments are accounted for either at cost or in accordance with standard. IAS 27 also outlines the accounting requirements for dividends and contains numerous disclosure requirements.

When an entity prepares separate financial statements, investments in subsidiaries, associates, and jointly controlled entities are accounted for either:

- at cost, or
- in accordance with IFRS 9 *Financial Instruments*.

The entity applies the same accounting for each category of investments. Investments carried at cost should be measured at the lower of their carrying amount and fair value less costs to sell. The measurement of investments accounted for in accordance with IFRS 9 is not changed in such circumstances.

IFRS 10 CONSOLIDATED FINANCIAL STATEMENTS

> ### Definition consolidated financial statements
>
> The financial statements of a group in which the assets, liabilities, equity, income, expenses and cash flows of the parent and its subsidiaries are presented as those of a single economic entity.

IFRS 10 was issued in May 2011 and applies to annual periods beginning on or after 1 January 2013. The objective of the standard is to set out the requirements for the preparation and presentation of consolidated financial statements when an entity controls one or more other entities. To meet this objective it:

- requires an entity that controls another (a parent) to present consolidated financial statements (subject to limited exemptions – see below).
- defines 'control', and confirms control as the basis for consolidation.
- provides guidance on how to apply the new definition.
- provides guidance on preparing consolidated financial statements.

With public limited companies quoted on the Stock Exchange, usually there is a parent company that controls several other companies. For investors, the main interest is not the financial results of only the parent company but all the other companies making up the group. In these instances the parent company must prepare group or consolidated accounts. The consolidated statements bring together the results of all the individual entities making up the group.

The standard's main contents are:

- the requirement that a parent entity (an entity that controls one or more other entities) must present consolidated financial statements.
- a definition of the principle of control, and the criterion of control as the basis for consolidation.
- the identification of the circumstances where an investor controls an investee and therefore must consolidate the investee by applying the principle of control.
- the accounting requirements for the preparation of consolidated financial statements.
- the definition of an investment entity and the exception to consolidating particular subsidiaries of an investment entity.

A parent need not present consolidated financial statements if it meets all of the following conditions:

- it is a wholly owned subsidiary or is a partially owned subsidiary of another entity and its other owners, including those not otherwise entitled to vote, have been informed about, and do not object to, the parent not presenting consolidated financial statements;
- its debt or equity instruments are not traded in a public market (a domestic or foreign stock exchange or an over-the-counter market, including local and regional markets);
- it did not file, nor is it in the process of filing, its financial statements with a securities commission or other regulatory organization for the purpose of issuing any class of instruments in a public market; and

- its ultimate or any intermediate parent of the parent produces consolidated financial statements available for public use that comply with IFRSs.

An investor consolidates an investee when it controls the investee. The investor controls an investee when it is exposed, or has rights, to variable returns from its involvement with the investee and has the ability to affect those returns through its power over the investee. This principle applies to all investees, including structured entities.

An investor must possess all of the following elements to be deemed to control an investee:

- Power over the investee, which is described as having existing rights that give the current ability to direct the activities of the investee that significantly affect the investee's returns (such activities are referred to as the 'relevant activities').
- Exposure, or rights, to variable returns from its involvement with the investee.
- Ability to exert power over the investee to affect the amount of the investor's returns.

Power is a key term and in many cases can be established by the voting rights (normally conferred by share ownership). In such cases, ownership of a majority of the voting rights confers power and control.

An investor evaluates all of the following factors to determine if it has power over the investee:

- relevant activities;
- how the relevant activities are directed; and
- the rights that the investor and other parties have in relation to the investee.

The term 'relevant activities' is a critical part of the requirement of the standard. It specifies which aspects of an investee's activities must be under the direction of an investor for that investor to have control for consolidation purposes. The standard defines relevant activities as activities of the investee that significantly affect the investee's returns.

Some non-exhaustive examples of possible relevant activities given in the standard include:

- selling and purchasing of goods or services;
- managing financial assets during their life (including upon default);
- selecting, acquiring or disposing of assets;
- researching and developing new products or processes;
- determining a funding structure or obtaining funding.

PREPARING CONSOLIDATED FINANCIAL STATEMENTS

If we consider a group of companies, each entity will prepare its own financial statements for the financial period: the separate financial statements. It then falls on the holding company to prepare consolidated financial statements for the entire group. If a group entity uses accounting policies other than those in the consolidated financial statements, appropriate adjustments should be made on consolidation.

Although there is some flexibility, the basic requirement is that each group entity's financial statements are drawn up to the same reporting date for consolidation purposes. Where reporting dates differ, additional financial information is prepared for consolidation purposes, unless impractical.

The main stages in preparing consolidated financial statements for a period are:

- combine like items of assets, liabilities, equity, income, expenses and cash flows from the financial statements of each group entity;
- eliminate intragroup transactions and balances;
- eliminate the parent's investment in each subsidiary and recognize goodwill and other business combination–related adjustments;
- allocate comprehensive income and equity between the parent and any non-controlling interests.

The elimination of intragroup transactions and balances is a similar principle to measuring 'family wealth'. Pocket money to children, the loan of a car to a spouse, funding a holiday for a child are not activities which impact on the total family income. To understand the financial performance and position of a group we must exclude those transactions that take place only among group members. The most common ones are:

NON-CURRENT ASSET TRANSFERS

During the normal course of business operations, non-current assets such as machinery may have been transferred from one group company to another for an agreed price. It is possible that this price is greater than the machinery's carrying amount on the balance sheet so a 'notional' profit will have been made by the group member selling the machinery.

Using the single entity concept the non-current asset should be stated in group accounts at the amount as if the transfer had not been made. In other words you must remove the profit element as a profit cannot be made between two members of the group of companies. This removal of the profit element will also involve an adjustment to depreciation.

Example

On 1 January a subsidiary sells equipment that has a carrying amount of £40,000 to a fellow subsidiary for £50,000. For the group accounts at the year end the notional profit of £10,000 must be eliminated.

INTERCOMPANY BALANCES

Members of a group usually trade with each other. An accounts receivable in the set of financial statements of one subsidiary will be matched by an equal accounts payable in the financial statements of another group company. For the individual companies this is correct but is misleading to show the group owing cash to and from itself. On consolidation the intercompany amounts must be cancelled.

UNREALIZED PROFIT

A member company may have sold goods it had manufactured during the year to a fellow group member at a profit. The manufacturing company making the sale will show a profit in its own financial statements. If the subsidiary purchasing the goods has inventory at the year end this is shown in its own financial statement at the price paid for the goods. However, the goods have not been sold outside the group so no group profit has been made. For the consolidated accounts, the inventory in the balance sheet and the closing inventory in the income statement must be reduced to the cost without the 'internal' profit.

Example

At the year end the parent has £200,000 of inventory that it purchased from its wholly owned subsidiary. The cost to the subsidiary of manufacturing these goods was £180,000 and it correctly shows in its own accounts a profit of £20,000. For the group accounts the 'profit' on the inventory must be eliminated by showing the inventory in the balance sheet and the income statement at its cost of manufacture of £180,000.

Definition – Non-controlling interests

Non-controlling interest is the equity in a subsidiary not attributable, directly or indirectly, to a parent.

Non-controlling interests used to be known as minority interest. There are occasions where the acquiring company has a controlling power, but there is a minor percentage of other investors. When a parent entity first obtains control over another entity, it recognizes any non-controlling interest in the new subsidiary's net assets. In subsequent periods the parent entity allocates to the non-controlling interest its proportion of:

- profit or loss.
- each component of other comprehensive income.

IFRS 3 BUSINESS COMBINATIONS

IFRS 3 became effective from 1 April 2004. A revised version was issued in 2008 and this became effective from 1st January 2009. The standard sets out the accounting requirements when an acquirer obtains control of another business (e.g. an acquisition or merger). Such business combinations are accounted for using the 'acquisition method', which generally requires assets acquired and liabilities assumed to be measured at their fair values at the acquisition date.

Definition – Business combination

The bringing together of separate entities or businesses into one reporting entity.

To make an acquisition one business will acquire another business either by offering its own shares, cash or a combination of both. This will give the acquirer (parent) control of the other company (subsidiary). This may be 100 per cent acquisition where the subsidiary is wholly owned or the subsidiary may only be partially owned but sufficient to give control. In a partial ownership there will be other owners and these are called non-controlling interests, previously known as minority interests.

Business combinations are accounted for using the 'acquisition method', which generally requires assets acquired and liabilities assumed to be measured at their fair values at the acquisition date. The procedure is:

- Identification of the 'acquirer'.
- Determination of the 'acquisition date' – the date on which the acquirer obtains control of the acquiree.

- Recognition and measurement of the identifiable assets acquired, the liabilities assumed and any non-controlling interest (NCI, formerly called minority interest) in the acquiree.

- Recognition and measurement of goodwill or a gain from a bargain purchase.

It is possible that intangible assets are being acquired and these can only be recognized if they meet the definition requirements and can be measured reliably.

Goodwill is initially measured as the excess of the cost of the business combination over the acquirer's share of the net fair values of the acquiree's identifiable assets, liabilities and contingent liabilities. An example illustrates the calculation.

Example – business combination

Active plc. wishes to acquire the assets and liabilities of Passive Ltd. An examination of Passive Ltd shows that it has the following assets and liabilities:

	£000
Non-current assets	45
Current assets	8
Liabilities	20

Active is acquiring both the assets and liabilities at fair value and the difference between these items is £33,000. One might assume that would be a reasonable acquisition cost. If Passive is a successful company it will want to be rewarded for this and may want to be paid £50,000. The difference between the assets and liabilities of £33,000 has been established and if Active pays the asking price it will have acquired 'Goodwill' which will be valued at £17,000.

The above requirements assume that it is always possible to identify the acquirer. The main indicator will be whether the acquirer has obtained control of the other entity. Guidance on whether there is control is given in IFRS 10 Consolidated Financial Statements.

The cost of a business combination is the total of the fair values of the consideration given by the acquirer plus any directly attributable costs of the business combination. Expenses such as fees of lawyers and accountants acting as advisers must be charged to the Income Statement and cannot be considered as part of the consideration.

Fair value is the amount which an entity will pay for an exchange between unrelated and willing parties (i.e. not in a forced sale). Fair value should be measured at the date that the exchange takes place, which in most instances is the date on which the acquirer gains control of the other entity.

The consideration paid may be:

- cash or other assets transferred to the acquiree;

- liabilities assumed by the acquirer, for example taking on the liability for a bank loan of the acquiree.
- the issue of equity instruments, such as ordinary shares.

There are instances where only a provisional fair value is measured at the acquisition date. If there are adjustments arising within 12 months of the acquisition date they can be set back to the acquisition date.

Having listed what is deemed as consideration we need to examine what the acquirer obtains for its money. At the acquisition date, the acquirer must recognize the acquiree's assets, liabilities and contingent liabilities at their fair value if they meet the following criteria:

- assets other than intangible assets should be recognized where it is probable that the associated future economic benefits generated by the use of the assets will flow to the acquirer and their fair value can be measured reliably;
- liabilities, other than contingent liabilities, should be recognized where it is probable that an outflow of economic benefits will be required to settle the obligation and their fair value can be measured reliably;
- intangible asset or contingent liability at fair value where they can be measured reliably. They should only be recognized in an acquisition where they meet the definition of an intangible asset as per IAS 38 *Intangible assets* and their fair value is capable of being measured reliably.

Having gone through the exercise of determining the value of the consideration it is paying and the cost of the identifiable net assets (assets – liabilities) it is acquiring, the acquirer is likely to find that the amount it is paying is higher than the value of the net assets it is acquiring. The acquiring entity in all probability, is acquiring the reputation of the acquired business, loyal customers, procedures and processes that are established.

These characteristics all contribute to the future economic benefits the acquirer hopes to enjoy but they are not specifically and individually identified. They come under the general description of 'Goodwill'. This is a complex and controversial topic and we explore it in detail in the next section.

THE ISSUE OF GOODWILL

Definition – Goodwill

An asset representing the future economic benefits arising from assets that are not capable of being individually identified and separately recognized.

> Goodwill is therefore an integrated part of the business and cannot be separated from it (IFRS 3).

The topic of goodwill has dominated business acquisitions and consolidated accounting for several years. Muller (2011) meticulously examined articles published in major accounting journals from 1933 to 2009 and concluded that goodwill is going to continue dominating the interest of researchers in this field of accounting literature.

To many the value placed on acquired goodwill is no more than a balancing amount. It is merely the difference between the net assets of the acquired company and the amount that the purchaser was willing to pay. Goodwill, in itself, has not been valued. The opposite view is that the acquirer has paid for something called goodwill and believes that is the value of it.

The other issue is the potential ephemeral nature of goodwill. Is it attached to the vendor of the acquired company and will disappear when the company is taken over? To some extent the accounting standard has addressed this by requiring an annual impairment test.

Discussion point

Given the nature of goodwill do you consider it should be recognized on the balance sheet of the acquirer?

The actual calculation of goodwill figure when there is a business combination causes no problems. A company acquiring another expects to pay for all the tangible noncurrent assets such as property, plant and equipment. It also expects to pay for the intangible assets. If the acquirer is also accepting any outstanding liabilities this will be deducted from the total assets. Even if the value of the tangible assets and intangible assets are added together the acquiring company usually pays more than this amount.

This is because the acquirer wishes to secure an operating, and possibly, an established and successful business. It is not just acquiring assets but all those other ingredients that make up that business. These are such things as reputation of the business, experience and knowledge of workforce, contacts with suppliers, customer base, and established systems and procedures. All of these ingredients fall under the heading of goodwill.

If the assets cannot be identified and separately recognized, the question arises as to how one places a value on it at the acquisition of another business.

We will work through a simple example to demonstrate this by using horizontal balance sheets.

Bigpin

Balance sheet before acquisition

	£		£
Noncurrent assets	3,000	Equity	2,400
Cash	2,000	Liabilities	2,600
	5,000		5,000

Bigpin agrees to pay £1,900 cash to acquire Smallpin. Having made the acquisition, Bigpin calculates the fair value of the assets it has acquired at £1200 for premises and £300 for machinery. Normally, there would be an extensive list of assets and liabilities being acquired but in this example we will assume that there are only tangible assets. Bigpin's calculations are as follows:

	£	£
Purchase price		1,900
Fair value of tangible asset		
Premises	1,200	
Machinery	300	1,500
Difference		400

As Bigpin paid more than the fair value of the tangible assets, the difference of £400 is assumed to be for goodwill. As £400 has been paid for goodwill this must be shown in the Balance Sheet of Bigpin with the other assets purchased.

If we add the acquired tangible assets of £1500 to the £3000 of non-current assets that Bigpin already owns, deduct the £1900 paid to Smallpin from the cash that Bigpin had and insert goodwill into the balance sheet, it will balance.

Bigpin plc.

Balance sheet after acquisition

	£		£
Noncurrent assets	4,500	Equity	2,400
Goodwill	400		
Cash	100	Liabilities	2,600
	5,000		5,000

That is a simplified example of the process of acquisition and the treatment of goodwill. The standard permits two methods for measuring goodwill, but both are based on the concept of residual value.

The accounting requirements for acquired goodwill are:

- Goodwill should be tested for impairment at least annually.
- Goodwill cannot be systematically amortized.
- Goodwill should not be revalued.
- Internally generated goodwill cannot be recognized.

Many successful companies have, over the years, built up excellent reputations, have good procedures, loyal employees and all the other ingredients that one connects with purchased goodwill. They cannot place this internally generated goodwill on their balance sheet. IAS 38 Intangible assets states that internally generated goodwill cannot be recognized as an asset because it is not an identifiable resource controlled by the company that can be measured reliably.

It is this criterion of being able to measure reliably that is critical. When a company purchases goodwill through the acquisition of another company we can calculate the amount it has paid. With internally generated goodwill a company would never be able to demonstrate how much it had cost. If you look at the Annual Reports of famous companies, the only goodwill that they will show on their balance sheet is that goodwill they have purchased.

There are those occasions when a company acquires another where the cost of acquisition is less than the fair value of the identifiable net assets acquired. In these circumstances, there is a 'negative' goodwill and the acquirer has made a gain which will be shown as such in the Income Statement. However, prior to the recognition of a gain from a bargain purchase, the company must reassess the identification and measurement of:

- the identifiable assets acquired and liabilities assumed;
- the non-controlling interest in the acquiree, if any;
- or a business combination achieved in stages, the acquirer's previously held equity interest in the acquire.

Non-controlling interest (NCI)

If less than a full acquisition is made, there will be some owners of the company who hold the minority of shares and therefore do not have control. The standard now allows the acquirer (parent) to measure any non-controlling in one of two ways.

1. At the NCI's proportionate share of the acquiree's (subsidiary's) identifiable net assets (this is the 'old' method).

2. At fair value (the 'new' method) known also as the full goodwill method.

The 'old' method concentrated on the parent's ownership interest and therefore only calculated the amount of goodwill acquired by the parent. This was calculated as the difference between the consideration paid by the parent and its share of the fair value of the subsidiary's net identifiable assets. This method did not refer to the NCI because it was only intended to recognize the parent's share of goodwill. The part of goodwill owned by the non-controlling interest is not recognized.

It is argued that the new method gives a full view of the goodwill of the subsidiary including non-controlling interests. It views the entire group as an economic entity with all equity holders, including non-controlling interest, as shareholders of the group even if they are not shareholders in the parent.

Example

In this example we will use the same basic figures for calculating goodwill but show the amount if there is a 100 per cent acquisition, the old method using an 80 per cent acquisition and the new method using an 80 per cent acquisition.

Bigone Corp acquires 100 per cent ownership of Smallone Corp for £500,000. The fair values of the assets acquired are £300,000.

	£000
Consideration	500
Net assets acquired at fair value	300
Goodwill (100%)	200

In the following calculation we calculate the goodwill by using the old method – that is only taking the group's share of goodwill into account. Note that the goodwill is only 80 per cent of the goodwill if there had been a 100 per cent acquisition. The same companies as above but Bigone Corp only acquires 80 per cent ownership. The consideration is £400,000.

	£000
Consideration	400
Net assets acquired (80% of £300)	240
Goodwill	160

Companies can use the old method if they wish or they can adopt the new (economic entity) method. This will show the full value of goodwill including that owned by the non-controlling interest.

	GROUP		NCI
	£000		$000
Consideration transferred for 80%	400	Net value (20% of £500)	100
Fair value of net assets (80%)	(240)	Net assets (20% of £300)	(60)
Goodwill	160		40

The goodwill using the new method is higher than the old method because the goodwill attributable to the non-controlling interest is included.

Where an entity decides to use the option to value non-controlling interests it can only be applied at the date of acquisition. Where this option is used the goodwill shown on the balance sheet will include the goodwill attributable to the non-controlling interest. The opposite side of the balance sheet will show the non-controlling interest including their share of goodwill.

Definition – Retained earnings

Net profits retained in the company after dividends and any other distributions have been made to investors.

Before we demonstrate some of these points with a worked example, we need to consider retained earnings. When a company acquires another company, the acquiree will have been in operation for a number of years. It will have been earning profits. A part of these profits will have been distributed to shareholders and a part will be retained in the business to finance future growth.

When the business is acquired, the acquirer purchases these retained profits. The rule is that any pre-acquisition retained earnings of a subsidiary are not aggregated with the parent company's retained earnings, only the post-acquisition retained earnings. Any retained earnings must be cancelled against the investment by the parent company in the subsidiary company. A simple example will demonstrate this.

EXAMPLE – RETAINED EARNINGS

HighCorp acquires LowCorp on 1 January 2012. It pays £40 million for 60 per cent of LowCorp at the date of acquisition. The share capital of LowCorp was £10 million and it had retained earnings of £30 million. By the end of the year LowCorp had retained earnings of £50 million.

The share capital and retained earnings of LowCorp will be eliminated against the cost of the investment in the consolidated financial statements. Using the old method for consolidation, the calculations are:

	£m	£m
Cost of investment		40
Less share of assets acquired		
Share capital	10	
Retained earnings	30	
	40	
60% share of assets acquired		24
Goodwill		16

Note that the pre-acquisition earnings have been included in our calculation. The post-acquisition earnings, that is, LowCorp's profit retained after the acquisition date will be included in HighCorp's retained earnings when the consolidated financial statements are prepared.

IAS 28 INVESTMENTS IN ASSOCIATES AND JOINT VENTURES

IAS 28 Accounting for investments in Associates was first issued in 1989. It has been superseded by IAS 28 *Investments in Associates and Joint Ventures* with effect from annual periods beginning on or after 1 January 2013.

The objective of IAS 28 is to set out the accounting requirements for investments in associates and for the application of the equity method in both associates and joint ventures. IAS 28 applies to all entities that are investors with joint control of, or significant influence over, an investee (associate or joint venture).

Definitions

An associate is an entity over which the investor has significant influence.
A joint venture is a joint arrangement whereby the parties that have joint control of the arrangement have rights to the net assets of the arrangement.

An investor may have a significant influence in another company that is neither a subsidiary nor a joint venture and, therefore, it does not appear in the consolidated financial statements. It is important that the user is made aware of the nature and implications of this investment.

IAS 28 establishes the concept of significance influence and the criteria to establish significant influence. It provides guidance on accounting for associates in the consolidated financial statements under the equity method and the disclosures required.

Definition – Significant influence

Significant influence is the power to participate in the financial and operating policy decisions of the investee but is not control or joint control of those policies.

The presence of significant influence in a business is assumed to be present where the investor has 20 per cent or more of the voting power. There are exceptions to this rule. For example, an investor may hold more than 20 per cent of the voting rights, but is unable to exercise significant influence because another investor holds the remaining voting rights. The reverse situation can occur where the investor has less than 20 per cent of the voting rights, but circumstances permit significant influence to be applied.

The existence of significant influence by an entity is usually evidenced in one or more of the following ways:

- Representation on the board of directors or equivalent governing body of the investee;
- Participation in policy-making processes, including participation in decisions about dividends or other distributions;
- Material transactions between the entity and its investee;
- Interchange of managerial personnel; or
- Provision of essential technical information.

Both accounting for associates and joint ventures must use the equity method. The reasoning for this is the recognition of income on the basis of distributions received may not be an adequate measure of the income earned by an investor on an investment in an associate or a joint venture. This is because the distributions received may bear little relation to the performance of the associate or joint venture.

The investor has joint control of, or significant influence over, the investee, and the investor has an interest in the associate's or joint venture's performance and, as a result, the return on its investment. To recognize this interest the investor, in its financial statements, includes its share of the profit or loss of the investee. The main requirements under this method are:

- On initial recognition the investment in an associate or a joint venture is recognized at cost, and the carrying amount is increased or decreased to recognize the investor's share of the profit or loss of the investee after the date of acquisition.

- The investor's share of the investee's profit or loss is recognized in the investor's profit or loss. Distributions received from an investee reduce the carrying amount of the investment. Adjustments to the carrying amount may also be necessary for changes in the investor's proportionate interest in the investee arising from changes in the investee's other comprehensive income. Such changes include those arising from the revaluation of property, plant and equipment and from foreign exchange translation differences.

IFRS 11 JOINT ARRANGEMENTS

In May 2011 the IASB issued IFRS 11 *Joint Arrangements* to replace IAS 31 *Interests in Joint Ventures*. The standard sets out the principles for financial reporting by entities that have an interest in arrangements that are controlled jointly. Such arrangements may be either a joint operation or a joint venture and have the following characteristics:

- There is a contractual arrangement binding the parties.

- Two or more of the parties have joint control.

- Joint control is the agreed sharing of control which exists only when decisions about the relevant activities have the unanimous consent of the parties sharing the control.

- In a joint arrangement, no single party controls the arrangement on its own.

- A party with joint control of an arrangement can prevent any of the other parties, or a group of the parties, from controlling the arrangement.

- An arrangement can be a joint arrangement although not all of its parties have joint control of the arrangement. An entity will need to apply judgement when assessing whether all the parties, or a group of the parties, have joint control of an arrangement.

- If facts and circumstances change, an entity shall reassess whether it still has joint control of the arrangement.

An entity must decide whether the type of arrangement in which it is involved is a joint operation or a joint venture. A joint operation is where the parties (joint operators) with joint control have rights to the assets, and obligations for the liabilities, relating to the arrangement. A joint venture is where the parties (joint venturers) have rights to the net assets of the arrangement.

A joint venturer should recognize its interest in a joint venture as an investment and account for it by using the equity method as explained in IAS 28 *Investments in Associates and Joint Ventures*.

Definition – Joint operation

A joint operation is a joint arrangement whereby the parties that have joint control of the arrangement have rights to the assets, and obligations for the liabilities, relating to the arrangement.

An entity that is a joint operator should recognize in its financial statements the following items relevant to the joint operation:

- its assets, including its share of any assets held jointly;
- its liabilities, including its share of any liabilities incurred jointly;
- its revenue from the sale of its share of the output arising from the joint operation;
- its share of the revenue from the sale of the output by the joint operation; and
- its expenses, including its share of any expenses incurred jointly.

IFRS 12 DISCLOSURE OF INTERESTS IN OTHER ENTITIES

IFRS 12 *Disclosure of Interests in Other Entities* was issued in May 2011 and applies to annual periods beginning on or after 1 January 2013. The objective of the standard is to require entities to provide a wide range of disclosures about their interests in subsidiaries, joint arrangements, associates and unconsolidated 'structured entities'.

The disclosures should enable users to of financial statements to evaluate:

- the nature of, and risks associated with, its interests in other entities; and
- the effects of those interests on its financial position, financial performance and cash flows.

Where the disclosures required by IFRS 12, together with the disclosures required by other IFRSs, do not meet the above objective, an entity is required to disclose whatever additional information is necessary to meet the objective.

IFRS 12 is required to be applied by an entity that has an interest in any of the following:

- subsidiaries;
- joint arrangements (joint operations or joint ventures);
- associates;
- unconsolidated structured entities.

CONCLUSIONS

The Annual Report and Accounts is one of the most important sources of information for people external to the company. In recent years the sophistication of the companies' websites has improved greatly and the amount of information is almost overwhelming.

However, the business world is complex and companies may enter into relationships which may make their transactions somewhat opaque. The standard setters have attempted in a raft of standards to encapsulate the various relationships to ensure that the user is not misinformed. But experience has shown that if a company wishes to obscure its transactions through various business relationships, it is very difficult to detect.

Where such frauds are found out it is often the size of the fraud and the status of the people involved is the most surprising. Often the fraud has continued for years without detection which suggests, no matter how sound the accounting standards and the vigilance of directors, auditors, investment analysts and others, Annual Reports and Accounts may not always be a window on the business.

RECOMMENDED FURTHER READING

Tombs, George (2007) *Robber Baron: Lord Black of Crossharbour*, ECW Press.

Mitchell, A. (1999), 'Maxwell's auditors and other mates', *Accountancy*, Vol 123 No. 1267 March 1999 p.80.

Amernic, Joel H. and Craig Russell (2007) *CEO-Speak: The Language of Corporate Leadership*. Mcgill Queens University Press.

Hussey, Roger and Woolfe, Sarah (1994) *Interim Statements and Preliminary Profit Announcements*. The Institute of Chartered Accountants in England and Wales.

CASE STUDY TIMBERTOPS PLC.

Timbertops plc. is preparing its consolidated accounts for the year ended 31 December 2012.

There are several issues on which it requires guidance and has asked your advice on the following:

A

It has investments in four companies in the form of equity shares and non-equity shares which carry no voting power.

Jade Co. Timbertops holds 60 per cent of equity shares and 10 per cent of non-equity shares.

X-Print Co. Timbertops holds 10 per cent of the equity shares and 95 per cent of the non-equity shares. In addition four of its directors are on the six person board of X-Print company.

Papersoft Co. Timbertops holds 40 per cent of the equity shares and 60 per cent of the non-equity shares.

Oak Mills Co. Timbertops holds 55 per cent of the equity shares but no non-equity shares.

Which of these companies should be part of the consolidated accounts?

B

X-Print sells some of its products to Timbertops. During the year, it sold products for £88,000 to Timbertops with the cost to itself being £76,000. Half of those products remain in the inventory of Timbertops at the year and at a value of £44,000.

At the end of the year the revenues and gross profit shown on the financial statement of the two companies were:

	Timbertops plc.	X-Print
Revenue	£1,450,000	£761,000
Gross profit	£521,000	£247,000

What would the consolidated revenues and gross profits be?

C

At the year end, there are the following balances for Accounts Receivable and payable in the financial statements of the companies.

	Accounts Receivable £	Accounts Payable £
Timbertops	220,000	195,000
Jade	85,000	46,200
X-Print	13,400	17,600
Papersoft	12,300	15,200
Oak Mills	24,800	28,200

Further investigations show that X-Print owes Timbertops £5400 and Oak Mills owes Timbertops £3200 and Papersoft £4700. What are the total amounts for accounts receivable and Accounts payable to be shown in the consolidated accounts?

CHAPTER 9
ANALYSING COMPANY PERFORMANCE

LEARNING OBJECTIVES

At the end of this chapter you should be able to:

- Explain the purpose and limitations of ratio analysis.
- Describe the external factors that contribute to analysis of companies.
- Calculate profitability, liquidity and gearing ratios.
- Conduct an analysis of a single company.
- Conduct an analytical comparison of two or more companies.

EXECUTIVE SUMMARY

Knowledge of the structure and content of financial statements is extremely useful and can be applied to analysing a company's performance and status. The main tools used come under the heading of ratios analysis. This can be subdivided into accounting ratios that are calculated using the financial statements and investment ratios based on the performance of the company's shares on the stock exchange.

A ratio describes a quantitative relationship between two values (usually expressed as x: 1 or x%). Ratios are widely used by various groups and individuals including present and potential investors, managers, lenders, trade unions, suppliers and other trade creditors but also by credit rating agencies, investment analysts and financial journalists.

There are many ratios but the main accounting ratios examine profitability, liquidity, working capital management and gearing. Some ratios concentrate on the cash flow statement and these are: cash flow from operating activities, cash recovery rate and cash flow per share. The main investment ratios are interest cover, earnings per share, price/earnings ratio and dividends per share.

Ratio analysis can only be useful if there are comparators such as the financial statements from previous years, the details of similar companies or industry averages. There are limitations to ratio analysis and it is imperative that you understand the accounting figures and the external factors that could influence the company's financial results.

CONCEPTUAL AND PRACTICAL ISSUES

Definition – Ratio analysis

A technique for evaluating the financial performance and stability of an entity, with a view to making comparisons with previous periods, other entities and industry averages over a period of time.

EXAMPLE

There are two companies and their revenue and gross profits for 2012 are:

	Company A	Company B
	£000	£000
Sales	90	180
Gross profit	25	40

From the above it is clear that company B makes the higher profit and this is to be expected as it is twice the size of A as measured by sales. The question is which company is the most profitable? To answer this we calculate the gross profit margin by expressing the gross profit as a percentage of sales.

	Company A	Company B
Gross profit margin	$\dfrac{25}{90} = 27.7\%$	$\dfrac{40}{180} = 22.2\%$

Although company B is the larger company with a higher profit, A is the more profitable, on a percentage basis. We could extend our analysis by comparing the performance of these two companies against the average for the industry in which they are operating. We could also calculate the ratios for a number of previous years and ascertain whether the ratios for 2012 are part of a trend or unusual in some way.

In the above example only one ratio has been calculated and we explain the major ones in this chapter. Although one ratio can be helpful, ratios are related and it is the appropriate combination of ratios that makes for a good analysis.

There are no set definitions of the various terms used in ratio analysis and there are different approaches to calculating them. We explain the main ratios and use the most common definitions of terms and methods of calculation. Where there are frequently used alternatives we make reference to them in the text.

Ratio analysis helps in the comparison between different size organizations, specific organizations and the relevant industry ratios. It also enables an analysis of corporate performance over a period of time. The main points are:

▪ The analysis is usually conducted on the financial statements of an organization. These may be the annual or interim report, but can also be internal financial statements if they are available. Usually the internal documents will provide much more detail and therefore are much more useful.

▪ The analysis is conducted for a single entity or a number of entities.

▪ There must be comparative figures otherwise the analysis will not be revealing.

One issue to be aware of is the definition of profit which a company uses. As required by accounting standards, the income statement shows the final figure of net profit. However, some companies calculate another figure for profit and they will use such terms as 'underlying profit'. Essentially the company has adjusted the accounting standards profit by those items which it considers to be a 'distraction'. Needless to say, the underlying profit is usually a higher profit than the one shown on the Income Statement and flatters any ratios calculated.

ACCOUNTING RATIOS

Accounting ratios are applied to the financial statements of a company. You may need to make adjustments to the financial statements, particularly if you are comparing with another company. The presence of International Financial Reporting Standards has greatly improved comparability but there are items where different accounting treatments are used. The main ratios discussed in this chapter are shown in Table 9.1 and subsequently examined in detail.

Ratio	Purpose
Return on net assets (RONA)	Measures the percentage return on the funds invested in the business
Net asset turnover	Measures the number of times the net assets been used during the year to achieve the sales revenue.
Net profit margin or Return on sales (ROS)	Measures the profit in percentage terms which a company makes on sales after deducting all expenses but before interest charges and tax
Gross profit margin	Measures gross profit as a percentage of sales and is a good indicator of how successful the business is in its basic trading operations
Current test	Shows the solvency of the company in the short term by comparing current assets and current liabilities:
Acid test	Shows the relationship between liquid assets and current liabilities
Payment ratio or accounts payable period	Measures the average time in days the entity is taking to pay its own debts
Collection ratio or accounts receivable period	Measures the average time in days trade debtors (accounts receivable), usually customers, have taken to pay the business for goods and services
Inventory turnover	The number of times in a financial period the inventory is used in generating sales
Leverage or gearing ratio	Refers to the relative proportions of equity and debt that a company has in its financial structure

Table 9.1 Main ratios

PROFITABILITY RATIOS

These concentrate on financial performance. The main ratios are:

– Return on net assets – RONA (also known as return on capital employed)

Return is defined as profit before interest and tax (PBIT), which is shown as operating profit in some financial statements or in smaller companies as net profit or net earnings. It is also known as EBIT – earnings before interest and tax.

Net assets are total assets – current liabilities. Some analysts prefer to use the total asset amount without deducting liabilities.

Return on Net Assets measures the percentage return on the investment of funds in the business. It provides information on how effective the business is in generating revenue from resources and management's ability to control costs. It is frequently referred to as the Prime Ratio and is regarded as the main measurement of the success of a company.

– Net asset turnover (also known as capital turnover)

Net asset turnover measures the number of times the net assets been used during the year to achieve the sales revenue. Generally the more frequently the net assets are 'turned over' the more successful the business is.

– Net profit margin (Also known as Return on Sales – ROS)

Net profit margin or ROS. This is the profit before interest and tax expressed as a percentage of the sales figure. It shows the percentage profit a company makes on sales after deducting all expenses but before interest charges and tax.

– Gross profit margin

Gross profit margin. This measures gross profit as a percentage of sales and is a good indicator of how successful the business is in its basic trading operations. For managers and investors, this is a key ratio in assessing business performance.

Liquidity ratios are used to evaluate the solvency and financial stability of a business. The main ratios are:

The current test shows the solvency of the company in the short term by comparing current assets and current liabilities: usually expressed as x:1. It demonstrates whether the company can pay its current debts.

The *acid test* is a liquidity ratio that shows the relationship between liquid assets and current liabilities, and is usually expressed as x:1. It is regarded as a more stringent test than the current test in assessing the solvency of a business. Liquid assets are all current assets except stock (inventories), which take longer to convert into cash.

Working capital ratios are used assess how effectively the organization has managed its working capital (i.e. current assets – current liabilities).

> ### Definition – Working capital
>
> The amount of funding required for the organization's day-to-day operations. It is the total of the current assets, for example, inventories, accounts receivable and cash, less current liabilities, for example, accounts payable, bank overdrafts.

The main ratios are:

The Payment ratio or Accounts payable period measures the average time in days the entity is taking to pay its own debts. The purchases amount on the Income Statement is the most appropriate figure but if this is not available the Sales figure may be used. The inventory figure from one year's financial statements can be used but if this is likely to fluctuate an average amount using opening and closing inventory can be calculated.

The Collection ratio or accounts receivable period is an efficiency ratio that measures the average time in days trade debtors (accounts receivable), usually customers, have taken to pay the business for goods and services over the year.

Inventory turnover is the number of times in a financial period the inventory is used in generating sales.

GEARING/LEVERAGE RATIOS

The ratio that analyses the financial structure of the business is known as the leverage ratio in some countries and the gearing ratio in others: it is exactly the same ratio. As with other ratios, however, there can be some differences in the calculation of the ratio.

Businesses fund their activities with the capital invested by the owners plus any retained earnings which are known as equity in incorporated entities. They may also have to borrow funds from banks and other financial institutions and these will form the long-term liabilities, frequently referred to as debt. As with all ratios definitions of these terms vary but equity is normally the risk capital and debt is the total of all liabilities over 12 months old. If you consider all the elements on the statement of financial position then you will see that equity + debt is equal to the net current assets also known as capital employed.

Leverage or gearing refers to the relative proportions of equity and debt that a company has in its financial structure. A highly leveraged company is one that has a high proportion of debt in relation to equity. A company that has a low proportion of debt in relation to equity is a low leveraged company. The importance of leverage is the potential risks or rewards, shareholders may enjoy in different economic conditions.

The different impact on high and low leveraged conditions is best explained by an example. To do this we will use two ratios: one is return on net assets and the other is return on equity. Return on net assets, or capital employed, we have already discussed in this chapter. This is the amount of earnings *before* interest expressed as a percentage of the net assets. With the ratio Return on equity we are going to define return as the earnings **after** interest before tax. In other words we are calculating what the shareholders receive on their investment, excluding long-term liabilities from our considerations. The formula is:

$$\frac{\text{Earnings after interest but before tax}}{\text{Equity}} \times 100$$

The calculation of the profitability and liquidity ratios is shown in the following example. We are excluding interest and tax and the gearing ratios are explained later in the chapter. The ratios are only calculated to one decimal place as greater accuracy is not normally required.

Summary Income Statement to 31 December 2012

	£	£
Revenue		115,000
Cost of sales:		
Opening inventory	44,000	
Purchases	80,000	
	124,000	
Less closing inventory	55,000	69,000
Gross profit		46,000
Operating expenses		23,000
Profit before interest and tax		23,000

Summary Balance Sheet as at 31 December 2012

	£	£	£
Current Assets:			
Cash	1,000		
Accounts receivable	18,000		
Inventory	55,000	74,000	
Non-current assets:		48,000	
Total Assets			122,000
Current liabilities accounts payable			12,000

	£	£	£
Long-term liabilities			40,000
Total liabilities			52,000
Owner's equity:			
Capital	47,000		
Profit for the year	23,000		70,000
			122,000

(continued)

Without comparators it is difficult to conduct a comprehensive analysis but comments can be made on the data we have (Table 9.2).

Profitability ratios	Formula	Ratio
Return on Net Assets %	$\dfrac{\text{PBIT}}{\text{NetAssets}}$	$\dfrac{23000}{110000} = 20.9\%$
Gross margin%	$\dfrac{\text{Gross profit}}{\text{Sales}}$	$\dfrac{46000}{115000} = 40.0\%$
Return on sales %	$\dfrac{\text{PBIT}}{\text{Sales}}$	$\dfrac{23000}{115000} = 20.0\%$
Net assets turnover	$\dfrac{\text{Sales}}{\text{Net assets}}$	$\dfrac{115000}{110000} = 1.05$ times
Liquidity ratios		
Current test	$\dfrac{\text{Current assets}}{\text{Current liabilities}}$	$\dfrac{74000}{12000} = 6.2:1$
Acid test (Quick ratio)	$\dfrac{(\text{Current assets} - \text{inventories})}{\text{Current liabilities}}$	$\dfrac{19000}{12000} = 1.6:1$
Working capital management		
Collection period	$\dfrac{\text{Receivables}}{\text{Sales}} \times 365$	$\dfrac{18000}{115000} = 57$ days
Payment period	$\dfrac{\text{Payables}}{\text{Purchases}} \times 365$	$\dfrac{12000}{80000} = 55$ days
Inventory turnover	$\dfrac{\text{Sales}}{\text{Inventory}}$	$\dfrac{115000}{55000} = 2.1$ times

Table 9.2 Calculation of main accounting ratios

THE PROFITABILITY RATIOS

Everybody has their own favourite profitability ratios but most will focus on the 'Big Three'. These are Return on Net Assets (also known as the prime ratio), Return on Sales and Net Asset Turnover and are shown in Figure 9.1.

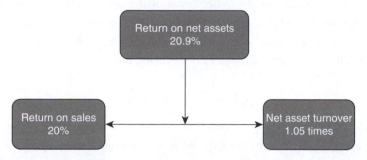

Figure 9.1 The profitability ratios

Allowing for rounding up of decimal places, the relationship of the ratios is that the return on sales multiplied by the net asset turnover equals the return on net assets. In the above diagram the 20 per cent for ROS multiplied by the 1.05 net asset turnover gives the 21 per cent return on net assets.

Let us put those calculations into a business perspective.

1. A company strives to improve its return on net assets as that is the key measure of its performance. It can only improve that ratio by improving one or both of the subsidiary ratios. A significant investment has been made in this company and the investors can look elsewhere if the return is considered insufficient.

2. The net assets turnover is a guide to the efficiency the company applies in using its net assets. An examination of the way that the company works may reveal that some assets are not being fully employed. Machinery may be idle or under used, building may be partly empty or too large for the amount of activity. If the company could reduce its net assets it may be able to achieve a turnover figure of 1.5 times. Multiply this by the return on sales ratio of 20 per cent and the return on assets jumps to an impressive 30 per cent.

   Another avenue may be to increase the sales volume without requiring additional net assets to meet the increased demand. If the Sales could be increased to £150,000 without requiring a further investment in net assets, the net asset turnover would be 1.36. Multiplying this by the return on sales ratio of 20 per cent gives a return on net assets of 27.2 per cent. Such an action may require the company to expand its working hours by adding another work shift.

3. Return on Sales ratio is calculated by expressing the profit as a percentage of the sales figure. To improve this ratio, it requires either an increase in the selling price of the products or a reduction of the costs incurred. To a large extent an

increase in volume of sales will not by itself increase the return on sales ratio unless the company strictly controls its operating costs.

Of course, the stage before the return on sales ratio is the gross profit margin and this is where a company's attention needs to be directed to impact on profit. The gross profit represents the difference between the selling price and the costs of the goods sold. If the gross profit margin is 40 per cent it will be that for £1, or £1 million of sales: volume will not in itself change the ratio. Attention must be directed at increasing the selling price or reducing the cost of sales.

THE LIQUIDITY RATIOS AND WORKING CAPITAL

Working capital is calculated by deducting the current liabilities from the current assets. It represents an investment by the company in its trading cycle. As a company must be alert to the amount of investment made in non-current assets such as buildings and machinery it must be even more aware of the investment in working capital. Absence of sufficient working capital can cause a company to become bankrupt. The use of ratios assists a company to manage its working capital and also reveals to investors the immediate financial health of the company.

Although there is no 'perfect' ratio, as a rule of thumb the current ratio is usually between 1.6:1 to 2:1 and the acid test about 1:1. The thinking behind these ratios is they indicate whether a company can pay its current liabilities from its current assets.

With a current ratio of 1.3:1 a company has £1.30 of current assets for every £1.0 of current liabilities. This suggests that if the company has to pay its current liabilities it should be able to do so from its current assets. If the ratio is 0.9:1 the company is unable to cover its current liabilities. This means it must try to obtain more funding, sell off some of its non-current assets or go bankrupt.

The deficiency of the current test is that a company may hold a very large inventory. This can be very difficult to sell in a hurry. The Acid Test omits inventories from current assets and is therefore more rigorous then the current test.

Our sample company has a current test of 6.2:1 and the acid test is 1.6:1. At first glance one may conclude that this company is financially very healthy because it has such significant coverage of its current liabilities. This is not the case.

The ratios reveal that the management is very poor at managing the finances of the company. The reason is that the £74,000 of current assets needs to be funded in some way. An excessive investment has been made and that money should be invested elsewhere to earn a better return.

Looking at the composition of the current assets, there is a modest amount of cash. The accounts receivable amount is larger but the collection period is 57 days and the payment period is 55 days both of which seem reasonable. For a company giving a month's credit the average time period is 45 days.

The only remaining figure is £55,000 for inventory which looks high compared to the other current assets. The inventory turnover is 2.1 times. This indicates that the company sells its inventory about twice in the year. If you consider a supermarket will sell a tin of beans every few seconds the ratio looks poor. However we need the following information:

1. What would be the usual turnover figure in this industry?

2. Does the company have to hold a large number of different products?

3. Is the amount of inventory being built up because a busy period is expected, for example, Christmas?

4. Does the balance sheet represent the usual level of inventory or is there some other factor influencing the amount?

5. Is the figure accurate? There could be obsolete inventory that should be written off and we discuss in an earlier chapter how profit could be manipulated by altering the closing inventory figure.

We have examined the current assets in detail but we have not investigated the non-current assets of £48,000. Unfortunately, we do not have a breakdown of this amount and there could be problems. If the company purchased property 40 years ago it is probably worth much more now. If it were to be revalued this would have a negative effect on the return on net assets. Also, we do not know whether the company has any intangible assets and the accounting treatment it uses.

THE PROCESS OF RATIO ANALYSIS

It is important not to rush into calculating and analysing ratios without an exploration of the context in which the study is taking place. This prior investigation is essential to understand the factors external to the chosen company. These factors contribute towards shaping its financial performance and position. Figure 9.2 illustrates these factors.

The main sources for information will be:

- Daily newspapers, for example, *Wall Street Journal*, *Financial Times*, for an overview and immediate information.

- 'Investment' Magazines specifically related to the activities of the share markets.

- General business magazines, for example, *Forbes*, *Business Week*, *The Economist*.

- Newsletters issued by several government and industry bodies and departments.

- The Internet and various websites.

- Companies which provide a substantial amount of information both in hard copy and on their websites. Use caution as they are likely to present information that favours their financial activities.

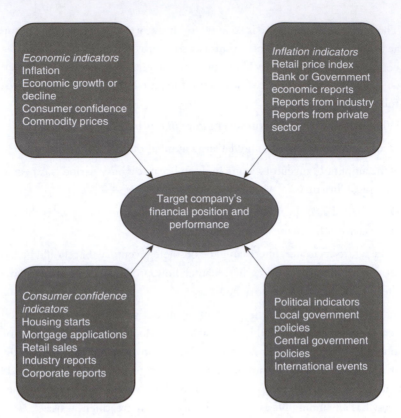

Figure 9.2 Factors influencing ratio analysis

From these sources you will be aiming to extract indicators of past performance, current events and predictions of future trends. Once the context is established, the financial statements can be investigated using the following procedure.

1. Acquire financial statements for several years, preferably a minimum of three years although five to ten years would be preferable. This should include annual and interim financial statements. It is helpful to obtain any internal financial documents if possible.

2. Scrutinize all the documents to see if there have been any significant changes over a period of time. Putting the key figures for the main figures such as revenue and earnings on a spread sheet helps the comparison. It is also useful to include aggregations such as total assets, net current assets and working capital.

3. If you have the published documents you must review the notes. You are looking for information on changes in accounting policies or accounting treatments that do not comply fully with the standards.

4. Examine the balance sheet, income statement and cash flow statement without calculating ratios. Your objective is to detect any items that look particularly large or unusual.

5. Identify and calculate the ratios that you consider to be the most important for your task and relevant to the company you are investigating.

6. If possible, obtain the ratios for a competitor and the industry averages. These are usually available in most libraries or on the Internet. Ensure that the definition of terms and method of calculation is comparable to your own.

7. Analyse and interpret the ratios using all the information you have collected. The process of interpretation may reveal additional information you require to complete your task.

8. If the management of the company has discussed their financial results and in an annual report they will have done so, compare it to your own interpretation. If there are differences investigate them.

A SINGLE COMPANY ANALYSIS

When investigating a company, in the absence of comparators such as other companies or information from previous years one is restricted to a same size analysis or a vertical analysis. In the former method revenue is considered as 100 per cent and all the costs and the profit are expressed as a percentage of that amount. We could express all the separate assets on the statement of financial position as a percentage of the total assets or the separate liability accounts as a percentage of total liabilities.

Table 9.3 shows the income statement figures for a single company. Management experience or other sources of information may indicate whether the

	Income statement for 2012	
	£	%
Revenue	10,000	100
Cost of sales	7,500	75
Salaries	600	6
Rent	200	2
Admin	180	1.8
Depreciation	400	4
Interest	100	1
PBT	1,020	10.2

Table 9.3 Same size analysis

percentage figures are acceptable. However, the analysis lacks depth and conclusions are impossible to make.

An analysis is greatly improved if a comparison with the previous financial period or, preferably, over an extended period of time can be made. One can conduct the same size analysis as above but it is helpful if percentage changes can be shown. Sometimes it assists focus if the analysis is for a few items only from the financial statement.

The following presentation of another company uses the sales figure with the comparison being the current year to the previous year. The change is shown not only in pounds but also in percentage terms which gives a better indication of the magnitude of the change (Table 9.4).

	Current year	Previous year	£ Change	% Change
Revenue	£70,150	£59,287	£+10,863	+18.3%

Table 9.4 Year to year change

The company has increased its revenue by £10,863 which appears excellent and the percentage change is an outstanding 18.3 per cent. If you have conducted prior research into the external factors affecting this company you will have a better perspective. If the industry and the economy generally are enjoying a boom the 18.3 per cent may not look so outstanding.

A comparison over several years is far more insightful than just with the previous period. With a trend analysis it is often helpful to first concentrate on two or three key items and compare them over several years. This reveals if there are any changes in their relationship. One can take the revenue each year and compare it to the gross profit and profit before interest and tax as in the following example (Table 9.5)

Year	1	2	3	4	5
Revenue	120	110	130	138	150
Gross profit	72	66	74	76	81
PBIT	12	11	11	12	13

Table 9.5 Comparison of revenue/profits over 5 years

On first examination it appears as if the company was losing sales with a reduction in gross profit and PBIT in Year 2. There is an apparent change of fortune in Year 3 with a boost of sales and increasing gross profit and PBIT for the remainder of the analysis. Superficially, there appears to be no major problems.

By calculating the gross profit margin and the return on sales the analysis is far more rigorous.

Year	1	2	3	4	5
Revenue	120	110	130	138	150
Gross profit margin	60%	60%	56.9%	55.1%	54%
ROS	10%	10%	8.5%	8.7%	8.7%

The gross profit margin has been declining. As the gross profit is calculated by deducting the cost of goods sold from the selling price, the decline in gross profit margin is due to one or a combination of the following factors.

(1) The selling price per unit has been reduced. This has resulted in an increase in the volume sold but we are making less gross profit on each item sold.

(2) To boost sales volumes the quality or packaging of the product has been increased, at a cost, and this cost has not been passed onto the customers.

(3) Special deals and discounts are being given to selected customers.

(4) New markets have been opened up where the usual selling price cannot be enjoyed.

The troubling feature is that the decline in the gross profit margin is continuous in years 3–5 suggesting that whatever strategy has been chosen it is still being pursued. Although this favours the revenue figures, the financial performance is suffering. Further investigations would need to be conducted to identify the strategy and decide whether it was appropriate.

This has been a brief introduction to the different forms of analysis and presentation you can make. These approaches are often best presented as a chart to assist the user in understanding the relationship of the date.

COMPANY COMPARISONS

The following hypothetical example emphasizes the interpretation of the ratios and uses simple calculations. The same procedures are used for a large, listed company but the volume of data and the variety of the transactions would be much greater. We are using the financial statements of two small companies that are not listed on a stock exchange and do not necessarily comply with international accounting standards.

SCENARIO

Company Zor has been in business for over 25 years but company Dow has been in business for only seven years. Both supply insulation material to the building industry

Income statements 2012

Zor and Dow

	Zor £	Dow £
Revenue	240,000	80,000
Less: cost of sales	130,000	47,200
Gross profit	110,000	32,800
Delivery costs	8,800	–
Wages	72,000	22,000
Advertising	12,000	4,000
Depreciation	5,000	1,300
Interest on loan	500	–
Operating costs total	98,300	27,300
Net profit	11,700	5,500

Note: Purchase of materials for the year were Zor £169,000 and Dow £44,800

Zor balance sheet as at 31 December 2012

	£	£
Non-current assets:		
Premises at cost		65,000
Vehicle cost	12,000	
Less depreciation	8,000	4,000
Total Non-current Assets		69,000
Current Assets:		
Cash	1,500	
Accounts receivable	35,000	
Inventory	144,500	181,000
Total assets		250,000
Accounts payable		28,960
Long-term Loan		50,000
Total liabilities		78,960
Owner's equity:		
Capital	160,000	
Profit for the year	11,040	171,040
		250,000

Dow balance sheet as at 31 December 2012

	£	£
Non-current assets		
Premises at cost		113,000
Current Assets:		
Bank	4,400	
Inventory	23,600	
Total current assets		28,000
Total assets		141,000
Current liabilities		
Accounts payable		12,080
Owner's equity:		
Share capital	124,000	
Profit for the year	4,920	128,920
Total liabilities & owners' equity		141,000

Using the above data, we can construct a table of the main ratios (Table 9.6).

Notes

1. In calculating the operating profit for Zor we added back the interest as we wish to know the profit that has been earned on the capital invested by the owner and the long-term loan. If Zor has a return of 5.51 per cent but paying a higher interest on the loan than this it's a poor position to be in. If we were only interested in the return the owner is receiving on the capital they have invested we would have used the profit after interest.

2. We have expressed the payment period and the collection period in number of days, although some prefer to express it as a percentage or a ratio.

3. For this exercise we have taken only the closing inventory amounts to calculate inventory turnover. Some claim that by calculating the average inventory (opening inventory + closing inventory divided by 2) you obtain a more accurate reflection of performance.

Analysis and interpretation

It is evident from the financial statements that Zor is the largest company, but that does not necessarily make it the best. We are interested in its financial performance and stability as reflected in comparing the two sets of ratios.

The first ratios we compare are the gross margin ratios. This is a good guide to how well the companies perform in buying and selling their product. Zor's ratio

Profitabilty ratios		Zor	Dow
Return on Net Assets %	$\dfrac{\text{PBIT}}{\text{Net Assets}}$	$\dfrac{12,200}{221,040}=5.51\%$	$\dfrac{5,500}{128,920}=4.27\%$
Gross margin %	$\dfrac{\text{Gross profit}}{\text{Sales}}$	$\dfrac{110,000}{240,000}=45.83\%$	$\dfrac{32,800}{80,000}=41\%$
Return on sales %	$\dfrac{\text{PBIT}}{\text{Sales}}$	$\dfrac{12,200}{240,000}=5.08\%$	$\dfrac{5,500}{80,000}=6.87\%$
Net assets turnover	$\dfrac{\text{Sales}}{\text{Net assets}}$	$\dfrac{240,000}{221,040}=1.09\text{ time}$	$\dfrac{80,000}{128,920}=0.62\text{ time}$
Liquidity ratios			
Current test	$\dfrac{\text{Current assets}}{\text{Current liabilities}}$	$\dfrac{181,000}{28,960}=6.25:1$	$\dfrac{28,000}{12,080}=2.3:1$
Acid test (Quick ratio)	$\dfrac{(\text{Current assets} - \text{inventories})}{\text{Current liabilities}}$	$\dfrac{36,500}{28,960}=1.26:1$	$\dfrac{4,400}{12,080}=0.36:1$
Working capital management			
Collection period	$\dfrac{\text{Receivables}}{\text{Sales}}\times 365$	$\dfrac{35,000}{240,000}=53\text{ days}$	N.A.
Payment period	$\dfrac{\text{Payables}}{\text{Purchases}}\times 365$	$\dfrac{28,960}{169,000}=63\text{ days}$	$\dfrac{12,080}{44,800}=98\text{ days}$
Inventory turnover	$\dfrac{\text{Sales}}{\text{Inventory}}$	$\dfrac{240,000}{144,500}=1.66\times$	$\dfrac{80,000}{23,600}=3.39\times$

Table 9.6 Two company ratio analysis

at 45.83 per cent is much higher than Dow's 41 per cent which might indicate that Zor is either able to charge more for its goods or buys them at a lower price than Dow from its suppliers.

Looking at the financial statements themselves it seems that Zor offers delivery and also allows its customers credit whereas Dow does not do this. Zor will charge more for these services whereas Dow is a cash business. It is also possible that Zor offers a higher quality product. A check on the Internet, a quick telephone call to the companies or obtaining the price lists could confirm this.

Although Zor's gross margin ratio is higher, the return (i.e. PBIT) on sales is lower at 5.08 per cent compared to Dow's 6.87 per cent. As Zor offers delivery and credit to customers it must be paid for in some way. Dow may therefore be competing more on price rather than services to customers.

The return on net assets, sometimes referred to as return on capital employed, is also known as the 'prime' ratio. It is the ratio that gives you the overview of the profitability performance. If we take Zor's figure we get a return of 5.51 per cent. In other words, the money invested long term in the business to acquire the net assets receives a return of 5.51 per cent. As a comparator we can look at the return if the decision were made to invest the £221,040 elsewhere. Current market rates may be lower but with Zor there is a risk element. The higher the level of risk then the greater the return you would expect.

Dow is not doing quite so well as Zor with a return on net assets of 4.27 per cent. If Dow wishes to improve this the company must look at the other two ratios. Dow's return on sales is 6.87 per cent and the net asset turnover is 0.62x. If we multiply these two amounts together the result is the prime ratio of 4.27 per cent. To improve the return on net assets the answer is in improving one or both of the other ratios.

We have explained the possible reasons for Dow's gross margin ratio being lower than Zor's but the return on sales being higher. This indicates that the problem may be with the value of net assets.

To explain this we need to look at the components of our net assets. The balance sheets reveal that the largest component for both companies is the premises, with Dow's being £113,000 against Zor's £65,000.

This is a huge disparity and the possible reasons are:

- Dow has premises that are much bigger than its current needs.
- Zor's premises may have been purchased many years ago and it is in the balance sheet at the original cost with no revaluation.
- Dow's premises may be in a much better location.

Having considered profitability we now consider liquidity, efficiency and the management of working capital. Zor has a very high current test of 6.25:1 and even the acid test is relatively high at 1.26:1. There are no perfect ratios as it depends on the circumstances but for the current test usually a ratio between 1.6:1 to 2:1 is considered healthy. The reason for this is at 1.6:1 it means that for every £1 of current liability the company has £1.60 of current asset. In other words, if all the people that the company owes money to wanted to be paid tomorrow, the company should be able to manage to do so.

Dow has a slightly high current test at 2.3:1 but the acid test is worrying at 0.36:1. Of course, Dow does not allow credit to its customers so there is no category of accounts receivable. Although there is cash in the bank, this is hardly sufficient to be able to pay debts in the short term. Its payment period of 98 days is considerably higher than Dow's which indicated financial stress.

The issue with both companies appears to be inventory turnover. To be able to investigate this we need to know the external factors. Are both companies building up their inventories in expectation of a large demand? Are these the usual ratios in the industry? Do suppliers only deliver in large amounts?

The above is only a brief analysis and there are many other ratios that can be calculated and also questions asked. What is required is a scan of the external factors. The analysis and interpretation of the financial statements of a large company would be similar to our example but would take much longer. It would involve a close examination of the accounting policies of the company and a thorough knowledge of accounting standards.

Ratio analysis is an excellent tool but it has its limitations. As we have seen in previous chapters the financial statements can be difficult to comprehend and the accounting treatments of certain items may not be suitable for the analysis. Decisions have to be made on how to treat non-current asset valuations and intangibles such as goodwill.

If there comparators are new companies or those operating in niche markets, there may not be other comparable companies or industry averages. Even if some data can be obtained, critical information such as the gross profit may not be disclosed. Even if comparators can be obtained, caution must be exercised because there are no agreed definitions of terms.

Finally, financial statements do not take account of non-financial factors. Hopefully the financial statements reflect the ability of the management and the success or otherwise of the strategies being pursued. It is essential that any ratio analysis begins with the scan of the external factors.

LEVERAGE OR GEARING RATIOS

Leverage, sometimes referred to as gearing, ratios assess the financial structure of the business. A knowledge of this is important as the profit of the company can change dramatically with shifts in the economy. The objective of the ratio is to investigate how a business funds its activities and the impact that can have on profit.

In addition to investments made by shareholders, known as equity, companies may have to borrow funds from banks and other financial institutions. These funds form the long-term liabilities, frequently referred to as debt. Equity is normally the risk capital and debt is the total of all liabilities over 12 months old. Equity + debt is equal to the net current assets also known as capital employed.

The relative proportions of equity and debt that a company has in its financial structure has an impact on profit in different economic conditions. A highly leveraged company is one that has a high proportion of debt in relation to equity. In times of increasing profit this is of great benefit to shareholders. A decline in profits will cause those shareholders grief. A company that has a low proportion of debt in relation to equity is a low leveraged company. This will not be so exciting to shareholders but is less risky when there is an economic downturn.

The two ratios that capture this are the return on net assets and the return on equity. Return on net assets, or capital employed, has already been discussed in this chapter. This is the amount of profit before interest and tax expressed as a percentage of the net assets. With the ratio Return on equity we are going to define return as the earnings after interest but before tax. In other words we are calculating what the shareholders receive on their investment, excluding long-term liabilities from our considerations. The formula is:

$$\frac{\text{Profit after interest but before tax}}{\text{Equity}} \times 100$$

Example

Foundation plc. is a low leveraged company and Contour plc. is a highly leveraged company. For 2009 they both have the same amount of profit before interest. The details for the two companies are as follows.

	Foundation plc.	Contour plc.
Equity	£600,000	£300,000
Debt	£300,000	£600,000
Profit before interest and tax	£60,000	£60,000
Interest charge on debt at 5%	£15,000	£30,000
Profit after interest but before tax	£45,000	£30,000

We can now analyse these two sets of figures by calculating the Return (Profit before interest and tax) on Net Assets (Debt + Equity) and the Return (Profit after interest but before tax) on equity.

	Foundation plc.	Contour plc.
Return on net assets	6.6%	6.6%
Return on equity	7.5%	10%

Although the two companies have the same profit before interest and tax (6.6%) the return that the shareholders receive is very different because of the amount of debt that Contour holds. If a company is enjoying high profits, the shareholders in the highly leveraged company will get a better return. This is because once the interest is paid the profit after interest relates to the much smaller amount of equity.

If there is an economic recession the shareholders in the highly geared company are the ones who are going to suffer. If profit before interest and tax is £30,000 the results would be:

	Foundation plc.	Contour plc.
Equity	£600,000	£300,000
Debt	£300,000	£600,000
Profit before interest and tax	£30,000	£30,000
Interest charge on debt at 5%	£15,000	£30,000
Profit after interest but before tax	£15,000	£0
Return on net assets	3.3%	3.3%
Return on equity	2.5%	0%

If you are a risk taker you may wish to invest in a highly geared company as in a booming economy you will do very well. The more pessimistic may decide to invest their funds in a less spectacular low-geared company.

INVESTMENT RATIOS

Shareholders are interested in the share price. Although the financial statements may provide information on the company, it depends on what the market thinks of the shares. These opinions will be based on the financial statements but also an analysis of external factors. One must also accept that rumour and greed may play a part in determining share prices.

MARKET CAPITALIZATION

The main ratio used to ascertain the value the market puts on a share price is the market capitalization. The formula is:

Current share price × Number of ordinary shares in issue

As share prices fluctuate, even on a daily basis, the 'value' of the company is always changing. At no stage is it possible to match the market valuation with the 'book value' of the company.

INTEREST COVER

One of the problems of leverage ratios is the different definition used. It is a useful technique but an alternative ratio, interest cover, reveals the effect of leverage but avoids the definitional problems. The ratio is calculated by using the formula:

$$\text{Interest cover} = \frac{\text{Profit before interest and tax}}{\text{Interest charge}}$$

What this ratio reveals is the number of times the interest charge could be paid out of the current earnings and we usually refer to the ratio as the number of times. If the interest charge can be paid, that is, is covered, several times from the earnings, the existing shareholders can have some confidence that they will receive a return even when the economy is bad.

As we demonstrated above, the low leveraged company has less risk in an economic downturn.

With a highly leveraged company the number of times that earnings can cover interest charges will be very few. In the worse situation there are insufficient earnings to cover interest and there is the danger that the company will go into bankruptcy.

Table 9.7 shows interest cover for both companies in a good economic situation and when the economy is poor.

	Foundation plc.		Contour plc.	
	Calculation	Interest cover	Calculation	Interest cover
Good economy	£60,000 £15,000	4 times	£60,000 £30,000	2 times
Poor economy	£30,000 £15,000	2 times	£30,000 £30,000	0

Table 9.7 Comparing interest cover

EARNINGS PER SHARE

Shareholders are interested in the amount of dividend the company pays. A company may pay out part of the earnings in dividends but retain some of the earnings in the company to fund growth. Although the retained earnings are kept in the company, they belong to the shareholders and are shown under the heading of Equity. The consequence of this is that the shareholder's shares will be more valuable, that is, there is capital growth.

The financial statements disclose the earnings for the financial period. An individual will hold only a portion of the total shares and is interested in the amount that their shares have earned.

IAS 33 Earnings per share requires companies to calculate and to disclose the basic EPS on the face of their Income Statement. The information that a company must provide is:

- details of basic and diluted EPS on the face of the income statement;
- the amounts used as the profit or loss for ordinary shareholders in calculating basic and diluted EPS;
- the weighted average number of ordinary shares used in calculating basic and diluted EPS;
- a description of those ordinary share transactions or potential ordinary share transactions that occur after the balance sheet date and would have had a significant effect on the EPS.

The basic EPS is calculated by dividing the profit or loss attributable to ordinary equity holders of the parent entity (the numerator) by the weighted average number of ordinary shares outstanding (the denominator) during the period. This is all ordinary shares in issue during the year. If a company has not issued further shares during the year, the calculation is shown in Example 1.

Example 1. Basic EPS calculation

Profit for year ended 31 December 2012	£7,000,000
Weighted average number of shares in issue	60,000,000
Basic EPS $\dfrac{£7.000,000}{60,000,000} = 11.7$ pence	

The other disclosure is the diluted EPS. Dilution arises where some individuals have the right to receive ordinary shares in the future in exchange for another type of investment. For example, they may have preference shares or convertible debt they can convert into ordinary shares in the future. If they choose to do this there will be more ordinary shares in issue so the EPS will decline.

The diluted EPS is a warning to existing shareholders that there is the risk that more ordinary shares may be in issued in the future. If that is the case the earnings per share they currently enjoy is not necessarily a good guide to the benefit they may receive in the future.

PRICE/EARNINGS RATIO (P/E RATIO)

Shareholders are interests in their current earnings per share but they are also interested in future performance. The P/E ratio reflects the stock market's opinion on the possible future earnings of the company. In the simplest terms the question being answered is how much is it worthwhile paying for that share now based on the current level of earnings.

The ratio is based on the earnings per share and the current market price of one share, the formula being:

$$\frac{\text{Current price of one share in the market}}{\text{Earnings per share}}$$

We can take the calculation of the basic EPS in Example 1 which was 11.7 pence and we will assume that the current market price is £1.17. If we apply the above formula the P/E ratio is:

$$\frac{£1.17}{£0.117} = 10$$

Sometimes the answer is referred to in years so in the above example the P/E ratio is ten years. This means that at the current level of earnings per share it would take ten years to recover the price paid for the share currently.

At first glance it would seem a good share as your money is returned in ten years, but we need to look at the future. Other things being equal, it would be preferable to purchase a share with a higher P/E ratio say of 15 years. This is because of the market predictions. The market believes that the company will prosper more in the future and is willing to pay for that future growth.

Generally, the higher the P/E ratio the better as it reflects the stock market's confidence in the company's financial prospects. The market is willing to pay more for the share than the current level of earnings would justify.

DIVIDENDS PER SHARE

A successful company pays dividends to its shareholders. The total amount of the dividend is shown in the financial statements. The individual shareholder wishes to know the dividend they get for each share they hold.

We can calculate both the dividend net which is the amount of dividend per share for the financial year and also the dividend yield. This latter ratio measures the dividend yielded on a share in relation to the current market price. The calculation of these two ratios is shown in the following example.

Example – Dividend per share

A company has 50,000 shares in issue and for 2012 it declares dividends of £10,000. Its current share price is £5.00 per share.

$$\text{Dividend net} = \frac{\text{Total dividends}}{\text{Number of ordinary shares}} = \frac{£10,000}{50,000} = 20 \text{ pence per share}$$

Once again, comparison with other companies or previous years will reveal whether this level of dividend is acceptable. However, the shareholder may have purchased the share several years ago at a much lower amount than the current market price.

The dividend yield ratio reflects the dividend as a return on the current price of the share. The formula is:

$$\frac{\text{Dividend net}}{\text{Current share price}} \times 100 = \frac{20 \text{ pence}}{£5.00} = 4\%$$

The investor has the choice of retaining the share and receiving a return of 4 per cent or selling the share and reinvesting the proceeds. If the investor believes that a higher return than 4 per cent can be obtained and the P/E ratio does not indicate that the stock market believes that earnings will increase in future years, the investor may decide to place their money elsewhere.

CASH FLOW RATIOS

The argument for the Cash Flow Statement is that it reveals the financial stability of the company without being distorted by the accruals and matching concepts. Also it does not have the deficiencies and differences in measurement methods as demonstrated on the balance sheet. It is possible for a company to make a profit but have a cash deficit so a sound method to measure financial worth is required.

Cash flow ratios assist users in assessing a company's ability to pay its current debts and the financial resources it has to undertake expenditures on assets. There are several cash flow ratios and the definition of the terms used and their components varies so caution must be used when making comparisons.

The cash flow ratios we discuss in this section fall into two general categories:

1. Ratios to test for solvency and liquidity:

    - operating cash flow (cash flow from operations to current liabilities);
    - cash interest coverage ratio;
    - cash flow to sales ratio.

2. Ratios that indicate the viability of a company as a going concern:

    - cash to capital expenditure (cash recovery rate);
    - cash to total debt ratio.

(OPERATING CASH FLOW) CASH FLOW FROM OPERATIONS TO CURRENT LIABILITIES

The purpose of this ratio is to assess how much cash is available to pay the company's current liabilities. The net cash flow from operations is taken from the Statement of Cash Flow and the current liabilities from the balance sheet. It is preferable, where possible, to calculate the average liabilities by adding the figure from last year's balance sheet to this year and dividing by two. The formula is:

$$\frac{\text{Cash flow from operating activities}}{\text{Average current liabilities}} \times 100 =$$

Example

A company has a total of £13,000,000 cash from its operating activities. On the balance sheet there are current liabilities of £14,800,000. The cash flow from operations to current liabilities is

$$\frac{£13,000,000}{£14,800,000} = 0.87$$

On its present performance the company is not generating sufficient cash from its operating activities to cover its current liabilities. This may be a matter for concern but this ratio varies radically, depending on the industry.

CASH INTEREST COVERAGE RATIO

The purpose of this ratio is to determine the company's ability to make the required interest payments. Some analysts prefer to also include the repayments required as in the example. The formula is

$$\frac{\text{Cash flows from operations}}{\text{Interest and repayments required}} = \text{Cash interest cover}$$

Example

A company has operating cash of £13,000,000. The total of its interest and repayments required is £14,500,000. The ratio is 0.89 which is dangerously low and any company with a cash interest multiple less than 1.0 runs an immediate risk of potential default. However, ratios vary due to the gearing of a company. A highly leveraged company will have a low multiple, and a company with a strong balance sheet will have a high multiple.

CASH FLOW TO SALES RATIO

The purpose of this ratio is to determine how successful a company is in converting its sales into cash. The higher the ratio is the more successful a company is considered to be. The formula is

$$\text{Cash flow to sales ratio} = \frac{\text{Operating cash flows}}{\text{Net sales}} \times 100$$

Example

A company has a cash flow from operations for the financial year of £2,900,000. The sales for the year as shown on the Income Statement were £3,700,000. The cash flow to sales ratio is

$$£2,900,000 = 0.78$$

In other words the company was able to generate 78 pence in cash for every £1 of sales.

CASH RECOVERY RATE (FREE CASH FLOW FORMULA)

The purpose of this ratio is to determine whether the company is successful in using its assets to generate a cash return. A company invests in the assets and, in the long term, those assets must generate more cash than they cost. The quicker the company can recover the cash that they invested in the assets, the lower the amount of risk. The cash flow figure is taken from that statement. Some people take the total assets and others only the non-current assets from the balance sheet. The formula is:

$$\frac{\text{Net cash flow from operations}}{\text{Average total assets}} \times 100$$

TOTAL DEBT (CASH FLOW TO TOTAL DEBT) RATIO

The purpose of this ratio is to indicate the length of time it will take to repay the debt, assuming all cash flow from operations is devoted to debt repayment. The lower the ratio, the less financial flexibility the company has and the more likely that problems can arise in the future. Total cash flow to debt is of direct concern to credit-rating agencies and loan decision officers. The higher the percentage ratio, the better the company's ability to carry its total debt.

The formula is

$$\text{Cash flow to total debt ratio} = \frac{\text{Cash flow from operations}}{\text{Total debt}}$$

Example

A company has operating cash flow for the year of £17,560. Its total debt is £20,728. Its cash flow to debt ratio is 0.85 which suggest that the company has severe financial problems.

CONCLUSIONS

Ratio analysis is a powerful tool but frequently abused as the limitations of the financial statements are not fully understood, the external factors are not scanned, and definition differences are ignored. It is essential in the analysis to suggest the reasons for a ratio changing over time or being different than competitors.

Accounting ratios can suffer both from deficiencies in the financial statements and also from changes to accounting standards. There is no value in conducting a trend analysis over several years without ensuring that no changes in accounting standards took place which would have affected the information disclosed. It is also necessary when comparing companies to ascertain whether they are using similar accounting treatments.

Investment ratios are widely used but rely only in part on the financial statements. They are also affected by the nature of the share market itself. Share prices move not only on the fortunes of a company but also hopes, fears, rumours and greed. A good understanding of investment ratios can only be gained by knowledge of how the market works.

Cash flow ratios have the advantage of using only the cash flow statement which gives a certain level of confidence in the credibility of the figures. However, by themselves there is not the depth of analysis that one gains from using all the financial statements.

RECOMMENDED READING

Leach, Robert (2010) *Ratios Made Simple*, Harriman House Ltd.

Walsh, Ciaran (2008) *Key Management Ratios*, Prentice Hall.

CASE STUDY KITCHEN RENEWALS

You own a consultancy agency, most of your clients being small to medium size. One of your new clients has a business, KitchenTops, which supplies granite and quartz counter tops for kitchens. The business has been in operation for about five years and your client, Tony Adelm wishes to expand into other activities which fit into his current operation.

He has observed that many of his customers cannot afford to replace their kitchen cabinets and also have new granite counter top and therefore choose only one: cabinets or countertops. He has been in negotiations with a company, Kitchen Updates, which offers cabinet resurfacing. Essentially, for the fraction of the cost of new cabinets, Kitchen Updates replaces the doors on the old cabinets and puts veneer on any visible surfaces. They can also replace handles and feedback from customers is very favourable.

The owner of Kitchen Updates intends to retire and has asked Tony if he wishes to buy the business. There have been no discussions on price but the owner has given Tony basic financial statements for 2012 to demonstrate that it is a 'good buy'. Tony has asked if you can have a look at the financial statements and tell him how it compares financially with his own business.

Unfortunately, these are both niche businesses and you are unable to obtain data from any other sources so you have to make an assessment on Tony's ratios compared to the financial statements for Kitchen Updates.

Your records show that Tony has no loans and carries very little inventory. He measures for the counter top and then orders from the stone supplier.

Prepare a report for Tony. This should give:

1. The comparison of the ratios for KitchenTops with those for Kitchen Updates.

2. Your explanation on what the ratios reveal.

3. The limitation of your analysis at this stage.

4. What further information you require.

5. Other factors Tony should consider before making a decision.

Kitchen tops ratios 2012

Return on net assets	23%
Profit margin before interest	8.7%
Capital turnover	2.64 times
Gross profit margin	17.4%
Current test	2.8:1
Acid test	1.9:1
Collection period	32 days
Credit period	35 days

KITCHEN UPDATES FINANCIAL STATEMENTS
Income statements for the year ending 31 December 2012

		2012
		£000
Revenue	520	
Less		
Wages	230	
Materials	<u>185</u>	<u>415</u>

Gross profit		105
Less Expenses		
Office expenses	28	
Depreciation	18	
Interest	8	54
Profit before tax		51

Kitchen updates

Balance sheet as on 31 December 2012

	Cost	Depreciation	Net book value
Non-current assets			
Machinery and vehicles	182	64	118
Current assets			
Inventory		20	
Accounts receivable		36	
Cash		15	71
	Total assets		189
Capital at beginning of year		96	
Add	Profit	51	
		147	
Profit withdrawn by owner		30	117
Add	Loan		80
			197
Less	Current liabilities		
Accounts payable			8
Total equity and liabilities			189

PART II
MANAGEMENT ACCOUNTING

CHAPTER 10
THE NATURE AND SCOPE OF MANAGEMENT ACCOUNTING

LEARNING OBJECTIVES

At the end of this chapter you should be able to:

- Describe the relationship between financial and management accounting.
- Identify the three purposes of management accounting.
- Explain the control loop and the importance of knowing the cost of activities.
- Explain the issues surrounding performance measurement.
- Describe the factors that determine the design of a management accounting systems.
- Classify costs in different ways.
- Distinguish between direct and indirect costs.

EXECUTIVE SUMMARY

One common need of managers is to know what 'something' costs and the reason. The 'something' for which managers wish to know the cost is usually a centre or department or the product or service being provided. Organizational performance is improved if control is exercised by comparing the cost with some form of benchmark and investigating differences. This enables managers to plan future activities, monitor and control the results, evaluate performance and make decisions.

There are four theoretical strands for management: contingency theory, agency theory, sociological theories, and psychological theories. Drawing on these theories, we propose a model where the management accounting system is influenced by the type and structure of the organization, the nature of the production activity, and the organizational constituents, that is, those interested in its performance.

A 'cost' can be classified in various ways depending on who wishes to use it and for what purpose. One classification which underpins several chapters is fixed and variable. A variable cost varies in total directly with changes in the level of activity. A fixed cost stays the same in total irrespective of changes in the level of activity.

An organization's output can be broadly divided into two types: continuous operations or meeting specific orders. Management accounting methods are driven by the nature of the output of the organization. The purpose of the available methods is to ascertain the cost of its activities. This aspect of management accounting is frequently referred to as 'costing' and is an essential foundation before the control and decision-making techniques.

Having determined the cost of activities, managers can use this information for planning, control and decision making. The techniques managers choose to use will depend on what actions they wish to take.

CONCEPTUAL AND PRACTICAL ISSUES

Financial and management accounting, in many organizations, use a common set of financial records. The main purpose of these records is to produce data for financial accounting and reporting to an external audience. Although the records may be suitably flexible to extract appropriate cost data, the core concepts of financial accounting tend to be pervasive. For example, in determining which transactions are deemed as *revenue expenses* and to be counted as costs in the current financial period's income statement and which transactions are *capital expenses* and will appear on the balance sheet of the organization.

The relationship of the two systems is most visible in the following:

1. Listed companies in many countries are required to produce interim financial statements either quarterly or half yearly. It would not be sensible for a company to disclose quarterly or half yearly financial information that was not compatible to the management accounting information available internally and did not produce information that enabled reasonable predictions of the annual financial results.

2. Management accounting, as with financial accounting uses the 'accruals' concept of accounting for transactions. This means that transactions are recognized when they take place and not when cash is received or paid, although the events may be simultaneous such as when you pay at the checkout at a supermarket. Often transactions are complex and accounting standards set out the requirements for these transactions to be recognized for financial accounting purpose but this also frames the cost for management accounting purposes. There is one departure from the accruals concept and we will examine this in Chapter 14 when we discuss capital budgeting also known as capital investment appraisal.

The accounting standards we discussed in earlier chapters define various financial transactions and how they should be recorded. Management accounting therefore uses the same concepts as financial accounting.

We do not wish to over emphasize the influence of financial accounting regulations on management accounting but it is important that you are aware that sometimes the reasons for unresolved issues may lie with financial accounting requirements and not the methods and techniques of managerial accounting. We will examine this issue more closely when we consider absorption costing in Chapter 11.

There are no legal requirements for organizations to implement a management accounting system. It is a voluntary activity and should serve the useful purpose of providing managers with information so that they can carry out their responsibilities and contribute to the success of the organization. To ensure that the information has value it must be generated in time for managers to be able to use

---

Discussion point

As management accounting information is so useful for understanding a company's activities, should it be required for it to be made available to the shareholders who own the company?

MANAGEMENT INFORMATION NEEDS

In a small business, the owner may be the only 'manager'. The management accounting system is likely to be rudimentary and may be little more than the financial accounting system with some important details added. The owner is likely to make all the decisions and performance measure will be of the entire business and not different parts of it. If there are 'managers' their role may be simply in following the instructions of the owner.

As a business grows, delegation of decision making will take place. Managers will need to receive quantitative and financial data to carry out their responsibilities of planning, control and decision making. Manager will need to know the cost of the products or services for which they are responsible or the costs of operating a specific area. There are likely to be boundaries to a manager's responsibilities and some mechanisms need to be in place to ensure integration of activities.

One common need of managers is to know what 'something' costs and the reason. Unfortunately, the term 'cost' is slippery and defies one simple explanation. It is therefore helpful to describe and classify the term in a variety of ways. At this stage we will use a very simple definition of cost. The last section of this chapter classifies cost in a variety of ways.

Cost – Definition

The value of resources applied in conducting the activities of an organization.

The 'something' for which managers wish to know the cost is usually a centre or department or a cost unit. A centre or department is usually under the control of a specific manager who will have the responsibility for the resources used. A cost unit can be defined as an identifiable unit of production or service such as a tin of paint or a bridge. Frequently, the term 'cost object' is used to refer to anything to which management wishes to attach costs. It may be a product, service, specific activity or organizational sub divisions such as departments or divisions of a company.

In addition to being precise as to what is being costed, it is important to specify the nature of the cost. It may be the cost of labour and material used in manufacturing a product. It could be the cost of maintenance or administrative overheads or the cost of running a machine on a particular piece of work. To complicate matters, the 'cost' for a particular unit of production or service can change depending on the level of activity and we will discuss this later in this chapter.

Knowing the actual cost is a start but managerial and organizational performance is improved if control is exercised by comparing this actual cost with some form of benchmark or standard and investigating differences. This enables managers to plan future activities, monitor and control the results, evaluate performance and make decisions.

In Chapter 13 we will examine planning and control techniques in detail but the actual cost could be compared to:

- Previous costs for the same activity. This will show whether we did better or worse than for a prior period of time. Unfortunately, all the errors and deficiencies in incurring the previous cost will obscure whether performance has improved.

- Costs for alternative courses of action. This could range from outsourcing or switching to different products or processes.

- Planned costs which will involve the careful calculation of predetermined costs for a specific period of time.

- The costs incurred by external organizations for the same activity. This information may be difficult to acquire but strategic competitiveness should be a part of an organization's portfolio.

Knowing the cost and having a comparator is valuable but decisions are also required. Whatever your responsibility level in an organization your performance will be aligned to corporate strategy. In a survey of 500 market leaders, three distinct strategies to be used by top performers in 2012 were identified (Heller Baird and Gonzalaz-Wertz, 2011). One of these was cost and complexity reduction to make operations more flexible, leaner and more accessible to customers.

Whether you are working in a service company, a manufacturing company or some form of public organization the benefits of cost and complexity reduction can decrease the financial outlay in bringing the product or service to the customer.

This focus of management accounting on contributing to the success of an organization leads us into the area of strategy. In Chapter 15 we expand on strategic management accounting but it is useful at this stage to discuss briefly at this stage how accounting and strategy are linked.

Making the best strategic decisions is essential to the continuing success of an organization. Possibly the best known work on strategy is Porter's Five Forces Model (Porter, 1985) and this is closely related to the application of management accounting information.

Porter's thesis is that a company has a choice of three strategies: cost leadership, differentiation, and focus or niche. Cost leadership and differentiation are the most important strategies for our current discussions.

Cost leadership is adopted where the organization offers products or services to the market at a low cost compared to competitors. Cost leadership gives an organization several advantages over its competitors. One is that the impact of competition is minimized by allowing the organization to increase profit margins at the prevailing level of industry prices. An organization may also become the price leader because competitors cannot compete when their costs are higher.

Product differentiation enables companies to improve its profit margins by charging premium prices or exempting it from a price-cutting war by its competitors. Customers are willing to pay more as they are perceived as different from competitors' products. It may be that the products carry a respected brand name or project a higher status of the buyer.

Once the corporate-level strategy has been decided, managers must implement it at the business or operational level. This will require planning, making decisions and controlling activities to achieve the desired strategy. Managers need management accounting to perform these functions.

By comparing actual performance with predetermined performance, management can make assessments and conduct investigations to remedy deficiencies and to promote good practices. The comparison is a stage in the control loop and provides management with information to make effective decisions (Figure 10.1).

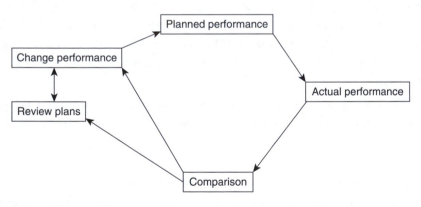

Figure 10.1 The control loop

As Figure 10.1 illustrates, plans should lead to action. The action is then measured and the actual performance compared with the plans. If there are differences, an investigation must be conducted and a decision taken. Frequently, the investigation is restricted to a detailed analysis of the actual performance but it is essential that the investigation should include a review of the original plans. Since the original plans were formulated there may have been both internal and external changes that have made the plans inoperable.

The basis of plans is the assumptions and decisions about future activity levels. An organization may be in an environment where activity levels have a certain degree of predictability, either because of constrained capacity of the organization or the stability of the marketplace.

Where the activity levels are judged to be reasonably consistent, the organization may determine that its priority is planning and controlling the actual costs of material and labour. Alternatively, and often additionally, it will also pay attention to period costs; that is those costs associated with a period of time rather than actual activity levels for example rent, insurance, salaries, administration costs.

Organizations that experience a turbulent environment and uncertainty in planning will need to examine various alternative courses of action and have the flexibility to change to meet fresh challenges.

Comparing actual performance against the plan is a critical stage in the control loop. Managers usually have some autonomy on how they run the area for which they are responsible. The metrics used to assess how they have performed as a manager are normally based on some form of comparison of actual costs, revenues, or profits against a predetermined amount. This is usually the financial components of the agreed strategy.

The measurement of a manager's actual performance is usually regarded as a reflection of how 'good' they are as a manager. Their future career, the resources under their control and possibly an incentive scheme will all be tied to managerial performance. However, actual performance is can be difficult to assess and is complicated both by measurement issues and human behaviour.

PERFORMANCE EVALUATION

An essential stage in the control loop is measuring actual performance against the plan. This is far more complex than it first appears as you are measuring the performance of people and how well they are carrying out their responsibilities. This requires a clear identification of the responsibility boundaries of a manager and also an understanding of how measuring performance can affect management behaviour.

The type of area for which a manager is deemed responsible will be set to meet the nature and purpose of the organization. These areas, also known as departments or centre will usually fall under one of the following headings.

1. A cost centre is where the manager is only responsible for the costs incurred and not the revenue. A manager could be in charge of a maintenance department or a warehouse where revenue is not generated. Managers may demonstrate improved performance by maintaining the quality of operations but reducing the costs or improving the quality while maintaining the cost level. There may even be circumstances where the manager is able to reduce cost levels and simultaneously improve quality.

2. A revenue centre is where the manager is responsible only for the revenue generated and not the costs incurred. This could be in a marketing department where sales people are given 'sales targets' against which their actual performance is compared. A more senior manager has the responsibility for controlling any costs incurred.

3. A profit centre is where the manager has the responsibility for both revenue and costs. Needless to say, the centre is expected to make a profit and the manager will be working towards a planned amount. The absolute amount of profit will be important, but this may also be expressed as a percentage of the sales figure or as a percentage return on the resources employed. These, and similar, percentage comparisons are valuable for tracing performance over time and for comparing to profit centres both within and external to the organization.

4. An investment centre is where revenue, costs and capital are the responsibility of a manager. In other words the manager is responsible for the funding decisions on machinery, equipment, buildings and other capital outlays.

Whatever the type of centre, a manager's performance and the way activities are conducted can be subject to close scrutiny and criticism. With cost centres, there is frequently the assumption held by senior management that its costs should be lower and will exert pressure for this to be achieved. Unfortunately, if the managers attempt to reduce costs this may lead to impairment in the services offered. For example a cleaning department may clean certain areas on alternate days instead of daily and this can lead to complaints from the user departments.

To avoid inter departmental arguments some organizations will make an internal charge to other parts of the organization for the services of a cost centre. For example, a printing department may start charging for leaflets and brochures it produces for other departments. The user departments may then decide to try for external competitive quotes and, if they choose this and accept them, this can reduce the 'income' of the printing cost centre so that it is making a 'loss'. If the cost centre is a vital internal resource, it cannot be allowed to fail. It will be the responsibility of the cost centre managers to ensure that the cost levels are competitive and consistent with the level of service provided.

Whichever type of structure an organization has, the management accounting system should be designed to provide the information which managers need. That same information can also be used as a measure on how the manager performed. It can be used to determine whether a manager contained costs, achieved the anticipated profit, and kept control of material wastage and other activities.

This dual nature of management accounting of providing information to meet the managers' needs and also assessing performance can lead to managers pursuing achievement of the performance measures without thought, although this could be in conflict with what is required to achieve organizational strategy.

For example, if the performance of a sales person is measured on the number of new customers obtained, there will be a tendency to concentrate on that and ignore maintaining a good relationship with existing customers. If employees are paid a bonus on the volume of work they achieve in a certain time, there may be a lack of attention to quality unless that is also measured in some way.

To better measure the performance that is required from employees, some companies construct a multifaceted array of key performance indicators (KPIs). The intention of these is to minimize attention being focused on just one aspect of performance to the detriment of other important aspects. But even here care needs to be taken and the SMART criteria technique has been advocated. This requires that a KPI must satisfy these five criteria: specific, measurable, attainable, and relevant and time bound. Hursman (2010) emphasizes that 'relevant' means relevant to the employee and not just the company

The problems of unwanted behaviours should not be over emphasized but managers need to be aware of them. Management accounting is not just about numbers. It is about the activities of people and their endeavours to use the resources for which they have a responsibility to achieve an agreed strategic goal.

THEORIES OF MANAGEMENT ACCOUNTING

Four theoretical strands for management accounting have been identified in the literature: contingency theory, agency theory, sociological theories and psychological theories (Gong and Tse, 2009). There is some overlap with these theories and in this section we will concentrate on contingency theory which has been the subject of many studies by researchers.

Contingency theory states that organizational structures and systems are a function of environmental and firm specific factors (Chenell, 2003). Various studies have been conducted over the years to identify the influencing factors. Gong and

Tse (2009) identified six groupings: environment; technical production; organizational structure; organization size; organizational strategy; national and organizational culture. They have listed the detailed factors under each of these headings which various studies have proposed as influential.

Using the research as a basis, we have devised Figure 10.2 which introduces the aspects that will be relevant to the following chapters.

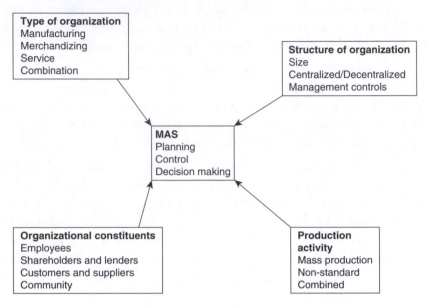

Figure 10.2 Factors affecting the design of MAS

TYPE OF ORGANIZATION

Management accounting is used in hospitals, banks, universities and manufacturing companies. Also by plumbers, electricians, landscape gardeners, charities and any other organization or individuals who need to know the financial consequences of the activities they undertake or the implications of those activities they plan to undertake.

These organizations have very different activities and may be pursuing very different strategies. Some will be manufacturers with substantial production facilities. Others will be merchandising companies that do no manufacturing but buy in their goods and sell them at a profit. A very large sector of the economy is service organizations and, within this category, there is a great diversity ranging from financial institutions to hospitals, hotels, airlines and others.

In profit-based organizations there will be a strong relationship between the costs of activities and the market price for goods and services as this will determine profits. In non-profit organizations, the total amount of funds available for a period of time or a specific range of activities may be decided at the commencement of a financial period. Managers must ensure that the costs for which they are individually responsible fall within those limitations. Strategies will have financial boundaries set on them by external factors, such as donations and government grants.

STRUCTURE OF THE ORGANIZATION

Small organizations may be controlled by the owner while larger organizations will have a formal structure that is established to ensure the efficient and effective management of activities. This is usually implemented by developing various centres or departments. The manager of a centre will normally participate in the objectives of that centre and you will be given some flexibility or discretion on operational achievement. The data that is regularly made available to managers should assist them in analysing their progress.

There is the danger of envisaging centres as self-contained units, isolated from other activities in the organization. This is not the case. It would not make sense for the sales manager to be pursuing ambitious sales targets, if the production manager does not have the resources to ensure the availability of goods. The structure must therefore aim at developing clearly defined areas of activity that are integrated into a functioning organization. Management accounting should contribute to this aim and in Chapter 13 we will explain budgetary control and how this integration may be achieved.

ORGANIZATIONAL CONSTITUENTS

Managers need information to plan, monitor and control the organization's performance. But there are many external groups that have an interest in that performance and their expectations may influence the nature of the cost information and the assessment of performance. These stakeholders may have differing objectives that influence their assessment of the organization's performance.

Commercial organizations quoted on a stock exchange have investors who will be conscious of the 'market' expectations for profit. All organizations have employees who will be concerned with job security and career progression. Customers, suppliers and even society have expectations and vested interests in the organizations.

LINK TO PRACTICE

Constituents' expectations

Although financial accounting is aimed at external audiences, management accounting contributes to the performance of managers in achieving the organization's financial performance which will become public. Managers will be aware of this and the reaction of various external users when reporting their key performance indicators.

The potential impact of external expectations on organizational financial performance was investigated in a project that examined the Central Bank of Norway and a large university hospital in the same country (Fallan, Petterson and Stemsrudhagan 2010). The research assessed society's expectations on the financial performance of each and the impact on the disclosure of financial results as revealed by their budgeted achievements

The managers responsible for the approval of budgets in the Bank were aware that society expected that the Bank would operate within its budget. The managers, therefore, set a budget at a high enough level to ensure that at the year-end there would be no spending in excess of the budgeted amount.

The hospital's mission was service to the community and their responsibility was seen by the community to treat as many patients as necessary even if that meant exceeding the budget. With changes in patients' treatments and increases in activity, a budget overspend was regarded as evidence that the Hospital required greater funding to satisfy the expectations of the community.

This unusual example demonstrates that a management accounting system is framed by the expectations of various groups and is closely connected to human behaviour. Those groups may have different objectives with those providing the funding seeking a good return on their investment and those using the products or services looking for competitive prices.

PRODUCTION ACTIVITIES

Organizations produce an output which may be readily identifiable or a performance measure can be devised. As explained earlier in the chapter this is known as a *cost object* although the term *cost unit* may be used to refer to one identifiable measure of output be it a bottle of detergent or a service such as a night in a hotel.

A specific definition of a cost unit is a quantitative unit of the product or service to which costs are allocated. The nature of the output will determine the cost unit. For example, a large accounting firm carrying out audits may consider the cost unit is a specific client: the audit job that the firm performs. A garage may also consider its cost unit as a repair job in so far as it does a specific task for an identified client. A construction company building a new hospital will consider this a cost unit although it may take several years to complete.

Other organizations may have output that is continuous. A paint manufacturer will not produce a can of paint specific for one customer but will produce daily, hundreds or thousands of cans of paint that may be purchased by anyone. The paint manufacturer will therefore want to know the cost of one can of paint. Service companies may also be offering an output that is, to all intent and purpose, continuous although there may be an identified customer. Usually that output is not tangible and a performance measure must be devised that is useful to the company. For example, a hotel may want to know the cost of an occupied room for one night.

An organization such as a recreation centre may offer clients a range of pursuits such as swimming, volleyball, badminton. The cost information they will most likely collect is the cost per hour or day for offering each of the different activities. Other organizations that are offering clients a standard service, such as a beauty salon, may wish to know the average cost of offering each of the standard services.

Frequently text books will refer to 'management accounting for service companies' as if it is a different system from that in manufacturing. This is not the case, although the management accounting system an organization uses will depend on several factors. Service organizations have environmental, economic and specific factors that will shape their system. Some of the following features of service organizations will be extremely influential in shaping their management accounting.

- The organizations are frequently national or international operations with a complicated management structure.
- A range of services may be offered, sometimes very different in nature.
- Products may be manufactured in addition to the services provision.
- It can be difficult to separate service organization's costs into fixed and variable elements.
- Specific costs are not easily traceable to certain revenue or output items.
- A substantial share of the costs are overheads.
- The activities can be highly complex.

CLASSIFYING COST

The building block of all management accounting systems is 'cost' but, as observed at the start of this chapter, this is hard to define with precision. If you were asked how much it cost to run your car each year you would need not only to calculate the petrol, oil, maintenance and repair costs, but also you should add in the costs of depreciation of the car, parking fees, and interest payment if you have it on a loan. If you were then asked to calculate the cost per mile of running the car, the calculations would be more complex as some costs, such as petrol would change depending on usage and other costs, such as tax, would stay the same.

To improve our analysis of the general term 'cost', we need some system of classifying 'costs' into useful categories. We also need to recognize that different information needs will require different methods to assemble our costs. To do this we need some form of classification and an understanding of how some cost may change at different levels of activity.

You will appreciate that in this chapter we are explaining concepts and methods individually. A large organization may have both production and service activities of varying natures. Not only will an array of costing methods and techniques be used but the classification of costs will be determined by the nature of those specific activities.

Classifications are useful for structuring a large amount of information so that it can be used in different ways and for various purposes. The population of a country can be classified by such factors as age, gender, economic standing and employment. This information can be used in determining various social policies, such as the number of schools, retirement benefits and hospital care.

Similarly a 'cost' can be classified in various ways depending on who wishes to use it and for what purpose. A purchasing manager may be interested in the cost of raw materials, a sales manager in the costs of running the sales department, the production manager in the total cost of one unit of output, the security manager in the hourly cost of offering 24-hour security.

In Table 10.1 we illustrate the basic types of cost classification, a brief explanation of that classification and some examples in the third column.

Classification	Explanation	Examples
Nature	This applies to materials, labour and overheads.	Raw materials, work in process, supervisory staff, depreciation, insurance.
Function	The purpose of the cost which is usually aligned to cost or profit centres.	Administration costs, production costs, distribution costs
Product costs	These are costs which can be directly identified with a particular product or service.	Raw materials or bought in parts in manufacturing, costs of staff in an accountants or lawyers office.
Period costs	These are costs that are related to a financial period.	Insurance for the buildings, salaries of administration staff.

Table 10.1 Types of cost classification

Adapted from Hussey and Ong (2012) Strategic cost analysis p25 business expert press

Direct cost	These are costs that can be identified with a specific cost object i.e. a particular product, department or other cost object.	Raw materials used in production and labour where it can be traced to that particular activity.
Indirect costs (Overheads)	These cannot be identified with an individual cost object but may be organization wide.	Supervisor salaries, heating in the buildings, telephone costs.
Variable costs	This is a behavioural classification and these costs change in total as activity changes.	Materials used in making the cost object.
Fixed costs	This is a behavioural classification and refers to those costs that stay the same in total regardless of changes in levels of activity.	Rent, insurance, depreciation
Mixed cost	A semi-variable cost that varies with volume, but not in proportion to volume.	Telephone bills that include a fixed charge for basic service plus a variable charge for long-distance calls.

You will note that these broad classifications can be merged to provide a more useful description of the type of cost. For example, raw materials can usually be identified with a cost unit which means that they are direct costs and, as such, they are variable. In other words, the more cost units you make the greater, in total, will be the cost of raw materials.

In addition to the above classifications, other terms are used which we briefly define below:

Opportunity costs are the benefits given up when one course of action is chosen over another. For example, imagine you have an evening job paying £10 per hour but decide to reduce your commitment by three hours per week so that you can attend an evening class. Not only will you have the cost of the evening class but you will also have the opportunity cost of £30 wages that you have forgone. This cost will be very relevant to your deciding whether to go to sign on for the evening class.

Sunk costs are past costs that were incurred through the acquisition of an asset or a resource. For example, a company may have purchased a few years ago a special packing machine. It now has the opportunity to outsource the packaging operation at a low price. The historic cost of the special machine is not relevant to the decision as to whether to outsource the function. It cannot be changed whatever decision is made as it is a cost that will not be incurred in the future: it has already been made.

Controllable costs can be influenced by a particular level of management. For example, the insurance that a company pays for the vehicles used by its sales staff cannot be controlled by the Sales Manager. However the amount of training undertaken in the department or the costs of promotional activities may be controllable at that level.

The identification of opportunity, sunk and controllable costs is not always easy. In Chapter 12 we explain incremental analysis and this expands and illustrates the above definitions. In Chapter 15 the relationship between strategy and management accounting will further illuminate this subject.

We will see in later chapter that the classification of a cost as to whether it is fixed or variable is extremely useful. In this chapter we will provide an introduction to both the direct/indirect classification and the variable/fixed classification. In later chapters we will extend these discussions to demonstrate how the concepts are applied.

DIRECT AND INDIRECT COSTS

In a manufacturing organization, materials and labour that can be identified directly with the product are likely to be significant. The increasing use of mechanization and robotics has, in some industries, reduced the amount of direct labour required. But be cautious! In some industries, where skilled labour is an essential part of the manufacturing process, the cost can be high. Generally, in service industries direct labour cost will be high and material cost low, or even insignificant. An accounting firm doing a major audit will have high direct labour costs but practically zero direct material costs.

Direct material costs will normally have the following characteristics:

- Detectable: This will often mean that they are visible, although with some direct materials, such as gases, this may not be the case and special equipment may be needed to detect them.

- Measurable: This can be by weight, volume, time or other appropriate method.

- Relatively valuable. Some costs are of small value and it is not useful to maintain records to calculate the costs to a specific cost unit. For example, in manufacturing, the costs of items such as glues, thread, screws are so minor that ordinary physical control are sufficient, for example, allowing a certain quantity for a specific level of production, with a reasonable allowance for wastage.

- Traceable – a system must be in operation to be able to record the quantity of materials to the specific product or service.

Calculating the cost of direct materials to specific cost units can cause difficulties. These fall under two heading: the practical and the price. On a practical basis, good records and work procedures are essential to ensure that materials are correctly received from the suppliers, stored in safe and secure conditions, and only issued when required by production. This usually safeguards the processing of the correct quantity of materials but there remains the problem of pricing, or determining the costs.

The delivery of materials may take place over a period of time and this does not necessarily synchronize with the quantities being issued to production. Prices will therefore vary over that period of time due to:

- inflation or deflation giving rise to price changes;
- variations in exchange rates if materials are purchased overseas;
- shortages in the supply of materials leading to price increases;
- temporary reductions due to special offers, discounts and so on.

The cost of direct labour is usually based on the remuneration system used in the company. It is essential that a sound record system is in place to charge the correct cost of labour to the appropriate activity. For example, in a manufacturing organization, piecework tickets or swipe cards may be used to record the times of different types of labour at various stages of the production process on a job. Time sheets are widely used in manufacturing and service industries. For example, employees in firms of accountants and lawyers will record their billable hours for each client's job.

In addition to those direct costs that can be identified with the production or service activity, there are also indirect costs which in many organizations are higher than the direct costs. Usually these overheads can be grouped under the following main headings:

- Production (manufacturing) overheads.
- Administration overheads.
- Selling overheads.
- Distribution overheads.
- Research and development overheads.

Different organizations may group their overheads to meet their own needs. Distribution overheads may be grouped with selling overheads but also may be classified as a direct cost for a particular job, for example, the delivery and setting up of specialized machinery to a foreign buyer.

The definition of research and development overhead is closely controlled by a financial accounting standard. The manner in which a company classifies such costs will depend on the nature of their activities and the requirements of the standard.

In a service organization, the overheads can be substantial. If you stay in a hotel, the costs of cleaning your room and the complimentary breakfast are insignificant. It is the property tax for the hotel site, the depreciation charge on fixtures, furniture and equipment, lighting and heating, the hotel staff you do see such as on the front desk. These are the costs of running the hotel.

If we wish to know the total cost of a cost object we need to ascertain:

- Direct material costs.
- Direct labour costs.
- Overhead costs.

Whether we are establishing the costs of building a bridge, manufacturing and installing a computerized system, conducting a surgical operation or defending a client on a murder charge there will be records of the direct costs incurred if the amount involved is worth recording.

The critical issue is how we share the total overheads for the organization over the various activities and the cost objects generated within one financial period. A manager needs to know the *full cost* of running a department, repairing a car for a client, transporting 100 meters of steel for 50 kilometres, or setting up an emergency hospital in a disaster area.

In some instances, the indirect costs may not be of overwhelming importance but usually they are. In Chapter 11 we explain the methods for sharing the indirect costs over the various cost objects. This enables us to ascertain the total cost including both direct and indirect costs.

FIXED COSTS AND VARIABLE COSTS

In Chapter 12 we will explain how the distinction between fixed costs and variable costs is extremely useful in short-term decision making. A crucial aspect is the definition of the terms.

A variable cost varies in total directly with changes in the level of activity.

A fixed cost stays the same in total irrespective of changes in the level of activity.

Both of these definitions need to be qualified. The behaviour identified applies only when activity levels are operating within a certain range. For each company this will be different and we discuss the concept further in Chapter 12.

The important features you should note with these definitions are as follows:

- It is where the change in activity levels changes the cost that is important. Costs can change for other reasons, such as increased labour rates, decreases in material prices, increases in rent and insurance.
- The assumptions of change are based on the short term.
- Activity-level changes that impact on cost, in practice, are within a restricted or relevant range.

- Activity levels can be measured by a method that is most appropriate for the organization.

A simple example of a variable cost is material cost. If you are making a product that requires 5 meters of material at £3.00 per meter, your cost for one cost unit is £15.00. If you make 2 units, it is £30.00; 3 units, £45.00.

If we consider fixed costs, such as rent or insurance, you must pay these whether you are operating at 100 per cent capacity or 5 per cent. These costs are fixed in relation to activity-level changes. You will realize that those costs that are considered direct costs must be variable costs: Those that are indirect will usually be fixed.

In this section we have concentrated on manufacturing organizations as the example for determining costs but similar issues of identifying and classifying costs can arise in very different types of circumstances as the following example (Akobundu, E., et al., 2006) shows.

LINK TO PRACTICE

Medical costs

In most societies the costs of health care are very substantial. Monitoring and controlling these costs present specific challenges. A study investigated the various methods used in previous cost-of-illness studies. They concluded that the studies, which covered 33 countries and 180 separate diseases, were inconsistent in their estimates of cost of illness raising concerns over the validity of the methods used. The authors analysed the costs into direct medical costs and indirect and non-medical costs.

Direct medical costs

Emergency dept./hospital services.
Outpatient doctors' services.
Drugs.
Diagnostic procedures/laboratory tests.
Other health care services.
Ancillary personnel.

Indirect and non-medical costs

Patient loss of productivity.
Care giving.
Transport costs.
Home remodelling.
Catch-all.
Although the previous studies had mostly captured the first typedirect medical costs, the majority of the studies omitted the indirect costs.

One can appreciate that in complex organizations, particularly services, there are significant problems in identify costs and relating them to specific activities. But such analysis can be critical, not only for profit organizations but those concerned with the provision of services to society.

Alzheimer's disease is becoming more prevalent with an aging population and the care of patients consumes resources. A study (Hux et al., 1998) in Canada estimated that the societal annual cost per patient was $9451 for mild disease, $16054 for mild to moderate disease, $25724 for moderate disease and $36794 for severe disease. Institutionalization accounted for 84 per cent of the cost of people with severe disease.

METHODS AND TECHNIQUES

Because of the ability to shape the management accounting system to fit the factors influencing the organization, there is flexibility in terms and definitions used. To provide a cohesive and coherent to the explanations, we have focused our chapters either on management accounting methods or management accounting techniques.

Management accounting methods are driven by the nature of the output of the organization. The purpose of the available methods is to ascertain the cost of its activities. This aspect of management accounting is frequently referred to as 'costing' and is an essential foundation before the decision making techniques can be explained later in this chapter.

To determine the total cost of a product or activity, a company selects either absorption costing or activity-based costing as its main method. Both of these are discussed in Chapter 11. Having decided an organization's output will either be continuous operations or meeting specific orders, this will determine the costing method that will be applied to ascertain the cost of the activity. The relationship is shown in Figure 10.3.

With continuous operation costing, the organization may be providing a service or manufacturing a product. The main distinction is that with manufacturing there is likely to be unfinished goods at the end of the financial period. A method is required to ascertain the costs incurred at this stage and this need is met by using process costing which is explained in Chapter 11.

Specific order costing covers three types of activity. We discuss job costing in detail and batch costing uses the same approach. With batch costing there are numerous identical items produced as a 'job'. For example, a company may manufacture pens, key rings and similar promotional items for customers. The items will carry the customer's name, trademark and any other message required. An order

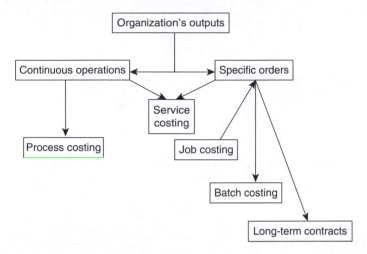

Figure 10.3 Management accounting methods

from a specific customer for 500 key rings will be considered as one job and costed as such.

Contract costing refers to those jobs that take a considerable time, such as building a bridge or a hospital. Records will be maintained to ensure that the costs incurred comply with the original plans. Where a job is in progress, the main issue is the calculation of profit at the end of a financial period and this is regulated by financial accounting. There is the issue where a company is considering an investment of funds in a project that will take several years to complete. A decision is required and the techniques used are explained in Chapter 14.

As we have explained previously, there are not specific costing methods for the service industry. However, the diverse nature of service organizations may mean that we are costing a specific order or a continuous operation. If the latter, there will not be any partly finished goods at the end of the financial period so process costing is not applicable.

The final twist with all of these methods is whether we wish to find the total cost, including overheads, or only the direct cost. Chapter 11 deals with the total cost approach and the alternative of excluding overheads, using variable costing, is explained in Chapter 12. Variable costing is also referred to as marginal costing.

Having determined the cost of activities, managers can use this information for planning, control and decision making. The techniques managers choose to use will depend on what actions they wish to take. In Figure 10.4 we have separated the techniques into planning/control and decision making, although there is some overlap.

In addition to the above techniques, an array of new techniques has developed which fall under the generic heading of Strategic Management Accounting. Possibly the best-known technique is the balanced scorecard and this and other

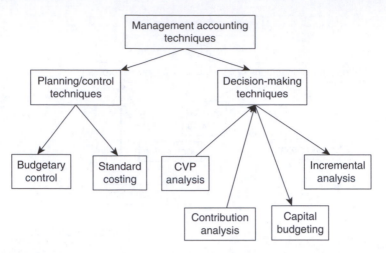

Figure 10.4 Management accounting techniques

techniques are discussed in Chapter 15. But the old techniques have not been forgotten. A study of UK manufacturing industry found that 'There are examples of "traditional" techniques such as absorption costing, standard costing and marginal costing as well as contemporary' techniques such as activity-based costing and throughput accounting' (Dugdale et al., 2005 p.3).

Having introduced the management accounting methods and techniques, we need to emphasize that it is the organization which will determine the most suitable for its own needs. Unlike financial accounting which is highly regulated, management accounting is a voluntary activity and evidence on what companies do is fragmentary. There are indications that there may be miscomprehensions as to what is or should be happening. This was demonstrated in a study in New Zealand.

LINK TO PRACTICE

Opinions of practitioners and educators on management accounting practices

A survey by Fowler (2010) in New Zealand examined and compared management accounting practitioners and educators on what methods and techniques are important in accounting. Surveys were conducted in 2001 and 2010. We extract below the top 10 practices chosen by each group in 2010.

Rank	Practitioners	Educators
1	Cash flow management	Performance evaluation
2	Product costing	Product costing

Source: Adapted from Fowler (2010) Table 1

Table Ranked importance of management accounting techniques

3	Operational budgeting	Behavioural implications
4	Variance analysis	Activity-based costing
5	Performance evaluation	Strategic management accounting
6	Customer profitability	Operational budgeting
7	ERP systems	Responsibility accounting
8	Standard costing	Cost volume
9	Capital budgeting	Absorption/variable costing
10	Cost volume	Activity based management

In subsequent chapters we discuss specific methods and techniques but it is for you to decide the appropriateness of their application in different organizations. It is always easier to appreciate the relationship with direct/indirect and fixed/variable costs with a real life example and we provide this in the case study at the end of the chapter.

CONCLUSIONS

Management accounting is for internal users and the system a company implements and operated should fit its needs. The system should generate relevant information in a timely manner to assist managers in planning, controlling and making decisions.

Cost is a term which is hard to define but the task is aided by classifying costs in various ways. Possibly, the most useful classification is the division of cost by their behaviour. This is a fundamental classification which greatly assists in decision making.

Management accounting can be considered as a series of methods and techniques. Methods are driven by the nature of the output of the organization. The purpose of the available methods is to ascertain the cost of its activities. This aspect of management accounting is frequently referred to as 'costing' and is an essential foundation before the decision-making techniques.

Techniques chosen by managers to use will depend on what actions they wish to take. Essentially they can be grouped into planning/control and decision-making techniques.

It is impossible to state categorically the management accounting practices an organization should adopt. Possibly best advice based on a study of management accounting practices in the UK food and drink industry. 'For educators, professional bodies and society generally the implication is that the gap between what purports to be 'best practice' and actual practice suggests that there is considerable room for improved dissemination of concepts and techniques' (Abdel-Kader and Luther, 2006, p.32).

RECOMMENDED READING

Bromwich, M. (1988) 'Managerial accounting definition and scope-from a managerial view', *Management Accounting*, 66(8), pp. 26–27.

Otley, D.T. (1980) 'The contingency theory of management accounting: achievement and prognosis', *Accounting, Organisations and Society*, 5, pp. 413–428.

CASE STUDY LAUNDRY NEWS

Although some illustrations have been given in this chapter, it is valuable to look at the range of costs that can be associated with a seemingly simple activity. This example, published in the magazine *American Laundry News* (2010) is taken from the service industry and illustrates the detail required to calculate the total cost of washing 1lb of linen.

Hotels and hospitals will usually have their own laundry facilities and these are usually considered as cost centres. It is essential to control the costs of this activity and a panel of experts discussed these issues in the magazine American Laundry News (2010) the costs that should be considered when calculating the cost per pound of processing linen. These are:

Direct linen-processing expenses:

- Production wages – those paid to hourly employees directly involved in processing/handling.

- Production benefits – Costs associated with holiday, vacation and sick pay; worker's compensation; health insurance and retirement costs; and employer's share of Social Security and unemployment benefits.

- Utilities – Costs associated with gas, electricity, fuel oil, steam, water and sewer.

- Linen replacement – Cost to replace stain, worn, torn and lost linen. It is typically 8 to 17 cents per pound processed.

- Chemicals – Costs associated with all laundry chemicals.

- Production supplies – Costs associated with any supplies used in linen processing. They include ironer pads, covers, aprons, flatwork-ironer tape, mending supplies, shrink-wrap, string, hamper liners, ironer wax and wax cloths.

- Linen distribution – Costs associated with clean/soiled-linen transport, including driver payroll/benefits, fuel, tolls, truck insurance, maintenance, repair, and amortization on vehicles.

- Equipment maintenance – Costs associated with keeping plant machinery and equipment operating. These expenses include engineering and maintenance payroll and benefits, equipment parts, and outside service contracts.

Indirect linen-processing expenses are any other expense needed to operate, including:

- Management payroll and benefits.

- Clerical payroll and benefits.

- Uniforms.

- Depreciation on equipment and buildings.

- Amortization on circulating linen.

- Rent (if applicable).

- Sales expenses.

- Office expenses.

- Taxes, insurance, licenses, permits, etc.

- Miscellany, including lease charges, safety, legal services, training, and travel and entertainment.

The costs above can be calculated but an essential element to the formula of cost per pound is the definition of the cost per unit, in the case the 'pound weight'. Is it a pound of dirty linen or a pound of clean linen after it has been processed? The latter will be considerably lighter because of the 'soil' factor. Or, instead of actual weighing is the weight calculated by estimating how much the washing machines hold in one load and how many loads are processed.

These are questions to be resolved by management but the accurate classification and definition of cost is essential to knowing what the cost per pound is. Without that reliable information management cannot conduct their responsibilities of planning, control and decision making.

This example immediately raises the following questions:

How do we calculate the direct costs for one pound of linen?

How do we charge the indirect costs to one pound of linen?

How do we determine what the costs should be?

If the cost per pound is considered too high how do we identify where the main problem lies?

CHAPTER 11
CALCULATING THE TOTAL COST OF ACTIVITIES

LEARNING OBJECTIVES

At the end of this chapter you should be able to:

- Explain total costing.
- Allocate overheads to production activities.
- Explain the purpose of predetermined overheads in determining the total cost.
- Calculate the full cost of a cost unit.
- Calculate the cost of a specific job.
- Describe process costing and the importance of equivalent units.
- Explain and apply the concepts of Activity-Based Costing (ABC).

EXECUTIVE SUMMARY

Manufacturing managers, at all levels, usually want to know the **total** cost of one unit, whether that is a tin of pet food or a specific one-off job. Both manufacturing and service managers want to know the cost of particular activities, whether that of running a department or carrying out a heart operation.

There are two main methods of organizational activity. This is job costing where an organization has a specific order which is a 'job' for a customer and process costing where the activity is continuous operations such as making cars.

Absorption costing, also known as full costing, has been the primary method used by companies particularly in manufacturing for ascertaining the costs of jobs and continuous outputs. Total cost means the direct costs of materials and labour that can be traced to the cost units plus a share of the indirect costs (overheads) for the entire organization.

Absorption costing enables the total overheads of the organization to be shared over the various production cost centres and the overheads for a particular production cost centre to be charged to the products passing through it.

Charging production cost centre overheads to the products passing through it is achieved by using an absorption rate or overhead charge out rate. The most frequently used rates are cost units, direct labour hours and machine hours.

Job costing, also known as specific order costing, identifies the direct material and direct labour cost with each job. To this is added the share of the overheads. As each job is specific to the customer and the period of time the job takes is crucial, either the direct hours or machine hours taken for the job are used as the allocation rate.

Process costing is used where there are continuous operations in manufacturing and a stream of homogeneous products flow from one process to the next until the production is complete. Units in one process which are not complete at the end of the financial period will not be transferred to the next process until completed. Process costing enables the cost of both the completed and incomplete units to be calculated at the end of a financial period.

Activity-based costing (ABC) has gained in popularity, particularly in the services sector where it is easier to identify work processes as discrete activities rather than cost units. The method calculates the total cost of a specified activity by assigning overheads through the use of cost drivers which are measures of activity. Overheads are collected in cost pools which are related to the major activity.

ABC as originally conceived has its weaknesses and time-driven ABC attempts to resolve these. First, managers are required to estimate on resources by each product, transaction or customer. Two estimates are required: the cost per time unit of supplying resource capacity and the unit time of resource capacity consumption by each, product, transaction or customer. This provides the additional information on how many minutes that staff members spend on activities in a particular time period.

All total costing methods, necessarily, use predetermined overheads to calculate costs. Unfortunately, financial predictions may not be accurate. The result may be that the overhead we are charging to the products and services will be incorrect.

Either the amount of overhead we charge will be too high. This technically is known as over absorption, over allocation or over recovery of overhead. Alternatively, the amount of overhead we charge will be too low. Technically this is known as under absorption of overhead. The accountant should take regular action to ensure that these problems do not escalate.

CONCEPTUAL AND PRACTICAL ISSUES

The initial issue in calculating the cost of something is determining what will be the cost unit or cost object. In the manufacturing sector this is normally evident. If you are making a car, a dining table or an iPod you have a tangible cost unit.

In the service sector it can be more complex. Even with our laundry example in the previous chapter, the dilemma arose as to whether a weighed one pound of soiled linen, or clean processed linen should be the cost unit or should a calculation based on a washing machine's assumed capacity to be the measure.

Some of the aspects of service operations that should be taken into account when identifying the cost unit are:

- The cost of materials is usually insignificant.
- Direct labour can be significant.
- Allocation of overheads is far more complicated than in a manufacturing organization.

It may be difficult to define the cost unit and hypothetical ones must be generated. For example, a hotel may decide on an occupied bed night; a transport company on a hybrid measure combining weight of cargo and distance mile.

In service organizations where an acceptable cost unit can be devised or where there are identifiable 'jobs', absorption costing can be applied for the allocation of overheads and the calculation of an allocation rate to arrive at the total cost. But given the differing characteristics of service organizations, new techniques, such as ABC, aimed at allocating costs to various activities, are attracting significant interest and application.

Whatever the type of industry and whether absorption costing or ABC is used, the essential problem is how we charge the indirect costs, the overheads, to the cost unit or activity. In most organizations overhead costs are substantial. We cannot claim that we know the total cost of a cost unit unless portion of the overhead cost is included. As we explain in this chapter, the difficulty is calculating that proportion without undertaking time consuming and expensive costing investigations.

One factor of total costing frequently overlooked by critics is that the purpose is to find the total cost at a given level of activity. If activity increases the total cost per unit will decrease as the fixed costs are spread over a greater number of items.

There is also the conceptual difficulty that fixed costs are period costs, for example, the rent for 2012. If these period costs are charged to a cost unit and all the products are not sold, the closing inventory to be carried forward to 2013 includes some portion of 2012 period costs. This is both a conceptual and practical aspect that can provoke consternation when looking at annual profits.

ABSORPTION COSTING

> ## Definition – Absorption costing
>
> The method used for charging overhead costs to cost units to ascertain the total cost of the unit. Overhead costs are charged to production centres using a process of overhead analysis and then charged to cost units using an overhead absorption rate.

In this section, we use the term 'absorption costing', also known as full or traditional costing, to mean a method designed to identify the material, labour and overhead costs incurred in generating a cost unit or running a department. The method was developed in the manufacturing sector and reflects the priorities of production facilities, although the technique is now used in other sectors.

Where costs such as direct materials and direct labour can be identified with the cost unit, they can be charged to it. For example, if you know the material cost is £1000 for 500 similar units the cost is £2.00 per unit. It is a simple matter to implement a system to record those costs. The issue is the overhead cost that cannot be identified with a cost unit.

Absorption costing provides answers to the following questions:

- How to share the total overheads of the organization over the various production cost centres;
- How to share the overheads for a particular production cost centre over the various products passing through it.

There is a two-step process. The first step is to share the overhead for the entire organization over both production and service centres. This will give you the cost for running that centre whether it is a production or service centre such as maintenance. A method must be used to charge the service centre overheads to the production centres. The reason for this is that finally the overheads must be charged to the cost units and these pass through the production centres.

The second step is to ascertain the amount of the production department's overhead which should be charged to the cost units passing through it. This is known as the absorption rate or overhead charge out rate and there are several ways of doing the calculation.

To explain the application of absorption costing, it is best to use a simple model of a manufacturing organization. This is illustrated in Figure 11.1 where there are a number of 'departments' or cost centres. Some of these are production cost centres, and others are service cost centres such as maintenance, canteen, and administrative support. For clarity, only one production cost centre A is shown.

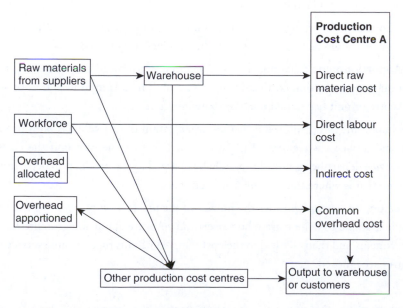

Figure 11.1 Absorption costing in manufacturing

Raw materials will be delivered from the supplier and a system must be in place to record the materials issued from the warehouse to all the cost centres. Similarly, records must be in place to record the labour hours worked in each of the cost centres. That gives the direct costs for Cost Centre A.

Some overheads may be identified directly with a cost centre as the activities of that centre necessarily incurred the cost. Examples are, the insurance on some highly specialized equipment, supervisors' salaries if they only work in A, depreciation of A's machinery, the cost of raw materials that are not sufficiently valuable to trace direct to the product. These overhead costs are allocated to Cost Centre A.

The second group of overheads is those which cannot be identified with a single cost centre, but must be shared over all the cost centres benefiting from them. These overhead costs may be, for example, the costs of cleaning, lighting, heating, insurance and property tax for the entire organization. These need to be shared in some way to each production department. The procedure for charging the overheads to the cost units is:

- Charge any overhead cost that can be identified with a particular production department;
- Share the common overhead cost over the production departments by preparing an Overhead Analysis Statement as shown below;
- Charge a share of the total overhead cost to each cost unit passing through it to give the total production cost of each cost unit.

You will find that organizations have may have their own terms for different stages in the procedure. The ones we will use are:

Allocation. Charging the entire amount of an overhead cost to a production cost centre or cost unit because it is directly incurring the cost.

Apportionment. Charging a part of a common overhead cost of the organization to a production cost centre or cost unit. The assumption is that the cost centre or unit has caused the cost to be incurred.

It is important to bear in mind that an organization most likely has both production and service cost centres. To find the total cost of one cost unit the costs of the service departments must ultimately be charged to the production departments because that is where the cost units are generated.

Before we start to consider the impact of the production process, we will use a simple example to demonstrate how overhead costs are apportioned to production departments and then charged to the cost units. With this first example service cost centres are ignored.

EXAMPLE OF OVERHEAD ANALYSIS STATEMENT AND ABSORPTION RATE

There are just two production departments in the factory. The following exhibit shows characteristics of the company.

	Total	Production Dept. 1	Production Dept. 2
Number of employees	20	15	5
Area (Sq. feet)	1,000	800	200

In total, for the financial period we have £220,000 of indirect costs which are made up of factory rent, canteen and maintenance. We can use the characteristics, shown above, of the two departments to apportion the overheads to them.

Overhead analysis statement

Factory overhead	Overhead £000	Basis of apportionment	Department 1 £000	Department 2 £000
Rent	100	Area	80	20
Subsidized canteen	40	Number of employees	30	10
Maintenance	80	Area	64	16
Total	220		174	46

You will appreciate that there is logic to this but, undoubtedly, some worrying questions come to your mind. Let us address these.

This is an arbitrary method. For example, we have charged canteen costs on the basis of number of employees but it could be that the majority of employees in Department 2 do not use the canteen. Similarly we have allocated maintenance on the basis of area but it could be that most of the maintenance work is carried out in Department 2.

We agree, but using the information already available, such as area, is a practical approach. We could collect information on who uses the canteen and where the maintenance is conducted, but will the cost of obtaining that information provide data that gives better data for planning, control and decision making? This is a decision that has to be made by management.

In defence of the arbitrary approach to allocating overheads we would argue that it is cost efficient and sensible to use a basis where we already have the information available without incurring further costs to obtain additional data. It could be argued that the approach is reasonable and, by and large, will reflect the departments' uses of the resources.

Secondly, if we wait until the end of the financial period so that we know the overhead costs reliably, it will be too late for the information to be of use to managers. We therefore use the planned, or budgeted overhead. In other words, we cannot wait until the end of the financial period to know what the actual overheads cost to do our calculations.

Using planned overhead costs can cause problems but it is necessary method. Imagine if you had your car repaired at the garage and they said they would not know what to charge you until the end of the financial period when they know their actual overhead costs. Good news for you but terrible for the cash position of the garage. The solution is to work with planned overhead costs. At the beginning of the financial period we must estimate what our overhead costs will be and use those figures for our calculations.

We have used the Overhead Analysis above to share the overheads over the two departments. We now need to find a way to charge these overheads to the cost units going through the department and we will use an absorption rate, also known as the overhead recovery rate or charge-out rate. This will allow us to answer the question of what is the total cost of a cost unit.

Definition – Absorption rate

The rate or rates calculated in a full costing system for the purpose of charging the overhead costs to the unit of production for a financial period.

There are several ways we can charge the overheads of a production department for a financial period to the cost unit. The choice of the absorption rate depends on the nature of the product and the resources we consider are being used. The three methods you are most likely to find in practice are:

THE COST UNIT

If all the units we produce are homogeneous, such as cans of paint, we can merely divide the department overheads by the number of units going through that department to give us an average overhead cost per unit. This is added to the direct material and direct labour cost to give the total cost per unit. You will find a worked example when we discuss process costing towards the end of this chapter.

LABOUR HOUR RATE

If you consider the costs of running the department are largely incurred to provide labour to work on the cost units then you can use labour hours. In the above example the overhead costs for Department 1 were £170,000. If management has determined that 25,000 hours of work should be carried out in that time the overhead labour rate is $£170,000/25,000 = £6.80$ per labour hour. If a cost unit required three labour hours then the share of overheads for the unit would be $£6.80 \times 3 = £20.40$. Note that this is NOT the direct labour cost but the share of overheads cost and this would be added to the direct costs to give the total production cost.

MACHINE HOUR RATE

You may work in an organization where the production process is highly mechanized in particular departments. If that is the case then you would charge the overheads to the cost unit on the basis of the machine hours incurred. For example, the overhead for department 2 is £50,000 for a set period of time. Management may have determined that this will provide a capacity of 20,000 machine hours. The machine hour rate is £50,000/20,000 = £2.50 per machine hour. If a job were to take 100 machine hours to complete then the cost of the overhead would be 100 × £2.50 = £250.

There are other methods for charging production department overheads to cost units. Two common methods are a percentage of the labour cost or the material cost. These have the advantage of the information already being available but are prone to fluctuations due to changes in labour rates and material prices.

One important aspect to remember is that not only will the overhead cost be a budget amount and not the actual, but the absorption rate will be based on the forecast of the level of activity as shown in the following formula:

$$\text{Absorption rate} = \frac{\text{Budgeted overhead costs}}{\text{Estimated activity levels}}$$

The key facts to remember are:

- Absorption rates are calculated for each department to charge the overheads to the product. Different departments may have a different method of allocation.
- The absorption rates will be based on the budgeted overhead cost and the anticipated level of activity in the coming financial period.
- Once the absorption rate is calculated at the beginning of the period it will be used to calculate the overhead cost of the cost unit.
- The overhead charge is added to the direct costs to obtain the total production cost.
- A cost unit will be charged overheads for every production department that it passes through.

SERVICE CENTRES

So far, we have considered only production cost centres. However, most businesses also have cost centres based in the factory that provide services to other cost centres. Examples of *service cost centres* include departments associated with the production areas, such as maintenance and quality control.

In a small organization where the services provided are not substantial, the costs may be allocated directly to the production cost centres on an arbitrary basis as described above. Unfortunately, we can have different scenarios. The simplest is where the service cost centre only serves the production cost centres. The other is where there are more than one service centre and they serve each other as well as the production cost centres. The following illustration demonstrates the actions to be taken in these circumstances.

ONE SERVICE COST CENTRE

In this example we assume that the individual overheads, for example, rent, heat, insurance have been apportioned over the three departments on a 'fair' basis. We also assume that the service department overheads are apportioned over the two production departments on the ratio of the total production overheads. Of course, another method could be chosen such as number of employees or value of machinery.

	Production Dept. 1 £	Production Depart 2 £	Service Dept. A £
Total overheads	20,000	40,000	6,000
Apportionment Dept. A	2,000	4,000	(6,000)
Total	22,000	44,000	0

The calculation for Production Department 1 is:

$$\frac{\text{Production Dept. 1 overheads}}{\text{Overheads Depts. 1 and 2}} = \frac{£20,000}{(£20,000+£40,000)} \times £6,000 = £2,000$$

TWO SERVICE COST CENTRES

In the following example, service department A gives support to the two production departments as well as Service Department B. However, Service department B gives support only to the production departments and not to Service Department A. In this case, A's overheads of £6000 are first charged to the two production departments and Service Department. B's overheads are then shared over the two production departments that it services.

	Production Dept. 1 £	Production Depart 2 £	Service Dept. A £	Service Dept. B £
Total overheads	20,000	40,000	6,000	2,000
Apportionment dept. A	2,000	2,000	(6,000)	2,000

Sub total	22,000	42,000	0	4,000
Apportionment dept. B	2,000	2,000		(4,000)
Total	24,000	44,000		

If we considered there was a need for a more sophisticated sharing of the service department overheads, we could use relevant criteria such as area, number of employees,

The result of these apportionments is that we now have all the overheads charged to the two production departments. The next stage will be to charge that overhead to the cost units passing through the production department. Once again, we could have chosen any method to share the service departments' overheads as long as it was logical and we had the relevant information.

Reciprocal services

In this situation both service departments benefit from the support of the other. Thus, the total overhead for service centre A cannot be apportioned to the production departments until a share of service centre B's overhead has been charged to it. But we cannot do this until service centre B is charged with its share of service centre A's overhead.

There are two methods for resolving this dilemma.

1. The elimination method which it can be argued leads to inaccuracies but it has the advantage of being simple.

2. The repeated distribution method which can claim to be fairer but is extremely tedious to apply.

We will restrict our discussion to the elimination method.

Under the elimination method, the costs of the reciprocal services are ignored. Normally, the overheads of the service centre which is the largest are apportioned to all the other centres. In this case it is service centre A. No return charge being made for service centre B. The reciprocal services are therefore ignored.

Possibly, it is the treatment of service centres that reflects most the arbitrary nature of absorption costing. But remember, the purpose of management accounting is to provide relevant information to managers in a timely manner. If the information does not serve that purpose, other methods of dealing with overheads and service centres must be used. This will usually increase the cost of running the management accounting system and possibly delay the issue of useful information.

Absorption costing has its critics and we discuss the alternative approach, ABC in a later section. Recent criticisms from researchers and the press have been spurred by the bankruptcies during the recent recession, particularly those in the auto industry in North America.

JOB COSTING FOR MANUFACTURING AND SERVICES

IDENTIFYING THE JOB

The purpose of job costing, also known as specific order costing, is to identify the cost of the job whether this is a tangible product or a particular service for a client.

You may have some preconceptions on what a job is. The following are examples of 'jobs':

The local garage repairing your car.

Building a new hospital.

Building a rocket for space exploration.

Making a film.

Providing security at an international convention of politicians.

A plumber repairing a leak for a customer.

A job has the following characteristics:

- It is an identifiable piece of work.
- It is carried out to a customer's specific requirements.
- Direct costs such as materials and labour can be identified with the job.
- A share of overhead costs must be charged to it.

We will omit long-term jobs from our discussions, such as building a hospital, as these are also affected by financial accounting regulations and have their own characteristics. We will concern ourselves with work that is of short duration, normally under a year. In these circumstances, each separate job is recognized as the cost unit.

We have already explained the principles of absorption costing. This involves identifying the direct material and direct labour cost with the job. To this is added the share of the overheads. As each job is specific to the customer and the period of time the job takes is crucial, either the direct hours or machine hours taken for the job are used as the allocation rate.

One example of job costing you will be familiar with is taking your car to the garage for a repair. Usually you will have an invoice that will list the parts fitted (direct materials) and also the time taken by the mechanic (direct labour) to diagnose the problem and carry out the repair. You will find that the rate charged for the mechanic's time is well above the actual pay rate. This is because it includes the allocation rate for the overhead. Garages usually use labour hour rate to charge overheads to the job.

Calculating the total cost

Following is a worked example that illustrates all the stages in arriving at the total cost of a job. We have simplified the calculations so that you can concentrate on the principles used.

WORKED EXAMPLE – EXCELSIOR DOORS

This is a small company that designs and installs remote controlled garage doors for commercial and private premises. The direct labour wage rate or cost is £10 per hour. The company uses total costing and has three production departments. With any job it does, the company adds 10 per cent to the production cost of the job to cover the administration and selling overheads and then adds a 5 per cent mark-up to allow for profit.

The following data is available for the next financial year:

	Factory	Fabrication department	Completion department	Installation department
Area (square meters)	4,000	2,000	1,200	800
Value of machinery	£100,000	£40,000	£30,000	£30,000
Number of direct employed	40	10	20	10
Budgeted labour hours	16,000	4,000	8,000	4,000
Budgeted machine hours	11,500	10,000	1,500	–

The above data will be used to share the factory overhead over the three departments using an arbitrary but reasonable basis and then to calculate the overhead absorption rate.

OVERHEAD ANALYSIS STATEMENT

Overhead	Factory amount £	Basis of allocation	Fabrication department £	Completion department £	Installation department £
Rent	20,000	Area	10,000	6,000	4,000
Heat and light	10,000	Area	5,000	3,000	2,000
Building insurance	20,000	Area	10,000	6,000	4,000
Machinery insurance	10,000	Value of machinery	4,000	3,000	3,000
Supervisors' salaries	64,000	Number of employees	16,000	32,000	16,000
Contract cleaning	16,000	Number of employees	4,000	8,000	4,000
	140,000		49,000	58,000	33,000

The company decides to use the machine hour rate in the Fabrication department as that department uses most of the machinery and few workers. The other two departments will use the labour hour rate as the use of machinery is comparatively lower.

Using the above data the machine hour rate in the Fabrication department is £49,000/10,000 hours = £4.90 per machine hour. The labour hour rate in the Completion Department is £58,000/8000 hours = £7.25 per hour and in the Installation Department £33,000/4000 hours = £8.25 per hour.

Let us assume that a client, Closet Stores Ltd., has agreed with Excelsior Doors the type of garage doors it requires and has asked for a quote for the job. Excelsior Doors will construct a Job Specification and the following is a typical example. Excelsior has calculated the direct materials will be £42,000 and direct labour is paid £10 per hour. It calculates that the job will require 450 paid labour hours in the machine department, 1200 hours in the Completion department and 650 hours in the Installation Department.

The job requires 1850 machine hours in the Fabrication Dept., 1200 hours in the Completion Dept. and 650 hours in the Installation Dept. Administration and selling overheads are calculated at 10 per cent of the total production cost.

Closet stores

Job specification

	£
Direct costs	
Direct materials	42,000
Direct labour	
Fabrication (450 hours)	4,500
Completion (1,200 hours)	12,000
Installation (650 hours)	6,500
Total direct costs	65,000
Overhead allocation	
Fabrication (1,850 machine hours @ £4.90)	9,065
Completion (1,200 labour hours @ £7.25)	8,700
Installation (650 labour hours @ £8.25)	5,363
Total production cost	88,128
Administration and selling overheads	8,813
	96,941
Profit mark-up (5%)	4,847
Selling price	101,788

You should have little difficulty with the calculations if you remember our explanation in the first part of the chapter. This job passes through the three departments and therefore the actual labour cost in each department must be charged at the rate of £10.00 per hour.

In addition, a charge must be made for the overheads. In the Fabrication Department, machine hours are considered most important and the overhead is calculated using the machine hour absorption rate. In the other two departments, labour hours are deemed to be most important but remember that the labour hour absorption rate for overheads must be used and NOT the wage rate.

In the final job specification we have rounded up the amounts to the nearest whole number. In practice, the company would round up the figures to the nearest ten or even one hundred.

There are two important points that need to be made on the managerial aspect of the Job Specification document.

1. It is both a plan and a control document. If Excelsior Doors wins this job it will use the Job Specification to control the progress of the job.

2. The figures are predictions but there is little scope for error. If the overheads are incorrectly predetermined, the profit could quickly turn into a loss.

In the above example, Excelsior Doors could have used a 'blanket' rate, also known as a factory wide rate, for factory overheads instead of the departmental rate. This would mean that the total overheads of £140,000 would be divided by the total predicted labour hours of 16,000 to give an overhead recovery rate of £8.75. If you multiply this rate by the total labour hours for the job the result is an overhead charge of $(450 + 1200 + 650$ labour hours$) = 2300$ hours $\times$ £8.75. This gives an overhead charge for the job of £20,125 compared to the amount on the job specification of £23,128.

Which one is right? The answer is that both are 'right' within the logic of the method you are using but you will find that a departmental rate is likely to give you more precise information for control and decision making than a blanket rate.

In some industries it is sometimes possible to negotiate the price of a job on a cost plus policy. The final selling price is calculated by adding an agreed fixed profit margin to the cost of the job. This approach has a number of weaknesses, as there is no incentive to control the cost of the job, it ignores market conditions and the total costs are dependent on the method of overhead recovery. If a client does enter into such a contract it is essential that the job specification is agreed in minute detail.

As a final note on specific order operations, remember the nature of the activity being undertaken. In some industries certain jobs are so repetitive and financially minor that the company does not need to cost each job. Everyday examples include oil changes for your car, dental visits and printing business cards. Although there is a customer (yourself) and the job is specifically for you, the service provider usually has a standard price based on previous experience. This 'average' cost is deemed sufficiently precise to provide a profit and attract customers.

Features of job costing

1. A job is clearly identifiable.
2. Different jobs may be worked on in the same financial period.
3. Costs are traced to the specific job.
4. A job can consist of either one 'product' or a number of similar units that make a batch.
5. The Job Specification is a prime document for detaining the costs involved in a job.

PROCESS COSTING

> ### Key definition – Process costing
>
> A costing method used where there are continuous operations in manufacturing and a stream of homogeneous products flow from one process to the next until the production is complete.

THE ISSUES

Process costing method is used where the production process is carried out in a series of separate stages with identifiable inputs and outputs at each stage. The finished output at one stage of production becomes the input for the next stage. Each stage or process can usually be clearly identified and is often contained in a separate department.

At each separate stage both direct and indirect costs are calculated. Direct costs for a particular process can be identified from the accounting records. Overheads will be allocated to the separate processes in the way described previously under total costing. The average cost of each cost unit can be calculated at each stage by simply dividing the total cost of that process for a period of time by the number of cost units produced in that period. The costs for the cost units are aggregated to give the final total cost for all of the processes that production goes through.

If you refer back to our discussion on overhead absorption you will see that we are using the basis of dividing total costs for a period of time by the number of cost units produced. This is because the cost units are all the same, such as identical packets of washing powder. Alternative methods such as machine hours or labour hours would not be relevant.

Although this method of costing is simple, an additional problem occurs at the end of each financial period. We will know the number of units completed during the financial period and transferred as inputs to the next process. But there are also a number of cost units which have not been completed by the end of the financial period for each of the separate processes. We will have to compute the cost of these incomplete units.

You will find that some accounting textbooks devote considerable space in demonstrating the calculations in detail. This is essentially to provide the required information for financial accounts. The usefulness of this calculation for the *management* of processes is debatable.

In our explanation of process costing, we use a simplified approach that demonstrates fully the principles without becoming entangled in the detail. In the following example we will assume that a company has two separate processes in the production flow. The completed outputs from Process 1 are transferred to Process 2 as the inputs for that process. For each process the direct materials, direct labour and a share of the overheads for that financial period are identified.

Worked example – complete and incomplete units

If there are no incomplete units at the end of the financial period, the calculations are straightforward. Assume that in the month of January a company that has two processes has the following information for Process 1.

Process 1	
Direct materials	£12,000
Direct labour	£3,000
Overheads	£5,000
Total production cost	£20,000

Number of completed units transferred to Process 2 during the period was 40,000. There were no incomplete units in Process 1 at the end of the period.

Average cost per completed unit for the period £20,000/40,000 = £0.50.

However, if all the units are not completed in Process 1 at the end of January they will remain in that process during February. At the end of January, we need to know the costs of the complete units that are transferred to Process 2 and the costs of the incomplete units that are retained in Process 1. Unfortunately, our accounting records will only show the total direct labour costs, direct material costs and share of the overheads for Process 1 for January. We must therefore devise a system to separate the costs of the complete and the incomplete units. Figure 11.2 illustrates the issues assuming that only 38,000 of the units are complete.

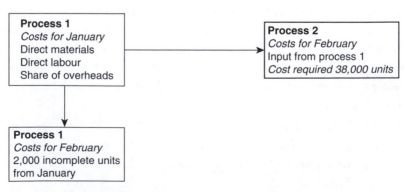

Figure 11.2 Process costing and incomplete units

Let us now introduce the problem of incomplete units and the concept of 'equivalent units'. If a unit is not complete at the end of the financial period, it will not be transferred to Process 2 but will remain in Process 1 to be completed. This will incur additional costs in the next financial period to complete the units. What we need to know is how much it has cost us in January in Process 1 to produce these incomplete units: the work in process (WIP).

The answer to finding the cost of incomplete units is to use the concept of equivalent units. If at the end of January, there were 2000 units that had been only 50 per cent completed, we would say that these were the equivalent of 1000 completed units. We have calculated that the cost of a completed unit is £0.50 so the cost of our 2000 incomplete units is $1000 \times £0.50. = £500$

You may have several comments on the above calculation. The first will be on the somewhat imprecise nature of the calculation. Although we could, with time and effort, obtain a more precise figure, it is highly doubtful is great accuracy would improve control of operations and decision making.

Your second comment may be on the assumption that 50 per cent completion of the unit means that 50 per cent of the cost has been incurred. We address this issue in the next example where we look at Process 2 for the same company but for the month of February.

WORKED EXAMPLE – TWO PROCESS PRODUCTION

The information we use to construct the following table is:

At the end of January 40,000 completed cost units have been transferred from Process 1. This represents the input to Process 2 at the beginning of February.

At the end of February there are 38,000 units completed and there are 2000 units incomplete that form Work in Process.

With the 2000 units in Process 2 that forms Work in Process, obviously all the costs are complete for Process 1 otherwise the units would not have been transferred. We need to calculate their value at the end of February.

Our records show that direct material cost for Process 2 has been completed. As far as direct labour and overheads are concerned the 2000 units are 50 per cent complete.

The first stage in the calculation is to divide the total costs for each item in column 2 by the number of effective units in column 5. This gives the average cost per unit which is entered into column 6.

In the final column 7 we enter the value of the work in progress by multiplying the equivalent units in WIP (Column 4) by the average cost per unit (Column 6). By adding this column we arrive at the total cost of the WIP.

Process 2 – Costs for February

1	2	3	4	5	6	7
Nature of cost	Total cost £	Number of completed units	Equivalent units in WIP	Effective units	Average cost per unit £	Value of WIP £
From process 1	20,000	38,000	2,000	40,000	0.50	1,000
Direct Materials	10,000	38,000	2,000	40,000	0.25	500
Direct labour	7,020	38,000	1,000	39,000	0.18	180
Overheads	9,750	38,000	1,000	39,000	0.25	250
Total	46,770				1.18	1,930

Reconciliation and summary

Value of completed units (38,000 × £1.18)	£44,840
Value of WIP (column 7)	£1,930
Total cost (reconciles with column 1)	£46,770

To recap on the various steps:

1. Previous process costs are always complete if products are transferred to the next process. Incomplete units will not be transferred to the next process.

2. The average cost per unit in column 6 is calculated by dividing the total cost per item (column 2) by the number of effective units (column 5).

3. Process 2 has 38,000 completed units at the end of the financial period. Of the remaining 2,000 units the costs are complete from Process 1 for materials but only 50 per cent complete for direct labour and overheads.

4. Where the output from one process is developed into two or more different products, the technique of joint process costing will be applied.

In some processes, some losses during production are unavoidable. Some of these losses are a normal part of the process. Sometimes losses are occurring due to breakdown in machinery, negligence of labour, poor quality raw material and so on. These are regarded as abnormal losses.

Normal is usually estimated on the basis of past experience of the industry. It may be in the form of normal wastage, normal scrap, normal spoilage and normal defectiveness. It may occur at any time of the process and is a cost of that process. If the defective units or materials can be sold as scrap, their value can be deducted from the cost of the process. If additional costs are required before the defective units can be sold these are regarded as part of the cost of the process.

Any loss caused by unanticipated conditions such as plant breakdown, substandard material, carelessness, accident and so on are regarded as abnormal losses.

In summary, the main features of process costing are:

1. The outputs of production are products that are identical.
2. The production process is continuous for a long period of time.
3. Costs are accumulated for a specific process that may be conducted in one department.
4. Products flow from one process to another.
5. At the end of a financial period there is usually an inventory of partly finished products.
6. The concept of equivalent units is used to value partly finished goods at the end of the production cycle.

The method of costing for processes is fairly straightforward and the attention given to it in some textbooks is misapplied. The information is important for financial accounting where it is essential to identify the full cost of the products and the value of inventory. There is evidence that the information is less useful for management accounting purposes.

LINK TO PRACTICE

Management control of processes

A study was conducted of three companies and their process costing practices. The researchers found that process costing practices were different from that described in management texts. In fact the companies paid considerable effort on developing accurate standard input costs and volumes rather than the information from process costing to help manage business operations efficiently and effectively.

Dosch and Wilson (2010)

A closer look at the limitations of process costing clarifies its weaknesses for day-to-day management planning and control.

1. Only historical cost is used and this not very informative for effective control.
2. Cost is determined by using averages which are generalized instead of being specific.

3. The calculation of the work in process cost is generally done on estimated basis which can be inaccurate.

4. Different products may be in the same process and common costs may be allocated to each product on an approximated basis.

Discussion point

Do you consider that process costing, despite its limitations, provides useful information for managers?

Definition

Activity-based costing seeks to ascertain the total cost by assigning overheads to major activities through the use of cost drivers which are measures of activity. Overheads are collected in cost pools which are related to these activities.

ACTIVITY-BASED COSTING

Absorption costing can be criticized. It involves considerable arbitrary decision in respect of overhead apportionment and different approaches can give different answers. It is also apparent that the method can be easily applied in a manufacturing environment but not so in a service organization where there is not a tangible cost unit and the overheads are significant but the material costs very small.

Not surprisingly, academics and consultants have searched for better methods. The alternative method, ABC, appeared in the late 1980s. Since then the use of the technique has spread both in the manufacturing and service sectors.

The first explanation of ABC as a valid alternative to absorption costing appeared in 1987 (Kaplan and Bruns). The authors demonstrated the value of the technique in the manufacturing sector where the proportion of the costs that were direct was falling and the indirect costs were increasing in importance.

With ABC the treatment of direct costs is exactly the same as with absorption costing. It is the method used to apportion the overheads which is different.

Predetermined overheads are still used. These will be the budgeted total costs for rent, insurance, electricity, power and other indirect costs. The way that these overheads are treated varies considerably compared to absorption costing.

ABC uses the concept of 'cost pools' instead of being based on functional departments or responsibility centres. Cost drivers are identified charge overheads to the products or activities so we do not have overhead absorption rates based on machine or labour hours. There are two main stages in implementing and operating ABC and we explain these separately.

ACTIVITY COST POOLS

The main *activities* in the organization are classified into activity centres. These can be defined as a unit of the organization that performs an operation that uses resources. It need not be based on an existing functional department. For example, a hospital spends a significant amount of money on medical supplies. As part of this process, orders have to be placed and this activity consumes resources. Conducting surgeries is a major activity which consumes substantial resources

COST DRIVERS

Cost drivers must be identified with each activity cost pool. A cost driver is any factor that causes a change in the cost of an activity or series of activities. Using our hospital example, it could be the number of orders placed for medical supplies. For a medical emergency service it could be the number of patients admitted.

A cost driver rate is then calculated by dividing the costs of the particular cost pool by the unit of activity. In our hospital example it would be the number of orders placed, or the number of patients admitted in an accident and emergency ward.

The final stage is assigning the costs of the cost pool to the product or service being provided. If the cost driver rate for orders for medical supplies is calculated at

£10 per order and in a financial period 500 orders are placed for supplies for heart patients, the total cost would be £5000 (Table 11.1).

Cost pool	Cost driver
Procurement of supplies	Number of orders placed
Machine set up costs	Number of different jobs run
Handling of materials	Quantity or weight of materials handled
Sales administration	Number of customer orders processed

Table 11.1 Examples of cost pools and drivers

ABC is a more sophisticated system than absorption costing and, it is claimed, should provide information about costs that is more comprehensive, reliable and useful than that provided by absorption costing. The method incorporates all relevant overheads and generates information that enables managers to make better decisions about the management of those activities and the possibilities of cost reduction.

There are barriers that prevent organizations adopting ABC in spite of its claimed benefits. One is the question of cost and the problems associated with organizational change. There is little inducement to undertake the substantial changes required to introduce a new system, if the business already produces product costing information that meets their needs. Even if the business is not entirely satisfied with its present system, the cost of implementing and managing a new system may seem too burdensome to make it worthwhile.

ABC is probably best suited for organizations where traditional total costing will not provide the information required. This can be due to the complex structure of the organization and the nature of the activities conducted. The method seems to have been particularly beneficial in the service industries, and ABC has been implemented by financial institutions, hospitals, and there is also some evidence that it is a better method than absorption costing in the hospitality sector.

Vaughn and Nelson (2010)

The emphasis in ABC on activities has generated an interest in investigating the efficiency in the use of the available capacity. Organizations have committed resources and need to assess the costs and management issues of unused capacity. Capacity cost can be defined as a fixed cost that is essential for the continuing activities of an organization. These costs tend not to vary from month to month and if capacity is not used fully, there may be opportunities for management to reduce these resources and thus decrease the amount of overhead.

As with absorption costing there are weaknesses in ABC not always understood by the non-financial manager. This may be particularly evident in ABC where a large component of the cost may be fixed and not variable and activity levels change. ABC, like absorption costing, relies on the accuracy of the predictions concerning the amount of the overhead and the level of the activity. For example, if an organization calculates that the overhead is £10,000 for a financial period and 1000 cost drivers, the application rate will be £10 per driver. However, if the actual activity level falls to 800 cost drivers the actual cost will be £12.50; a significant difference in the cost.

A further issue is the nature of the cost drivers. These are usually 'transactional' cost drivers where the number of times an activity has been carried out is important, for example the number of machine set ups or the number of purchase orders raised. This assumes that the activities are homogeneous: all machine set ups take the same time to carry out. Further analysis may show that there are differences in the *time* taken for set ups and we may improve our cost information if that is built into our model.

LINK TO PRACTICE

The use of ABC in United Kingdom's largest companies

A survey was conducted in 1994 and repeated in 1999 to assess the use and development of ABC in the United Kingdom's largest companies. The following table extracted from that study shows the comparison.

	1999 survey		1994 survey	
	N	%	N	%
Currently using	31	17.5	74	21.0
Currently considering adoption	36	20.3	104	29.6
Rejected ABC after assessment	27	15.3	47	13.3
No consideration to date	83	46.9	127	36.1
	177	100.0	352	100.0

Table 2 ABC adoption status

Source: Innes, J., Falconer, M. and Sinclair, D. (2000).

The authors concluded that the adoption status had not changed significantly over that period either in total or by sector. They observed, from their analysis, that companies in the financial sector and the larger companies had the higher adoption rates.

If ABC does become more widely practiced we can expect to see further modifications and refinements. This may also relate back to absorption costing and different methods of allocating overheads. However, the essence of the two approaches is shown in Table 11.2.

Absorption costing	ABC
Establish budget for overhead cost for the forthcoming financial period	
Identify cost or profit centres over which total overheads will be shared	Identify activity pools to which overheads will be collected
Decide on allocation rate for each cost centre. This will most likely by machine hours, labour hours or cost units	Decide on the cost drivers for each activity pool. This is a factor that is capable of numerical measurement such as the number of orders placed to purchase supplies
Charge direct costs to the job, process, service or activity	
Charge indirect costs to products, jobs or service using the allocation rate	Charge indirect costs to the activity pool using the cost driver
Add direct costs and indirect costs to find total cost or product, job, process or activity	

Table 11.2 Comparison of absorption costing and ABC

Time-driven ABC

Kaplan, Anderson and Steven (2004) highlighted the weaknesses of ABC. One issue has been that the compilation of the time taken by various activities in an organization has been derived from interviews and surveys with individuals undertaking those activities. In a large organization this can be very time-consuming and expensive. It is also an exercise that organizations would not wish to repeat frequently so the original estimates become outdated. One could also question the credibility of the data. There could be an understandable tendency for individuals to over-estimate the time to demonstrate how hard they work!

The authors also questioned whether traditional ABC was suitable for complex operations. They pointed out that even shipping products could require a range of different approaches that could not be captured by a constant cost per order distributed.

The authors have proposed a model which simplifies ABC in two ways. First, managers are required to estimate resources by each product, transaction or customer. Two estimates are required: the cost per time unit of supplying resource capacity and the unit time of resource capacity consumption by each product, transaction or customer. This provides the additional information on how many minutes that staff members spend on activities in a particular time period.

The authors have also given guidance on how managers may best estimate these figures and then calculate the cost-driver rates. The claim is that time-driven ABC overcomes the difficulties and costs of implementing and maintaining a traditional ABC system and provides managers with cost and profit information quickly and inexpensively.

There have been several articles on variations on time-driven ABC and examples of organizations that have implemented it successfully. The proponents of the method write strongly in its favour but we would not take this as encouragement for all organizations to adopt it. As we observed in Chapter 10, it is for the organization to decide on which system best meets its needs. In doing so, it would change and mould the system so that it fits the organization and not for the organization to fit the system.

PREDETERMINED OVERHEADS

In the above discussions on both absorption- and activity-based costing, we have referred to the indirect costs without specifying the period of time in question. We have explained that an organization cannot wait until the end of a financial period when the actual overhead amount is known. To do so would delay decision making and even the timely invoicing of customers.

For this reason, overhead costs for the financial period, usually for a year, are predicted through a budgetary control system. Using these predictions of the overhead costs and activity levels, the allocation rate, whether machine hour, cost unit or any other basis, is calculated and applied using the predicted figures. The formula is:

Budgeted overhead costs for the coming financial period = Allocation rate

Estimated allocation base, for example, machine hours

Unfortunately, no matter how carefully budgets are determined, our financial predictions based on our strategy may not be completely valid. Also, we can expect that some of our predictions will not be 100 per cent accurate. If that is the case, the overhead charged to the products and services will be incorrect and we will be in one of the following two positions:

1. The amount of overhead charged will be too high. This is known technically as over-absorption or over recovery of overheads.

2. The amount of overhead charged will be too low. Technically this is known as under absorption of overhead.

The following example illustrates these points.

A company budgets for overhead costs for the coming financial year of £15,000. It also budgets for an activity level of 5000 cost units. The variable cost of each unit is £6.00. It uses the allocation rate of £3.00 (£15,000/5000) to charge out overheads. The total cost of one unit is assumed, therefore, to be £9.00.

At the end of the financial period the actual overheads are, in fact, £15,000 as budgeted. If, in addition, the level of activity is different than predicted we have the following scenarios.

Actual activity level Cost units	Charge out rate based on prediction	Overhead charged to production
6,000	£3.00	£18,000 (over absorption)
4,000	£3,00	£12,000 (under absorption)

At the higher level of activity, the overhead cost is in actual fact £2.50 (£15,000/6000 units) per unit and at the lower level of activity £3.75 (£15,000/4000 units). This is because overheads are fixed costs and stay the same in total but change per unit as activity levels change.

If managers are making decisions on the predicted costs of a unit, wrong choices will be made. They will be very surprised at the end of the year that their performance does not meet, or surpasses, expectations. To avoid the peril of these positions, the accountants will keep a track regularly on the overheads and activity levels that were budgeted and those that are actually incurred. Adjustments will be made to correct the position as the financial period progresses. However, there is a link between management accounting and financial accounting that we will expand on in the next section.

CRITICISMS OF TOTAL COSTING

Previously, we examined the concerns expressed on inventory valuations and we return to those again. Certainly, parts of absorption costing are arbitrary but the main concerns are aimed at the inclusion of period costs in closing inventory. Should, for example, depreciation on factory machinery be charged in total to the profit for the year or is it a part of the cost of the item and can therefore be transferred to the next year in closing inventory? A simple example will explain the issue.

For a manufacturing company with one product, the activities for Years 1 to 3 are shown in the following table.

Detail	Year 1	Year 2	Year 3
Number of units made	1,000	1,000	800
Variable costs per unit	£2.00	£2.00	£2.00
Fixed manufacturing cost	£5,000	£5,000	£5,000
Number of units sold	1,000	800	600
Selling price per unit	£10.00	£10.00	£10.00

The income statements for the two years would appear as follows:

	Year 1 £	Year 2 £	Year 3 £
Sales	10,000	8,000	6,000
Opening inventory			1,400
Variable costs	2,000	2,000	1,600
Fixed (period) costs	5,000	5,000	5,000
Total costs	7,000	7,000	8,000
Less closing inventory	–	1,400	3,300
Cost of goods sold	7,000	5,600	4,700
Profit/loss for period	3,000	2,400	1,300
Return on sales	30%	30%	21.7%

Closing stock Year 2

Total cost divided by number of units manufactured £7000/1000 = £7.00 per unit

Closing inventory is 200 units @ £7.00 = £1400

Closing stock Year 3

Total costs divided by number of units manufactured £6600/800 = £8.25 per unit

Closing inventory is 400 units @ £8.25 = £3300

On the face of it, Year 2 is reasonably successful as it still shows a return on sales of 30 per cent although the profit has reduced. This is because, through the use of absorption costing, part of the period costs have been transferred to Year 3 as part of closing inventory. That year is a financial disaster.

Through the years, commentators have questioned the use of absorption costing for the calculation of closing inventory. The arguments have become stronger because it is claimed that prior to the 2008 recession the big three auto makers in North America continued high production levels thus maintaining profits although their market was declining. The high number of units lowered the cost per vehicle and the closing inventory carried part of the period costs to the successive year.

The debate on the use of absorption costing was reignited by Foster and Baxendale (2008) who espoused the use of variable costing for the valuation of inventory. Financial accounting regulations require the use of absorption costing but it is worthwhile to consider the strengths and weaknesses of the method and the alternative of variable costing.

There is no easy answer but the following list of points are worthy of debate.

1. Absorption costing does what it sets out to do which is to calculate the total cost of the product. Closing inventory is therefore valued at its total cost which is correct.

2. In some industries the variable costs of manufacture are negligible.

3. Inventory values do not make sense unless period costs are included.

4. If only variable costs were used the inventory values shown on the balance sheet would be understated.

5. Investors should realize that if a company is continuing full production when there is a declining market, there are going to be problems.

6. Many people do not understand variable costing and will misunderstand the financial information.

7. Conceptually, period costs are for a specific period of time and should be charged against the profit for that period.

8. Companies can enhance profits with absorption costing by manufacturing items for inventory.

Discussion point

Given the potential problems caused by inventory valuation when using absorption costing, do you consider an alternative approach is required?

CONCLUSIONS

Managers need to know the total costs of their activities on a regular basis. Absorption costing has been the traditional method of calculating the total cost, but ABC is increasingly being used, particularly in service industries. The latter method has been improved by the application of a time-based approach.

Calculating direct costs causes few problems but the difficulty is with overheads. To ensure that the information is timely, predetermined overhead rates are calculated. The usefulness of this information relies on the accuracy of both the budgeted overheads and the predicted levels of activity.

Although the total cost of manufacturing units is essential information for management, it presents a conceptual issue. At the year end the closing inventory will be valued at the total cost, that is, including the overheads which are mostly fixed costs. These fixed costs relate to a period of time and should be charged to the sales in that period to calculate profit. However, the total cost of the closing inventory properly includes overheads and will therefore be charged to the following period.

A proposed answer to this dilemma is to use variable costs for the calculation of the closing inventory. It can be argued that by doing so the closing inventory is undervalued as the fixed costs are an integral part of the cost. In addition financial accounting regulations require the total cost.

RECOMMENDED READING

Foster, B. and Baxendale, S. (2008) 'The Absorption vs. Direct Costing Debate,' *Cost Management*, July/August, pp. 40–48.

Kaplan, R. S. and Anderson, S. R. (2004) 'Time-driven activity-based costing,' *Harvard Business Review* 82 (11), pp. 66–69.

CASE STUDY PREMIER CABINETS

Premier Cabinets designs and fits high-end kitchen cabinets to meet a client's particular needs. It has three departments Construction, Finishing and Installation. The detailed budget for the company for the next year has been prepared and the company wishes to allocate these amounts over the three departments.

The first five items the company has been able to allocate from its own records. The remainder of the items have to be allocated to each department using a fair but arbitrary basis.

Overhead Analysis

	Total	Construction	Finishing	Install
	£	£	£	£
Indirect materials	10,200	8,200	1,000	1,000
Maintenance	10,200	9,500	500	200

	Total	Construction	Finishing	Install
	£	£	£	£
Depreciation – machinery	8,150	6,650	1,000	500
Insurance – machinery	4,500	3,500	500	500
Power	6,500	5,500	500	500
Not allocated				
Rent (area)	60,000			
Cleaning (Area)	6,000			
Light and heat (Volume)	2,650			
Building depreciation (volume)	15,900			
Indirect wages (No. of employees	19,600			
Canteen (No. of employees)	23,800			
Building insurance (volume)	5,300			
Supervision (No. of employees)	42,000			
Total overhead	214,800			

(continued)

The company has drawn up the following information to assist in the allocation of overheads to the three departments
    Details of departmental structures

	Construction	Finishing	Install
	£	£	£
Area – square metres	5,000	2,000	3,000
Volume cubic meters	25,000	10,000	18,000
Number of employees	10	20	5
Budgeted labour hours for year	20,000	40,000	10,000

It has received an enquiry from a prospective client. A discussion on the design with the client allows Premier to make some calculations on the costs which it will incur.

Direct materials	£18,500
Wages	
Construction	£3,500
Finishing	£1,000
Install	£1,500

In addition it has calculated the following labour hours which are required to work on the job.

Construction	420 hours
Finishing	600 hours
Install	210 hours

Based on this information, calculate the total cost of the job to Premier Cabinets.

CHAPTER 12
CALCULATING VARIABLE AND INCREMENTAL COSTS

LEARNING OBJECTIVES

At the end of this chapter you should be able to:

- Explain cost behaviour at various levels of activity.
- Apply the high/low method to differentiate between fixed and variable costs.
- Calculate the contribution margin.
- Explain and apply CVP analysis.
- Apply contribution analysis.
- Demonstrate incremental costing.

EXECUTIVE SUMMARY

In decision making the assumed differing behaviours of fixed and variable when activity levels change are fundamental to various management accounting techniques. It is assumed that variable costs in total vary directly with changes in the level of activity and fixed costs in total stay the same irrespective of changes in the level of activity.

The division of variable/fixed costs can be used to calculate the Break Even Point (BEP) of production. This technique allows you to answer the question 'How many units do we have to produce and sell to break even, that is to make neither a profit nor a loss?'.

A more sophisticated approach is CVP Analysis. This is a most powerful tool for assisting short-term decision making. It uses the same basic assumptions that costs can be classified as either fixed or variable and that both costs and revenues are linear throughout the relevant range of activity. This difference between the selling price and variable cost per unit in known as the contribution margin. This concept can be used in management decisions on changes in selling prices, variable costs and fixed costs.

The calculation of the contribution margin can be used in such decisions as:

- Dropping a product line where the rule is if a product/division/department/factory is making a contribution to fixed overheads. It should not be discontinued unless there are other reasons to justify it.

- Pricing a special order where the rule is, assuming other things being equal, if an activity makes a contribution to fixed overheads it is worthwhile undertaking.

- Selecting the most profitable alternative where the rules are if the number of units sold is not material to your decision, select the alternative that gives the largest contribution per unit but if the number of units that are sold is material, select the alternative that gives you the largest total contribution margin.

- Dealing with a resource scarcity where the rule from is that if there is a scarce resource select the alternative that gives the largest contribution margin per dollar of scarce resource.

In certain situations requiring comparison of alternatives, it is quite possible that not only variable costs will be affected but also fixed costs. In this instance we are not only interested in variable costs but any costs that may be *relevant* to that particular decision, and this may include certain fixed costs.

Incremental Analysis, assumes that some fixed costs will change. The relevant costs are those that change. Relevant costs include opportunity costs and should be included. Sunk costs are irrelevant and should be excluded.

CONCEPTUAL AND PRACTICAL ISSUES

There are several stages in decisions making. First, specifying the problem or opportunity to be investigated. Secondly, identifying the feasible alternative options and selecting the decision model you intend to use. Next, collecting both quantitative and non-qualitative data in a form that will assist in making a decision. Finally, aggregating all the relevant information and comparing the various options.

In conducting the financial analysis the selected option will be calculated on a cost/benefit measure. You should incorporate any non-financial characteristics where possible as these may have a significant impact on the financial decision. Industry structure, market composition, ownership structure, demand and supply variables, interest rates, political changes, inflation or deflation, management compensation, regulatory changes and globalization can all influence the cost decisions you are making.

In the previous chapter we discussed total costing and how the total cost per unit included both the variable and fixed costs. This costing method has the great advantage in identifying the total cost of a cost unit but only at a specified level of activity. If the activity level changes, the total cost will change.

Many management decisions are concerned with actions and strategies which involve changes in activity levels. Questions such as 'If the activity level changes how will that affect our profits?' or 'How many units must we make to ensure a profit?' are the essence of managerial decision making. Variable or marginal costing provides the information for such decisions.

However, it is evident that the assumptions on cost behaviour can only hold in the short term. Property taxes, insurance, salaries tend to increase year after year irrespective of activity levels. Also, decisions about organizational change can involve fixed costs. Our final section on incremental costing argues that some decisions involve changes in both variable and fixed and this must be recognized.

COST BEHAVIOUR

FIXED AND VARIABLE COSTS

Few organizations have the good fortune to be in an environment where stability is the norm. Change is a feature of business life, whether it is changes in labour costs, material prices or consumer demand. Changes in costs can occur for a variety of reasons but we are interested in changes that are due to changes in levels of activity. The key definitions are:

Definition – Variable costs

Costs which remain the same per unit but in total change directly with changes in the level of activity.

The above definition can be shown diagrammatically (Figure 12.1).

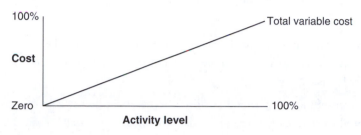

Figure 12.1 Variable cost behaviour

At zero activity there will be zero cost. As activity increases so does the total variable cost.

A simple example of a variable cost is direct material cost. If you are making a unit of a product that requires five metre of material at £4.00 per metre your cost for one cost unit is £20.00. If you make two units the total cost of direct materials is £40.00, 3 units £60.00 and so on.

The assumption is that the variable cost per unit stays the same regardless of changes in activity. Of course, the supplier of the materials may decide to increase the price. This is a decision which is not related to activity so our assumption holds true. There is also the possibility that as activity increases and more materials are required, the supplier may reduce the price above a certain order level. These issues will be discussed in the later section on the relevant range.

Definition – Fixed costs

Costs which in total remain the same irrespective of changes in the level of activity.

Figure 12.2 illustrates the above definition.

The fixed cost is assumed to be the same at zero activity and at 100 per cent of a firm's capacity.

If you consider fixed overhead costs, such as rent or insurance, you must pay these whether you are making 20 or 2000 units in the financial period. Changes in

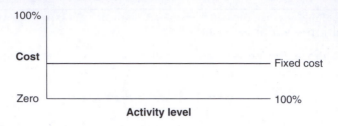

Figure 12.2 Fixed cost behaviour

activity levels will not result in changes to these costs. However, these costs may be subject to price increases, for example the landlord increasing the rent irrespective of activity levels.

Those costs that are defined as 'direct' costs must be variable costs. Labour in the production area is therefore usually defined as a variable cost. The more products that are manufactured the greater will be the labour cost. However, the reverse is not always true. Although production is declining, union agreements, company policy and government regulations may prevent a reduction in the labour force. In such circumstances labour can be a variable cost as production increases but show a tendency to be fixed as production falls.

Having given that word of caution, the following table demonstrates the way that variable, fixed and total costs are assumed to behave where production activity fluctuates. Our variable costs are £5.00 per unit and the fixed costs for a financial period are £10,000. Table 12.1 shows the differences in costs if activity fluctuates in the financial period.

Number of units	Variable costs		Fixed costs		Total costs	
	Total £	Per unit £	Total £	Per unit £	Total	Per unit
1,000	5,000	5.00	10,000	10.00	15,000	15.00
500	2,500	5.00	10,000	20.00	12,500	25.00
200	1,000	5.00	10,000	50.00	11,000	55.00
2,000	10,000	5.00	10,000	5.00	20,000	10.00
2,500	12,500	5.00	10,000	4.00	22,500	9.00

Table 12.1 Cost behaviour and changing activity levels

The above contrived and somewhat dramatic example demonstrates the impact of fluctuating activity and the substantial changes in the total cost per unit. It is doubtful that in real life organizations experience such massive swings in activity levels. However, in a competitive environment with tight profit margins even a slight decrease in activity can increase the total cost per unit and erode profits.

The example also demonstrates the impact on the total cost per unit when activity increases as the fixed costs are spread over more units. Both manufacturing and service organizations therefore concentrate on increasing productivity levels and thus reducing their total cost per unit. We discussed in the previous chapter the danger of maintaining production levels when there is a declining market. The fixed costs are merely being transferred into closing inventory for the next financial period.

Changes in technology can also have an influence on cost structures. In manufacturing there has been a decline in labour as mechanization has increased. Direct material may be the only significant variable cost. In service companies, direct labour may be the only substantial variable cost with little or no material cost. Even in the service sectors, the introduction of automated processes and procedures is changing this.

Having pointed out some weaknesses in the general assumption that variable costs respond directly and symmetrically to changes in activity levels, whether increasing or decreasing, there is an added complication. Research demonstrates that, in reality, is not the case. A phenomenon has been identified known as 'sticky cost' behaviour.

Studies have found that, as expected, total costs increase with activity increases but they decrease more slowly in response to equivalent activity decreases. A study of a sample of US, UK, French, and German firms revealed that operating costs are sticky in response to changes in revenues (Calleja et al., 2006).

On average, total operating costs increase by around 0.97 per cent per 1 per cent increase in revenues, but decrease by only 0.91 per cent per 1 per cent decrease in revenues. The research also concluded that costs tend to be less sticky over longer time-horizons and when firms sustain larger drops in revenue.

STEPPED COSTS

The assumption that fixed costs remain the same can only be acceptable in the short term. It is recognized that as activity increases above a certain level so additional operating capability must be added. This could be an extension to the factory, additional machinery, transport or supervision.

In the following example it is assumed that the company adds more machinery at 60 per cent activity and there is a further smaller amount at 80 per cent activity (Figure 12.3).

MIXED COSTS

Some costs are a mix of fixed and variable. The cost for the supply of power, for example, may well consist of a standard charge for the delivery of the power and a

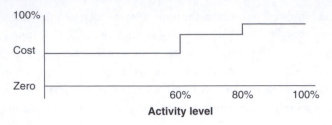

Figure 12.3 Stepped costs

variable cost representing the amount used. Sometimes, the cost of a service may decrease with greater usage. There are three methods that can be used to separate the total cost into the fixed and variable elements. They are:

Account Analysis

This is a frequently used method and requires management to use its professional judgement and experience to determine the division of the total cost into its fixed and variable elements. A manager with experience of the behaviour of costs incurred in production can make reasonable estimates.

Scatter graphs and regression analysis

Cost information from previous periods on a weekly or monthly basis and the division of the costs at various levels of activity can be identified.

High-low method

This is a popular method because it is a simple calculation and has an appealing logic. Using cost information from previous periods, the costs and activity at the highest level and the lowest level during the period are identified. The following formula is then used:

$$\frac{\text{Cost (highest level of activity } - \text{ lowest level of activity)}}{\text{Number of units (highest level of activity } - \text{ lowest level of activity)}}$$

The above formula is applied in the following table:

	Cost	Number of units
Highest level of activity	£50,000	5,000
Lowest level of activity	£40,000	3,000
Difference	£10,000	2,000

Assuming that fixed costs stay the same then the difference in the total costs of £10,000 must be due to variable costs and the increased activity of 2000 additional units. The variable cost per unit must be £10,000/2000 = £5.00. If we know the total cost and the total variable cost, the difference between the two must be the fixed cost. Proof is given by expanding the above table.

	Number of units	Total variable cost (Units × VC per unit)	Total Cost	Fixed cost Total cost – variable cost
Highest level of activity	5,000	£25,000	£50,000	£25,000
Lowest level of activity	3,000	£15,000	£40,000	£25,000

The distinction between fixed and variable costs is extremely useful in making decisions. The following survey of UK companies in the food and drink industries demonstrates the importance and we expect the pattern would be similar for many industries. The survey also reveals the extent of the application of techniques we discussed in previous chapters.

LINK TO PRACTICE

Costing systems in the food and drink industry

	N.	Frequency of use		
		Rarely/never	Sometimes	Often/very often
Separation of variable and fixed costs	116	24	28	48
Plant wide overhead rate	115	65	12	23
Departmental or multiple plant wide overhead rates	113	63	24	13
Activity-based costing	114	76	13	10
Target costs	112	55	21	24
Cost of quality	111	68	18	14
Regression/learning curve techniques	111	95	4	2

Table 2 Management accounting practices

Adapted from Abdel-Kader, M. and Luther, R (2006) *Management Accounting Practices in the UK Food and Drink Industry*. Chartered Institute of Management Accountants

BREAK EVEN ANALYSIS

One issue most organizations confront is the level at which activity must occur so that they do not make a loss or, preferably, they make a targeted amount of profit. The assumption that fixed and variable costs behave differently in periods of fluctuating activity can be used to identify the number of units to be produced and sold in order to break even. A product is said to break even when it makes neither a profit nor a loss. The formula used is:

$$P£0 = SP(x) - VC(x) - TFC$$

Where

$P = $ Profit

$SP = $ Selling Price per Unit

$VC = $ Variable Cost per Unit

$TFC = $ Total Fixed Cost

$X = $ number of units

The number of units required to break even (B/E) can be found by conducting the following calculation.

$$B/E = \frac{TFC}{SP - VC} = \text{Number of units}$$

The selling price (SP) per unit minus the variable cost (VC) per unit gives the contribution margin or contribution per unit. This is a very important concept which will be used in several examples.

A simple example will demonstrate the calculation. An organization makes a product where the variable costs are £6.00 and the fixed cost for the period is £10,000. The selling price is £8.00.

$$\frac{£10,000}{£8.00 - £6.00} = 5000 \text{ units}$$

The mathematics is easy to understand but the intriguing question is the nature of the difference of £2.00 between the selling price and the variable cost. This is the contribution margin and is the amount that each unit contributes towards the total fixed cost. It is not until the total fixed cost has been recovered do we start to make a profit. In this example the BEP is 5000 units.

The above relationships can be shown in the form of a break even graph or chart. A basic example is shown below. The activity levels are shown on the horizontal (X) axis and the pounds on the vertical (Y) axis. The total fixed costs stay the same throughout the entire activity. Thus, if the activity is zero the fixed cost is the same as if the activity were 100 per cent.

At zero activity, the variable costs are zero but the total costs will equal the fixed costs. As activity increases the variable costs will increase in a linear relationship and this is demonstrated by the total cost line.

Obviously, at zero activity the revenue is zero and this is plotted as such. Once again we will assume that revenue increases in a linear fashion. The point where the revenue line and the total cost line intersect is known as the BEP. Above that point we make a profit and below that point we make a loss (Figure 12.4).

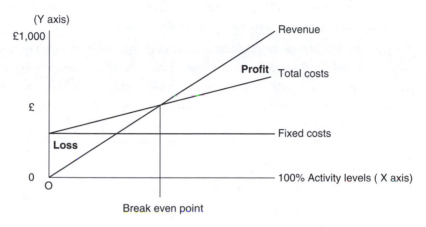

Figure 12.4 Break even graph

It is easy to identify the BEP in the above chart, both in terms of pounds and volumes. It is also possible to plot on the chart the margin of safety.

Definition – Margin of safety

This is the difference between the level of actual or planned level of activity and the break even point.

The margin of safety measures the amount by which the level of activity can reduce before the company arrives at its BEP and then starts to make losses. The margin of safety can be measured in units of production or sales, sales value or in percentage terms.

In structuring the above chart we have made some major simplifying assumptions about cost behaviour. We have assumed that fixed and variable costs and even revenues will be perfectly linear over the full range of activity. This is highly unlikely and the revenues and costs may change.

As discussed above, fixed costs are likely to demonstrate a stepped progression. As activity increases, at certain levels a company will have to expand its capacity. This may mean increasing factory space or introducing more machinery or equipment. These additions will cause an increase in the fixed costs.

Variable costs are also likely to change over the full range of activity. It is not to do primarily with changes in price. Direct labour costs in the first few periods may be higher per unit because the workforce has a learning curve before they reach optimum efficiency. Material usage may also vary because of changes in production efficiency and wastage at different levels of activity.

Finally, our revenue may change because at higher levels of production because we offer discounts to our customers above a certain quantity purchased.

Because our simplifying assumptions are not valid over the complete range of activity, we can only make decisions and draw conclusions where the costs behave according to our assumptions. This range of activity where our assumptions are deemed to hold good is known as the relevant range.

Definition – Relevant range

The range of two activity levels between which valid assumptions can be made about cost behaviour. Outside this range, the assumed relationship between fixed costs, variable costs and revenues may not apply.

CVP ANALYSIS

The break even analysis shows us the level of activity where neither a profit nor loss is made, but the underlying concepts can be used to expand this basic information. Cost Volume Profit (CVP) analysis uses the same basic assumptions that costs can be classified as either fixed or variable and that both costs and revenues are linear throughout the relevant range of activity.

If our selling price and variable cost per unit are assumed to remain the same the difference, the contribution margin, between the two will remain the same per unit but will increase or decrease in *total* as activity changes. For example, when the contribution per unit is £2.00, the total contribution margin for ten units would be £20 and for 50 units the total contribution margin would be £100.

The contribution per unit or contribution margin and can be expressed as:

$$CM = SP - VC$$

Where SP is the selling price per unit and VC is the variable cost per unit. This is a most powerful tool for assisting short-term decision making. Before we go any further we can use basic data to demonstrate the usefulness of the contribution margin.

Where our revenue is £8 per unit and our variable costs per unit is £6 the contribution margin is £2. This is not a profit! It is a contribution towards covering the total fixed cost and, once those have been recovered, the profit. If our fixed costs are £16,000 and our contribution margin is £2 per unit our BEP is £16,000/£2 per unit = 8000 units. If we wished to make a profit of £4000 then the total number of units we would need to make and sell is:

$$\text{Total Fixed cost} + \text{Target profit} = £16,000 + £4,000 = £20,000/£2 = 10,000\,\text{units}$$

Contribution margin can be thought of as that part of the selling price per unit that goes towards recovering the total fixed cost. Once the total fixed costs have been recovered, in other words you have reached break even; the unit contribution margin is the amount each unit sale adds to profit.

If the contribution margin of a product is known, it is easy to calculate the BEP and the profit or loss at different levels of activity. You can also quickly see how any increase or decrease in the revenue or variable cost per unit immediately impacts on the contribution margin and your BEP.

For example, you may have a product with a selling price of £15 and the variable costs are £11. The contribution margin is £4. In a financial period the fixed costs are £60,000.

1. How many products do you need to sell to break even?
    Answer: £60,000/£4 = 15,000 units

2. You can increase the selling price to £16 and thus increase the contribution margin to £5.
    The BEP is now £60,000/£5 = 12,000 units

3. You can reduce the variable costs to £10 per unit by investing in more machinery thus increasing your fixed costs to £66,000 in a financial period. The selling price is £16 per unit.
    New contribution margin is £6 per unit so BEP is £66,000/£6 = 11,000 units.

These are only simple examples but illustrate the flexibility of the technique. Once it is established that variable costs stay the same per unit, several types of decisions can be explored. But remember that we are using a short-term decision-making technique that makes several assumptions.

We have used a production example to explain the concept of contribution margin but the technique is valuable in a wide range of activities including to measure efficiency in the operating room of a hospital.

This study emphasizes the information value of CVP analysis and the simplicity of its application. It should be remembered that the identification of variable costs and the prediction of their behaviour during different activity levels may be difficult.

We can take a further step in our CVP analysis by calculating the Contribution Margin Ratio. This is the percentage of contribution margin divided by the selling price per unit:

$$CMR = \frac{SP - VC}{SP} = \frac{CM}{SP}$$

where

CMR = contribution margin per unit

SP = selling price per unit

VC = variable cost per unit

CM = contribution margin per unit

The important principle in the application of this technique is that the contribution margin ratio will be the same for one unit or for the total production. This means that it can be used to ascertain the amount of sales pounds needed to earn a specific amount of profit by using the following formula:

$$\text{Total sales in pounds} = \frac{\text{Target profit (TP)} + \text{Total fixed costs (TFC)}}{\text{Contribution margin ratio (CMR)}}$$

The following example shows the calculation of the contribution margin ratio (CMR) for one unit and the calculation of the sales pounds needed to achieve a certain amount of profit.

Example

A company has a product with a selling price of £10 and variable costs of £6. In the financial period its fixed costs are expected to be £160,000 and it has budgeted for a profit of £40,000.

Contribution margin ratio $= SP - VC = £10 - £6 = £4$.

$$\frac{£4}{£10} = 40\% \text{ or } 0.4$$

Sales in pounds to achieve £40,000 profit $= \dfrac{TP + TFC}{CMR} = \dfrac{£200,000}{0.4} = £500,000$

Proof		
Sales	50,000 units at £10 each	£500,000
Less:		
Variable costs £6 each		£300,000
Fixed costs		£160,000
Profit		£40,000

MULTIPLE PRODUCT ANALYSIS

So far in this chapter we have assumed that there is only one product. In reality there is likely to be several products. The question is how do we apply the concepts of break even and contribution margin in such a situation? If a company has a range of products that are basically similar with differences in variable costs and contribution margins, the weighted average contribution margin can be used as in the following example.

WORKED EXAMPLE – TWINNERS PLC.

Twinners plc. produces a similar product with two model types: the 'Standard' and the 'Leader'. Three 'Standard' models are sold for every one 'Leader'. The budgeted fixed costs for the financial period are £500,000 and the revenue and variable cost per unit figures are:

	Standard model	Leader Model
	£	£
Selling price	90	120
Less Variable costs	70	80
Contribution margin	20	40

$$\text{Weighted average contribution margin} = \frac{3(\pounds20) + 1(\pounds40)}{4 \, \text{units}} = \pounds25.00 \, \text{per unit}$$

To break even the company would have to sell the following number of units:

$$\text{BEP in units} = \frac{\text{Total fixed costs}}{\text{Weighted average CM}} = \frac{\pounds500,000}{\pounds25.00} = 20,000 \, \text{units}$$

The total of 20,000 units would comprise the ratio of 3:1 units so the Standard would sell 15,000 (20,000/4 × 3) units and the Leader would sell the remaining 5000 units.

Proof	Standard	Leader	Total
Number of units	15,000	5,000	20,000
Sales	£1,350,000	£600, 000	£1,950,000
Variable costs	£1,050,000	£400,000	£1,450,000
Contribution margin	£300,000	£200,000	£500,000
Less fixed costs			£500,000

You will note that in this example we have not allocated the fixed costs to the two different models but deducted them from the total contribution. We will see the application of this approach again later in the chapter.

PROCEDURE FOR CVP ANALYSIS

CVP analysis must be set in a context. It can appear easy to calculate the contribution analysis and make a decision, but it must be tied into the economic environment in which the company operates and be related to the company's strategy.

In Chapter 15 we discuss strategic management accounting but we will use some of the terms in describing the procedure for CVP analysis. You can refer to these later.

PROCEDURE FOR CVP ANALYSIS

1. Macro analysis of the industry. This will assess the current state of the industry, the markets, the competitors and a prediction of future trends.

2. Micro analysis that attempts to determine the company's best strategy.

3. Business strategy analysis which will be a detailed assessment of the company's mission and vision statement. It would also be useful to complete a value chain analysis which is discussed in Chapter 15.

4. If the data is available, a CVP analysis of the company's financial performance for the last five years.

LIMITATIONS OF CVP ASSUMPTIONS

We have emphasized the limitations of our assumptions, but that does negate the concepts of break even and contribution margin and the value of the techniques. These concepts are extremely useful for assisting in making a range of decisions irrespective of the limitations which are:

Fixed costs

In practice these will not stay at the same level over the full range of activity. As activity increases a stage will be reached where a company must invest in additional resources. This will introduce an incremental element of fixed cost which behaves in a stepped manner which we explained previously.

Variable costs

Variable costs per unit are unlikely to stay the same over the full range of activity. In the early stages labour costs per unit may be higher as productivity is low as the employees have to go through a learning curve. We then enter the relevant range where the variable costs are linear but they may increase per unit at the upper end of activity due to overtime payments or excess wastage due to human error. Similarly, direct material costs per unit may fluctuate but decrease as activity increases as volume discounts and other reductions may be possible.

Discretionary costs

Some costs are fixed and there is very little that can be done easily to change, for example, the property tax or the depreciation on machinery. There are some costs, such as advertising, research and employee training which may be considered to be discretionary. Managers may decide to increase or decrease such costs irrespective of activity levels. In a declining market, employee training will often be the first sacrifice.

Activity measurement

There may be more than one method for measuring activity. We have used the general term 'a unit of production', but in some industries such identification may not be so easy. For example, in the transport industry, fuel costs will be influenced by the distance to be travelled and the weight of the load to be transported. In such cases a hybrid unit may be required.

Inventory

We assume that the amount sold exactly equals the amount produced and there is no inventory. If a company maintains low or constant inventory levels then there is no problem. If there are significant changes in inventory levels during the financial period it may be necessary to build this into the analysis.

CONTRIBUTION ANALYSIS

FINANCIAL CONTRIBUTION STATEMENTS

This is a term that is used loosely to refer to the concept of what can be termed as either a contribution margin statement or a variable cost statement. In other words, a financial statement that concentrates on variable costs and ignores fixed costs. This approach changes your product cost and the cost of inventory.

WORKED EXAMPLE – TWOTOES LTD.

In the following example, we show the product cost per unit figure using both total costing and variable costing for a company that produced 10,000 units in the financial period and sold 9500 at £6.00 per unit with the remaining 500 units going into the inventory at the end of the period. Direct materials are £4.00 per unit and variable overhead £1.00 per unit

Using full costing the fixed overhead of £12,000 has been charged to the cost unit on the basis of the number of units produced.

Total costing

Cost per unit

	£
Direct costs	4.00
Variable overheads	1.00
Fixed overhead (12,000/10,000)	1.20
Total full cost per unit	6.20

Value of closing inventory is 500 units at £6.20 per unit = £3100.

Variable costing

Cost per unit

	£
Direct costs	4.00
Variable overheads	1.00
Total variable cost per unit	5.00

Value of closing inventory is 500 units at £5.00 per unit = £2500.

	Total costing		Variable costing	
	£	£	£	£
Sales (9,500 at £6.00)		57,000		57,000
Production cost of goods made (10,000)				
Direct costs	40,000		40,000	
Fixed costs	12,000		12,000	12,000
Total cost of production	52,000		52,000	
Less closing inventory (500 units)	3,100		2,500	
Cost of goods sold		48,900		49,500
Profit		8,100		7,500

As the closing inventory under variable costing excludes the fixed overhead there are two differences when compared to the total cost approach. The value of our closing inventory is lower and our profit is lower. This is because the fixed period costs have been written off in the financial period.

The significance of the difference in costing methods on inventory valuation and profits is not important in many companies as inventories are maintained at a low and consistent level. It should also be noted that for financial accounting and reporting purposes companies are required to use total costing for inventory valuation. However, it is important that you should realize the distinction and the main guidelines are:

- If the units produced are equal in number to the units sold there is no difference in profit.
- If the units produced are higher than the units sold, total costing will give a higher profit.
- If the units produced are lower than the units sold, variable costing will give a higher profit. This would only occur if there was an opening inventory.

DROPPING A PRODUCT LINE

A major strategic decision made by any company will be whether to drop a product line, or close a division, or a factory. Often, this will not just be a financial decision. A company will be considering its strategic position, the possible loss of goodwill of customers and suppliers, the actions of competitors and the response of the workforce. However, financial information will be a major factor influencing the decision.

The problem will be the treatment of fixed costs and the following example demonstrates the issues. We use the figures for Twinners plc. example explained under Multiple Product Analysis. We will make a slight change, however and delete the contribution margin line and allocate the total fixed costs of £500,000 based on the ratio of the number of units sold.

	Standard	Leader	Total
Number of units	15,000	5,000	20,000
Sales	£1,350,000	£600,000	£1.950,000
Variable costs	£1,050,000	£400,000	£1,450,000
Fixed costs	£375,000	£125,000	£500,000
Total costs	£1,425,000	£525,000	£1,950,000
Profit/(loss)	(£75,000)	£75,000	£0

The total impact on the bottom line is the same as if we had not allocated the fixed costs: we have broken even. The problem arises where managers without much financial knowledge receive this information. An immediate response is to suggest that the product line 'Standard' is dropped as it is making a loss. Of course, if Standard was dropped all the fixed costs would be charged to Leader and it would make a substantial loss.

The questions to ask in these situations are:

1. Do we need to allocate the fixed overheads?

2. If we discontinue any one of the models will this lead to a reduction in fixed overheads?

3. Is the model making a contribution to overheads?

The allocation of fixed overheads may be on a reasonable basis but the issue is whether we can reduce fixed costs by dropping the Standard model and whether this model is making a contribution. In the absence of other information we will assume that there will be no reduction in fixed costs and as the Standard model makes a significant contribution of £300,000 towards covering fixed costs then the model should be retained.

As a general guideline we can state:

If a product/division/department/factory is making a contribution towards fixed overheads, it should not be discontinued.

PRICING SPECIAL ORDERS

Frequently managers are confronted with the possibility of winning a large order but only if a reduction in the normal selling price can be negotiated. Obviously, the manager will have to consider the impact on other customers, the possibility of this 'special deal' being repeated and on the larger strategic direction of the company. To assist in the decision the application of the contribution margin can be very useful. We will use the example from the last section but restrict our discussions to the Standard model.

Number of units	15,000
Sales (£90 per unit)	£1,350,000
Variable costs	£1,050,000
Fixed costs	£375,000
Total costs	£1,425,000
Profit/(loss)	(£75,000)

Let us assume that a new customer offers to buy 8000 units but at £80.00 per unit instead of £90.00. With variable costs of £70.00 per unit, this would give an additional contribution of £80,000 £(80 − 70 × 8000 units). If fixed costs remain at the same level this £80,000 would clear the current 'loss' and put the 'Standard' into a profit position on a total cost basis.

There are several issues that need to be investigated before a final decision can be made. These are:

- Is there spare capacity to allow the order to be fulfilled?
- Will there be any impact on fixed costs?
- Will the customer expect future deliveries at this price?
- Will other customers expect to enjoy the lower price?
- How does this fit in with the strategy of the company?

Of course, if the company uses total costing the increase in the number of Standard units will lead to a greater allocation of fixed overheads.

If the above questions can be answered satisfactorily, the guideline is:

If a 'special order' makes a contribution to fixed overheads it is worthwhile undertaking.

SELECTING THE MOST PROFITABLE ALTERNATIVE

Usually a company will have a range of products and may wish to concentrate its attention on that product that makes the most 'profit'. Once again, the contribution margin can be used to rank the products that produce the greatest benefits.

We can repeat the details from the example of Twinners plc. which had two models of their product with the following unit selling price and costs.

	Standard model	Leader Model
	£	£
Selling price	90	120
Less variable costs	70	80
Contribution margin	20	40

Given the choice of receiving £20 contribution margin to fixed costs or £40 it is safe to say that most would choose the latter. Assuming that it is just as easy to sell the Leader model as it is to sell the Standard model and there are no significant barriers, the general rule for ranking products is to concentrate on making the product that gives the highest contribution margin per unit first, in order to cover the fixed costs the fastest and start making the business a profit as quickly as possible. The fixed costs do not need to be considered in this decision because it is assumed that they remain unchanged by the choice of model produced.

One must be cautious in jumping to decisions based on contribution per unit data. What must also be considered is the size of the market for each product and the total contribution that can be generated. If either 8000 units of the Standard model or 5000 units of the Leader model can be sold in one month, the total contribution margin for each product will be:

Total contribution margin = Contribution margin per unit × Number of units sold

	Standard model	**Leader model**
Total contribution margin	£20 × 8000 = £160,000	£40 × 5000 = £200,000

If one has to choose between the models, it is better to generate £200,000 contribution from the Leader model towards fixed overheads. If a reasonable prediction of sales can be made it makes more financial sense to rank products on the basis of the total contribution margin. The guideline is:

Choose the product with the largest contribution per unit unless the number of units that can be sold differ among products. In this case you select the alternative that gives the largest total contribution.

UNIT CONTRIBUTION AND TOTAL CONTRIBUTION

We have concentrated on unit contribution but there are situations where a decrease in unit contribution can be offset because it leads to an increase in total contribution through an increase in the sales volume. Using the Standard model the present situation is:

Sales volume	15,000
Selling price per unit	£90
Variable costs per unit	£70
Contribution margin	£20

Imagine the scenario where the Sales Director proposes that the quality of the product can be improved but at an additional cost of £2. Unfortunately, the market is very competitive and the selling price cannot be increased but the sales volume will increase to 20,000 units. The comparison is:

Old design 15,000 units × £20 = £300,000 contribution margin

New design 20,000 units × £18 = £360,000 contribution margin

Although the proposal appears worthwhile, an examination of the fixed costs would need to be made to ensure that they would not increase and to verify the sales prediction.

LIMITING FACTORS

A company cannot expand indefinitely with just the same products. Usually the size of the market limits growth. But there may be some scarcity of resource or other limiting factor, such as shortages of materials or labour, a restriction on the sales demand at a particular price, or the production capacity of machinery.

Where a company experiences a limiting factor, whether it is a ceiling on sales growth or a shortage of materials, managers must ensure that the contribution margin per limiting factor is maximized. The formula that is used is:

$$\text{Contribution margin per limiting factor} = \frac{\text{Contribution margin per unit}}{\text{Limiting factor per unit}}$$

Using our example of Twinners plc. again we will assume that variable costs represent a limiting factor that could be direct materials or direct labour. We will assume that material is in short supply and the Standard model requires 3.5 lbs. of material and the Leader model requires 4 lb. If we divide our contribution margin per unit by the materials per unit, we obtain the following result.

	Standard model	Leader model
Contribution margin per unit	£20 = £5.72	£40 = £10
Limiting factor per unit	3.5 lbs.	4 lbs

If there are no other considerations, it is best to concentrate on the Leader model that gives a contribution margin of £10 per unit compared to £5.72 from the Standard model. If we find that there is a restricted demand for the Leader model, once that demand was met we would switch the limited resource to the production of the Standard model. The guideline is:

If there is a limiting factor, select the alternative that gives the largest contribution margin per pound of scarce resource.

INCREMENTAL ANALYIS

In this chapter we have concentrated on variable costs and the contribution margin. When comparing alternative courses of action we have assumed that fixed costs will not be affected. This is a very narrow approach and there are situations where fixed costs are important. An alternative to variable costing that does not omit potentially important fixed cost data is Incremental Analysis also known as Relevant Costing.

When conducting incremental analysis, we are concerned only with costs relevant to the decision we have to make. The information that is relevant is where:

1. the costs or benefits relate to the future; and

2. the costs or benefits differ between the alternatives.

When calculating relevant costs, we ignore irrelevant costs. Irrelevant costs include fixed costs that do not change in the future. However, where fixed costs are likely to change where certain decisions are made, they should be included. The technique removes the constraints of total costing but is not an alternative to it. It also completely disregards the fixed/variable cost classification that we have used so far.

We also take into account relevant costs such as **opportunity costs and sunk costs**. Opportunity costs are the benefits foregone when we choose one alternative over another. For example, if you have to give up your job to go back to college, then the salary foregone is the opportunity cost of your decision to return to college.

Sunk costs are costs that have been incurred in the past and, thus, are irrelevant as they cannot be changed. However, there is a psychological tendency for decision makers to include sunk costs as relevant in an effort to 'recover' sunk costs (Kahneman and Tversky, 1979) or a tendency to accelerate commitments to sunk costs (Whyte, 1986). In this respect, managers and management accountants must take care to separate sunk costs from future differential costs.

Possibly one of the most confusing aspects of sunk costs is the issue of depreciation which managers see as an on-going cost – even into the future – until the asset is completely written off. An example below of Oldtimes demonstrates that the acquisition of an asset in the past cannot influence a future decision although there is a current depreciation cost.

Worked example – Oldtimes

Oldtimes have a press machine which costs £20,000 when it was bought ten years ago. Its remaining life is ten years. The annual operating costs of the press machine are £60,000 per annum. A new and far more efficient press can be purchased for £12,000 but it will have a life of only one year. Its operating costs would be £40,000.

The decisions are:

	Keep old press £	Buy new press £	Difference £
Depreciation over next 10 years	10,000		10,000
Write off old press immediately		10,000	10,000
Depreciation of new press		12,000	12,000
Operating costs	60,000	40,000	(20,000)
Total cost	70,000	62,000	(8,000)

The depreciation does not change. It is going to be £10,000 written off over the next ten years or, if the old press is disposed of, £10,000 written off immediately. As these amounts are the same there is no difference. The purchase of the old press is therefore a sunk cost and should not appear in our calculations.

By buying the new press, the company will make cost savings of £8000 and the purchase would be the correct decision. Of course, the old press could possibly be sold. If so, the amount received would appear as a further benefit if the new press were purchased.

A further example of the incremental analysis technique completes this section.

Worked example – Maisie Exeter Ltd

Maisie Exeter Ltd. manufactures insulation tape for domestic use. It supplies the tape to hardware retailers at £6 per metre. Its variable costs are £2 per metre. Its current production output is 6000 metres per month and it is contemplating increasing that production by 50 per cent per month. Fixed costs would not be affected.

The only change in the figures will be the 50 per cent increase in revenue and variable costs. The contribution margin is £4 per metre and an extra 3000 metres will give an additional contribution margin of £12,000.

Upon further investigation, the company determines that the increased production will also increase fixed costs by £10,000 per month. Our analysis so far shows that the additional contribution margin covers the additional fixed costs to give a profit of £2000. But as fixed costs will also change we may wish to draw up a simple statement of all the relevant revenues and costs.

Incremental cost statement

	£
Incremental sales (3000 metres £6)	18,000
Incremental variable costs (3000 metres @ £2)	(6,000)
Incremental fixed costs	(10,000)
Profit	2,000

Not surprisingly, we arrive at the same conclusion using the two techniques. Managers sometimes wonder which is the best technique: Contribution Analysis or Incremental Analysis. Both of the techniques are concerned with identifying the relevant costs when making the decision. The relevant costs are those that change. In Contribution Analysis the assumption is made that only variable costs will change and fixed costs remain the same. In Incremental Analysis there is the realization that some fixed costs will change.

The questions you need to ask when selecting the appropriate technique are:

1. What is the decision that needs to be made?
2. What are the alternatives?
3. What cost information do we have or can obtain?
4. Can we classify the costs into fixed and variable components?
5. Will only the variable costs change?
6. Will some of the fixed costs change?

If you have the information and only variable costs change, use Contribution Analysis. If fixed costs are also likely to change use Incremental Analysis. Contribution Analysis does have the advantage of being very flexible in its application. Incremental Analysis has the advantage of ensuring that all relevant costs, both fixed and variable, are taken into account.

CONCLUSIONS

The concepts of fixed and variable costs have underpinned most management accounting techniques. CVP analysis, contribution analysis and various forms of variable costing are valuable tools. The calculation of the contribution margin continues to be a valuable guide for management when making decisions.

The lessening importance of variable costs and the increasing importance of fixed costs mean that the latter increasingly must be included in deliberations. Incremental Analysis, which also goes under the titles of differential costing and relevant costing attempts to address the balance. The focus is not on the fixed and variable cost distinction but on which costs change where there are alternative courses of action.

RECOMMENDED READING

Guigdra, F., Horrigan, J. O. and Craycraft, C. (1998) 'CVP analysis: a new look.' *Journal of Managerial Issues.* Vol 10, No 1, pp. 74–85.

Adelman, R. L. (1983) 'The marginal contribution break-even point.' *The CPA Journal*. Vol 53, No 10, Retrieved, 6 February 2013 from ABI?INFORM Global (Document ID: 212251886).

CASE STUDY GREEN PASTURES LTD

Cynthia Chard is the owner of Green Pastures Ltd which has for several years manufacturing garden furniture. Her main products have been chairs, tables and sun-umbrellas. She is contemplating extending the business by manufacturing and selling garden ornaments. She has sketched the designs for the ornaments: one being a small boy fishing (The Robert) and the other being a small girl smelling a posy of flowers (The Chanel).

The impetus for this decision has arisen from two factors:

1. There is space in her current factory to permit additional manufacturing.

2. Her main stream output generates scrap material which could be used for the ornaments. At present, she is able to sell the scrap materials for £2.00 per pound.

She has asked you to help her determine whether the project is worthwhile. The difficulty is that Cynthia, although extremely entrepreneur and a good sales person, has little financial knowledge. Currently she sells the scrap material at £2.00 per pound and considers that any price above that must give her a 'profit'.

After discussions with her you manage to ascertain the following information:

1. She has done market research and she believes in a year she can sell 1000 of each of the models. Comparing to similar products she believes she can sell the Robert for £40 and the Chanel for £55.

2. She considers that the ornaments will have a longer season that the garden furniture and it would be easier to store any inventory which remains unsold at the end of the prolonged season.

3. The Robert would require1.5 lb. of materials and The Chanel 2.0 lb.

4. She can use existing labour to make the models when there is a lull in the demand for garden furniture. They are all part-time employees, working irregular hours and they would be pleased of the opportunity to earn extra income. She would pay them £6.00 for each Robert and £7.00 for each Chanel.

5. The models will need finishing and presentation packaging and she believes this will cost £3.00 for The Robert and £4.00 for the Chanel.

6. She argues that there will be no delivery costs as the models will be delivered at the same time as the garden furniture. Her logic is that the vans will be delivering anyway so how can there be an additional cost.

7. Similarly, she argues that there are no manufacturing overheads as the factory is there anyway with empty space, so how can there be an additional cost. The new venture should only take about 10 per cent of the factory space. Last year she believed it cost about £250,000 to run the factory.

8. Similarly she argues that no administrative costs will be involved as it is only a matter of adding a small amount of additional information on the existing records.

Cynthia asks whether you agree that it is better to make the ornaments than to sell the scrap material and to give her the figures so support your recommendations. In particular she wants to know which of the ornaments is the most profitable.

In preparing your report for Cynthia you want to give her the facts but also you are aware that her financial knowledge is limited. You also want to include in your report any misgivings you may have about the way she views the project.

After you have sent Cynthia your report she phones you to say that there is a manufacturing problem and the supply of materials for the first month is limited for technical reasons. In view of this she has decided to concentrate the manufacturing on the model which is the most profitable. How do you respond?

CHAPTER 13
PLANNING AND CONTROL

LEARNING OBJECTIVES

At the end of this chapter you should be able to:

- Discuss the use of budgets in planning and control.
- Prepare a production budget.
- Explain the potential impact of budgetary control on managers' behaviour.
- Explain the value of flexible budgets.
- Discuss how standard costs are developed.
- Calculate and interpret direct material variances.
- Calculate and interpret direct labour variances.
- Discuss techniques for understanding variances.

EXECUTIVE SUMMARY

Organizations seek to achieve both short-term and long-term strategies by monitoring and controlling progress towards them. The strategies will, in part, be expressed financially and comparisons will be regularly conducted of actual performance against the plans. An analysis may provide information that suggests that plans be revised or provide evidence that actual performance does not meet expectations and corrective action must be taken.

Two techniques, budgetary control and standard costing, are widely used for planning and control purposes. Both of the techniques require plans to be made of required performance and regularly financial reports are produced which compare actual performance for a period of time against the plans. Where there are differences, which are known as variances, between actual performance and the plan, the techniques provide signposts to the possible problems.

Budgetary control is found in some form in most manufacturing and service organizations. There are various approaches to setting budgets but the final analysis is the comparison of planned performance with actual performance and the identification of the differences. The variances are performance measures, both for the organization and individual managers. Because of the importance of budgets in identifying managers' performance, the consequences for human behaviour, such as setting slack budgets, is frequently observed.

Budgets may be fixed for the financial period. These are sometimes referred to as static budgets. Budgets may also be flexible and adjusted to the level of activity which took place in the financial period.

Standard costing is a technique routinely used in large manufacturing organizations for product costs, it can also be found in the service sector. The technique is very close to the daily production process and may be integrated with the budgetary control system in an organization. The basic standards are direct materials and direct labour, although some companies expand on this to calculate sales and overhead variances.

CONCEPTUAL AND PRACTICAL ISSUES

Budgetary control is less of a pure accounting technique and more of a management tool. It is linked to strategy and is used not only as part of the planning process but also to measure managerial performance.

Budgets are normally set for one year, and expressed on a monthly basis to show the expected financial performance. This requires a considerable degree of forecasting ability by managers. If the budget period starts in January 2016 you may be asked in early autumn of 2015 to contribute to setting the plans for your own area for the year 2016. One of the aspects of a good system is that budgets are disseminated *prior* to the commencement of the financial period.

In constructing the budgets, individual budgets are set for the main functions. The budgets for the functions must be integrated. For example, the production department must be making plans to satisfy the prediction of the sales department. Once functional budgets are integrated a master budget can be prepared showing the expected financial performance for the entire organization.

Needless to say, the path of integration can become a highly politicized process. For a manager, the functional budget lays down the performance they are required to achieve for the coming year. By setting out the organizational *financial and managerial strategies* and the actions that must be taken to achieve them, managers at all levels are making business plans that help to meet the financial objectives.

Although some organizations adopt a system where all the budgets are determined at the highest level, it is usual for individual managers to be involved in setting the budget for their own function. As the actual results for the period are compared to the budget, it is not surprising that some managers attempt to set budgets which are going to reflect favourably on their abilities to perform. It is also possible that some managers will wish to build 'slack' into their budget so they will not have to work so hard to achieve the planned performance.

Research shows that where managers participate in the budgeting process, the system is improved and the commitment of managers to achieving the budget is greater. It must be remembered, however, that the directors of a company will be seeking to respond favourably to the expectations of investors and lenders. A participative system that does not deliver the financial results that some constituents demand will not continue for long.

BUDGETARY CONTROL SYSTEMS

Definition – Budget

A budget is a formal document which is a financial representation of the strategy of an organization.

A typical budget:

- relates to a defined time period (usually 12 months divided into shorter periods);
- is designed and approved well in advance of the period to which it relates;

- shows expected income and expenditure;
- identifies responsibility levels for various parts of the budget;
- includes all capital and revenue expenses likely to be incurred in furthering the organization's strategic objectives; and
- is not an accounting exercise but a managerial planning and control system.

LINK TO PRACTICE

Although a budgetary control system requires considerable resources, a study of the UK food and drink industry by Abdel-Kader and Luther (2005) concluded that almost all of the companies in their survey used budgeting for planning and control. The following table demonstrates the use made by the participants of various aspects of the budgeting system.

	N	S1	S2	S3	S4	S5
Budgeting for planning	120	2	3	13	28	56
Budgeting for controlling costs	120	3	5	19	25	48
Activity-based budgeting	116	35	25	21	8	11
Budgeting with "what if?" analysis	118	17	16	36	23	8
Flexibility budgeting	117	29	16	23	19	13
Zero-based budgeting	117	52	19	14	9	7
Budgeting for long-term plans	117	14	21	26	26	14

Table 2 Use of Budgetary Control System

Source: Abdel-Kader, M. and Luther, R (2006) *Management Accounting Practices in the UK Food and Drink Industry.* Chartered Institute of Management Accountants.
S1, never; S2, rarely; S3, sometimes; S4, often; S5, very often.

The authors pointed out that the vast majority of respondents used budgeting for planning and controlling costs. Flexible budgeting was used by about one-third of the companies but 29 of the 117 respondents never used flexible budgeting and 16 companies rarely used it.

In this chapter we explain both static(fixed) budgets and flexible budgets.

Functional budgets will be constructed based on departments or some other identifiable area of activity. These functional budgets will be integrated to form the Master Budget that encompasses all of the organization's operations and activities.

In most organization the first stage will be to establish the sales budget. This will allow the production budget to be set to meet the sales demand. From this the other resources required can be identified and, finally, a Budgeted Cash Flow, Income Statement and Balance Sheer can be drawn up. This flow is shown in Figure 13.1.

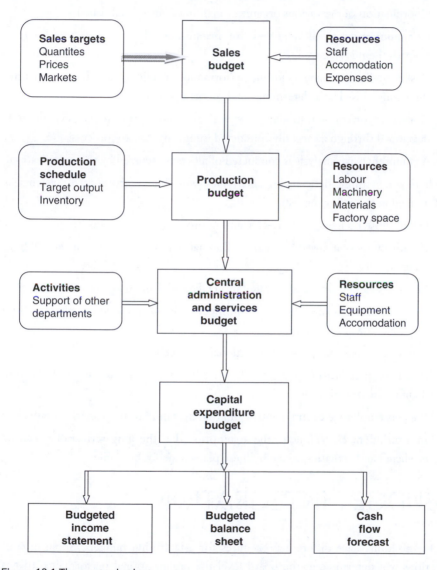

Figure 13.1 The master budget

There are several claimed advantages of a budgetary control system. A company may not enjoy all of them but should attempt to benefit from as many as possible of the following:

▪ Strategic formulation and implementation is enabled by the formal planning process.

- Control and assessment of actual performance is ensured by the regular and frequent comparisons with planned performance.

- Corrective action can be taken in a timely manner where actual performance is unacceptable or unforeseen economic events intrude.

- Coordination of the various organizational functions is established.

- Communication to all managers of organizational objectives and progress towards them is achieved.

- Responsibility of managers for the performance of activities and functions within their control is clearly determined and reported upon.

- Consensus on organizational objectives and motivation to achieve them is developed through a carefully conducted budgetary control process.

- A comprehensive analysis is conducted of all costs incurred by the organization.

There are definite deficiencies and issues with budgetary control systems as described in the following list:

- Establishing budgets is a time-consuming process.

- If static budgets are used and activity fluctuates, the reported variances will have no credibility.

- Managers can become demotivated if they consider the budgets are unrealistic.

- Once managers realize that they will meet their budget amounts there is little incentive to work harder.

- The system may encourage dysfunctional work behaviour.

- It is a complex process requiring skills both in setting plans and implementing them in the organization.

- Budgets emphasize central control and that may inhibit managerial initiative.

- In a turbulent environment, the assumption that the long-term future can be predicted and activities driven by these plans may not be viable.

BUDGET INTEGRATION

Organizations have different procedures for establishing budgets. Some organizations will determine at the board level the organizational performance that is required and then instruct managers what they must do. This 'top down' approach has become less common and usually, discussions and consultations will take place at various levels. Sometimes, organizations will use a 'bottom up' approach where functional managers construct their own budgets. These are then integrated into the master budget. This can only be successful where there is agreement on the economic and political climate facing the organization and the strategy that it is to be followed.

Whatever approach is used, at some stage budgets are constructed for individual functional areas. This allows an analysis of the costs for each area and also reveals the area's contribution to the overall strategy of the organization. It is essential that these functional or operational budgets are integrated otherwise problems will arise such as more products may be made than can be sold, or the machinery or labour is not available to meet the planned output for the month.

The setting of functional budgets is therefore an iterative process. It is usual to start by establishing the Sales Budget on a monthly basis for the coming year. This will quantify the products or services to be sold and put those in financial terms. Having established the sales budget, attention can be given to the production budget. This will show the quantities required to meet the demands of the sales budget and a decision will be made on the inventory levels to be held.

The sales budget will be based on forecasts of the quantities to be sold in different geographic areas as this may affect the price received in overseas markets. The organization may also be offering a range of services and products so a quantitative budget will be required for each one. The quantitative sales budget will then need to be converted into a financial budget. At this stage the accountant may work with the sales team determining whether there are any special taxes or import duties; volume discounts or similar regulatory requirements that may affect selling prices. At a later stage the accountants will also have to resolve the problems of foreign exchange rates.

With the sales budget in place, it is then possible to conduct an analysis of the costs that will be incurred on resources to achieve the level of sales. The analysis of the costs and the decisions made must be in line with organizational strategy and the detailed information will incorporate such information as:

- Number of sales people required and the costs of salaries, cars and other travelling expenses.
- Office space and equipment required.
- Commissions paid to agents.
- Special promotions and discounts.
- Advertising budget for print, television and other outlets.

With the sales budget in place it is possible to generate the production budget. The items to be made each month will be determined by the sales budget but a decision will be needed on the amount of inventory to be held. With the quantities to be manufactured established, the amount of materials and labour can be decided. There will also be decisions required on machine capacity, storage facilities, and internal transport. Some of these may require senior managers to decide on fresh expenditure on equipment.

The Purchasing Manager will draw up a purchases budget to show the quantities of materials required and the cost. There will also be a purchasing department budget to show the cost of running that department. Similarly the Personnel Manager will be consulting with the Sales and Production Managers on the number of people they require, the sought for skills and the remuneration.

Discussion point

Given the number of managers involved and the data are predictions of the future, what reliability do you consider can be placed on budgets?

It is possibly easier to understand budget integration in a manufacturing organization where there is a separation between sales and production departments but integration is essential. Our first example is the construction of a production budget where the sales volumes are a given. The second example is more complex as it is a smaller company and the difficulties of integration and decision making are exemplified.

CONSTRUCTING A PRODUCTION BUDGET – COSYKIDS

Cosykids manufactures car seats for children. It has only one model and a budget for the sales volume for the first four months of the year has been produced. The production manager will use these forecasts to develop his own budget.

For this example we are going to concentrate on the materials budget. Each car seat requires two meters of metal tubing, three meters of fabric and one meter of padding material. In addition, there is the harness which is outsourced to another manufacturer.

In addition to meeting the monthly sales volume, it has been decided that an inventory level of 5 per cent of the following month's sales volume must be carried. In Month 1 the commencing inventory is ten seats. The forecast of sales for month 5 is 300 seats.

Cosykids quantitative production budgets

	Month 1	Month 2	Month 3	Month 4
Sales (given)	200	600	1,200	500
Closing inventory at 5% of following month	30	60	25	15
Monthly output	230	660	1,225	515
Less beginning inventory	10	30	60	25
Production units required	220	630	1165	490

Production materials budget

	Month 1	Month 2	Month3	Month 4
Production units required	220	630	1165	490
Meters of fabric	660	1,890	3,495	1,470
Meters of padding	220	630	1165	490
Meters of tubing	440	1,260	2,330	980
Harness	220	630	1165	490

The above information can be given to the purchasing manager but, as you can imagine, there are likely to be several issues under discussion with all managers, such as:

1. Do we have space to store the material?

2. Can we secure discounts?

3. How do we store the car seats if the sales targets are not met?

4. Can we phase production so that we have a stable number each month? This will be very important for hiring labour and machine capacity.

In the above example we have considered only the material direct costs. There will also be labour costs which can be even more complex with decisions to be made on whether skilled or unskilled labour is required and the wage rate to be paid. The production manager also has the problem of determining the overheads for the department – the indirect costs. There may be supervisors' salaries, maintenance costs and depreciation of machinery all specific to that department. The production manager can expect that a share of the factory overheads will also be allocated to the budget. These probably will be uncontrollable as far as the production manager is concerned.

Even with this simple budget you will realize that the purchasing manager must be involved for the supply of materials, and the personnel department responsible for employment of workers. There is also the funding for machinery and the acquisition of other resources to be resolved. You will also appreciate that the more detailed the information, the better will be the analysis and control. There can be a tendency to concentrate on the direct production costs such as materials and labour with insufficient effort spent on the analysis of overhead costs and how these support the organizational strategy.

A SMALL SERVICE COMPANY – IRONGRIP

Irongrip is a consultancy that advises homeowners and commercial organizations on the security of their premises. There is substantial demand for their work but Irongrip has difficulty in recruiting knowledgeable consultants.

On average each consultant billed clients for 1200 hours at £120 per hour The Company currently employs ten consultants and their salaries are £95,000 each. Last year's figures reveal that travel and related expenses for the consultants averages 20 per cent of salaries. Administrative and promotion costs are £20,000 monthly. The Income Statement for the last year is as shown.

Income Statement for last year

	£
Revenue	
CP fees	1,440,000
Costs	
CP consultants salaries (10×£95,000)	950,000
Travel and related expenses	190,000
General office expenses	240,000
Total costs	1,380,000
Profit	60,000

At a recent meeting of directors it was agreed that the profit was too small given the buoyancy of the market. It was decided that the company should aim for a profit of £500,000 and an aggressive strategy of expansion should be pursued. None of the Directors had financial training but believed the target profit figure could be achieved by:

Recruiting two more consultants.

Increasing salaries to £100,000 per annum

Increasing the billable hours each consultant to 1300 hours and the charge out rate at £130 per hour.

Having made this high-level strategic decision, the Board passes the information to the Office Manager who is responsible for financial matters. The Office Manager, who is responsible for costs, decides it is more helpful to reverse the budget. In other words, to start with the profit, add on the planned costs and thus arrive at the figure of required sales. The workings are shown in the following table. Given the somewhat speculative strategy, the Office Manager decides to work to the nearest £000 and to add 10 per cent to general office costs to allow for the increased workload and inflation.

Office Manager's Working Budget

	Budget £000
Targeted profit	500
Add on planned costs	

Consultants' salaries (12 × £100,000)	1,200
Travel and related expenses (20% of salaries)	240
General office expenses	264
Required revenue	2204

The planned revenue of the Directors is:

Number of consultants	12
By billable hours	1,300 hours
By charge out rate	£130
Total revenue	£2,028,000

This demonstrates that there is a shortfall in revenue of £176,000 if the targeted profit is to be achieved. This also does not allow for the fact that the Office Manager allowed for an increase in office expenses but not travel!

The calculations, however, enable us to reassess the strategy on revenue generation. Each consultant should generate (1300 hours × £130) £169,000 in revenue. Deduct the salary of £100,000 and travel expenses of (20%); a consultant generates a 'gross profit' of £49,000. To achieve the target profit through an increase in the revenue, we need to either:

▪ Employ 3.5 more consultants which may be difficult to achieve.

▪ Increase the revenue generated by the 12 consultants by approximately £15,000 each consultant. This could be achieved by either increasing the billable hours to 1415 for each consultant or the charge out rate to £141 per hour or a combination of the two.

Any revenue generating option can have implication for cost. This in turn can have an impact on strategy. Budgets both contribute towards the development of strategy and reflect the financial implication of strategic proposals. Whether the company starts with the sales budget or a target profit plus costs, the strategy and the budget go hand in hand.

BUDGET VARIANCES

Usually, the actual performance of an organization throughout the year will not correspond exactly with the original budgets. Actual performance may be better or worse than the original budget. These differences are known as variances and may be either an adverse (unfavourable) variance or a favourable variance.

When we name a variance as adverse or favourable we are identifying its impact on the budgeted profit. Where the actual costs are lower than the budget there will be a favourable variance because profit will be higher than budgeted. Where actual costs are higher the variance is adverse as actual profit will be lower than budgeted. With sales the reverse is true. If actual sales are higher than the budget the variance is favourable: if lower the variance is adverse.

For example, if your actual costs are £10,000 higher than planned costs, this will mean that your budget profit is reduced by the £10,000. If your sales are £5000 lower than planned then your actual profit will be unfavourably affected compared to your budget.

The aim of the budget system is, by the end of the financial year, to ensure that your actual performance meets the budget. To assist in this, managers normally receive a budget report on a monthly basis comparing their department's actual performance against the budget. The report will show the planned amount for the month, the actual performance, and the variance. Some reports may also show the same information for the year to date.

Below is a simple example showing the performance for one month. This budget report has only six lines of information and you can expect to see budgets with many more items identified.

	Budget £000	Actual £000	Variance £000
Revenue	2,100	2,260	160F
Cost of goods sold	(1,400)	(1,580)	180U
Administration overheads	(350)	(340)	10F
Distribution overheads	(180)	(185)	5U
Advertising overheads	(90)	(120)	30U
Profit	80	35	45U

We budgeted for a profit of £80,000; the actual profit was only £35,000 due to aggregate variances of £45,000 unfavourable. There are serious problems we need to identify which are the important variances and the above budget can be redrafted to make it more informative.

First, a line is added to show 'Gross Profit' and the Gross Profit Percentage which we discussed in the first part of this book. This is the difference between the cost of the goods sold or manufactured and the price received for them. It is a key indicator of performance. A subtotal of the operating costs is also added. The following table shows the redrafted budget.

Redrafted Monthly Budget Report

	Budget £000	Actual £000	Variance £000
Revenue	2,100	2,260	160F
Cost of goods sold	(1,400)	(1,580)	180U
Gross profit	700	680	20U
Gross profit percentage	33.33	30.09	
Administration overheads	(350)	(340)	10F
Distribution overheads	(180)	(185)	5U
Advertising overheads	(90)	(120)	30U
Operating costs	620	645	25U
Profit	80	35	45U

The first four lines are revealing. The revenue has increased but the cost of making the goods has increased out of proportion. The result is that our gross profit margin has dropped by over 3 per cent which is critical.

Until we have more information from the managers responsible for the various activities, it is not possible to make firm statements but several questions arise.

1. Was the increase in revenue due to an increase in volume sold or a price increase?

2. Was the design or materials used changed thus leading to the unfavourable Cost of Goods Sold variance? Alternatively, had production not been informed in advance that there were changes anticipated and thus unanticipated costs were incurred by production to meet the sales requirements?

3. The small unfavourable variance on Distribution overhead could be caused by a volume increase in sales – more to be delivered.

4. The larger unfavourable variance in Advertising costs could have been incurred by a decision being made to promote the product.

More investigations are required to answer these questions and variance analysis provides the signposts as to where you should look. In the next section we discuss more fully the investigation of variances.

Investigating variances

The Budget Reports will go to individual managers who are responsible for the activities of various departments. To some extent they will know the background to the events that have led to the favourable or unfavourable variance. They may not be aware of the financial impact and the connections with other departments.

The budget report will demonstrate the financial consequences of the events that have occurred and illuminate some aspects that would not otherwise be apparent. It also allows managers to concentrate their attention on where the financial impact is important.

In conducting variance investigations it is essential that both favourable and unfavourable variances are examined. It is just as important to know why some things went right as to find the reasons for the bad news. However, this does not mean that every variance should be investigated. This would be too time consuming and some filters need to be established to focus attention on variances that matter. The following methods are used in practice.

POUNDS AND PERCENTAGES LIMITS

A general rule can be set that any cost variance under a certain amount will not be investigated. If we take our limit as $£15,000, in the above example only the advertising overheads will be investigated. Taking an absolute amount can be misleading. You could have actual expenditure of say £32,000 where the budget was for only £20,000. This difference falls under our guidelines as it is only £12,000 but may be worth investigating as it suggests there is a problem.

Using percentages can resolve this dilemma. A rule could state that any variance under £15,000 or 10 per cent of the original budget amount is not examined. Our £12,000 would pass the absolute amount hurdle but would be captured by the percentage limit.

RECURRING VARIANCES

Variances may fall within the limits that have been set but it is valuable to keep an eye on the frequency of the variance over a period of months. Let us take the case where the monthly budget for a cost is £25,000. The following table shows the actual cost for each month and the variance for the first four months of the year.

Variances

Month	Actual cost	Variance
January	£27,000	£2,000U
February	£28,000	£3,000U
March	£28,000	£3,000U
April	£29,000	£4,000U

Although the variance may fall within any pound and percentages limits that have been set, it should be investigated. If a variance is frequently different from the original budget it suggests there may be a problem. It may be that the original budget figure was poorly set or that circumstances have changed and an overspend is acceptable.

In this example, there is the worrying feature that the variance shows an upwards trend. Action needs to be taken now to ensure that there is proper control and that the variance is not even greater in May. If you see the trend of a variance increasing or decreasing over a period of time, you need to investigate.

EXPERIENCE

The methods we have described above are useful but remember that the responsible managers have knowledge and experience. They will have been involved in setting the original budgets, discussing their integration with colleagues and, if problems have arisen, may have already investigated them or discussed the situation with colleagues. The Budget Report, however, establishes the hard, financial facts of activities and displays an integrated and comprehensive picture of the activities that have occurred and how this compares to the strategic plan that was made.

FLEXIBLE BUDGETS

Definition – Flexible budget

A budget which is adjusted for the actual level of activity in the financial period.

So far in this chapter we have been explaining static, or fixed, budgets. With these budgets amounts are set at the beginning of the year and are not changed. Static budgets are appropriate where activity levels are reasonably consistent or are controllable by the manager. In other words, once the budget has been agreed, it is unlikely that there will be any events that will affect the plan for the forthcoming financial period.

The static budget, however, can be very misleading. For example, because of an unexpected buoyant market, a company will sell more items than was predicted. This will show as a favourable variance when actual revenue is compared to the original static budget. This is the good news. Most likely, this growth in sales volume will cause an increase in actual production and distribution variable costs to support the sales. With a fixed budget these actual costs will give rise to as unfavourable variance.

The reason for variances is easy to explain but the conclusions that are drawn may be misleading. The information required by managers is what the costs should be if the activity level achieved is not what was planned. For example, the production department may have been instructed temporarily to increase their production by 10 per cent. One would expect that their materials and labour will increase by this amount and these costs will therefore be higher than the static budget and an unfavourable variance will arise.

Where a company anticipates fluctuating activity a flexible budget gives much better information thus improving monitoring and control. The flexing of the budget refers only to variable costs and if there is a cost variance it can be assumed to be due to an increase or decrease in activity. Fixed costs are not normally flexed as they should remain the same regardless of any changes in activity within the relevant range.

The flexed budget

A flexible budget is drawn up in the same way as a static budget. The sales are predicted and the variable costs to support those sales. It is important in doing this that the volumes and the revenue and variable costs per item are detailed. At the end of the month, the actual number of items sold and made are known. The budget can then be flexed so that the financial figures reflect a budget for the attained levels of activity instead of the original predictions.

WORKED EXAMPLE – STATIC AND FLEXIBLE BUDGETS

The following example compares a static and flexible budget. The static budget was set for 40,000 units to be produced and sold. The planned revenue and costs per unit for this level of activity are shown in the first column. By multiplying the budgeted level of activity (40,000 units) by the revenue or cost per unit, the static budget in column two is calculated. For example, Direct materials at £1.30 per unit multiplied by 40,000 units gives the static budget of £52,000.

At the end of the month, the actual number of units produced and sold is 45,000. With the fixed budget the actual results for 45,000 units are compared against the revenue and costs for 40,000 units. This is shown in Table 13.1.

The company may be very happy with these results. The actual profit is £9000 more than was budgeted. This favourable result is due almost entirely to the sales performance. The question arises as to whether the variable costs unfavourable variances are acceptable. As more units were sold and made, increases are reasonable but we need to prepare a flexible budget to ascertain whether these are under control. The calculation of the flexed budget is the total budgeted sales or cost amount divided by the budgeted number of units. The resulting budgeted amount per unit is then multiplied by the actual number of units for the financial period.

The results are given in Table 13.2.

The comparison reveals that the company did not do as well as originally thought with the actual profit performance being $4500 lower than it should have

	Static budget	Actual performance	Variance
Number of units	40,000	45,000	
	£000	£000	£000
Revenue (£6.00 per unit)	240	270	30F
Variable costs			
Direct materials (1.30 per unit)	52	65	13U
Direct labour (1.50 per unit)	60	68	8U
Variable overheads (£0.50)	20	18	2F
Total variable costs	132	151	19U
Fixed Overheads			
Lighting and heat	12	14	2U
Depreciation	25	25	–
Insurance	30	30	–
Total fixed overheads	67	69	2U
Total costs	199	220	21U
Profit	41	50	9F

Table 13.1 Static budget

been at that level of activity. The main message we can draw from the flexed budget are:

1 The sales team did well in beating their budgeted volume and maintaining the unit price at $6.00.

2 Direct material cost was actual $65,000 whereas at that level of activity it should have been $58,500. We need to investigate whether there was a wastage issue or did the growth in sales result in more materials having to be purchased at a higher price.

3 Direct labour was close to budget but a saving of $4500 was made on variable overheads. It is worth examining this to ascertain the reasons.

Fixed overheads should have remained the same but the one to investigate is light and heat. It is possible that the original budget was not correct or a part of that cost is variable and fixed. It may be that the increased production elevated that variable element.

The above example demonstrates that flexible budgeting provides more useful information where there is fluctuating activity. However, there are disadvantages. The production manager has planned originally to manufacture 40,000 units but is called upon to increase this by 5000 units. This means more materials have to be ordered and there is the danger that there would not have been sufficient capacity

	Flexible budget	Actual performance	Variance
Number of units	45,000	45,000	
	£000	£000	£000
Revenue (£6.00 per unit)	270	270	–
Variable costs			
Direct materials (1.30 per unit)	58.5	65	6.5U
Direct labour (1.50 per unit)	67.5	68	0.5U
Variable overheads (£0.50)	22.5	18	4.5F
Total variable costs	148.5	151	2.5U
Fixed Overheads			
Lighting and heat	12	14	2U
Depreciation	25	25	–
Insurance	30	30	–
Total fixed overheads	67	69	2U
Total costs	215.5	220	4.5U
Profit	54.5	50	4.5

Table 13.2 Flexible budget

on the machinery. In other words, the planned coordination of activities can be disrupted. If there is a strong strategy underpinning these actions, there is no problem and proper coordination of all the activities should have been achieved.

Some companies use a reverse procedure to determine what the actual cost per unit is at the actual level of activity instead of using a flexible budget. In the above example the planned unit cost for materials was $1.30. In the reverse method, the actual cost of $65,000 for direct materials is divided by the actual volume of 45,000 units. The actual cost per unit is therefore 1.44 per unit which can be compared to the budgeted cost of $1.30 per unit. An investigation can now be conducted to ascertain the reasons why the actual material cost per unit is greater than the budgeted cost per unit.

Although flexible budgets can be useful especially when there is fluctuating activity, the following are the reasons that they are not used more widely.

▪ It may be difficult to identify variable costs with precision.

▪ Fixed costs are so substantial that flexible budgets would not provide useful information.

▪ In a multi-product company, it may be difficult to separate the various factors making up the cost.

- The company may be operating a standard costing system which provides better information more quickly.

- Managers usually know beforehand if there are likely to be issues and advised the management team and action has been taken. For example, the Sales Director will know if budgeted volumes will not be achieved and informed relevant managers of the downturn.

- Some issues will be those of policy and an analysis of the decisions to be made will have already been made in great detail. If sales volumes are down it may be decided to use cheaper materials and thus reduce the selling price. A technique such as contribution analysis will have been used.

Finally, the static budget has been agreed to by all managers and endorsed by the Board. It has been established after much analysis and discussion. The budget reflects the corporate strategy of the organization and failure to achieve its aims may result in a loss of confidence by lenders and investors and, at the worse, bankruptcy. Flexible budgets can be a useful tool but need to provide the information that managers need. Other methods and techniques may better settle those needs.

BUDGET BEHAVIOUR

Much has been written about the behavioural aspects of budgetary control systems, from the setting of budgets to the interrelationship between the technique and individuals and groups. It is claimed that budgetary control is improved in an organization where the process is participative with managers involved in establishing the budgets for their own particular function or level of responsibility.

The level of participation can vary and some method for ensuring the integration of all the functional budgets is required. Where there is substantial participation the dilemma is that managers are establishing the targets against which they will subsequently be measured. There is an understandable temptation to build some slack into the budget. A manager may 'pad' a budget by submitting cost targets higher than is realistic to ensure that there is some budgetary slack. In this way a manager can be confident that they will achieve budget. There is also an aspect of 'empire building' in setting budgets. In some organizations the status of a manager is reflected in the size of the budget they control.

At the other end of the time scale there are behavioural traits connected with the year end. If a budget is not spent by the end of the year, funds are not carried forward to the coming year. A manager may go on a spending spree as the 'money is there'. Additionally, there is a belief that if the budget is not spent, senior managers will decrease the budget next year in line with the actual expenditure.

STANDARD COSTING

> **Definition – Standard costing**
>
> Standard costing is a system of cost ascertainment and control in which predetermined standard costs and income from products and operations are set and periodically compared with actual costs incurred and income generated in order to establish any variances.

The basis of standard costing is that the total cost of any item is the price per unit multiplied by the quantity used. In this chapter we are going to concentrate on material and labour costs, although the principles can be used for overhead costs. The technique is clearly appropriate for manufacturing companies and in depth research into 41 UK manufacturing companies gives a good insight into company practices.

> ## LINK TO PRACTICE
>
> ### Use of standard costing in UK manufacturing
>
> The results of a survey of 41 UK manufacturing companies found that most (29) use standard costs and, of those that do not, eight have only limited manufacturing operations or are engaged in contract work. The conclusion is that only four companies (less than 10%) do not employ standard costing where this might be expected.
>
> All (29) 'standard costing companies' set standards for materials, most (26) set standards for labour and about two-thirds (20) set overhead recovery rates. However, standard cost variances often do not appear as part of P&L information. Over half of these 'standard cost companies' base P&L reports on actual costs; some 'add back' variances while others frequently update material standards so that they approximate actual costs.

Although not necessarily appearing in the P&L most of these companies calculate some material and labour variances for control purposes

Source: Dugdale, D. Jones, C. and Green S. (2005) *Contemporary Management Accounting Practices in UK Manufacturing.* Chartered Institute of Management Accountants.

It would seem that standard costing is the usual management accounting technique applied in manufacturing companies and labour and material standards are the most common, but overhead recovery rates are used by the majority of companies. On the basis of this survey it appears that standard costing is restricted to internal management control systems and the data does not find its way into the financial accounting system through the Income Statement.

The extent of the application of the technique in manufacturing is not surprising. The following simple example demonstrates the valuable information which can be generated.

Imagine that we are going to make some apple juice. We plan to make five gallons of juice which will take 20 lbs of apples. So that our juice is cheaper than the shop bought juice we plan to buy apples at 50 pence per pound. Our planned cost for apples for the juice is therefore £10. This is our standard cost to make the required amount of apple juice.

Unfortunately, we could not purchase the quality of apples we required so we purchased 25 lbs of an inferior quality. The price was 45 pence per pound. Let us put this information into financial terms.

Plan	20 lbs × 50 pence per lb =	£10.00
Actual	25 lbs × 45 pence per lb =	£11.25

We can see that by purchasing more apples, even at the lower price meant that we spent £1.25 more than we planned. This is an unfavourable variance because our costs are higher. We need to know the detailed breakdown of this decision but before doing so we need to explain how companies set their standards: in our example the number of pounds of apples and the price per pound. One of the following methods is usually employed.

- Prior experience is adopted as the standard. Although this may reflect the successes of the past it may also include the deficiencies and also does not take into account changes in both internal and external conditions that may have taken place.

- Taking past experience as the base but updating it for changing conditions. This 'after the event' approach still embraces the faults of the past.

- If the data is available comparison with other organizations. This is a more analytical approach but valid comparisons must be used.
- The standards that the company wishes to achieve in order to pursue its strategic plans. This is the most rigorous but time-consuming method.

Where a company uses the strategic approach, standard cost is the planned unit of cost that is calculated from technical specifications and economic and market conditions. The technical specifications specify the quantity of materials, labour and other elements of cost required, and these are then related to the prices and wages that are expected to be in place during the period when the standard cost will be used.

To determine the appropriate standard for both usage and price of a resource, a careful analysis must be conducted of a range of information. To set standards for materials and labour, the organization will refer to:

Materials – quantity and price

    Analysis of past data

    Job specifications which should list required materials

    Engineering plans that provide a list of material

    Chemical formulas

    Recipes or other documents specifying materials required

    By time and motion studies

    In price lists provided by suppliers

    The expected economic environment

    The predicted actions of suppliers, competitors and customers

Labour – quantity (hours) and rate

    Analysis of past data

    Time and motion studies

    Contracts that set labour rates

    Prevailing rates in the area or industry

    The expected economic environment

    Changes in labour supply and demand

As a procurement manager you can expect to be involved in the materials pricing standard. As an engineer, chemist, or production manager you will assist with the quantity of the materials. Similarly with labour standards, a range of managerial knowledge and experience may be necessary to assist in setting standards.

At this stage you will realize that standards are going to be set for the cost of the inputs, the labour and materials, and you therefore need to know the price for the inputs and the amount of usage for a certain level of production. For materials, it is necessary to determine the amount of materials required to make one unit. The price of the materials is then set to establish the standard cost for materials.

Setting standards for labour requires a different approach. With this input we are interested in the time in which it is planned direct labour will take to complete a certain volume of work. This is usually measured in standard hours or standard minutes. The important point is that a standard hour is a measure of production output, rather than a measure of actual time.

For example, a company may determine that 500 cost units should be produced in one hour. In an eight-hour day the actual total production is 4500 cost units. That actual output can be converted into standard hours as follows:

$$4500 \text{ units}/500 = 9 \text{ standard hours of production.}$$

You will appreciate that if you have managed to achieve nine standard hours of production in eight actual hours, labour is being very efficient. In the next section we will examine how this achievement can be measured in financial terms and integrated into a cohesive analysis of the activities.

Direct cost variances

Direct materials variances. Predetermined standards are set both for the usage level of direct materials for a given level of production and the price allowed per unit of direct materials. This allows us to calculate three variances

$$\text{Total direct materials variance } (SQ \times SP) - (AQ \times AP)$$

$$\text{Direct material price variance } (SP - AP)AQ$$

$$\text{Direct materials usage variance } (SQ - AQ)SP$$

Where

$SQ = $ Standard quantity

$SP = $ Standard price

$AQ = $ Actual quantity

$AP = $ Actual price

The total direct materials variance reveals whether your actual total cost is as planned. If not, the subsidiary variances will show whether we paid more or less per unit of materials than we planned or we used more or less materials than we planned. This could be due to poor planning, a change in market conditions that may require a new strategic approach or a deviation from the original strategy.

Of course, you may have purchased a much higher quantity of materials than you planned but at a much lower price. One may compensate the other so that there is no total cost variance. For this reason all three variances should be calculated.

The relationship between usage and price, and the formulae we use can be shown in a diagrammatic form (Figure 13.2).

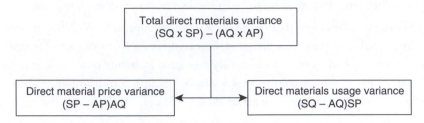

Figure 13.2 Direct materials variances

Note that we always put the standard (plan) first and then deduct the actual figure. If the answer is positive it is a favourable variance, if it is negative it is an unfavourable variance.

WORKED EXAMPLE – COFFEETIME LTD

We can now use a more complex example to illustrate the use of material cost variances. Coffeetime Ltd makes wooden coffee tables and has set the following standards for each table:

Standard quantity of timber for each table = 2 metres

Standard price per metre = £3.00

During the financial period a total of 90 coffee tables were made. The actual usage of materials was 210 metres and the price paid per metre was £3.05.

The only piece of information missing is the quantity of timber that should have been used for 90 tables. This is calculated by multiplying the production quantity (90) by the standard quantity for one table (two metres) to give the standard of 180 metres. We can now apply the three formulae:

Total direct materials variance

$$(SQ \times SP) - (AQ \times AP)$$

$$(180\,metres \times £3.00) - (210\,metres \times £3.05)$$

$$£540 - \$640.50 = \$100.50(U)$$

Direct material price materials variance $(SP - AP)AQ$

$$(\$3.00 - -\$3.05) \times 210\,metres = \$10.50(U)$$

Direct materials usage variance $(SQ - AQ)SP$

$$(180\,metres - 210\,metres)\$3.00 = \$90.00(U)$$

This organization has some problems to resolve. It has a total unfavourable variance of $100.50. The difference between actual and planned price accounts for only $10.50 and the main issue is the quantity of materials that has been used to give the adverse variance of $90.00.

Summarizing our direct materials variance analysis:

Direct materials usage variance	(£90.00) (U)
Direct materials price variance	£10.50 (U)
Total direct materials variance	£100.50 (U)

Direct labour variances. Direct labour variances use the same principles as material variances except hours are used as the measure. As with materials, the reasons for the actual total cost of direct labour differing from the plan is either we paid more or less per hour for labour than we planned or we required more or less labour hours than we had planned for that level of production.

The terms we use for the sub-variances are direct labour rate; that is how much we paid per hour and direct labour efficiency variance (sometimes referred to as the labour productivity variance). This is the difference between the actual production achieved, measured in standard hours, and the actual hours worked, valued at the standard labour rate.

The relationship between these calculations and the formulae we use can be shown in a diagrammatic form (Figure 13.3).

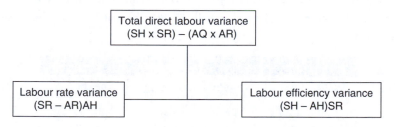

Figure 13.3 Direct labour variances

where

SH = standard hours

SR = standard rate per hour

AH = actual number of hours worked

AR = actual rate per hour

We will continue the example of the coffee tables. The standard set is that one person should make one table every four hours. The standard wage rate is $15.00 per hour. It took the workforce 350 actual hours for which they were paid a total of $5600, that is, $16 per hour.

The calculations are:

Total direct labour variance

$$(SH \times SR) - (AH \times AR) =$$

$$(90 \text{ tables} \times 4 \times \$15.00) - (350 \text{ hours} \times \$16) =$$

$$(360 \times \$15) - \$5,600 = \$200(U)$$

Labour Rate Variance

$$(SR - AR)AH$$

$$(\$15.00 - \$16.00)350 = \$350(U)$$

Labour Efficiency Variance

$$(360 - 350)\$15.00 = \$150(F)$$

The summary of these findings is

Labour Rate Variance $350(U)

Labour Efficiency Variance $\underline{\$150(F)}$

Total direct labour variance $200(U)

One could hypothesize that a higher level of skilled labour was used leading to the favourable efficiency variance but the higher rate we paid led to a total labour rate variance of $350 (U).

We can now put together our material and labour variances to show a profit statement and how the variances impact on our planned profit. In Table 13.3 we assume that the company planned to sell the 90 tables at $85 each but received $86.00 each.

	Plan	Actual	Variance
Sales	7,650	7,740	90 (F)
Timber cost	540	640.50	100.50 (U)
Labour costs	5,400	5,600	200(U)
Total costs	5,940	6,240.50	300.50 (U)
Profit	1,710	1,499.50	210.50 (U)

Table 13.3 Labour and material variances

From the above table we can see how the line-by-line variance aggregates to the total variance and shows why the actual profit is $210.50 lower than the planned profit. The breakdown of the main variances into their subdivisions suggests where the problems may lie. The variances have given you signposts to direct you investigations. Both favourable and unfavourable variances should be investigated.

In a properly implemented and operated system a company should enjoy the following advantages:

- Implementing standards requires a thorough examination of the organization's production and operations activities. Every stage in production is minutely examined and the most cost effective and efficient procedures are established.

- The technique is very flexible and a full-blown system covering all aspects of the organization is not always needed. Standards may only be set for material usage if that is a significant cost and close control is required.

- Responsibility for performance is identified with specific managers.

- A viable and credible benchmark is established against which actual performance can be compared.

- The setting of standards encourages the coordination and integration of the various functional activities.

- Managers who are properly trained and understand the use of standards will be more effective.

Disadvantages of standard costing:

- In a turbulent economic environment or where the organization is breaking new frontiers it may be impossible to gather sufficiently robust data to set viable standards.

- Even with a fairly simple system, implementing and updating a system can be costly.

- If any of the standards become out of date or lose their relevance the entire system has reduced credibility.

- Busy managers may suffer from information overload and ignore the data.

CONCLUSIONS

Planning and control are essential management activities. Budgetary control systems, in one form or another, are found in many organizations. There are undoubted drawbacks to the system. Forecasting can be uncertain, the process is time consuming, and managerial behavioural responses can be disruptive. Unfortunately, there is no alternative which is more useful. Budgetary control systems do compel organizations to be forward looking, integrates the various functions, clearly sets out activities and provides information to investigate and take action where there are problems.

Standard costing suffers from fewer issues. The main failing of most systems is their complexity and keeping the standards up-to-date. With computerized systems it is reasonably simple to devise a myriad of standards covering all activities and to issue variance reports on a weekly, if not daily, basis. This usually results in information over load for the managers. The other weakness of the system is keeping the standards up-to-date, particularly in a volatile environment.

RECOMMENDED READING

Yuen, D (2007) 'Antecedents of budgetary participation: Enhancing employees' job performance' *Managerial Auditing Journal* 22.5 pp. 533–548. http://search.proquest.com/docview/274716342?

Edwards, John Richard; Boyns, Trevor; Matthews, Mark. (2002) 'Standard costing and budgetary control in the British iron and steel industry: A study of accounting change'. *Accounting, Auditing & Accountability Journal* 15. 1 pp. 12–45. http://search.proquest.com/docview/211232620?

CASE STUDY SAM WAYS AND STANDARD COSTING

Sam runs a small business making cabinet frames which are sold to furniture manufacturers and incorporated into their products. He sells the frames to several companies but he is concerned about his costs that appear to be always increasing. He has asked you to consider the feasibility of introducing a standard costing system but he stresses that it must be simple and relevant to his needs. He adds that none of his staff have any financial training and his knowledge has been 'picked up' over the years. Any system must therefore be worth the cost of running it.

He states that his normal quarterly sales are 10,000 frames and he has already told his employees that is the target for the next quarter. His secretary, Wendy May, is also in charge of purchasing and he suggests that you see her. The workshop is run by Mat Ford who is responsible for all production including the hiring of labour and you also interview him. The main comments from both are given below.

Wendy.   Purchasing the materials is really easy because we just use the one type of board. I only do the job because my uncle works for the supplier so it's easy for me to phone him and they deliver the next day whatever we want. Each frame should take 1.5 metres of material so for the 10,000 frames I will order 15,000 metres of material. The list price is $4.50 per metre but it does fluctuate. However, my uncle always gets me a discount so you can reckon on paying about 5% less than $4.50 per metre but that's not a promise because it can change almost daily.

Mat. *It's simple production. You just cut on the machines and glue and fix to a standard pattern so standard costing should work. We pay our workers £10 per hour and we reckon that they should manage to work 2 metres of material every hour. We are using 15,000 metres so that should take us 7,500 hours take or leave a few either side.*

At the end of the following Quarter, Steve contacts you and says that he has some actual figures for the month. They produced less than the 10,000 expected and only made 9500 frames. Unfortunately, Wendy's uncle had unexpectedly left the company which supplied the materials so they had to go to a different supplier. The board was not so good and was more expensive. They needed 15,200 metres for production of 9500 frames and the total material cost was £69,160.

Mat had told him that because of a virus, several workers were off sick and they had to use untrained labour. Fortunately, they had only paid £9.80 as the average wage which was a saving and the total wages bill was £76,440.

He has asked if you can analyse the figures and explain whether standard costing would help him control the costs in this situation and, if so, how would you implement the system.

CHAPTER 14
CAPITAL BUDGETING

LEARNING OBJECTIVES

At the end of this chapter you should be able to:

- Define capital budgeting and identify when it should be used.
- Explain the time value of money concept.
- Summarize the strengths and weaknesses of the various techniques
- Evaluate investment opportunities using the techniques explained in this chapter.

EXECUTIVE SUMMARY

A company deciding to make a substantial investment for a number of years may be less concerned about profit and more about ensuring that it will recover its cash investment. Capital budgeting, also referred to as capital investment appraisal, is a method using either profit or cash for evaluating projects that require significant up-front funding and will not show a return for several years.

There are different approaches to capital budgeting and one could not make the claim that one is superior to the others. It will depend on the amount of funding, the length of time, the nature of the project and the financial expertise available. The main techniques are:

PAYBACK PERIOD

The purpose of this cash-based technique is to find out how long (usually measured in years) it will take to get the original investment back. If there is a choice of projects, the one that provides the fastest payback is chosen, although the alternative may give a greater return but over a longer period.

DISCOUNTED PAYBACK PERIOD

A more sophisticated cash-based approach than the above as it takes into account the time value of money. This can be critical where there are projects with different timings in the cash flow return.

NET PRESENT VALUE

This uses the time value of money and compares the initial investment to the future cash flows which are adjusted to today's values. If there is a positive net present value, financially it would make sense to embark on the project. Where there is a choice of projects, the choice would be the project that gives the greatest positive net present value.

INTERNAL RATE OF RETURN

Very similar in approach to the net present value technique but provides the results in the form of a percentage return on the investment.

ACCOUNTING RATE OF RETURN

This uses the profit basis and has the advantage of simplicity and providing information in the form that management would find familiar and relate to other performance measures it uses.

Evidence from various surveys indicates that the techniques using discounting are most popular, at least by the larger companies. However, companies may use several techniques at one time depending on the nature of the project and the context. Companies may also use the undiscounted payback technique to filter possibilities and use a more sophisticated technique to make the final decision.

Definition – Capital expenditure (CapEx)

Funds used by a company to acquire or improve non-current assets such as property, machinery or equipment. These expenditures can include everything from replacing a machine to building an additional factory in another country.

CONCEPTUAL AND PRACTICAL ISSUES

A company assessing the investment of a large sum of money for a prolonged period of time usually has various courses of action. At the simplest, one course of action is not to make the investment and the other to make it. Alternatively there may be other opportunities, with varying time spans, different amounts of required investments and the promise of a range of financial returns with dubious levels of certainty.

These long-term decisions are strategic in nature and the deliberations and investigations are for internal purposes only and not for external disclosure. The project may even be termed highly confidential and aspects of it given fictitious names so that even internal people working on the project do not know the complete picture.

Capital budgeting is the procedure of selecting one project from several potential investment projects or making a decision on one project. This may be to replace some highly specialized machinery, repair it or to continue without changes. Alternative opportunities require evaluation and, depending on the selection, the expectation is that the project will be of financial benefit to the company.

Management requires a sound technique that allows them to assess and compare the alternatives with some confidence. There are a range of techniques available but none provide an absolute answer. All of the techniques are based on projections of returns arising from the investment and their validity is only as good as those projections. Even with excellent predictions, management will still have to determine its strategic policy and evaluate data in the context of other factors that influence the success, or otherwise, of the company.

In using these techniques, some simplifying assumptions are made. The most popular techniques are based on projections of cash flows. It is usually assumed that the future cash flows take place at the end of each year of the project life. Companies may carry out their calculations on a quarterly or half yearly basis, but in this chapter we use the annual basis. Secondly, it is assumed that the initial cash investment is usually made on day 1 of the first year, although it is possible that the investment is stepped in stages.

There are four stages to the cash flow techniques:

1. Determine the amount of funding required and whether this will be sourced internally or externally or both.

2. Decide the return required from the project. This is sometimes referred to as the hurdle rate.

3. Predict the amounts of the annual net cash flows (the difference between the cash inflows and outflows).

4. Decide the timing of the movements of cash flows.

Definition – Time value of money

The concept that a specific sum of cash is worth more if it is received sooner rather than later. The reason for this differences is that cash received sooner can be invested to earn interest.

Some of the cash-based techniques use discounting which applies the concept of the time value of money. This involves converting future cash flows into present day values. For example, assume a friend wanted to borrow money from you now and promised to pay you £1000 in a year's time. The first question is whether you are confident that you would receive the money in 12 months' time. The second question is what would you do with the money if you did not lend it to your friend?

If interest rates were 10 per cent you may decide to invest £909 now. In one year's time you would receive the return of your £909 plus 10 per cent interest of £91: a total of just over £1000. You may believe that your friend will pay you £1000 in one year's time, but looking at the time value of money and current interest rates you would only lend your friend £909 now. In reaching that decision we have taken the £1000 in one year's time and discounted it at a 10 per cent rate to give today's value of £909.

Of course, the greater the length of time before your friend pays you the £1000 the less you would be willing to lend him that amount today. The promise of paying £1000 in five years' time is only worth £621 now and in ten years' time £386. There are formulae, tables, calculators and computer programmes that will provide the discounted amounts at different interest rates and over different time periods. An abbreviated version is shown in Table 14.1 and this will be used in the examples we work through in this chapter.

Future	Interest rate			
Years	1%	5%	10%	15%
1	0.990	0.952	0.909	0.870
2	0.980	0.907	0.826	0.756
3	0.971	0.864	0.751	0.658
4	0.961	0.823	0.683	0.572
5	0.951	0.784	0.621	0.497
6	0.942	0.746	0.564	0.432
7	0.933	0.711	0.513	0.376
8	0.923	0.677	0.467	0.327
9	0.914	0.645	0.424	0.284
10	0.905	0.614	0.386	0.247

Table 14.1 Discounted cash flows

Discussion point

If you were lending money to a friend what other information would you consider critical before you decide?

A major issue in discounting techniques is the discount rate that should be used. This desired rate of return, also known as the hurdle rate, is the minimum rate of return which a company requires from its investment. This is taken as the rate of return the company could earn by investing the same amount in the best available alternative investment that bears the same risk.

Definition – Hurdle rate

The minimum amount of return a company expects from an investment.

It can be difficult to identify the alternative investment opportunity so a company may resort to other methods. One is to use the cost of capital. This is the costs that the firm will incur, usually interest, in raising the funds needed for the investment.

It may be that the funding will come from a mixture of equity and debt. In this instance the weighted cost of capital would be used. The WACC for a company is a function of the cost of equity and cost of debt. Cost of equity means the return expected by shareholders. Cost of debt means the average return expected from holders of debt. The weighted cost of capital is a weighted average of the returns expected by all providers of capital. Ignoring complications of preferred shares and taxation the formula is:

$$WACC = D/(D+E) \times i + E/(D+E) \times r$$

where i is the interest rate,

r is the required return on equity,

D is the amount of debt capital,

E is the amount of equity capital.

Several companies have a strategic approach where it has decided formally the minimum return a project must make before it will contemplate undertaking it. If there are several potential projects they will be screened to discard the ones that do not make the minimum rate. Further investigations are conducted to consider other factors which will influence the final decision (Figure 14.1).

The above techniques, when applied to the same problem, can provide different indicators as to which is the best project in which to invest. The answers are all

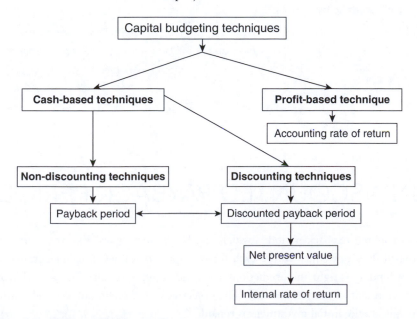

Figure 14.1 Capital budgeting techniques

'right' and the differences are due to the assumptions made, the funding strategy of management and the availability of data. It is therefore critical that a company determines its capital budgeting policy, which of the techniques it will use, and work with the results that it generates.

LINK TO PRACTICE

Use of techniques

Possibly the most extensive study in the UK demonstrating the trends in the use of techniques was conducted by Pike (1996). Surveys were conducted with the UK's largest 100 companies four times between 1975 and 1992 and the following table shows the results

	1975	1980	1986	1992
Payback	73	81	92	94
Average accounting rate of return	51	49	56	50
Internal rate of return	44	57	75	81
Net present value	32	39	68	74

Table 2.2 Evaluation techniques used

Pike found that in 1975, 11 companies used 4 different methods and this has increased to 36 by 1992

Adapted from Pike, Richard (1996). A longitudinal survey on capital budgeting practices. *Journal of Business Finance & Accounting*, 23(1) pp. 79–92.

UNDISCOUNTED PAYBACK PERIOD

Undiscounted payback period is widely used. The main feature of the technique is that it does not adjust future cash flows to present values. Smaller companies, where funding is tight and predictions are difficult, often require the payback from the investment as soon as possible. The objective of the technique is to determine how quickly the initial investment is repaid.

If there is only one potential project and the cash return over its life does not recover the initial investment, the project is not worth undertaking. If there are two or more projects, the one that returns the investment the quickest is preferred as long as the initial investment is recovered.

Worked example – Conblock

Conblock manufactures concrete blocks and wishes to expand its activities. It owns three empty sites in Lowstoft, Hillville and Downside. It has access to funding to a maximum of £100,000 and decides to open a new concrete plant on one of the sites. A plant has a normal economic life of five years. The company has conducted some market research and the following is a brief summary

Lowstoft. Market is not large but there are plans to extend the town in two to three years' time and that should increase sales significantly.

Hillville. There are large developments currently taking place so there is an immediate market. Once the current phase of development takes place the market may diminish.

Downside. A fairly stable market with no indications of great growth prospects and it may take some time to become established.

Discussion point

Based on the above information which project do you consider most favourable and why?

Table 14.2 shows the original investment required and the positive cash flow over the five-year period. The main characteristics of the layout are:

- Year 0 is a conventional way of referring to the start of year 1. Year 1, 2, 3, etc. means the end of year 1, 2, 3, etc.

- Net cash flow is the difference between the cash flow in, for example from sales, and cash flow out for costs.

- Negative cash flow in any year is shown in brackets. The initial investment is cash going out and is shown in year 0 in brackets.

- It is assumed that cash flows during a year will be received evenly throughout the year.

Without the application of a capital appraisal technique, management could spend some time arguing which is the best investment. Lowstoft gives the greatest cash return of £35,000 but the main positive cash flows are towards the end of the five years and these are only predictions. Downside appears enticing as it is claimed

Year	Lowstoft £	Hillville £	Downside £
0	(100,000)	(100,000)	(80,000)
1	15,000	30,000	20,000
2	20,000	35,000	22,000
3	30,000	35,000	25,000
4	35,000	15,000	25,000
5	35,000	10,000	10,000
TOTAL	35,000	25,000	22,000

Table 14.2 Cash flow for three potential projects

to be a stable market. Also, it only requires an investment of only £80,000 but gives a cash return of £22,000.

Such arguments could continue for ever and management needs to have a policy on the CapEx techniques it uses. Management may decide that they will select the project which returns the initial investment the quickest. In this case the undiscounted payback period would be used. The lengths of time taken for the initial investment to be recovered are:

Payback periods

Lowstoft	4 years
Hillville	3 years
Downside	3.52 years

Hillville is the answer with the shortest payback period. Such a result may seem counter intuitive but the purpose of the technique is to identify which project returns the initial cash investment in the shortest period of time. Further research may reveal marketing, technical, distribution and employment factors that weigh against Hillville as the final selection but the company has firm evidence of the financial aspects.

The calculation for Downside is best explained in Table 14.3 which shows the annual cumulative position. With more complex examples, it is usual to use the format shown below to compare the alternatives.

In year 3 there was negative cumulative position of £13,000. The positive cash flow of £25,000 in year 4 would have cleared this deficit and left a surplus of £12,000. Assuming that the cash flows in at regular intervals during the year, the calculation is:

Year	Net cash flow £	Cumulative £
0	(80,000)	(80,000)
1	20,000	(60,000)
2	22,000	(38,000)
3	25,000	(13,000)
4	25,000	12,000
5	10,000	22,000
Total	22,000	

Table 14.3 Cumulative cash flow for downside

$$\frac{\text{Year 3 cumulative position}}{\text{Year 4 net cash flow } 25,000} = \frac{(13,000)}{25,000} = 0.52 \text{ of a year.}$$

Discussion point

Does the financial information change your original opinion on the best project?

The main *advantages* of the payback period are as follows:

- Non-financial managers can easily comprehend the technique which may not be the case with the more sophisticated techniques.

- If it is difficult to make acceptable predictions of future cash flows, the technique focuses on the short-term return.

- The technique is useful where other factors introduce a high level of risk. These could be political, technical, economic or environmental.

- Where other investment opportunities are expected to become available in the future it may be advantageous to free up the proposed investment as soon as possible.

The technique does have some drawbacks. The two critical ones to this technique are concerned with the calculation of the return on the investment. Any cash flows after the initial investment is recovered are ignored. A long-term project, say for 15 years, may cover the initial investment in the first five years. The cash returns from the other ten years would be ignored.

The second criticism is that the technique ignores the time value of money. It does not make sense to invest £1000 now in order to receive £1000 in several years' time. Any investment is expected to earn a return.

DISCOUNTED PAYBACK PERIOD

The purpose of discounted payback is the same as undiscounted payback: to identify the project which most quickly returns the initial investment. However, the concept of the time value is applied and the future cash flows are discounted to present values.

To illustrate the technique we use the same example as above and assume that the company has selected a discount rate of 5 per cent. As the calculations are slightly more complex, Tables 14.4–14.6 show each project individually.

Year	Net cash flow £	Discount rate 5%	Net present value £	Cumulative net cash flow £
0	(100,000)	0	(100,000)	(100,000)
1	15,000	0.952	14,280	(85,720)
2	20,000	0.907	18,140	(67,580)
3	30,000	0.864	25,920	(41,660)
4	35,000	0.823	28,805	(12,855)
5	35,000	0.784	27,440	14,585
	35,000		14,585	

Table 14.4 Lowstoft – Discounted payback period

Year	Net cash flow £	Discount rate 5%	Net present value £	Cumulative net cash flow £
0	(100,000)	0	(100,000)	(100,000)
1	30,000	0.952	28,560	(71,440)
2	35,000	0.907	31,745	(39,695)
3	35,000	0.864	30,240	(9,455)
4	15,000	0.823	12,345	2,890
5	10,000	0.784	7,840	10,730
	25,000		10,730	

Table 14.5 Hillville – Discounted payback period

Year	Net cash flow £	Discount rate 5%	Net present value £	Cumulative net cash flow £
0	(80,000)	0	(80,000)	(80,000)
1	20,000	0.952	19,040	(60,960)
2	22,000	0.907	19,954	(41,006)
3	25,000	0.864	21,600	(19,406)
4	25,000	0.823	20,575	1,169
5	10,000	0.784	7,840	9,009
	22,000		9,009	

Table 14.6 Downside – Discounted payback period

The payback periods are:

$$\text{Lowstoft} \quad 4 \text{ years} + \frac{(£12,855)}{£27,440} = 4.47 \text{ years}$$

$$\text{Hillville} \quad 3 \text{ years} + \frac{(£9,455)}{£12,345} = 3.77 \text{ years}$$

$$\text{Downside} \quad 3 \text{ years} + \frac{(19,406)}{20,575} = 3.94 \text{ years}$$

This brings the three projects much, closer with Hillside still the front runner with 3.77 years but closely followed by Downside with 3.94 years. This is a difficult decision for management. There are so many 'What ifs' with the crucial one being the confidence placed in the predictions. Two of the projects are hovering around the four-year mark in a five-year time frame and it may be other non-financial factors which determine the final selection.

The discounted payback period has most of the benefits and drawbacks of the undiscounted technique but does have the advantage of applying the time value of money concept. However, this introduces a major issue that is present in discounting techniques: deciding the discount rate to be used.

This issue is also present in the next technique: the calculation of the net present value. However, we are now illustrating a technique which calculates the return for the entire life of the project and not only the period when the initial investment is recovered.

NET PRESENT VALUE

The objective of the *net present value (NPV)* technique is to convert all future cash flows over the entire life of a project into present-day values. It differs from the discounted payback period technique as the purpose is to consider the return over the entire period and not the project which gives the quickest return.

The term Net Present Value means the difference between the cash outflows and the cash inflows over the life of the project. The NPV of these future cash flows are shown in amounts and not percentages. To decide if a project is worth undertaking there are three simple rules.

If the NPV is positive the return is greater than the discount rate. When there is a positive net present value this shows that the project has met the discount rate and has an amount of cash above this measured in present values. The higher the amount of the positive NPV the better the project is.

If the NPV for the life of the project is negative the return is lower than the discount rate used. For example, Conblock used a 5 per cent discount rate. If a higher discount rate were used some of the projects would show a negative return.

If the NPV is zero the return is the same as the discount rate.

If you refer back to the discounted payback period calculations for the three projects, the final row of each table shows the Net Present Value for the project and these are:

Lowstoft	£14,585
Hillville	£10,730
Downside	£9,009

All of the NPVs are positive which means that the projects have recovered the required rate of 5 per cent and, in addition, have generated cash above this. Lowstoft is the most financially successful project as the net present value is £14,585.

We summarize the results of our investigations in Table 14.7.

Technique	Undiscounted payback	Discounted payback	Net present value
First position	Hillville	Hillville	Lowstoft
Second position	Downside	Downside	Hillville
Third position	Lowstoft	Lowstoft	Downside

Table 14.7 Summary of Conblock's results

All of the techniques give the right answer based on the criterion the management used. These are:

Undiscounted Payback. How quickly do we recover our cash using undiscounted cash flows?

Discounted Payback. How quickly do we recover our cash using discounted cash flows?

Net present value. Which project recovers the most cash over its entire life using discounted cash flows?

Discussion point

Given the information in Table 14.7 and the prior information and calculations, what would be your advice to the company?

INTERNAL RATE OF RETURN

One issue with the NPV technique is that the results of the calculations are not easily discussed either in reports or management meetings. A positive NPV shows the recovery of the discount rate in percentage terms plus the final net present value in money terms. The project Lowstoft therefore makes 5 per cent and £14,585. It is much more elegant and informative if this could all be expressed in percentage terms.

The internal rate of return (IRR) technique shows the total return on the investment as one comprehensive percentage figure. When evaluating a single project, the project is financially worthwhile if the IRR is higher than the cost of capital. When comparing projects, the project with the highest IRR is preferred.

To illustrate the technique we will use the example of Lowstoft. As it has a positive NPV we know that the percentage return is above 5 per cent. What we need to know is how much above. This is where some guessing is required before we can do the calculation.

We could continue to continue to do the calculations using an increasing discount rate, for example, 5 per cent, 6 per cent, 7 per cent. This would be tedious. However, we know that if there is a negative net present value the project has not met the discount rate. From this we can move on to the second stage of the calculation, but Table 14.8 shows the first stage where we have 'guessed' at 15 per cent.

We know that a discount rate that gives a zero NPV is somewhere between 5 per cent and 15 per cent. Rather than continuing to guess, we can use the following formula.

Year	Net cash flow £	Discount rate 5%	Present value £	Discount rate 15%	Present value £
0	(100,000)	0	(100,000)		(100,000)
1	15,000	0.952	14,280	0.870	13,050
2	20,000	0.907	18,140	0.756	15,120
3	30,000	0.864	25,920	0.658	19,740
4	35,000	0.823	28,805	0.572	20,020
5	35,000	0.784	27,440	0.497	17,395
	35,000		14,585		(14675)

Table 14.8 IRR for Lowstoft

$$\text{Positive rate} + \frac{(\text{Positive NPV} \times \text{range of rates})}{(\text{Positive NPV} + \text{Negative NPV}}$$

$$= 5 + \frac{(£14,585)}{(£14,585 + £14675)} \times 10(15\% - 5\%)$$

$$= 5 + (0.49846 \times 10)$$

$$= 9.98\%$$

Some managers find it more helpful to know that the investment has a return of 9.98 per cent. You can calculate the IRR for the other two projects and the consequent ranking should be the same as for our NPV calculations.

ACCOUNTING RATE OF RETURN

This is a non-cash technique with the objective of calculating the average profit over the life of a project and expressing it as a percentage of the average investment. It is favoured by some companies because it reflects other performance measures which are also based on profit. As profit can be defined in various ways, it is essential that a company ensures consistency in the use of a definition. The formula used to calculate the ARR is:

$$\text{Accounting rate of return} = \frac{\text{Average net profit}}{\text{Average investment}}$$

It is important to remember that with this technique we are not considering inward cash flows or revenues, the return is profit. This means that all costs of the project have been covered.

Worked example – single project

A company is considering submitting a proposal to supply and operate specialized machinery on a major road building project. The project is considered to be of strategic benefit as it is hoped that it will allow the company to expand into new markets. The company's cost of capital is 5 per cent.

The cost of the machinery will be £800,000 and has a life of five years when the project ends. The predicted profits for the five years are:

Year 1 £90,000

Year 2 £80,000

Year 3 £60,000

Year 4 £40,000

Year 5, $30,000

Total £300,000

The accounting rate of return is:

$$\frac{£300,000/5 \text{ years}}{£800,000} = 7.5\%$$

Discussion point

How could you improve the financial analysis to assist the company to make a decision?

Worker example – Comparison of two projects

A company has two potential projects and has decided to evaluate them using the ARR. To demonstrate the different result if the net present value technique is used we add in the issue of depreciation which is a non-cash item. As both of the projects are considered speculative a discount rate of 15 per cent is used.

Each project requires an initial investment of £200,000 and will last for two years. The net profit before interest and tax is given for each year. We have also included the amount of depreciation charged each year before calculating the profit. Depreciation is £100,000 annually being 50 per cent of the investment. Depreciation is a non-cash calculation and needs to be added back to profit to obtain the cash movement (Table 14.9).

$$\text{ARR for project A} = \frac{£24,000}{£100,000} = 24\%$$

$$\text{ARR for project B} = \frac{£22,000}{£100,000} = 22\%$$

	Project A	Project B
Year 1		
Net profit before interest and tax	£2,000	£42,000
Depreciation charged	£100,00	£100,000
Year 2		
Net profit before interest and tax	$46,000	£2,000
Depreciation charged	£100,000	£100,000

Table 14.9 Accounting rate of return example

These are very close results and with some uncertainties in predictions, the company may find it difficult to choose. However project B has most of the profit in year 1 so it is interesting to calculate what the net present value technique demonstrates. We are calculating the cash flows in each instance by adding back the depreciation to the profit and assuming the cost of capital is 10 per cent (Table 14.10).

Project A			
Year	Cash flow	Discount rate 10%	Present value
0	(200,000)		(200,000)
1	102,000	0.870	88,740
2	146,000	0.756	110,376
Net present value			(884)
Project B			
0	(200,000)		(200,000)
1	142,000	0.870	123,540
2	102,000	0.756	77,112
Net present value			652

Table 14.10 Net present value calculations

If the discount rate is 15 per cent neither project looks attractive despite the results of the accounting rate of return.

The above example has not been contrived to prove that cash is better than profit in deciding on capital investment projects. A company must decide which technique best fits its policies and strategies. The Accounting Rate of Return does have the great advantage in the familiarity of the terms, the ease of calculations and the relationship with other performance measures used by the company.

One factor which can be important to the company and is captured by the ARR technique is taxation. In some countries there are tax reliefs and incentives for capital investments. These can have a significant effect on the calculations and the decisions made.

USE AND LIMITATIONS OF TECHNIQUES

Given the array of techniques, the question is which one do companies use and how is it used. There have been several surveys, possibly the largest in the United Kingdom being by Pike (1996) which we referred to at the beginning of this chapter.

Surveys from other countries have a similar pattern, although there are differences in application. The evidence, however, is that discounting techniques are now the most frequently used when making capital budgeting decisions.

An Australian study (Kalyebara and Ahmed, 2011) surveyed the top 490 companies on the Australian Stock Exchange almost 20 years after the Pike study. They received 205 useable replies and their analysis contains companies of various sizes unlike Pike's study that gave the results for the top 100 companies. However, the responses to the question 'What techniques of capital budgeting do you use?' show the dominance of discounting techniques (Table 14.11).

Technique	Number	Per cent
Net present value	66	32
Profitability index	2	2
Internal rate of return	55	27
Payback period	53	26
Accounting rate of return	18	9
Other techniques	8	4

Table 14.11 Use of capital budgeting techniques

Adapted from Kalyebara and Ahmed (2011) Table 4.

No matter how sophisticated the techniques and how credible the cash projections there is always the element of risk. Pike (1996) ascertained the trend in the risk analysis conducted by the companies in his survey (Table 14.12).

Firms which:	1975	1980	1986	1992
Shorten payback period	25	30	61	60
Raise required rate of return	37	41	61	65
Use probability analysis	9	10	40	48
Use sensitivity analysis	28	42	71	88
Use beta analysis	0	0	16	20

Table 14.12 Risk appraisal techniques

Adapted from Pike (1996) Table 2.3 Risk appraisal techniques- trend (response: 98 companies).

Definition – Beta analysis

A statistical measure of the volatility of an investment in relation to the market as a whole. Beta is a key component for the capital asset pricing model (CAPM), which is used to calculate cost of equity. Generally, the higher a company's beta is, the higher it's cost of capital discount rate and thus the lower the present value placed on the company's future cash flows.

Any technique which uses discounting has to decide on the required rate of return (hurdle rate). A study by Block (2005) demonstrates that the nature of the industry determines the metric used to set the hurdle rate.

LINK TO PRACTICE

Determining the hurdle rate

Block's study analysed the metric used as the hurdle rate by the nature of the industry. He used three metrics as shown on the following table.

	WACC %	Return on stockhoders equity %	Required rate in EPS %	Other %
Energy	94.7	5.32	–	–
Technology	98.2	–	1.8	–
Manufacturing	78.9	11.6	9.5	–
Retail	68.7	6.7	23.1	1.5

Table Hurdle rate by type of industry

	WACC %	Return on stockhoders equity %	Required rate in EPS %	Other %
Finance	70.6	19.6	6.9	2.9
Healthcare	75.4	12.8	8.1	3.7
Utilities	47.4	52.6	–	–
Transportation	77.2	14.1	8.7	–

(Continued)

Block, S. (2005, Table 7 p.61)

His further analysis identified the primary goal of the firm as broken down by industry. He had three categories of goals: stockholder wealth maximization; growth in earnings per share; return on stockholders' equity. The analysis demonstrated that the goal of the firm decided on the metric it used for determining the hurdle rate. This is further support for our argument in Chapter 10 that the perceived constituents interested in the organization will influence the management accounting practices it adopts.

Attempting to reduce risk in the planning stage is admirable but the final stage is judging if the project was successful, that is, the project made the return that was required. This requires some form of audit.

> ## Definition – Post Completion Audit (PCA)
>
> A formal procedure which systematically monitors the progress of an investment project by comparing actual performance with budgets and assessing the worth of the investment technique in the context of the final outcomes.

The post-completion audit serves several useful purposes. It should assist managers in better understanding of capital budgeting thus leading to selecting better projects and improving cash projections. It also deters managers from promoting their pet projects by over-stating potential cash flows. Against managerial tendencies to promote projects by over-stating potential cash flows. The audit also reveals where there were implementation problems.

Evidence as to the extent and thoroughness of these audits is fragmentary. Undoubtedly, they require a substantial amount of effort with data being reviewed many years after the decision was taken. Many changes may have taken place both economically and within the company which can make comparisons difficult. There is also the problem that cash discounting will most likely to have been used to select the project but its subsequent success or otherwise will be measured using the accruals basis and profit or loss.

The study by Kalyebara and Ahmed (2011) asked their 205 respondents what methods of audit did they use and the results are shown in Table 14.13.

Method	Number	Per cent
Reconcile profits with estimates	62	23
Reconcile costs with estimates	65	24
Reconcile production volumes with estimates	47	18
Reconcile time of installation with estimates	38	14
Reconcile rate of return with estimates	49	18
Others	6	2

Table 14.13 Post completion audits used

Adapted from Kalyebara and Ahmed (2011), Table 1

Some of these of course are non-financial measures and would not be comparable with the capital budgeting technique used.

Although the techniques are widely used there are severe critics. A very thorough review of the surveys and the techniques themselves has been given by Ghahremani et al. (2012). The thrust of their paper is to illustrate the problems of the traditional techniques which they regard as being:

1. The use of a narrow decision focus usually set by the investing department.

2. The failure of the techniques to consider non-financial benefits.

3. With discounting techniques they argue that benefits should be discounted at the market risk-adjusted discount rate like the WACC, but the investment cost should be discounted at a reinvestment rate similar to the risk-free rate.

4. Their short-term focus as major projects may continue for years and this can influence the discount rates at different times.

5. The assumptions that the current competitive position will remain unaltered if the investment is not undertaken. This is incorrect as competitors will be changing and the current condition is not stable.

Their solution to these weaknesses is the use of real options. The term 'real' is used because it is applied to tangible asset investment and not financial instruments. The option is the choices which become available with a business investment opportunity. These choices include expanding projects or ceasing them if certain criteria are not satisfied. It is claimed using the technique provides better decision-making information than the use of traditional techniques.

We leave the final words to Adler. He regarded the techniques' limitations as 'narrow perspective, exclusion of non-financial benefits, over-emphasis on the short-term, faulty assumptions about the status quo, inconsistent treatment of inflation, and promotion of dysfunctional/cheating behaviour' (Adler, 2006 p. 4).

CONCLUSIONS

Whatever capital budgeting technique is chosen, that data should not be used by itself to justify a capital investment decision. It is a highly important but must be placed in the context of all the other information that is available. Capital investment decisions are about predicting future long-term events and the apparent specificity of the financial numbers should not tempt people into believing in certainties.

The arithmetic simplicity of the techniques and apparent precision of the numbers can be misleading. It is easy to accept that the results produced by a spread sheet are factual and not merely forecasts. The issues with capital budgeting are making the predictions, taking strategic and external factors into account and, if using discounting, to determine the appropriate rate.

In making the predictions it is easy to be over optimistic or pessimistic. It is essential that some form of sensitivity analysis takes place. This should incorporate both cash in and out predictions with varying levels of adjustments.

RECOMMENDED READING

Maral Ghahremani1, Abdollah Aghaie1 & Mostafa Abedzadeh1 (2012) *International Journal of Business and Management*, Vol. 7, No. 17 Published by Canadian Centre of Science and Education 98.

Burns, R. M. & Walker, J. 'Capital Budgeting Surveys: The Future is Now.' *Journal of Applied Finance*, Vol. 19, No. 1/2 pp. 78–90. http://search.proquest.com/docview/201488717?

Pike, Richard H. (1986) 'The Design of Capital Budgeting Processes and the Corporate Context.' *Managerial and Decision Economics* 187. http://search.proquest.com/docview/230089361?

Les Oakes project

Les Oakes owns a small Canadian engineering company. It is facing fierce competition in the domestic market and the financial performance of the company has begun to stagnate. Over the last three years Les has designed and patented a new model of valve fittings for electric pumps. The intention is that the valve fittings would be sold to pump manufacturers for them to assemble into their products.

He cannot see a strong market in Canada for the valve fittings but considers that there is a large, unexploited market in Europe. He has been in discussions with three pump manufacturers in Germany, three in Hungary and two in the United Kingdom.

These discussions were very encouraging so he employed a marketing consultant to assess the potential sales for the next ten years. The consultant has informed Les that there is a good potential market in Europe but is likely to reach its maximum growth in six years' time. The predictions of sales figures for Les's share of the market are as follows:

European Sales projections

Year	Canadian $
1	400,000
2	600,000
3	800,000
4	1,000,000
5	1,200,000
6–10	1,400,000

Les has decided that the company has to develop this new valve but is uncertain as to the strategy to follow. He calculates that he can raise $2,000,000 to invest in the new project. He is anxious that if the project is not successful the company will be bankrupt. He is also aware that the company's future does not look healthy and that the new product could be an excellent opportunity.

Les has kept his management team informed of progress and has now called a meeting to agree their strategy. The Sales Manager,

Production Manager and Accountant comprise the management team and attend the meeting.

The Accountant has provided preliminary data showing the cash flows relevant to the project. To achieve the predicted level of sales, the factory would have to be extended and new equipment and machinery installed. This would involve a capital investment of CA$2,000,000. Once in production the variable costs will be 60 per cent of the sales figure. The annual fixed costs will be CA$400,000.

The Sales Manager states that she considers the sales figures from the external consultant are approximately 10 per cent higher than what is supported by the evidence she has been able to collect. She argues that the annual sales predictions should all be reduced by 10 per cent.

The Production Manager states that even if sales were 10 per cent lower this would have no impact on the production facilities required. He suggests that if there is a doubt about the sales figure they should develop the project in two stages. This would mean a capital investment of $1,000,000 at the start of the project and a further $1,200,000 at the beginning of year 4. In the first three years they could only produce 60 per cent of the sales figure predicted by the external consultant. There would be a savings on fixed costs in those first three years and they would be only $250,000 per annum instead of $400,000. If the sales were as originally predicted they could invest the remaining $1,200,000 and from year 4 onwards they would be meeting the predictions of the European consultant.

Les is uncertain what he should do? He needs the cash back as soon as possible. Should he accept the sales figures of the European consultant or take the advice of the production manager and implement the project in two stages. What are the financial implications of any decision he makes? What other factors should he take into account?

Advice Les on what he should do. You can assume that the discount rate is 10 per cent.

CHAPTER 15
STRATEGIC MANAGEMENT ACCOUNTING

LEARNING OBJECTIVES

At the end of this chapter you should be able to:

- Explain the concepts and practices of strategic management accounting.
- Describe the components of the Value Chain Analysis.
- Discuss the construction and application of the Balanced Scorecard.
- Explain target costing, Kaizen costing and life cycle costing.
- Describe the relationship between Activity-Based Management and Activity-Based Costing.
- Explain Total Quality Management and its strengths and weaknesses.
- Explain the Theory of Constraints and the calculations involved.

EXECUTIVE SUMMARY

Traditional management accounting has been criticized for being too concerned with the past and internal process. The information being supplied to management did not assist them in making strategic decisions.

Because of these criticisms several techniques were developed which aimed to be forward looking with an external focus. They cannot be claimed to be the sole preserve of the management account and some of them are designed to strengthen team building and the participation of every employee in the company.

Value Chain Analysis was developed by Porter (1985), but there have been additions, modifications and other claimed improvements by consultants and academics over the years. It is a technique that enables an organization to focus on each separate operation and to ensure that it adds value to the product or service. The essence of the technique is the process of value added that is contributed by the entire industry of which the organization is one part.

First conceived by Kaplan and Norton (1992) the Balanced Scorecard has grown in popularity and there are various versions. They are very similar in that a variety of financial and non-financial measures are used and compared to a 'target' value. These measures are presented in a single report (the Scorecard) which is a succinct summary of actual performance compared to the critical success factors of the business. The Scorecard is balanced as it uses both financial and non-financial measures.

Three cost reduction techniques widely used are Target costing, Kaizen costing and Life cycle costing. Target costing is the opposite of the cost plus approach. In target costing the price customers are likely to pay (the market price) is first determined, the required profit is then deducted from this to give the target cost, that is, the total cost for manufacturing the product. Target costing focuses on the design stage and Kaizen costing on the production stage. Life cycle costing is concerned with all costs over the entire life of the product or projects

Activity-Based Management is closely related of Activity-Based Costing and also concentrates on activities. Organizations undertake activities which consume resources. If these activities are analysed and monitored costs can be controlled at source. For instance, some activities can be enhanced and some may be eliminated. The activity is deemed value-added if the customer is willing to pay for it. Non-value adding activities should be eliminated is this would not affect the customer's perceived value of the product/service or impair the functioning and operation of the organization.

Total Quality Management is a philosophy rather than a technique. It is assumed that all processes, procedures and practices can be improved. To bring about these improvements TQM encourages employee empowerment. The first stage in implementing TQM is to identify customers and analyse their expectations. Measures are devised to make these expectations achievable in the production process. The measures can be both quantitative, for example the time taken for a repair to be conducted or qualitative, for example the image the customer yearns for in buying the product or service. Management and shop floor work together to attempt to bring about the required changes.

The Theory of Constraints regards an organization as a system which consists of multiple linked activities, some of which act as constraints on efficiency and output. The presence of these bottlenecks will result in supplies being delayed to customers, the expensive build up on inventories, and some activities not working at full capacity because of bottlenecks. Five steps are required to apply the technique and thus increase productivity

Throughput accounting applies the theory of constraints by providing measures in an attempt to cut costs. It is assumed that the only variable cost is materials and all other costs are 'conversion' costs that are fixed in the short term, including direct labour. The focus is on generating more throughput and material costs are deducted from the selling price to calculate the 'throughput' figure for a product.

CONCEPTUAL AND PRACTICAL ISSUES

Definition – Strategic management accounting (SMA)

Management accounting which includes non-financial information and internally generated information as well as information on relevant factors external to the firm.

At the beginning of the twentieth century, most accounting was financial accounting and, to a lesser extent, cost accounting. The latter was concerned with identifying the costs of products and processes within the company. It was internally orientated and focussed on what had happened. In particular, the role of cost accounting was to establish the total cost incurred in production.

Management accounting developed from cost accounting after the Second World War and expanded its range of methods and techniques to provide useful information. The costing of manufacturing processes and the tangible assets associated with them shifted to knowledge-based assets and strategies to manage those intangible assets. Managerial thinking changed and the practice of imposing systems and decisions from top-down without question developed into more participative styles.

These developments, and other changes, led to the re-thinking of strategic formulation and the cost information required. The new business environment of organizational empowerment, competitive capabilities and core competencies required the collection and reporting of cost and other quantitative and qualitative data that is future-orientated and identifies changes in the external environment.

Although valuable new management accounting methods and techniques were being developed some questioned whether the needs of management for information were met. The first to raise doubts publicly was Simmonds (1981) who encouraged management accountants to provide information which was of greatest value to the business. Accountants should change their perspective from a pure financial focus to a broader business perspective.

The call for management accountants to improve the information they generated was taken up by others. In 1987 Johnson and Kaplan (1987) claimed that management accounting was falling behind the needs of the modern accounting environment and that the accounting information was not relevant to managers.

In the United Kingdom Bromwich (1988) suggested the way in which strategic management accounting should develop. The role would be to evaluate:

- the company's competitive advantage or value added relative to its competitors;
- the benefits the company's products yield over their lifetime to customers;
- the benefits which sales yield to the company over a long decision horizon.

Any developments in strategic management accounting were slow to take place. In 1996, the journal *Management Accounting Research* published a special issue on the subject. It concluded that:

- there were less than 20 key articles on this subject in the mainstream academic journals;
- a comprehensive conceptual framework was absent;
- empirical evidence on practices was limited.

Since 1996, progress has been made, at least judging by the number of articles on Strategic Management Accounting and the many courses offered by universities and colleges.

Discussion point

Do you consider that SMA is an integral part of the accounting discipline or is it a multidisciplinary subject?

If we look for a conceptual framework that underpins many of the techniques explained in this chapter, then it is to be found in the works of Prahalad and Hamel (1990) on core competencies. Their argument is that the company's overall strategy should be based on the areas where it has significant competitive advantage. As competitors would have difficulty in matching these core competencies, they can be strategically exploited.

Definition – Core competencies

The skills and technologies that have been developed throughout an organization. It is the aggregate of the learning processes by individuals and groups across the learning organization

---

For strategies to be successful, the core competencies must be capable of being recognized and articulated in such a way that they can be managed. Once this is accomplished, the information needs to be communicated throughout the organization so that the competencies can be managed effectively and thus contribute towards strategy development.

Although many articles now appear on the use of strategic management accounting in different types of industries and various types of organizations, 'the term SMA is open to a number of variations, reflecting the fact that there is still no agreed conceptual framework about what constitutes SMA' (Ma and Tayles, 2009, p.2).

Many of the subjects we have discussed in earlier chapters can fall under the heading of SMA. This depends on the time frame being examined, the extent of external comparisons and the links with strategy. However, several techniques have emerged in recent years which are departures or extensions of existing practices. These are examined below.

VALUE CHAIN ANALYSIS

Definition – Value chain analysis

This technique analyses each stage of the business process, from the initial inputs to the eventual end-user. The objective is to deliver maximum value at the least possible total cost.

Value chain analysis is used in many disciplines and cannot be claimed to be the prerogative of the accountant. However, an accountant can contribute a specific skill set. A company may have constructed an excellent strategy but this has to be implemented at every stage in the organization's operations.

Value chain analysis is a technique that enables an organization to focus on each separate operation and to ensure that it adds value to the product or service. The value chain was developed by Porter (1985) but there have been additions, modifications and other claimed improvements by consultants and academics over the years.

The essence of the technique is the process of value added that is contributed by the entire industry of which the organization is a part. Using a simple example, the initial value added analysis may appear as in Figure 15.1.

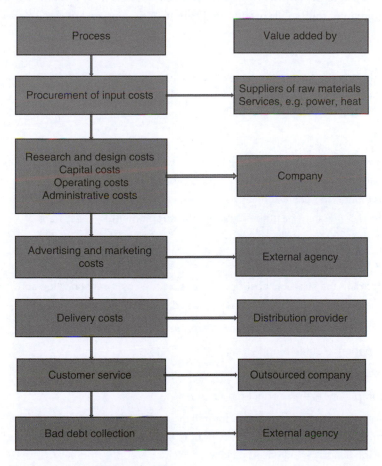

Figure 15.1 Simple value chain analysis
Source: Adapted from Hussey and Ong (2012), Table 6.1.

The above is a simplified layout. An in-depth value chain analysis would require significantly more detail and would reflect the nature of the industry and the structure and practices of the company.

The analysis of the value chain reveals the company's current and potential competitive advantages. The aim is to find opportunities for adding value and identify potential activities where cost reduction may take place. Improvements may include improving the cost and timing of the inputs to the company as well as enhancing internal operations. Deliveries to customers, repairs and maintenance, and methods of debt collection should also be scrutinized.

It should not be assumed that value chain analysis is a technique to be used only by large companies. Walker and Scott (2011) conducted a value chain analysis of a dairy farm in New Zealand. It is a normal size operation in that country and it milks 400 cows on 114 effective hectares. The opinion of the authors that the only strategy open to the farmer was to strive for cost leadership by minimizing the cost per kilogram of milk solids produced. Their analysis consisted of three steps:

LINK TO PRACTICE

Value chain analysis in dairy farming

Step 1

Identify and describe the strategically relevant processes or value activities and list the resources or assets needed by each value activity. Revenue is are determined to each value activity. The farm's value activities were identified as land ownership, pasture management, supplementary feed, herd management and milking.

Step 2

Determine the strategic cost drivers causing the costs in each value activity. These can be classified as structural cost drivers, for example:

- economies of scale, scope or the amount of vertical integration;
- experience or learning;
- technology used or available;
- complexity of the product range.

The main structural cost drivers for milking are technology and scale. The farm has made a significant investment in a 50-bale rotary shed. The benefits are significant. An increased milking capacity has supported land acquisitions, reduced milking time and thereby saved labour, and given a 20,000 kilogram increase in milk solids from less stressed cows.

Executional cost drivers are also identified and include:

- continuous improvement of staff;
- use of total quality management techniques;
- capacity utilization;
- plant layout and design and linkages with suppliers and customers.

Example of executional cost drivers are the farm reducing costs by spreading out fertilizer itself and changing from its older practice of mixing seed with fertilizer to complete pasture renewal methods that increase grass growth. The farmer and staff are continually learning and improving the procedures.

Step 3

Analyse the information to develop sustainable superior profits or competitive advantage by either controlling the strategic cost drivers better or by reorganising the value chain to improve the product. In this case, that means producing more milk solids and revenue.

The study raised the interesting point that value chain concepts were already being used by the farmer, a finding also of previous studies. It may be that the practices of Value Chain Analysis have been applied by good managers for many years. Academics and consultants have only conceptualized and structured the concepts.

> **Discussion point**
>
> Are advice and recommendations from academics and consultants merely the conceptualizing, packaging and promoting of good management practices which already exist?

THE BALANCED SCORECARD

> **Definition – Balanced Scorecard**
>
> A strategic planning and management technique used to focus business activities based on the vision and mission of the organization.

There are several variations and offshoots of the original Balanced Scorecard which was first conceived by Kaplan and Norton (1992). They are very similar in that a variety of financial and non-financial measures are used and compared to a 'target' value. These measures are presented in a single report (the Scorecard) which is a succinct summary of actual performance compared to the critical success factors of the business. The balance is the balancing of the tension among the various factors being measured, in both financial and non-financial terms.

Four critical success factors (CSFs) or perspectives have been identified which, it is claimed, capture the strategy of the organization. For each of these factors, the organization has to develop three to five measures. The factors are:

1. Financial perspective – The measures normally used for this factor are ratios such as Return on Investment (ROI). This demonstrates whether the organization has met its financial objectives.

2. Customer perspective – Measures such as growth in market share, number of new customers, and customer satisfaction survey demonstrate whether, the organization seeks to ascertain whether the customers' expectations are being met.

3. Internal business process perspective – There are three areas of attention: innovation, operations and post-sales service. The perspective demonstrates the effectiveness and efficiency of managing the internal operations or value chain. It shows the organization's success in improving critical business processes.

4. Learning and growth perspective – There are four areas that are measured: goal congruence, measured by satisfaction ratings; Skill and process development, measured by the percentage of employees trained; workforce empowerment, measured by the percentage of line workers making management decisions; enhanced information system capabilities, measured by the percentage of processes with real-time feedback. This perspective assesses the organization's abilities in adapting, innovating and growing.

Some companies have added an environmental perspective.

The aim of the Scorecard is to ensure that there is a balance in all aspects of the analysis. This means obtaining a balance among the four dimensions so that one critical success factor does not predominate between quantitative and non-quantitative measures. Such measures should be forward looking as well as retrospective and both short term and long term.

The relationships among the four dimensions can be shown in a form of a diagram or strategy map. This is a diagram which shows the primary strategic goals, usually in a box with text, which are being pursued by an organization or management team.

LINK TO PRACTICE

Example of a balanced scorecard

Perspective	Measures	Example of targets
Financial	Return on investment Profitability Revenue growth Revenue mix Cost reduction	Return on investment 15% Increase in operating income — 5% Growth in sales revenue — 20% Share of revenue from wholesale customers — 30% Decrease in administrative cost — 3%
Customer	Market share Customer acquisition Customer retention Customer profitability Customer satisfaction	Market share – 30% New customers per month 1,000 Repeat customer rate 50% Average customer profit – $1,000 Rating of 4.9 - on a 5 - point scale
Internal	Process quality measures Order processing time Number of computers Lead-times Amount of scrap	Zero defects Process time reduced to three minutes Number of computers increased by 30% Lead time reduced by 80% Non-recycled scrap reduced by 90%
Innovation and learning perspective	Amount spent on research Number of training programmes Employees trained Employee retention Employee productivity Number of new products	Total amount $100,000 Five programmes per month Every employee one per month Increased by 20% Number of transactions – 18 per day Increased by 20%

Source: Adapted from Werner and Xu (2012)

Implementing a Balance Scorecard requires a substantial amount of work and is best carried out by a team of managers from different areas of the organization. The setting of targets can be a difficult process and a significant amount of investigation must be conducted beforehand. The following six points illustrates the process.

Implementing a balanced scorecard

Stage 1 – Preliminary evaluation
The evaluation of the external environment and the organization and its strategy. This also includes the financial position, human and capital resources and the procedures and processes being used.

Stage 2 – Implementation plan
Meetings with managers to explain the project discuss its objectives and gain support.

Stage 3 Developing objectives, measures and buy-in
Achieving consensus on objectives and to establish a cause-and-effect linkage across objectives at both senior and middle-level management.

Stage 4 Measures and targets
Establish a clear, unambiguous measure for each target so that managers know what they are expected to achieve.

Stage 5 Agreement
Middle and senior managers should agree the responsibilities for each area and objective and understand the method for measuring performance.

Stage 6 Top management support
Top management should have been involved throughout the process but it is essential that they understand, agree and sign off on the system.

There are difficulties in implementing and maintaining a Balanced Scorecard. By its implementation we are contemplating significant organizational change and there can often be strong resistance. Implementation can be time consuming and expensive. The measures and targets may be difficult to set and open to criticism at the time they are established or later when they are in operation.

Implementation is also a long process and it is frequently found that participants suffer from 'system innovation syndrome'. This is where the team responsible for implementing the Balanced Scorecard and other managers become exhausted by the exercise. Short-cuts are taken, inappropriate and ambiguous measures and targets are set, and some managers retain the old methods. Some of these issues can be avoided by following the advice Upton (2012).

Performance measures

Carefully assess the financial and non-financial measures you are using.

- Use of multiple financial and non-financial performance measures reflects business unit strategy more fully, but consider managers' limited cognitive ability to process so many measures.

- Managers look for ways to simplify complex judgements and decisions. Managers will ignore unique business unit measures and focus on measures used commonly across all business units.

- Improving the consistency and consensus of evaluations can engender confidence in the outcomes of the BSC, leading to improved effectiveness.

Common-measures bias is a problem because it:

- Ignores critical aspects of business unit strategies; and

- Sends a message to unit-level managers to focus only on common measures.

Increase manager involvement in selection of performance measures:

- An important use of BSCs is in strategy evaluation. Managers will seek information supporting strategic choices while ignoring disconfirming information. This tendency is known as motivated reasoning.

- Counter motivated reasoning by involving managers in performancemeasurement selection. Managers will take more notice of measures they have selected. If the measures point to a flawed strategy, then managers are less likely to ignore those signals.

Source: Upton (2012)

Common-measure bias

Consider these ways to combat the common-measures bias

- Ensure all measures are given adequate weight in performance evaluations.

- Require managers to justify their BSC-based judgements and decisions.

- Provide objective assurance reports that all performance measures are relevant and reliable.

- Ensure adequate training in the BSC. Managers who understand the BSC concepts and structure will pay closer attention to all performance measures.

- Stress the strategic importance of all performance measures – provide strategy maps to clearly show the strategic links between measures.
- Design standard operating procedures that step managers through all measures during performance evaluation sessions.

Source: Upton (2012)

Presentation

- For managers evaluating more than one business unit, tabular presentation of BSC results improves consistency of judgements.
- Graphical presentation of results does not appear to enhance the decision quality of managers.

Source: Upton (2012)

COST EVALUATION AND REDUCTION

This section describes three techniques, each concerned with cost reduction and evaluation. What differentiates them is the time span they are concerned with and the focus of the analysis. The definitions of the three techniques are given below.

Definition – Target costing

The setting of target costs for each product and each product-related activity, starting with the design of the product and culminating with the sale of the product.

Definition – Kaizen costing

The analysis of the costs of a product when it is in production with the objective of reducing the costs. This can be achieved by lowering the purchase cost of materials, continuously improving the production process and strict scrap controls.

> **Definition – Life cycle costing**
>
> A technique to determine the total of all the costs of a product, service or asset over a defined period of time. The costs include acquisition, installation, operation, production, maintenance, refurbishment and disposal.

The relationship of the techniques is shown in Figure 15.2. The process boundaries set for each of the techniques are usually more flexible than denoted with target costing and kaizen costing often overlapping. The process of each of the techniques is discussed in more detail in the subsections.

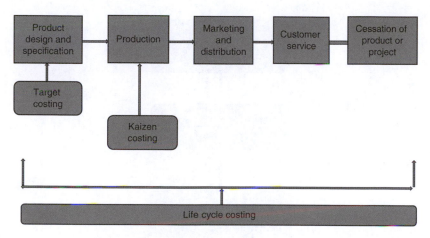

Figure 15.2 Techniques for cost control

One method of pricing products or services is to add on to the cost (variable and fixed) a percentage amount to derive the market price. This is known as the cost-plus model. This method can only be used if the market is non-competitive or only slightly competitive.

This method has the great advantage that you know you are going to make the required profit as long as you can sell the product or service. The problem is that changes may have occurred in the market environment where the company has operated or intends to do so. There may be competition from others who have adopted the strategy of cost leadership. Customers may place a different value on the product or service than the company has and will attempt to drive down the market price.

TARGET COSTING

The alternative to the cost-plus model is to use target costing, also known as price-led costing.

This technique ensures that the product is introduced to the market with a specific functionality, quality and selling price which can be produced at a life cycle cost to generate an acceptable level of profitability (Cooper and Slagmulder, 1997).

A company using target costing collects market research data to ascertain the price customers are willing to pay given the product's functionality, quality and alternatives provided by competitors. The profit the company requires is deducted and the balance is the target cost. The following diagram illustrates the process where the company has determined the market price is £5.00. It is seeking a profit of 25 per cent and assumes that the design costs will be 80 per cent. This is a figure commonly quoted in the literature although disputed by Cooper and Slagmulder (2004) (Figure 15.3).

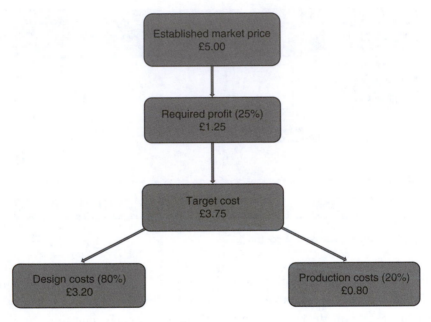

Figure 15.3 The process of target costing

One area which is frequently not investigated is that of design of the product. Comparatively small changes in design can lead to considerable reductions in subsequent production costs. Value engineering is performed to redesign the product and *kaizen* costing (also known as continuous improvement) is performed to streamline its manufacturing and distribution processes. It is essential that designers and production managers share their expertise in order to achieve the target cost.

In implementing target costing it is important that you have a good grasp of the relationship of the components of fixed and variable costs and how they behave in the long term and short term. It may be that by increasing fixed costs, for example by greater mechanization, variable costs in the form of labour can be reduced.

Variable or fixed costs may also be reduced by outsourcing but this is a decision which must be reflected in the company's strategy.

An article by Swenson et al. (2003) researched the practices of four large companies using target costing. We summarize below the information on a project being considered by Caterpillar which they detailed (Table 15.1).

The team had to find an additional 0.8 per cent in savings to achieve the 5.4 per cent cost reduction target. The team sent a questionnaire to the operational groups to identify potential cost savings. The responses did not identify specific solutions but areas where cost reduction efforts were most likely to succeed.

Target costing is not a complex technique although it requires a change in management thinking and philosophy in a company where the model has always been cost plus pricing. In summary, the stages of Target Costing are described below:

- Calculate the target cost that satisfies the market price and the organization's target profit.

- Evaluate the types of actions that may be implemented in different departments or areas to bring actual costs in line with the target cost.

- Assess whether the reduction in costs in one area may lead to a consequential increase in costs in other areas.

- Set targets for each area in discussion with managers.

- Monitor the cost reductions to ensure that the actions implemented produce the required results.

KAIZEN COSTING

Kaizen costing may be used in manufacturing or the service sector. Kaizen encourages everyone in the company to continually reconsider how the task is undertaken and whether there is a better way of doing it.

Kaizen Costing concentrates on the production phase and on achieving continuous, incremental improvements over a period of time to reduce costs. The emphasis is on the process of production rather than the product. The principles are used in the service sector. For example, a hospital may use the technique to reduce waiting times.

Generally, the technique only considers those production costs which can be directly controlled by the shop floor. The design and development phase is excluded completely from the analysis.

Companies establish their own procedures but normally there is a two pronged approach with senior management and a work cell group. In one model management will set the cost reduction targets for the product. This may be done half yearly or even quarterly. The work cell group sets its targets and negotiation takes place.

Once there is agreement between management and the work cell the latter has considerable freedom in identifying ways to achieve these targets. Progress is monitored and if the cost reductions are not achieved the reasons are sought. Costs are incrementally reduced for each period until the target profit is met.

Kaizen is not merely a technique for reducing costs. It is claimed that it empowers the workers, develops an organizational culture of learning, and create a pride in work. Others argue that the requirement to continuously bring about improvements increases worker stress.

Cooper and Slagmulder (2004) conducted research at Olympus Optical Co. Ltd in Japan. They identified two categories of Kaizen costing; General Kaizen costing and Product-specific Kaizen costing. General Kaizen costing technique focuses on the way a product is manufactured; the assumption being that the product's design is already determined. As mentioned above, management sets the cost-reduction goals and the workers have the responsibility of identifying ways to achieve them.

Product-specific Kaizen costing enables the rapid redesign of a new product to correct any cost overruns. The authors provide the example of product-specific continuous improvement with a new camera entering mass production.

LINK TO PRACTICE

Introducing a new camera

The total costs were 15 per cent higher than originally specified. Although there was an extremely tight deadline Olympus Optical reduced costs, without sacrificing the productǆs functionality and quality, in the following ways:

1. Decreasing the number of parts in the product,
2. Replacing certain materials with cheaper ones,
3. Managing supplier costs, and
4. Transferring production overseas where overall costs were lower.

This example demonstrates that, given the target and the commitment significant savings can be achieved. However, to be effective, Kaizen costing must be a philosophy adopted by the entire organization. Once the cost-reduction target is agreed, the work cell should be held responsible for achieving it. It should be part of organizational culture that the work cell attempts to achieve the agreed target cost by improving processes.

Life cycle costing

Life cycle costing is applied broadly, including the management of long-term assets such as property as well as the environmental costs of various activities. It is sometimes referred to as the 'cradle to grave' technique.

The purposes for which organizations could choose to use life cycle costing are the acquisition of a system or project on long-term budgets and operating results, and also to compare among competing suppliers of products and services. Repair costs, maintenance and warranties were all other concerns that encourage management to look at the life cycle costing. We will confine our discussions to products and services over their anticipated life time.

Companies are increasingly concerned with the life cycle cost when they either purchase an item or manufacture it. For example, if a company is implementing a new computerized system there are additional costs apart from the initial cost of purchasing it. There will be the training costs of staff to operate the system, the possible costs of the supplier for maintenance, breakdowns and upgrades. There is also likely to be the less quantifiable costs of the disruption caused during the implementation period. There may even be costs associated with running the old system and the new system until there is confidence in its efficiency. Finally, there may be costs associated with the abandonment or dismantling of the system, for example, a nuclear power plant.

Four distinct categories of life cycle costs have been proposed and the importance of each will vary from company to company and over time. The categories are:

1. research and development cost;
2. production and construction cost;
3. operation and maintenance support cost;
4. retirement and disposal cost.

Retirement and disposal costs have become increasing important as environmental legislation compels companies to remedy damage that is caused by their operations. However, this underlines the problem that many life cycle costs will be incurred for several years into the future. To complete a proper analysis the time value of money concept has to be applied.

Life cycle costing is future orientated and compels managers to examine the long-term financial implications of the strategic decisions they are making. It also encourages managers to examine and question the costs incurred at every significant stage in the entire life of the product.

Unfortunately, there is usually little subsequent effort to monitor actual performance and to conduct a post-audit. Although managers will have carefully predicted the costs to be incurred over the life of the asset, few ensure that actual costs are compatible with predictions. This lack of control and monitoring may be because accounting records which may consolidate the costs of maintenance and similar expenditures under one heading for the entire department or organization.

ACTIVITY-BASED MANAGEMENT (ABM)

> ### Definition – Activity-based management
>
> A technique with the objectives of maximizing value-added activities while eliminating or minimizing non value-added activities.

ABM is a logical follow on for companies using Activity-Based Costing. The technique attempts to improve organizational efficiencies and effectiveness by:

1. reducing costs,

2. creating performance measures,

3. improving cash flow and quality and,

4. producing enhanced value products.

ABM analyses an organization into a set of related activities that create and deliver value to customers. The most basic concept in ABM is that of an 'activity', thus, its relationship with ABC. People undertake activities which consume resources – so controlling activities allows you to control costs at their source.

ABM regards some activities as value-added as the customer is willing to pay for them. Activities are non-value adding if their elimination would not affect the customer's perceived value of the product/service or impair the functioning and operation of the organization. If we consider typical non-value added activities in a manufacturing environment, the obvious ones are:

- Storage and internal transport of raw materials, work in process and finished goods. These can be significant and may be reduced by using systems such as 'Just-In-Time' deliveries of supplies and configuring the production lines to reduce movements of work in process and finished goods.

- Idle time and down time. It may be more financially beneficial to conduct regular maintenance and employ progress chasers to ensure that capacity is functioning at its most efficient.

The above examples are from a manufacturing environment but you can apply the principles to any type of activity. A key factor to concentrate on is the wastage of time. This is costly and often means that the customer is also waiting. In some service industries, customers may regard waiting as a normal part of the activity but usually rapid service is expected.

An analysis of customers and their profitability using Activity-Based Management can be very fruitful as shown in the following case investigated by Plowman (2007).

In this case, the largest increment of costs was incurred whenever a customer interacted with the Call Centre; with the above customer segment this was twice. The solution was to avoid actions that would lead to the customer contacting the Call Centre.

A statistical analysis was conducted to identify those customer categories which caused the company to incur high costs. The company then developed a marketing and service strategy for attracting and retaining the more profitable customer categories.

TOTAL QUALITY MANAGEMENT (TQM)

> ## Definition – Total Quality Management
>
> An integrative philosophy for continuously improving the quality of products and processes in an organization. The premise is that all organization members are responsible for the quality of products and processes with the objective of meeting or exceeding customer expectations.

TQM is not specifically a technique which accountants can call their own although they can make a useful contribution. Whether you are in accounting, marketing, production, or any other function you will be involved in TQM if your organization decides to implement it.

Continuous improvement assumes that all processes, procedures and practices can be improved. Frequently, the best suggestions for improvements are generated by the employees doing the specific job. TQM encourages employee empowerment but, at the same time the essential integration of processes and procedures must be obtained. The use of multi-departmental teams can minimize possibilities of disruptions through partial implementation of improvements.

All members of the organization are aiming to achieve the quality expected by customers but the customers have to be identified. The immediate buyer may not be the final user of the product or service. Some would argue that there are even internal customers as employees are frequently completing their work to satisfy the next stage in the production process. There is also the issue that customer can perceive quality as:

- Luxury compared to other products or services even if you have to wait for it.
- Delivery at the time promised and the price agreed.
- Consistency in that the product or service is exactly the same no matter at which outlet you purchase it or at what time.
- The availability of spare parts or quick service time.

Given these differing opinions the first stage in implementing TQM is to identify customers and analyse their expectations. Measures must then be devised to make these expectations achievable in the production process. The measures can be both quantitative, for example, the time taken for a repair to be conducted. Measures can also be qualitative, for example, the image the customer yearns for in buying the product or service.

There is plenty of guidance on implementing and operating TQM. As it is a philosophy, some of the advice has a crusading approach, although most studies agree on what should be done and where the failures are most likely to occur.

Different sources have emphasized various characteristics of a successful TQM operation. (Powell, 1995) has constructed a list of 12 factors.

1. **Committed leadership:** a near-evangelical, unwavering, long-term commitment by top managers to the philosophy, usually under a term similar to Total Quality Management, Continuous Improvement (CI) or Quality Improvement (QI).

2. **Adoption and communication of TQM:** using tools like the mission statement, and themes or slogans.

3. **Closer customer relationships:** determining both internal and external customers' requirements, then meeting those requirements no matter what it takes.

4. **Closer supplier relationships:** working closely and cooperatively with suppliers and ensuring they provide inputs that conform to customers' end-use requirements.

5. **Benchmarking:** researching and observing best competitive practices.

6. **Increased training:** usually includes TQM principles, team skills, and problem-solving.

7. **Open organization:** lean staff, empowered work teams, open horizontal communications and a relaxation of traditional hierarchy.

8. **Employee empowerment:** increased employee involvement in design and planning, and greater autonomy in decision making.

9. **Zero-defects mentality:** a system in place to spot defects as they occur, rather than through inspection and rework.

10. **Flexible manufacturing:** (applicable only to manufacturers) can include just-in-time inventory, cellular manufacturing, design for manufacturability (DFM), statistical process control (SPC) and design of experiments (DQE).

11. **Process improvement:** reduced waste and cycle times in all areas through cross departmental process analysis.

12. **Measurement:** goal-orientation and zeal for data, with constant performance measurement, often using statistical methods.

A somewhat similar study was conducted by Black and Porter (1996) with the aim of developing an empirical framework for TQM. The survey included members and participants of the European Foundation for Quality Management, containing both US and other non-European companies operating in Europe.

In total 204 correctly completed questionnaires were returned, a response rate of 44.2 per cent.

There were ten main factors identified and the one that was most distinctive was Strategic Quality Management. This had the following sub-factors:

- Process control and improvement of core processes, in accordance with design;
- Active leadership by management in quality issues;
- Inclusion of employees' well-being considerations in improvement activities;
- Senior executive commitment to quality through involvement and communication;
- Development/implementation of long-term plans/strategies focused on quality;
- Analysis of performance and cost data to support improvement priorities.

A more recent study by Dayton (2003) was intended to identify the current critical success factors in TQM systems in US corporations. The research sought to ascertain whether US quality assurance professionals would agree that the ten TQM critical factors would be similar to those identified by Black and Porter and whether Strategic Quality Management would be deemed the most important factor

The survey tool was sent to approximately 1000 members of the American Society of Quality. A total of 402 usable surveys were returned. Both of the hypotheses were supported and Strategic Quality Management was considered to be the most important factor.

There are many claimed benefits of TQM. Companies that have implemented it have spoken of the time and cost in doing so but have also expressed pleasure at the visible improvements. The gains that organizations claim to have made include:

- Reputation as a quality organization;
- Reduction in costs without lowering quality;
- Increases in financial measures such as profit margins and return on investment;
- The ability to charge higher prices for products and services than previously;
- Better customer retention levels and a decrease in returned goods and repairs under guarantees;
- Increase in presence in new markets, both nationally and internationally;
- Better working relationships with suppliers sometimes leading to reduced purchasing costs and better delivery times;
- Speedier response times to changes in the market and customer preferences.

On the other hand, organizations have found problems in introducing TQM. Consequently, they have abandoned the attempt or decided on partial implementations. The difficult issues have been:

- Agreeing which customer they are trying to satisfy and how do those customers perceive quality. There may be a customer chain and if the final customer is not satisfied the displeasure may result in a lowering of sales or other customers in the chain seeking alternative suppliers.

- Identifying appropriate measures of quality and being able, on a regular basis, to collect, analyse and feedback this data to employees.

- Attempting to achieve employee empowerment, but at the same time ensuring integration of all the process and functions.

- Seeking continuous improvements but also attempting to benefit from the gains of consistency and standardization of procedures and practices.

Although TQM has its supporters the technique is 'fraught with pitfalls for firms that lack the requisite complementary resources' (Powell, 1995 p.33). It may be that these pitfalls are being experienced. In an article entitles 'The Demise of Total Quality Management' Dayton (2003 p.393) concluded:

> The absence of senior management valuing and living the TQM process coupled with organizational inflexibility and inertia and the negative publicity beginning to be associated with TQM (negative publicity due in a large part because many divergent ideas and consulting schemes were inappropriately clumped under the TQM banner) provided an environment that weakened and eroded the foundations of TQM.

Definition – Theory of constraints

A technique for identifying the most important constraint on achieving a goal and then systematically improving that constraint until it is no longer the limiting factor or constraint. In manufacturing, the constraint is often referred to as a bottleneck.

THEORY OF CONSTRAINTS

The assumption is that a system consists of multiple linked activities, one of which acts as a constraint (i.e. the 'weakest link in the chain'). It is also assumed that in current manufacturing practices direct labour has reduced as a proportion of total cost and is now a fixed cost. The only variable cost is materials and all other costs are 'conversion' costs that are fixed in the short term.

Almost every manufacturing organization will have a bottleneck or binding constraint. This will result in a mismatch between the amount of inventory produced in a period and the customer demand. This leads to insufficient supplies of the product and customer dissatisfaction or a build-up of inventory which suggests wasted resources.

The theory of constraints is applied within an organization by applying the following five focusing steps.

1. Identify the system's bottlenecks.

2. Decide how to exploit the system's bottlenecks. Ensure that the full capacity of the bottleneck is being used.

3. Subordinate everything else to the decisions made in Step 2. The production schedule must be determined by the capacity of the bottle neck. This will mean that for a temporary period the non-bottleneck activities will be working at less than full capacity. The production capacity of the bottleneck resource should determine the production schedule for the organization as a whole.

4. Exploit and elevate the bottleneck's capacity. Investigate all means of exploiting the full capacity of the bottleneck without incurring cost. If the constraint has not been removed capital expenditure may be required.

5. Be alert to new bottlenecks. Step 4 may lead to a new constraint. If so, the five steps are repeated. The final constraint is probably the strength of market demand.

The performance measure used in the Theory of Constraints is known as throughput accounting. It is a management accounting technique but, unlike cost reduction techniques that attempt to cut costs, throughput accounting focuses on generating more throughputs.

Throughput is calculated by deducting direct material costs from the selling price and assumes that direct labour is a fixed cost.

WORKED EXAMPLE

A company produces three products. The details are as follows.

	Product 1	Product 2	Product 3
Selling price per unit	£156	98	114
Direct material cost per unit	£108	78	78
Maximum demand (units)	45,000	25,000	30,000
Time on the bottleneck resource (hours per unit)	3	2	1.5

There are 200,000 bottleneck hours available each month.

1. Calculate the throughput per unit.
   Selling price – Direct material = throughput per unit

2. Calculate the throughput return per hour of bottleneck resource. This equates to Throughput per unit in Step 1 divided by the number of hours for each unit on the bottleneck.

3. Using the return per hour, rank the units.

4. Without exceeding the maximum demand for a product, allocating the bottleneck resource (hours per unit) to each one in order. This is the optimum production plan.

5. Calculate total throughput for each product. Return per hour of bottleneck resource (Step 2) × number of hours (Step 4).

	Product 1	Product 2	Product 3
Step 1 Throughput per unit	£48	£20	£36
Step 2 Return per hour of bottleneck resource	£16	£10	£24
Step 3 Rank units	2	3	1
Step 4 Allocate bottleneck resource (hours)	135,000	20,000	45,000
Total throughput for each product	£2,160,000	£200,000	£1,080,000

Although product 1 generates the highest throughput per unit at £48, product 3 generates the highest return of £24 of the scarce resource of bottleneck hours. Product 3 is given priority followed by Product 1 and the remaining 20,000 bottleneck hours (200,000–180,000) are allocated to Product 3.

CONCLUSIONS

Strategic Management Accounting has become popular and the topics discussed in this chapter can be found in most books and university and college courses bearing the name. Some of the techniques would rely heavily on accounting skills whereas others are interdisciplinary.

It is difficult to ascertain the success of some of these techniques. Value Chain Analysis and the Balanced Scorecard are well established. The cost reduction and valuation techniques appear to be effective. Questions are raised in the literature and in surveys on the use of techniques, such as Total Quality Management, which rely heavily on philosophy and cultural change.

Despite the plethora of advice on how to implement the techniques in an organization, it would seem that the practice frequently does not match the philosophy.

RECOMMENDED READING

Nair, Mohan (2000). 'The keys to implementing activity-based management', *The Journal of Corporate Accounting & Finance*; March/April 11, 3 pp. 37–42.

Dayton, Nick A. (2003) 'The demise of total quality management (TQM).' *The TQM Magazine* 15, 6 pp. 391–396.

Ward, Keith (2012) *Strategic Management Accounting*, Routledge.

Hussey, R and Ong, A. (2012) *Strategic Cost Accounting*. Business Expert Press.

CASE STUDY QUALITY UTENSILS – QU LTD.

Steeve Burg is the Managing Director of a small company, Quality Utensils Ltd., which manufactures various kitchen accessories, such as cutting boards, ladles, whisks, serving spoons. They also have recently commenced manufacturing sets of utensils for barbeques and camping. Steeve accepts the criticism of some of his managers that this is a speculative venture, but he is concerned that profit margins on kitchen utensils are declining.

Although the sales of the kitchen items remain reasonably consistent, demand for the barbeque and camping items fluctuate considerably. Steeve had thought that sales would be to a large extent seasonal, but was surprised that demand could vary considerably both in the summer and winter months. These fluctuations led to either high levels of inventory or insufficient to meet the circumstances when there was high demand. He is also having some issues with getting materials from his suppliers when there is an unexpected surge in demand.

As well as the high inventories, there are labour problems. The work in producing the items is highly skilled and many of the workers have been with QU Ltd for several years. Because of the fluctuations in demand at times overtime is available and at other times there are fears of redundancies. This had depressed morale.

Another issue is the competition posed by goods manufactured in China and at much lower prices than those set by QU. Although Steeve believes that the quality of his goods is far superior, there is no denying that the foreign imports are posing a considerable threat.

Steeve's son, Mitch, has recently finished an MBA in Business at a US University. Mitch is home for the vacation, with his friend Christian Bird, and Steeve discusses with them the business problems the company is facing.

'It's no good worrying vaguely about things', Mitch says 'You need to get your thoughts in order and put them on paper'. Mitch explains that they have been studying the Balanced Scorecard at University and suggest that his father completes one and discusses it with his senior managers at their next meeting.

Complete a Balanced Scorecard for the company and advise Steeve on its potential benefits and the problems he still has to consider.

GLOSSARY

ABSORPTION COSTING

The method used for charging overhead costs to cost units to ascertain the total cost of the unit. Overhead costs are charged to production centres using a process of overhead analysis and then charged to cost units using an overhead absorption rate.

ABSORPTION RATE

The rate or rates calculated in a full costing system for the purpose of charging the overhead costs to the unit of production for a financial period.

ACCOUNTING STANDARDS

Regulations governing financial accounting and reporting. These pronouncements are issued by a national or international standard-setting body and there is normally some form of national legal procedure that will ensure compliance with the requirements of the standards by organizations.

ACCRUALS ASSUMPTION OR CONCEPT

Financial statements must be prepared on the accruals basis. Transactions and other events are recognized as they occur and not when cash or any other consideration such as cheques are given or received. These transactions and events must be recorded in the accounting records when they occur and not when payment is made or received.

ACTIVITY-BASED COSTING (ABC)

A costing method used to ascertain the total cost by assigning overheads to major activities through the use of cost drivers which are measures of activity. Overheads are collected in cost pools which are related to these activities.

ACTIVITY-BASED MANAGEMENT (ABM)

A technique with the objective of maximizing value-added activities while eliminating or minimizing non value-added activities.

ASSET

A resource controlled by the enterprise as a result of past events and from which future economic benefits are expected to flow to the enterprise.

BALANCED SCORECARD

A strategic planning and management technique used to focus business activities based on the vision and mission of the organization.

BETA ANALYSIS

A statistical measure of the volatility of an investment in relation to the market as a whole. Beta is a key component for the capital asset pricing model (CAPM), which is used to calculate cost of equity. Generally, the higher a company's beta is, the higher its cost of capital discount rate and thus the lower the present value placed on the company's future cash flows.

BORROWING COSTS

Those costs directly attributable to the acquisition or construction of qualifying assets are capitalized.

BUDGET

A formal document which is a financial representation of the strategy of an organization.

BUDGET VARIANCE

The difference between the budgeted financial performance and the actual performance for a financial period.

BUSINESS COMBINATION

The bringing together of separate entities or businesses into one reporting entity.

CASH EQUIVALENTS

These are short-term, highly liquid investments that are readily convertible to known amounts of cash and which are subject to an insignificant risk of changes in value.

CAPITAL EXPENDITURE

Funds used by a company to acquire or improve non-current assets such as property, machinery or equipment. These expenditures can include everything from replacing a machine to building an additional factory in another country.

CONSOLIDATED FINANCIAL STATEMENTS

Consolidated financial statements, also known as group statements, are the aggregated financial results of a parent company and its subsidiaries. They provide an overall view of an entire group of companies as opposed to one company's stand-alone position.

CORE COMPETENCIES

The skills and technologies that have been developed throughout an organization. It is the aggregate of the learning processes by individuals and groups across the learning organization.

COST

The value of resources applied in conducting the activities of an organization.

DEBENTURE

A long-term loan usually taken by an organization and repayable at a fixed date. Some debentures are irredeemable securities. Most debentures pay a fixed rate of interest which must be paid before a dividend is paid to shareholders.

DEPRECIATION

A portion of the full cost of an asset which it is considered has been 'used up' during the financial period. It is an annual charge to the Income Statement and reduces the carrying value on the balance sheet.

DERECOGNITION

The removal from the Statement of Financial Position of an organization of assets and liabilities that had previously been recognized.

DERIVATIVE

A complex financial instrument whose value depends on (or is derived from) the value of another basic underlying variable or asset.

DISCLOSURE

The publication of financial and non-financial information to those interested in the financial, operational and economic activities of an organization.

ENTITY

A circumscribed area of economic activities whose financial information has the potential to be useful to existing and potential equity investors, lenders and other creditors who cannot directly obtain the information they need in making decisions about providing resources to the entity and in assessing whether the management and the governing board of that entity have made efficient and effective use of the resources provided.

EQUITY

A contract which evidences a residual interest in the assets of an entity after deducting all of its liabilities. If we put this in the terms of the accounting equation then Assets – Liabilities = Capital (Equity).

FAIR VALUE

The value agreed with a sale at arm's length with willing buyer/seller.

FINANCIAL INSTRUMENTS

Any contract which gives rise to a financial asset of one entity and a financial liability or equity instrument of another entity.

FINANCIAL PERIOD

The period of time between one balance sheet date for which financial statements are prepared and the next balance sheet date. The period is normally 12 months and annual financial statements are prepared. In some countries, companies may be encouraged, or required, to publish summary financial statements more frequently, either quarterly or half yearly.

FIRST IN FIRST OUT (FIFO)

This method assumes that items purchased or manufactured first are sold first. The result of this is that the value of inventory at period end is the most recently purchased or produced.

FIXED COSTS

Fixed costs in total stay the same irrespective of changes in the level of activity.

FLEXIBLE BUDGET

A budget which is adjusted for the actual level of activity in the financial period.

GOODWILL

An asset representing the future economic benefits arising from assets that are not capable of being individually identified and separately recognized. Goodwill is therefore an integrated part of the business and cannot be separated from it.

GROSS PROFIT MARGIN

This is calculated by expressing the gross profit as a percentage of revenue and is a good measure of the performance of a company in buying and selling goods.

$$\text{Gross profit margin} = \frac{\text{Gross profit}}{\text{Revenue}} \times 100$$

HEDGING

Reducing risk by taking action now to reduce the possibility of future losses, usually with the possibility of not enjoying any future gains.

HURDLE RATE

The minimum amount of return a company expects from an investment.

IMPAIRMENT

The position when an asset's recoverable amount falls to an amount less than its carrying amount.

INITIAL MEASUREMENT

The determination of the monetary amounts of economic transactions and events that are to be recognized and entered into the records of the organization at the date of the transaction or event.

INTERNAL AUDIT

An examination of the procedures and records of an organization carried out on its own behalf to ensure that its own internal controls are operating satisfactorily. The internal audit may also be used to conduct investigations to detect any possible theft or fraud.

INVENTORY

The products or supplies held by a company at any one time. For a manufacturing company inventory could consist of raw materials required for production, items known as work in progress which are part way through the production process and finished goods awaiting delivery to customers.

JOINT OPERATION

A joint arrangement whereby the parties that have joint control of the arrangement have rights to the assets, and obligations for the liabilities, relating to the arrangement.

KAIZEN COSTING

The analysis of the costs of a product when it is in production with the objective of reducing the costs. This can be achieved by lowering the purchase cost of materials, continuously improving the production process and strict scrap controls.

LEDGER

Traditionally a book containing accounts of a similar type. For example, the Debtors Ledger would contain a separate account for each customer who received goods on credit.

LIABILITY

A present obligation of an entity resulting from past events, the settlement of which is expected to be an outflow from the entity of resources embodying economic benefits.

LIFE CYCLE COSTING

A technique to determine the total of all the costs of a product, service or asset over a defined period of time. The costs include acquisition, installation, operation, production, maintenance, refurbishment and disposal.

MANAGEMENT ACCOUNTING

The methods and techniques for collecting, compiling and processing financial, quantitative data and non-quantitative data within an organization to assist managers in planning, control and decision making.

MARGIN OF SAFETY

This is the difference between the level of actual or planned level of activity and the breakeven point.

NET REALIZABLE VALUE (NRV)

The estimated sales value of the goods minus the additional costs likely to be incurred in completing production, if necessary, and any other costs necessary to make the sale.

NON-CONTROLLING INTERESTS

This is the equity in a subsidiary not attributable, directly or indirectly, to a parent. It is the partial ownership of a company which does not give the shareholder the control of the company. Previously, the term 'minority interest' was used.

POST-COMPLETION AUDIT

A formal procedure which systematically monitors the progress of an investment project by comparing actual performance with budgets and assessing the worth of the investment technique in the context of the final outcomes.

PROCESS COSTING

A costing method used where there are continuous operations in manufacturing and a stream of homogeneous products flow from one process to the next until the production is complete.

QUALIFYING ASSET

An asset which necessarily takes a substantial period of time to get ready for its intended use or sale.

RATIO ANALYSIS

A technique for evaluating the financial performance and stability of an entity, with a view to making comparisons with previous periods, other entities and industry averages over a period of time.

RECOGNITION

The process of incorporating economic transactions and events into the financial statements of an organization. Both the nature of the transaction or event and the timing need to be recognized, that is, in which financial period it should be recognized.

RECORDING TRANSACTIONS

Entering into the records of the organization the economic transactions and events. These records are still sometimes referred to as the 'books of account', although it is now normal practice to maintain these records on a computerized system even for a small business.

RECOVERABLE AMOUNT

Recoverable amount is the higher of fair value less costs to sell and 'value in use'.

RELEVANT RANGE

The range of activity levels between which valid assumptions can be made about cost behaviour. Outside this range, the assumed relationship between fixed costs, variable costs and revenues may not apply.

RETAINED EARNINGS

Net profits retained in the company after dividends and any other distributions have been made to investors.

REVENUE

Revenue arises from the sale of goods, the provision of services and the use of assets yielding interest, royalties and dividends. It is the gross inflow of economic benefits, for example, cash, receivables and other assets arising from the ordinary operating activities of an enterprise.

SENSITIVITY ANALYSIS

This is a technique of altering assumptions or predictions when making decisions.

SIGNIFICANT INFLUENCE

This is the power to participate but not to be able to control the financial and operating policy decisions of the investee.

STANDARD COSTING

A system of cost ascertainment and control in which predetermined standard costs and income from products and operations are set and periodically compared with actual costs incurred and income generated in order to establish any variances.

STRATEGIC MANAGEMENT ACCOUNTING

Management accounting which includes non-financial information and internally generated information as well as information on relevant factors external to the firm.

TARGET COSTING

The setting of target costs for each product and each product-related activity, starting with the design of the product and culminating with the sale of the product.

THEORY OF CONSTRAINTS

A technique for identifying the most important constraint on achieving a goal and then systematically improving that constraint until it is no longer the limiting factor or constraint. In manufacturing, the constraint is often referred to as a bottleneck.

TIME VALUE OF MONEY

The concept that a specific sum of cash is worth more if it is received sooner rather than later. The reason for this differences is that cash received sooner can be invested and earn interest.

TOTAL QUALITY MANAGEMENT (TQM)

An integrative philosophy for continuously improving the quality of products and processes in an organization. The premise is that all organization members are responsible for the quality of products and processes with the objective of meeting or exceeding customer expectations.

TRIAL BALANCE

A list of all the closing balances on the accounts of an organization with debit balances in one column and credit balances in the other. If the double entry bookkeeping has been done properly, the two totals should agree.

VALUE CHAIN ANALYSIS

This technique analyses each stage of the business process, from the initial inputs to the eventual end-user. The objective is to deliver maximum value at the least possible total cost.

VALUE IN USE

The discounted future cash flows expected from an individual asset or a cash-generating unit.

VARIABLE COSTS

Variable costs in total vary directly with changes in the level of activity.

WEIGHTED AVERAGE

This method calculates the average cost of items at the beginning of the period and the cost of similar items purchased or produced during the period.

WORKING CAPITAL

The amount of funding required for the organization's day-to-day operations. It is the sum of current assets minus the sum of current liabilities.

REFERENCES

Abdel-Kader, M. and Luther, R. (2006) *Management Accounting Practices in the UK Food and Drink Industry*. Chartered Institute of Management Accountants.

Accountancy Live (2013) *Deloitte US Fined $10 Million Over Standard Charter*. 19 June. www. accountancylive.com/croner/jsp/CronerZoneChannel.do?cache=false&channelId=-601014

Accounting Standards Board (1999) *Statement of Principles*. December. London.

Accounting Standards Board (2005) IAS 8 *Accounting Policies, Changes in Accounting Estimates and Errors*.

Accounting Standards Steering Committee (1975) *The Corporate Report*. London.

Adams, Roger (2013) 'Integrated Reporting' *AB International*, May, pp. 22–24.

Adler, Ralph W. (2006) 'Why DCF Capital Budgeting is Bad for Business and Why Business Schools Should Stop Teaching it'. *Accounting Education: An International Journal*, Vol. 15, No. 1, pp. 3–10.

Akobundu, E., Jing, J., Blatt, L. and Mullins, C. D. (2006) 'Cost-of-Illness Studies: A Review of Current Methods'. *Pharmacoeconomics*, Vol. 24, No. 9, pp. 869–890.

Alexander, David and Jermakowicz (2006) 'A True and Fair View of the Principles/Rules Debate'. *ABACUS*, Vol. 42, No. 2, pp. 132–164.

American Laundry News (2010) 'Measuring Costs Per Pound?' Vol. 36, No. 7, pp. 16–19.

Asare, Stephen Kwaku and Wright, Arnold M. (2012) 'Investors', Auditors', and Lenders' Understanding of the Message Conveyed by the Standard Audit Report on the Financial Statements'. *Accounting Horizons*, Vol. 26, No. 2, pp. 193–217.

Ball, Ray (2009) 'Market and Political/Regulatory Perspectives on the Recent Accounting Scandals 2009'. *Journal of Accounting Research*, Vol. 47, No. 2, May, pp. 277–323.

Bent, David and Richardson, Julie (2003) *The Sigma Guidelines*, Toolkit Forum for the Future. http://www.projectsigma.co.uk/Toolkit/SIGMASustainabilityAccounting.

Black, Simon A., Porter, Leslie J. (1996) 'Identification of the Critical Factors of TQM'. *Decision Sciences*, Vol. 27, No. 1, pp. 1–22.

Block, S. (2005) 'Are There Differences in Capital Budgeting Procedures between Industries? An Empirical Study' *The Engineering Economist*, Vol. 50, pp. 55–67.

Bromwich, M. (1988) 'Managerial Accounting Definition and Scope-from a Managerial View'. *Management Accounting*, Vol. 66, No 8, pp. 26–27.

Bromwich, M., Macve, R. and Sunder, S. (2010) 'Hicksian Income in the Conceptual Framework'. *Abacus*, Vol. 46, No. 3, pp. 348–376.

Bruce, R. (2013) *The Bruce Column – Uncertain Weather Ahead*. http://www.iasplus.com/en/news/2013/01/bruce-column-future-of-ifrs

Calleja, K., Steliaros, M. and Thomas, D. C. (2006) 'A Note on Cost Stickiness: Some International Comparisons'. *Management Accounting Research*, Vol. 17, No. 2, pp. 127–140.

Canadian Center of Science and Education 98. Capital Budgeting Technique Selection through Four Decades: With a Great Focus on Real Option.

Chenell, R. H. (2003) 'Management Control Systems Design within Its Organizational Context: Findings from Contingency- based Research and Directions for the Future'. *Accounting, Organizations and Society*, Vol. 28, No. 2–3, pp. 127–168.

Clarke, F. L. (2010) 'Alas, Poor Hicks Indeed! Sixty Years of Use and Abuse! – Commentary on Bromwich et al.' *ABACUS*, Vol. 46, No. 3, pp. 377–386.

Cooper, R. and Slagmulder, R. (1997). *Target Costing and Value Engineering*. Portland, Oregon: Productivity Press.

Cooper, R. and Slagmulder, R. (2004) 'Interorganizational Cost Management and Relational Context'. *Accounting, Organizations and Society*, Vol. 29, No. 1, pp. 1–26.

Dayton, Nick A. (2003) 'The Demise of Total Quality Management (TQM)'. *The TQM Magazine*, Vol. 15, No. 6, pp. 391–396. http://search.proquest.com/docview/227596085?accountid= 14789.

Deloittes (undated) *UK Airlines Start to Value Landing Slots as Assets on Balance Sheets*. Retrieved 21 January 2013. http://www.deloitte.com/view/en_gb/uk/969833d0303fb110VgnVCM1000 00ba42f00aRCRD.htm.

Dugdale, D., Jones, C. and Green, S. (2005) *Contemporary Management Accounting Practices in UK Manufacturing*. Chartered Institute of Management Accountants.

Dzinkowski, Ramona (2013) 'A New View from America?'. *Accounting and Business International*, June, p. 30.

Elkington, J. (1998) *Cannibals with Forks: The Triple Bottom Line of 21st Century Business*. Capstone Publishing.

Evans, Lisa (2003) 'The True and Fair View and the Fair Presentation "override" of IAS 1'. *Accounting and Business Research*, Vol. 33, No. 4, pp. 311–325.

Fallan, L., Pettersen, I. and Stemsrudhagen, J. (2010) 'Multilevel Framing: An Alternative Understanding of Budget Control in Public Enterprises'. *Financial Accountability & Management*, Vol. 26, No. 2, p. 190. Retrieved 26 December, from ABI/INFORM Global (Document ID: 2048747931).

Financial Accounting Standards Board (1978) Concepts No. 1. *Objectives of Financial Reporting by Business Enterprises*.

Financial Accounting Standards Board (2010) *Exposure Draft: Proposed Accounting Standards Update*. July.

Financial Reporting Council (2005) *The Implications of New Accounting and Auditing Standards For The 'True and Fair View' and Auditors' Responsibilities*. London.

Financial Reporting Council (2006) *Auditor's Reports on Financial Statement in the UK*. London.

Financial Reporting Council (2010) *Corporate Governance Code*. London.

Financial Reporting Council (November 2012) *Foreword to Accounting Standards*. London.

Fischer, J. (1995) 'Contingency-based Research on Management Control Systems: Categorization by Level of Complexity'. *Journal of Accounting Literature*, Vol. 14, pp. 24–53.

Fisher, L. (2013) ' Importance of Ethics'. *Accounting and Business International*, March, pp. 23–25.

Foster, B. and Baxendale, S. (2008) 'The Absorption vs. Direct Costing Debate'. *Cost Management*, July/August, pp. 40–48.

Fowler, Michael (2010) 'Teaching and Practice Gap'. *Chartered Accountants Journal*, Vol. 89, No. 11, December, pp. 36–38. 3p.

Ghahremanil, M., Aghaiel, A. and Abedzadehl, M. (2012) *International Journal of Business and Management*, Vol. 7, No. 17, pp. 98–119.

Global Reporting Initiative (2011) *Sustainability Reporting Guidelines*, www.globalreporting.org/Pages/default.aspx

Gong, Maleen Z. and Tse, Michael, S. C. (2009) 'Pick, Mix or Match? A Discussion of Theories for Management Accounting Research'. *Journal of Accounting – Business & Management*, Vol. 16, No. 2. pp. 54–66.

Heller, Baird C. and Gonzalez- Wertz, C. (2011) 'How Top Performers Achieve Customer-Focused Market Leadership'. *Strategy & Leadership*, Vol. 39, No 1, pp. 16–23.

Hicks, J. R. (1946) 'Income'. Chapter XIV of *Value and Capital*, 2nd ed., Clarendon Press.

Hoffman, L. and Arden, M. H. (1983) 'Legal Opinion on True and Fair View'. *Accountancy*, November, pp. 154–156.

Humphrey, C. and Turley, P. (1992) *The Audit Expectation Gap in the United Kingdom*. London: Institute of Chartered Accountants in England and Wales.

Hursman, A. (2010) 'Measure What Matters: Seven Strategies for Selecting Relevant Key Performance Indicators'. *Information Management*, Vol. 20, No. 4, pp. 24–28.

Hussey, R. and Woolfe (1994) *Interim Statements and Preliminary Profit Announcements*. London: Institute of Chartered Accountants in England and Wales.

Hux, M. J., O'Brien, B. J., Iskedjian, M., Goeree, R., Gagnon, M. and Gautier, S. (1998) *Canadian Medical Association Journal*, Vol. 159, No. 5, September.

ICAEW (2012) *The Future of Financial Reporting*.

IFAC (2012) *Code of Ethics for Professional Accountant*, http://www.ifac.org/sites/default/files/publications/files/2012-IESBA-Handbook.pdf

International Accounting Standards Board (2010). *Project Summary and Feedback Statement*.

Innes, J., Falconer, M. and Sinclair, D. (2000) 'Activity-based Costing in the U.K.'s Largest Companies: A Comparison of 1994 and 1999 Survey Results'. *Management Accounting Research*, Vol. 11, pp. 349–336.

International Accounting Standards Committee's (IASC) (1989) *Framework for the Presentation and Preparation of Financial Statements*, IASC.

International Accounting Standards Committee (1997) *IAS 1 Framework for the Presentation and Preparation of Financial Statements*, IASC.

International Ethics Standard Board for Accounting (2012) *Handbook of the Code of Ethics for Professional Accountants*, IESBA.

IIRC (2012) *Integrated Reporting (IR) Prototype Framework*, http://www.theiirc.org/wp-content/uploads/2012/11/23.11.12-Prototype-Final.pdf

Jensen, M. and Meckling, W. (1976) 'Theory of the Firm: Managerial Behavior, Agency Costs, and Ownership Structure'. *Journal of Financial Economics*, Vol. 3, pp. 305–360.

Johnson, Gary G. and Hicks, Mary Beth Hicks (2012) 'An Investigation of the Decision Influences that Lead Nations to Adopt and Require Implementation of International Financial Reporting Standards'. *International Journal of Business, Accounting, and Finance*, Vol. 6, No. 2, Fall, pp. 116–142.

Johnson, H. T. and Kaplan, R. S. (1987) *Relevance Lost: The Rise and Fall of Management Accounting*. Boston: Harvard Business School Press.

Kahneman, D. and Tversky, A. (1979) 'Prospect Theory: An Analysis of Decisions under Risk'. *Econometrica*, Vol. 47, No. 2, pp. 263–291.

Kalyebara, Baliira and Ahmed, Abdullahi D. (2011) ' Determination and Use of a Hurdle Rate in the Capital Budgeting Process: Evidence from Listed Australian Companies'. *The IUP Journal of Applied Finance*, Vol. 17, No. 2, pp. 59–72.

Kaplan, R. S. and Anderson, S. R. (2004) 'Time-driven Activity-based Costing'. *Harvard Business Review*, Vol. 82, No. 11, pp. 66–69.

Kaplan, R. S. and Norton, P. (1992, Jan/Feb) 'The Balanced Scorecard – Measures that Drive Performance'. *Harvard Business Review*, pp. 71–79.

Kaplan, R. S. and Bruns, W. (1987) *Accounting and Management: A Field Study Perspective*. Harvard: Harvard Business School Press.

Keller, A., Smith, K. and Smith, L. (2007) 'Do Gender, Education Level, Religiosity, and Work Experience Affect the Ethical Decision-making of U.S. Accountants?' *Critical Perspectives on Accounting*, Vol. 18, No. 3, pp. 299–314.

Lee, Gap Teck, Ali, Azhan Md and Bien, Dora (2009) 'Towards an Understanding of the Audit Expectation Gap'. *The ICFAI University Journal of Audit Practice*, Vol. 6, No. 1, pp. 7–35.

Lee, T. H., Gloeck, J. D. and Palaniappan, A. K. (2007) 'The Audit Expectation Gap: An Empirical Study in Malaysia'. *The Southern African Journal of Accountability and Auditing Research*, Vol. 7, No. 1, pp. 1–15.

Liggio, C. (1974) 'The Expectation Gap: The Accountant's Waterloo'. *Journal of Contemporary Business*, Vol. 3, pp. 27–44.

Liu, Lan Yan Jun (2006) *The Use of Activity-based Planning (ABP) in the UK Crown Prosecution Service*. Chartered Institute of Management Accountants.

Ma, Yi, and Tayles, Mike (2009) 'On the Emergence of Strategic Management Accounting: an Institutional Perspective.' *Accounting and Business Research*, Vol. 39, No. 5, pp. 473–495.

Macario, A. (2006) 'Are Your Hospital Operating Rooms "efficient"?: A Scoring System with Eight Performance Indicators'. *Anesthesiology*, Vol. 105, No. 2, pp. 237–240.

Macve, Richard (1981) *A Conceptual Framework for Financial Accounting and Reporting*. London: The Institute of Chartered Accountants in England and Wales.

Madalina, Gîrbina, Nadia, Albu and Catalin, Albu (2011) 'The Role of the Accounting Professional Bodies in Social and Environmental Reporting'. *Annals of the University of Oradea, Economic Science Series*, Vol. 20, No. 1, pp. 622–628.

McGregor, W. (1992) 'True and Fair View – An Accounting Nachronism'. *Australian Accountant*, Vol. 62, No. 1, February, pp. 68–71.

Muller, Victor O. (2011) 'Trends in Academic Research on Consolidated Accounting'. *Journal of International Business and Economics*, Vol. 11, No. 2, pp. 98–106.

O'Connell, Vincent (2007) 'Reflections on Stewardship Reporting'. *Accounting Horizons*, Vol. 21, No. 2, June, pp. 215–222.

O'Keeffe, Irene and Hackett, Fiona (2012) 'True and Fair: A Moving Target'. *Accountancy Ireland*, Vol. 44, No. 3, June, pp. 28–31.

O. Müller, Victor (2011) 'Academic Research on Group Accounting over the Past Fifty Years'. *International Journal of Business Research*, Vol. 11, No. 1, pp. 145–155.

Otley, D.T. (1980) 'The Contingency Theory of Management Accounting: Achievement and Prognosis'. *Accounting, Organizations and Society*, Vol. 5, pp. 413–428.

Perrin, Sarah (2013) 'Hoogervorst reaches ou't'. *AB International Edition*, January, pp. 30–31.

Pike, Byron and Chui, Lawrence (2012) 'An Evaluation of the FASB's Conceptual Framework from a User's Perspective'. *Academy of Accounting and Financial Studies Journal*, Vol. 16, No. 1, pp. 77–94.

Pike, Richard (1996) 'A Longitudinal Survey on Capital Budgeting Practices'. *Journal of Business Finance & Accounting*, Vol. 23, No 1, pp. 79–92.

Plowman, B. (2007) 'Activity Based Management: Driving Profitability'. *Accountancy Ireland*, Vol. 27, No. 2, pp. 23–25.

Porter, B. A. (1993) 'An Empirical Study of the Audit Expectation-Performance Gap'. *Accounting and Business Research*, Vol. 24, pp. 49–68.

Porter, B. A. and Gowthorpe, C. (2004) *Audit Expectation-Performance Gap in the United Kingdom in 1999 and Comparison with the Gap in New Zealand in 1989 and in 1999*. The Institute of Chartered Accountants of Scotland Edinburgh.

Porter, M. E. (1985) *Competitive Advantage*. New York, NY: The Free Press.

Powell, T. C. (1995) 'Total Quality Management as Competitive Advantage: A Review and Empirical Study'. *Strategic Management Journal*, Vol. 16, 15–37.

Powell, Joanne (2012) 'Ethics and the Education of Chartered Accountants'. *Accountancy Ireland*, Vol. 44, No. 3, pp. 58–61.

Prahalad, C. K. and Hamel, G. (1990) 'The Core Competence of the Corporation'. *Harvard Business Review* Vol. 68, No. 3, 79–91.

Ramanna, Karthik and Sletten, Ewa (2009) *Why Do Countries Adopt International Financial Reporting Standards?*. Harvard Business School, Working Paper 09–102. pp. 1–46.

Segarra, M. (2012) 'Lots of Trouble'. *CFO*, Vol. 28, No. 2, March, pp. 29–30.

Siegel, Philip H. and Jackson, Pamela Z. (2011) 'An Analysis of Marketing and Accounting Educators Ethics' Preferences'. *Journal of Legal, Ethical and Regulatory Issues*, Vol. 14, No. 1, pp. 25–42.

Simmonds, K. (1981) 'Strategic Management Accounting'. *Management Accounting*, Vol. 59, No. 4, pp. 26–29.

Stuart, Thomas (2012) 'Ethics and Accounting Education'. *Issues in Accounting Education American Accounting Association*, Vol. 27, No. 2, pp. 399–418.

Swenson, Dan, Shahidansar, I., Bell, Jan and Andil-Woon, Kim (2003) 'Best Practices in Target Costing'. *Management Accounting Quarterly*, Vol. 4, No 2, pp. 12–17.

The Auditing Practices Board (2006) *Ethical Standard for Reporting Accountants*, October.

Upton, D.R. (2012) 'Experimental Balanced Scorecard Research: Implications for Practitioners'. *Management Accounting Quarterly*, Vol. 13, No 4, pp 25–31.

US Environmental Protection Agency (June 1995) *An Introduction to Environmental Accounting As A Business Management Tool*. http://www.epa.gov/ppic/pubs/busmgt.pdf

Vaughn, P., Raab, C. and Nelson, K. B. (2010) 'The Application of Activity- based Costing to a Support Kitchen in a Las Vegas Casino'. *International Journal of Contemporary Hospitality Management*, Vol. 22, No. 7, pp. 1033–1047.

Walker, Pamela and Scott, Colin (2011) 'Value Chain Analysis of a Dairy Farm'. *Chartered Accountants Journal*, July, pp. 42–43.

Werner, M.L. and Xu, F. (2012) 'Executing Strategy with the Balanced Scorecard'. *International Journal of Financial Research*. January, Vol. 3, No. 1, pp. 88–94.

Whyte, G. (1986) 'Escalating Commitment to a Course of Action: A Reinterpretation'. *Academy of Management Review*, Vol. 11, No. 2, pp. 311–321.

Zeff, Stephen, A. (2012) 'The Evolution of the IASC into the IASB, and the Challenges it Faces'. *Accounting Horizons*, Vol. 26, No. 2, pp. 193–217, DOI: 0.2308/acch-50138

Zeff, Stephen A. and Nobes, Christopher A. (2010) 'Commentary: Has Australia (or Any Other Jurisdiction) 'Adopted' IFRS?'. *Australian Accounting Review*, Vol. 20, No. 2, pp. 178–184.

INDEX